CATHOLIC SOCIAL TEACHING
AND THE UNITED STATES ECONOMY

Catholic Social Teaching
and
The United States Economy

Working Papers for a
Bishops' Pastoral

Edited by
John W. Houck
and
Oliver F. Williams, C.S.C.

University Press of America
Washington, D.C.

Copyright © 1984 by

University Press of America,™ Inc.

4720 Boston Way
Lanham, MD 20706

3 Henrietta Street
London WC2E 8LU England

Library of Congress Cataloging in Publication Data
Main entry under title:

Catholic social teaching and the United States economy.

"Essays . . . first presented and discussed at a major
symposium organized by the Center for Ethics and Religious
Values in Business of the College of Business Administra-
tion of the University of Notre Dame"—Foreword.
"Co-published by arrangement with the Notre Dame Center
for Ethics and Religious Values in Business"—T.p. verso.
Includes index.
1. United States—Economic policy—1981-
—Congresses. 2. Church and social problems—United
States—Congresses. 3. Church and social problems—
Catholic Church—Congresses. I. Houck, John W.
II. Williams, Oliver F. III. Notre Dame Center for
Ethics and Religious Values in Business.
HC106.8.C38 1984   261.8'5   84-20883
ISBN 0-8191-4374-X (alk. paper)
ISBN 0-8191-4375-8 (pbk. : alk. paper)

Co-published by arrangement with the
Notre Dame Center for Ethics and
Religious Values in Business

Cover design by Ann E. Mercer

Dedicated
to
The U.S. Catholic Bishops' Committee
on
Catholic Social Teaching and the United States Economy

If the trumpet give forth an uncertain sound,
who will answer? (1 Cor. 14:8)

Contents

Foreword

ARCHBISHOP REMBERT G. WEAKLAND, O.S.B.
Chairman, U.S. Bishops' Committee on Catholic
Social Teaching and the U.S. Economy

THE ESSAYS OF THIS VOLUME WERE FIRST PRESENTED AND discussed at a major symposium organized by the Center for Ethics and Religious Values in Business of the College of Business Administration of the University of Notre Dame. The conference, which was open to the public and attended by over two hundred and fifty persons, was convened specifically for the U.S. Bishops' Committee charged with writing a pastoral letter on the economy. As chairman of the Bishops' Committee, I have the privilege of saying thanks to Father Hesburgh and the entire Notre Dame community. It was their idea to hold the conference. They came to us wanting to be of service as a Catholic university by helping the bishops to clarify many of these complex issues. I especially want to thank Father Oliver Williams and Professor John Houck who convened this symposium for us and who selected the authors and planned the program. The Committee is indeed grateful for the amount of effort, work, and expertise they brought to this task. I also want to say a special word of thanks to all those listed in the Preface who funded this important work.

My gratitude is extended to all of the authors included in this volume. With very little to work from, they gave us exactly what we wanted. We desired expertise in the facts from those who are well qualified and that is what we were given by our fifteen authors. At the same time, we wanted others to try to be bishop and attack the problem from the point of view of Catholic social teaching. Some of the essays included here fulfilled that charge well. I have to say all of the essays printed here have been of special help to the Bishops' Committee and I trust many readers will better understand our final document with the aid of these studies.

The Committee has consulted with a number of people and I think we have heard from all the major areas of concern. Business executives, labor leaders, economists, public officials, theologians, and a number of organizations working directly with the poor or for social concerns were all well represented in our deliberations. The Office of the Campaign for Human Development brought in several groups of people, including three black women, who talked to the Committee about how the economic system looks from their point of view, that is, from the perspective of those who are affected by it.

Reflecting on our many consultations and discussions, I feel some crucial trends are discernible. Three points are worth noting. I think these points will help to understand our pastoral letter on the economy.

First, I believe that we are in a special moment—a new moment in the history of the Church in the U.S.A. More and more, Catholics today are being challenged by the Bible and are becoming deeply scripturally based in their Catholic spirituality. Encouraged by the Second Vatican Council, people are confronting those "tough texts" in the Bible which deal with discipleship and are reflecting on the lifestyle we all enjoy here in the United States. We all need to examine our lifestyle in the light of the Gospel and our world situation. This is something which concerns everyone and touches the whole fabric of our society and the economic structures that support it.

Second, I think that the Church here in the United States is under special pressure from Third World nations and the Churches of the Third World who have taken up these issues before we did. I am thinking of the documents from the General Conference of Latin American Bishops at Medellín, Colombia, and at Puebla, Mexico. We cannot help but react to their statements, for we are deeply involved with them as a Church. In this light we have an obligation to look at ourselves and who we are. The work of our brother bishops in Latin America has been a good challenge to us and forces us to delve more carefully into global economic and social problems. It goes without saying that the speeches of Pope John Paul II have been a special source to us here in the United States. The encyclical, *Laborem Exercens*, was issued in September 1981, after we had begun our work on the Committee, but its teaching is central in our document.

Finally, I hope we have made it clear that we sincerely do not want to make the pastoral letter a political instrument of either the Democratic or Republican party. To be sure, we cannot help but say things that will have ramifications for public policy; in a document on the economy that is inevitable. However, it would be unfair to say we began our process with any sort of political agenda. We began our work on the Committee as convinced faith-people seeking to explore the economic situation in the United States and its impact abroad from the perspective of our faith tradition.

As you read the pastoral letter, remember that it is just a beginning. Unlike the recent one on nuclear ethics (*The Challenge of Peace: God's Promise and Our Response*), ethical reflections on the economy do not lend themselves to a neat package. Many have noted that the nuclear statement is just the opening round in a long discussion. Imagine what our draft on the economy will be! We have made a beginning with the hope that later statements by future generations of bishops will continue the reflections. When you receive our first draft which will be available at the annual meeting of the bishops on November 12, 1984, please help us and share your comments with us. Reflect on the pastoral with your faith community or academic colleagues. We truly need your help. After receiving responses and critiques, if all goes as planned, we hope to have a second draft prepared for a June 1985 meeting of the U.S. bishops, and a final version written for November 1985. Meanwhile, there is much work to be done. I do hope you will remember our work in your prayers.

Preface

IN THE CLOSING PAGES OF *THE PROTESTANT ETHIC AND the Spirit of Capitalism*, Max Weber expressed serious misgivings about the future of capitalism in the United States. He feared that as people abandoned the interplay between religious and business values, civilization would be on the decline:

> . . . in the United States, the pursuit of wealth, stripped of its religious and ethical meaning, tends to become associated with purely mundane passions. . . . For of the last stage of this cultural development, it might well be truly said: "Specialists without spirit, sensualists without heart; this nullity imagines that it has attained a level of civilization never before achieved."

Committed to affirming and improving the role of business in society, the Center for Ethics and Religious Values in Business of the University of Notre Dame takes Weber's warning as a challenge for continued reflection and action. To focus attention on religious thinking and the business world, the Center sponsors a biennial symposium on some aspect of the theme.

The 1980 Symposium resulted in the book *The Judeo-Christian Vision and the Modern Corporation,* which includes such scholars as James Gustafson, John C. Bennett, Michael Novak, Kirk Hanson, Denis Goulet, Christopher Stone, James Schall, S.J., Edward Trubac, Burton Leiser, William Sexton, Kenneth Jameson, Charles Wilber, Catherine Cleary, and Elmer Johnson. Of the conference, *The New York Times* reported: ". . . there would be no facile resolution of the conflict between the values of a just society and the sharply opposing values of successful corporations."

The 1982 Symposium examined John Paul II's encyclical letter *Laborem Exercens*. The meeting brought together eighteen distinguished scholars and corporate and labor leaders. In a lively and fruitful three days, some 150 persons shared in the discussions, which *Newsweek* characterized as a "free marketplace of ideas" exploring a religious vision of business power. The 1982 conference resulted in the volume, *Co-Creation and Capitalism: John Paul II's Laborem Exercens*, which includes essays by Michael Novak, Stanley Hauerwas, David Hollenbach, S.J., Bernard Murchland, Joseph A. Pichler, J. Bryan Hehir, Denis Goulet, Ernest Bartell, C.S.C., Andrea Lee, IHM, Amata Miller, IHM, George C. Lodge, Mark J. Fitzgerald, C.S.C., and Elmer W. Johnson.

The Center for Ethics and Religious Values in Business is under the co-directorship of Oliver Williams, C.S.C., and John Houck, both of the Department of Management, College of Business Administration. It evolved from the University of Notre Dame Joint Committee on Business, Theology and Philosophy founded in 1976.

The Center seeks to build bridges between business, business studies and the humanities. Its programs are designed to strengthen the Judeo-Christian ethical foundations in business and public policy decisions by fostering dialogue between academic and corporation leaders and by research and publications.

Publications developed by the Center include: *Full Value: Cases in Christian Business Ethics*, *A Matter of Dignity: Inquiries into the Humanization of Work*, *The Judeo-Christian Vision and the Modern Corporation*, and *Co-Creation and Capitalism: John Paul II's Laborem Exercens*. Articles have appeared in *California Management Review, Business Horizons, Theology Today* and the *Harvard Business Review*.

For the conference, *Catholic Social Teaching and the U.S. Economy*, and the publication of this volume, we are most grateful for the encouragement and financial support provided by the Indiana Committee for the Humanities, The National Endowment for the Humanities, and the General Electric Foundation; and at the University of Notre Dame: the College of Business Administration and the Center for Continuing Education.

We wish to thank at Notre Dame Deborah K. Buscoe, Janice Coffield, Patricia Flanigan, Jacqueline Marnocha, Phyllis Sandfort, Kristina Strom and John Lawless for their help. We are especially indebted to two graduate assistants, Dale T. Wolberg and Charles A. Schwartz, for their research and editorial assistance. We wish to acknowledge the contributions of: Peter Lombardo, Assistant Director, Center for Continuing Education; Michael Garvey, Assistant Director, Information Services; Sister Elaine DesRosiers, O.P., Director of Educational Media; Daniel Jenky, C.S.C., Director of Campus Ministry; Calvin Bower, Chairperson, Department of Music; and David E. Schlaver, C.S.C., Editor and Publisher of Ave Maria Press.

For guidance and support we wish to recognize our president, Father Theodore M. Hesburgh, C.S.C.; our dean, Frank K. Reilly; our associate deans, Yusaku Furuhashi and Vincent Raymond; and our chairperson, Robert P. Vecchio.

Our special gratitude goes to the copy editors, Katharine Terry Dooley and Mary Dooley Houck, both of whom serve generously in a voluntary capacity.

Finally, it is our pleasure to dedicate this volume to the U.S. Catholic Bishops' Committee charged to draft the pastoral letter on Catholic Social Teaching and the United States Economy: Archbishop Rembert Weakland, O.S.B. (chair), Archbishop Thomas Donnellan, Bishop George Speltz, Bishop William Weigand and Bishop Peter Rosazza. Their task is a most difficult one. The openness, fidelity and resourcefulness of the Committee more than meet the challenge!

John W. Houck
Oliver F. Williams, C.S.C.
Co-directors, Center for Ethics
    and Religious Values in Business
University of Notre Dame
Notre Dame, IN 46556
August 1984

One

The Making of a Pastoral Letter

OLIVER F. WILLIAMS, C.S.C.

"THERE IS TROUBLE IN THE LAND." WITH THAT NOTE A
recent television program opened a penetrating discussion of the
economy of the United States. Concern about unemployment, the
development of a permanent "marginalized group" who lack marketable skills, and the suffering endured by many of the least advantaged
as plants close and the economy enters a new phase are just a few of
the burning domestic issues. Sensitive Americans are also deeply trou-
bled about the growing economic dilemmas of Third World nations
as they strive to find a place in the world economy. What does Catholic social teaching have to say to the present economic situation in the
United States and the world?[1]

It is this question which has been the focus of a special committee
appointed by the U.S. bishops to write a pastoral letter to be titled
"Catholic Social Teaching and the United States Economy." The
schedule calls for the presentation of the first draft of the pastoral at
the November 1984 meeting of the U.S. bishops in Washington, D.C.,
discussion of a second draft at the June 1985 session, and the submission of the final draft at the November 1985 bishops' meeting.

The History of the Document

In their November 1980 meeting the U.S. bishops approved a
Pastoral Letter on Marxist Communism.[2] That letter was designed to

1

be a "Christian reflection on the Marxist world view," hence it was quite abstract, avoiding any discussion of political, economic or military actions of Marxist regimes. After completing this pastoral, the bishops accepted a motion from their ranks to begin drafting a similar document on capitalism.[3] As a result of this vote in November 1980, the U.S. bishops' ad hoc Committee on the American Economy was formed under the chairmanship of Archbishop Rembert Weakland, O.S.B., of Milwaukee, Wisconsin. Archbishop Thomas Donnellan of Atlanta, Georgia; Bishop George Speltz of St. Cloud, Minnesota; Bishop William Weigand of Salt Lake City, Utah; and Auxiliary Bishop Peter Rosazza of Hartford, Connecticut were also assigned to the committee.[4] Committee consultants (who meet regularly with the committee) are: Rev. Michael Lavelle, S.J., an M.I.T. trained economist, representing the Conference of Major Superiors of Men; Sister Margaret Cahill, O.P., also an economist, representing the Leadership Conference of Women Religious; Dr. Donald Warwick of Harvard University; and Dr. Charles Wilber of the Economics Department at the University of Notre Dame. Four staff members of the U.S. Catholic Conference in Washington, D.C. also serve as regular consultants: Thomas Quigley, Rev. Bryan Hehir, Ronald Krietemeyer and Msgr. George Higgins. In addition, Rev. John R. Donahue, S.J. of the Jesuit School of Theology (Berkeley) and Rev. David Hollenbach, S.J., of the Weston School of Theology (Cambridge, MA) have served as consultants in the areas of biblical studies and Catholic social teaching.

Although the pastoral on Marxism was primarily a theoretical analysis, the bishops' committee soon came to the conclusion that a similar document on capitalism was not feasible. There is no one theoretical position on capitalism and, in any event, the real concern of the prelates was the United States economy and its global effect, not some construct called "capitalism." The bishops were cognizant of the growing unrest in American society and they took it to be their duty to address this turbulence in the light of the Catholic social teaching.

Public Response

The business press made little pretense; they did not appreciate the Catholic bishops involving the church in discussions on the economy. Although the bishops' committee had conducted a number of hearings with a wide spectrum of experts on different aspects of the problems to be addressed, it was not until the first set of public hearings was announced that the proposed pastoral letter attracted widespread press interest. On December 12, 13 and 14, 1983, the public discussion was held at the University of Notre Dame and organized by two of its faculty, Professor John Houck and Father Oliver Williams, C.S.C. Papers were presented by 15 well-known scholars and practitioners representing a wide spectrum of viewpoints. (All the papers are included in this volume.) Several days before the opening of the Notre Dame symposium, both *Fortune* and *Business Week* registered their opinions.

Perhaps the most biting critique was in the column of *Fortune*'s managing editor, Daniel Seligman. He reasoned that the bishops will make a case for socialistic solutions, since "socialism gives them a role to play, while capitalism—reliance on impersonal market forces—leaves them out in the cold." Seligman went on: "Continuing to act out the axiom that God intended them to be social planners, the bishops are once again on the secular stage and once again threatening to unclarify the issue."[5] Later, *Fortune* published three letters on the Seligman piece, all of which were very critical of the editor.[6]

Business Week, while more moderate in tone, was equally disparaging. Their writer tended to see the force of the pastoral letter as just another proclamation for the liberal Democratic agenda.[7] Although concern for the poor on the part of the Jews and Christians antedated Republicans and Democrats by over a thousand years, the *Business Week* writer assumed that the solutions offered by the bishops' committee would be a clone of the Democratic party strategies. In any event, the two-page article revealed little sympathy for the work of the bishops' committee.

The Wall Street Journal ran a brief item on November 18, 1983 titled "The Bishops' Agenda." Obviously not impressed with the church's past track record, the *Journal* article concluded on a sarcastic note, speculating on the contents of the letter. "Perhaps it will illuminate the hidden dangers that exist in human tendencies to accumulate savings and invest them in factories and farms. Of course, we are fully prepared for a recommendation of unilateral disinvestment."[8]

The New York Times, reporting on the symposium, captured the spirit of the meeting: "contentiousness is commonplace here at Notre Dame, the home field of the Gipper. And when dozens of business leaders, theologians and academics lined up against each other at the university this week, the debate over the economy was fought as hard as any gridiron encounter." *The New York Times* writer was impressed that the Notre Dame conference included "people with various shades of opinion," but he noted a dilemma with this approach: "The attempts at even-handedness left some of the participants a little frustrated. 'I have a feeling we haven't captured the sense of urgency among the poor,' Bishop William K. Weigand of Salt Lake City said at one point."[9]

The *Los Angeles Times*, analyzing the Notre Dame meeting, observed that "About one-third of the major speakers represented conservative viewpoints; the remainder voiced moderate-to-liberal positions." This writer noted a prediction "that the letter will make the antinuclear statement seem like 'a Sunday-school picnic' by comparison."[10]

Church Involvement in Social and Political Issues

A recent editorial in *The Wall Street Journal* captured the mood of some of the faithful when it severely criticized mainline Protestant churches and the American Catholic Church. "The mainline Protestant churches and the American Catholic Church failed to devote sufficient resources to creating a sturdy moral answer to aggressive modern secularism. . . . Catholic and Protestant church leaders chase secular political goals while neglecting the needs of their congregations for moral and spiritual nourishment."[11]

There is no question that "moral and spiritual nourishment" are essential to the mission of the church. How is it that the churches are increasingly involved in social and political issues? How are these concerns part of the church's mission? These are crucial questions for many today and some background may be helpful.

The overarching Catholic vision was stated in systematic form by Thomas Aquinas (1225-1274) and this perspective continues to guide the church today.[12] Aquinas, drawing on the biblical teaching and the writings of the Church Fathers, wove an enduring tapestry with an Aristotelian and neo-Platonic philosophic framework. All of creation flows from God and finally will return to him. The goal of life on this earth is to become the sort of person who will finally enjoy the vision of God in the next world. "Man's ultimate happiness consists solely in the contemplation of God. . . ."[13]

Becoming the sort of person who might enjoy this vision, becoming virtuous, is only thought to be possible because of a gift of God (a supernatural gift of grace). Appropriating the virtues over a lifetime is the *Means* to the *End* of human life. Then one is oriented properly to God and may see him in the next life. For Aquinas, however, all creation is fundamentally good and being properly oriented to God entails as well the appropriate orientation toward the natural good.[14] Aquinas highlights the key biblical virtues—faith, hope and charity—but he also stresses the need to form character in Aristotle's four cardinal virtues—wisdom, justice, temperance, and fortitude.

For Aquinas, then, moral and spiritual nourishment was crucial, for this was the way one prepared for life in the next world. The focus was on personal morality and in this context the medieval theologians wrote much about just prices, trade and usury. The efforts of the moralist were largely directed to individual Christians and were designed to insure that each kept faithful to a path of personal virtue.

While the churches have never forsaken their role of shaping the character of individual Christians through preaching, teaching and liturgy, there has been a new realization that the Christian mission also entails criticizing the unjust social structures and transforming the world. Aquinas lived in an era when it was generally assumed that society was static. People most often remained in the socio-economic group where they were born, as lord, peasant, craftsman or merchant. "Justice" was understood to mean that each person was entitled to whatever their particular role in society required. Thus, in "justice," a lord had considerably more material goods than a peasant. Viewing the world in terms of the analogy of the human body, each class of society was seen to have a different role to perform in society, but all were united in an organic unity.

How is it that transforming the world and hence involvement in social and political issues have come to be understood in the church as an integral part of its mission, as a "constitutive dimension of the preaching of the Gospel"?[15] On one level, it could be argued that in the United States only in recent years have Catholics assumed positions of power in business, government and the wider society. It would have made little sense to speak of changing the social structures to the immigrant parents or grandparents of the current generation of American Catholics. As a result of education and the upward mobility of their parents, present-day Catholics are often very influential in the United States. In 1891 Pope Leo XIII issued the encyclical (a pastoral letter written by the pope as the chief shepherd of the church) *Rerum Novarum*. This encyclical was published in face of the impact of the industrial revolution and the church's growing concern over severe working conditions and the exploitation of the workers. American Catholics were largely blue collar people, and the pastoral championed their cause — political and economic rights. Today the descendants of these poor workers probably do not need to hear a comforting word but rather a challenging one — a call to continue to fashion a world that is more humane for the poor and the powerless!

Unlike the United States, Europe has long had a tradition of Catholics being directly active in social and political issues. Theologians reflecting on the relationship between temporal progess and salvation have deepened our understanding of the Kingdom of God. The Jews of Jesus' time believed that in some ways the Kingdom of God was already present. It was experienced in the historical acts of God (cf. 2 Samual 7:12-16), yet it was also future (cf. Judges 8:23). Jesus preached that where people are conforming their lives to the will of God, there the Kingdom is coming (Matthew 6:9-13). In his many stories, Jesus portrays the characteristics of the Kingdom — peace, justice, forgiveness, and harmony. Following the resurrection, the disciples of Jesus came to realize that the Kingdom of God had come into the world in the very person of Jesus, the Christ. The church today has come to realize that human work furthers the Kingdom of God. Pope John Paul II in the 1981 encyclical, *Laborem Exercens* (On Human Work), reiterates this point.

> Let the Christian who listens to the word of the living God, uniting work with prayer, know the place that his work has not only in earthly progress but also in the development of the Kingdom of God. . . .[16]

Tying "earthly progress" with the Christian vocation is now a well-established fact in Roman Catholic teaching. "Moral and spiritual nourishment" that simply focused on personal virtue to the exclusion of a social dimension would indeed be a deficient diet in the Catholic context.[17] John Paul II quotes the Second Vatican II document "The Church in the Modern World" to make this point: "People are not deterred by the Christian message from building up the world, or impelled to neglect the welfare of their fellows. They are, rather, more stringently bound to do these very things."[18]

In *Laborem Exercens* John Paul II brings together the traditional emphasis in Christian teaching on the need to become virtuous persons with the relatively recent focus on transforming the world. Work has a subjective and an objective dimension and the development of the Kingdom of God entails both. John Paul understands the Book of Genesis to mean that the most important purpose of work is to develop the human qualities of the person (the subjective dimension of work). When Genesis speaks of human "dominance" over nature, this is indeed an invitation for humankind to share in the work of creation, to be co-creators and transform the world (the objective dimension of work).

> . . . Man ought to imitate God, his creator, in working, because man alone has the unique characteristics of likeness to God.[19]
>
> Man shares by his work in the activity of the creator.[20]

To be sure, salvation is more comprehensive than present liberation from dehumanizing environments. Insofar as the Kingdom of God reaches the human heart, it overcomes sin and floods a life with the love that strikes at the root of social and political injustices. Yet, because God has acted and continues to act to realize his Kingdom on earth, his creatures are called to respond and mirror his love by actively changing the world in accord with his intentions. The Kingdom of God will come finally and completely only in God's good time.[21]

At root, this discussion of the development of the Kingdom of God draws on the theological issue of how the divine and human contribute to the economy of salvation. While no exhaustive explanation is possible for such a mystery, the work of theologians such as Walter Kasper and H. Richard Niebuhr is most helpful.[22] Knowing who God is, his mighty deeds in the past and his present work, Christians are called to conform their action to God's action. Sometimes called the "indictive/ imperative" approach of biblical ethics, this style helps to understand how the human response is a sign and a mediation of God's activity, while in no way exhausting all of the divine initiatives. The human response is indeed essential, yet no one plan of action can be construed to be God's plan or *the* plan.

Recent church documents stress the primacy of the spiritual, yet these documents are misunderstood if this emphasis is taken to mean a flight from social and political concerns.[23] The church vision here is one of integral humanism which considers the concrete person emeshed in social and political structures. Redemption affects all creation and efforts to overcome unjust aspects of the world are part of the spiritual task. The Gospel proclamation is one of love but also one of justice and peace. Thus the emphasis on the spiritual is not meant to imply that the Christian can escape from involvement in the world but rather it calls for a more profound engagement with it. That which is truly human is spiritual. Pope John Paul has repeatedly taught that Christ and the church shed light and offer hope to the person in his or her world. The mission of the church is to speak and act in the concrete situation.

> Man in the full truth of his existence, of his personal being and also of his community and social being — in the sphere of his own family, in the sphere of society and very diverse contexts, in the sphere of his own nation or people . . . , and in the sphere of the whole of mankind — this man is the primary route that the Church must travel in fulfilling her mission: *he is the primary and fundamental way for the Church*, the way traced out by Christ himself . . .[24]

Thus it is clear that while the Roman Catholic Church can never forsake its role of shaping the character of Christians by its preaching, teaching and liturgy, this task does not exhaust its mission of providing "moral and spiritual nourishment."[25] A recent statement of the Administrative Board of the United States Catholic Conference outlines this other important dimension.

> The church's role in the political order includes the following:
> — education regarding the teachings of the church and the responsibilities of the faithful;
> — analysis of issues for their social and moral dimensions;
> — measuring public policy against Gospel values;
> — participating with other concerned parties in debate over public policy; and
> — speaking out with courage, skill and concern on public issues involving human rights, social justice and the life of the church in society.[26]

Economic Life and Catholic Social Teaching

In Catholic moral life the church, speaking through legitimate authority, is understood to be endowed by Christ with special competence to interpret tradition, Scripture and the natural law. In practice, church statements contain various types of assertions. For example, the recent pastoral letter on nuclear ethics, *The Challenge of Peace: God's Promise and Our Response*, approved in May 1983 by the U.S. Catholic Bishops, distinguishes between three sorts of moral assertions: universally-binding moral principles, previous magisterial teaching, and concrete applications to specific cases. In this latter category, the pastoral suggests that a diversity of views might be expected, all based on the same moral principles, for "prudential judgments are involved based on specific circumstances which can change or which can be interpreted differently by people of good will".[27]

To understand the church's response to economic life, one must keep in mind the type of distinctions regarding moral assertions that are employed in *The Challenge of Peace*. Reading church encyclicals or pastoral letters of decades past will most often tell one more about the dominant threats to human dignity in that era than about how to be moral in the present situation. Church documents though written on a particular problem and reflecting the dominant thought patterns of the time, serve to build up a body of teaching which achieves greater authority as it is applied to new situations.

For example, Thomas Aquinas, synthesizing much of the religious thought up to his time, expressed the dominant religious perspective on trade in the thirteenth century. Merchants were likely to succumb to greed, which not only destroys the virtuous character of the individual but also erodes the moral fabric of the community. Thus trade and wealth creation were suspect and most often discussed in connection with the sin of avarice. Unfortunately, this bias against commerce, although it may have made sense in a particular historical context, is often prevalent in religious thinking in later ages.

A thinker who has had a profound influence on how people have come to understand commerce is Adam Smith (1723-1790). Smith asked a very simple but ingenious question: Why are some nations noticeably wealthier than their neighbors? In his famous work, *An Inquiry into the Nature and Causes of the Wealth of Nations*, published in 1776, Smith related his observations. Some nations were wealthier because they used an effective division of labor in making products and because they utilized the free competitive market. His notion of the market mechanism continues to underpin what have become known as capitalist economies.

In civilized society he stands at all times in need of the cooperation and assistance of great multitudes, while his whole life is scarce sufficient to gain the friendship of a few persons. . . . Man has almost constant occasion for the help of his brethren, and it is in vain for him to expect it from their benevolence only. He will be more likely to prevail if he can interest their self-love in his favour, and show them that it is for their own advantage to do for him what he requires of them. Whoever offers to another a bargain of any kind proposes to do this. . . . It is not from the benevolence of the butcher, the brewer, or the baker, that we expect our dinner, but from their regard to their own interest.[28]

The prevailing mercantile view looked to the quantity of precious metals to measure wealth. Smith rejected this understanding, for he saw that real wealth was a nation's productivity, "the value of the annual produce of its land and labour." Increased productivity (wealth) was not an *end* in itself but a *means* to increase the quality of life of people. Smith accepted the Judeo-Christian vision which portrayed a land where all might enjoy the good things of creation. His insight was that this vision, while far from realized in any nation, was gradually becoming a reality in those places which utilized incentives, economic action based on self-interest (profit motive), and a market economy. Smith assumed that the *self* that was self-interested would be shaped by moral forces in the community so that economic self-interest would not degenerate into a crass selfishness. His vision was one of an acquisitive economy enabling a humane community.

At their best, all the church statements which reflect on and offer guidance to capitalist economies are attempts to be the moral force envisioned by Adam Smith insuring that an acquisitive economy does not degenerate into an acquisitive society. For example, Pope Leo XIII in *Rerum Novarum* put the Church squarely on the side of the workers in the struggle for recognition of labor unions. In 1908 30 Protestant denominations formed the Federal Council of Churches in America and this group championed social reforms such as adequate working conditions, child-labor laws and a living wage. Protestant writers including Congregationalist Pastor Washington Gladden in *Applied Christianity* (1886) and *Church and Modern Life* (1908), and Baptist Walter Rauschenbusch in *Christianity and the Social Crisis* (1910) and *Theology of the Social Gospel* (1917) argued for reform. Monsignor John A. Ryan was most influential in Catholic circles, writing *A Liv-*

ing Wage (1906) and *Distributive Justice* (1916). Ryan drafted a crucial document of the National Catholic Welfare Conference (the predecessor of the United States Catholic Conference) issued in 1919 by the U.S. bishops and often cited as the forerunner of some of Franklin Roosevelt's New Deal policies. Titled *Social Reconstruction: A General Review of the Problems and Survey of Remedies*, Ryan's document offered a moral perspective on the economy and made suggestions for such reforms as minimum-wage laws, child-labor laws, the right of labor to organize and unemployment and health insurance. For the most part, Ryan's suggestions have become public policy in the United States.

In 1931 Pope Pius XI issued *Quadragesimo Anno.* While its proposed alternative model of society is of dubious value today, the role of the church as an agent of change in the socio-political order was clearly established. Three principles enunciated in the document have been dominant in all subsequent Catholic social theory: the need to protect the dignity of the person; the concern that organizations be no larger than necessary — subsidiarity; and the focus on the necessity for mediating structures (family, professional associations, church, etc.) between the person and the state.

Quadragesimo Anno outlined a vision of society and its relationship to the state which has continued to develop in Catholic social thought. Society is comprised of all the various groupings that people find necessary or helpful — families, churches, unions, professional associations, business corporations, social clubs, neighborhood associations, and so on. The role of the state is to be *in the service of* society; that is, its role is primarily to facilitate the cooperation and well-being of all these groupings or "mediating structures" as they are often called today. The encyclical uses the verbs *direct, watch, urge,* and *restrain* "as occasion requires and necessity demands" when describing the role of the state (para. 80). The 1961 encyclical of Pope John XXIII, *Mater et Magistra,* employs similar terms: the role of the state is to "encourage, stimulate, regulate, supplement and complement" (para. 53).

Catholic social thought is ever vigilant against collectivist tendencies which tend to obliterate legitimate mediating structures. This defense of personal rights is clearly evident in the 1981 encyclical, *Laborem Exercens,* where Pope John Paul II vigorously defends the solidarity of workers and their right to come together in organizations to defend common interests. Eschewing the model of interest-group pluralism which tends to view the world exclusively through the prism of one set of interests, Catholic social thought repeatedly returns to the notion of the common good as the appropriate context in which to consider one's own interests. John Paul II emphasizes this point in *Laborem Exercens.*

> Just efforts to secure the rights of workers who are united by the same profession should always take into account the limitations imposed by the general economic situation of the country. Union demands cannot be turned into a kind of group or class "egoism," although they can and should also aim at correcting—with a view to the common good of the whole society—everything defective in the system of ownership of the means of production or in the way these are managed.[29]

Society is often *identified with* the state in socialist theory and practices. Thus the state has control of all aspects of life—the arts, sciences, politics, economics, etc. Some would argue that in time the appropriate social structures will transform persons so that state control will be unnecessary. People will be almost selfless. Catholic social theory could never accept this perspective. Assuming that human nature is flawed, one of the roles of the state, according to this religious perspective, is to facilitate the growth of desirable character traits and mute those that are less noble. Yet there is a confidence in the goodness, the cooperative dimension of the person, so that the social constraints of the state are designed to enhance human freedom and curtail selfishness for the common good.

This confidence in the fundamental goodness of the person underlies the church's basic strategy of appealing to the consciences of those who control wealth and power in order to bring about basic changes in society designed to alleviate the plight of the poor. Pope Paul VI in *Populorum Progressio* (Development of Peoples) argues for a new international economic order but he appeals for strategies of negotiation and consensus rather than any violent means. His *Octogesima Adveniens* (1971) echoes a similar theme. Pope John Paul II, in his address in Oaxaca, Mexico also makes this point: ". . . it is not just, it is not human, it is not Christian to continue certain situations that are clearly unjust. You must implement real, effective measures on the local, national, and international levels, following the broad line marked out by the encyclical *Mater et Magistra* (Part III). And it is clear that those who can do the most are the ones most obligated to collaborate in this effort."[30] Again, speaking in Brazil, John Paul says:

So the church of the poor speaks like this: You particularly the ones who in decision-making have power, you, on whom the world situation depends, do everything so that the life of each man in your country may become "more human," more worthy of man.

Do everything so that at least gradually the abyss that divides the few "excessively rich" from the great multitudes of poor, those who live in want, may disappear.[31]

"A Preferential But Not Exclusive Option for the Poor"

In 1968 at the Second General Conference of Latin American bishops at Medellín, Columbia, the assembled pastors took a bold step in publicly stating their intention of focusing the Church's efforts to do all that is necessary to help the poor organize and overcome injustices. In 1971, Paul VI in *Octogesima Adveniens* spoke of the "preferential respect due to the poor."[32] To be sure, this focus on the poor is not a new idea for Christianity. Jesus began his ministry by reading a text from Isaiah which summarized his central concerns: "He has sent me to bring good news to the poor, to proclaim liberty to captives and to the blind new sight, to set the downtrodden free, to proclaim the Lord's year of favor" (Luke 4:18). The Hebrew Scriptures tell of how God and all his people ought to regard the poor:

He will free the poor man who calls to Him, and those who need help,
He will have pity on the poor and feeble, and save the lives of those
in need . . . (Ps. 72:12-13).

What is significant about this "option for the poor" is that it signals a commitment by the bishops to promote social justice in the economic and political arenas.

In January 1979, another General Conference of Latin American bishops was held at Puebla, Mexico and attended by Pope John Paul II. The document from this assembly has a chapter entitled "A Preferential Option for the Poor," which not only stresses the need for a change in people's minds and hearts but also for a change in those structures of society which impede the progress of the poor.[33] Pope John Paul, speaking at Puebla, encouraged the bishops to speak out against injustice but he also warned against any movement that would present Christ as a political revolutionary. A year later in Brazil, John Paul spoke of "a preferential but not exclusive option for the poor."[34]

John Paul, throughout his writings, is trying to steer a course between simply supporting the status quo where it may be unjust and unabashedly encouraging violent revolution. To the rich and the powerful, he counsels concern for the poor and the environment that nurtures them. To the poor, he preaches "solidarity,"[35] taking a stand and collectively reacting to exploitative situations and systems.

> In order to achieve social justice in the various parts of the world, in the various countries and in the relationships between them, there is a need for ever new movements of solidarity of the workers and with the workers. This solidarity must be present whenever it is called for by the social degrading of the subject of work, by exploitation of the workers and by the growing areas of poverty and even hunger. The church is firmly committed to this cause for she considers it her mission, her service, a proof of her fidelity to Christ, so that she can truly be the "church of the poor."[36]

The church is not at all interested in provoking open confrontations between workers and authorities, for that would likely lead to much bloodshed. There is, however, in the theme of solidarity an acknowledgement that often a prudent and well planned confrontative stance is necessary. The underlying theme of *Laborem Exercens* is that, beneath all the conflict and competition among various social groupings, there is a mutuality of interests shared by all co-creators of the world.[37] The person is primarily *homo faber*, a "maker;" and solidarity underlies all socio-economic differences. There is no such thing as inevitable class struggle for Catholic social teaching. The struggle is always *for* justice, not *against* others. Marxists notions of inevitable struggle are erroneous.

> Even if in controversial questions the struggle takes on a character of opposition toward others, this is because it aims at the good of social justice, not for the sake of "struggle" or in order to eliminate the opponent. It is characteristic of work that it first and foremost unites people. In this consists its social power: the power to build community.[38]

How the Bishops Decided What to Say

One thing is certain: any pastoral letter from a national bishops' conference will rely on the current Vatican teaching. In the case of the economy, the 1981 encyclical, *Laborem Exercens*, has surely had a major influence on the U.S. bishops' letter. This is not simply because the bishops must submit to the pope's teaching under holy obedience, but rather because the Vatican teaching, for the most part, is already a product of consensus among the prelates. Authority in the Church is best understood on the analogy of a lens. As a lens focuses light, so church authority focuses the best insights of the community for the faithful. *Laborem Exercens*, written for the global community, is necessarily general and overarching. The task for a national bishops' conference is to bring this teaching down to the situation of its own country.

Not surprisingly, the U.S. bishops' pastoral on the economy has an opening chapter explaining why the church must speak to issues of the economy at this moment. The mission of the church as necessarily entailing improving social and political structures of society is discussed. Drawing from the Bible, the document presents a vision of God's intentions for humankind followed by a summary of the highlights of past Catholic teaching on socio-economic issues. The document concludes with four applications of the teaching: 1. Employment and Unemployment—the need to create jobs. 2. Poverty and Welfare—providing an adequate income for the poor and disadvantaged. 3. Trade with Third World Countries—how to narrow the gap between rich and poor nations. 4. Principles for Cooperation—consideration of the strengths and weaknesses of planning.[39]

The volume contains all the papers presented at the Notre Dame Conference in December 1983. The purpose of the conference was to assist the Bishops' Committee in their task of applying Catholic social teaching to the four areas described above. The authors were asked to help clarify for each of the topics the principle issues, the major policy options, the trade-offs involved in the major policy options and an ethical analysis of the moral and religious values at stake for the major policy options. Obviously, no one author could do all of these tasks, but for each topic the three (or five) authors collectively met the assignment. The 15 papers included are designed to assist in understanding the bishops' pastoral letter. Following the outline of the conference, the volume is divided into four sections and each section has an introduction which highlights the salient issues.

The Notre Dame meeting was open to the public and was attended by over 250 persons. Economists, government officials, labor leaders, theologians, business executives and a host of other constituencies were represented. Although it was impossible for all those attending to offer comments at the sessions, all were invited to submit written comments for the bishops' committee. A number wrote lengthy reports to the Committee after the Notre Dame conference.

A crucial ecclesiological principle was given full exercise at the Notre Dame meeting: the conviction that the Spirit is present in the entire community of faith. The church is the whole "People of God," and listening to a plurality of perspectives from all segments of the world is essential to the process of discerning the truth. This process is part of the mission of the church. The Second Vatican Council states the task: "For it is her (the Church's) task to uncover, cherish, and ennoble all that is true, good, and beautiful in the human community."[40] The openness to read the "signs of the times" is a quality conveyed particularly well with two images used a number of times in the Vatican II decree "The Dogmatic Constitution on the Church."[41] These images, the "People of God" and the "Pilgrim Church," are rooted in the experience of the Hebrews who were freed from slavery and led to the Promised Land. During this period, which in important ways is paradigmatic for all future times, the people were pilgrims on a journey, following the Lord with their best lights, often in the face of hardship and darkness. They persevered because of their faith and because they discerned God's will in their new circumstances. The church as "People of God" is continually searching for the truth to speak to the times. With its biblical vision as the context, the church brings all possible resources—intellectual, moral and spiritual—to bear as it formulates its teaching. Because the church understands itself as the People of God, one can expect a modest tone when making particular applications of principle in the pastoral letter. There will also be ample time for corrections before second, third and final drafts of the letter.

A Consensus Document?

Gregory Baum, theologian and resource person for the Canadian bishops when they wrote their 1983 economic statement, argued a provocative point in a *National Catholic Reporter* article entitled "Should Church Critique of Economy be Prophetic or Based on 'Consensus'?"[42] For Baum, the attempt by the U.S. bishops to gain a consensus among Catholics on economic questions is a foolish endeavor. "The search for 'a broad consensus' in the rich nations may at this particular time prevent the church from offering a prophetic message." The difficulty with this sort of proposition is that it fails to deliver the kind of nuanced analysis which might have the possibility of ultimately *producing* the food, housing, participation, shelter and jobs that a "preferential option for the poor" entails. A society of 200 million people is not going to have quality of life unless many of the most talented are drawn into the task.

The final document must be both prophetic in its challenge to the rich and powerful and consensual in seeking solutions to complex problems. For example, in research I have done on sugar-cane workers in a Third World nation it became clear that the major problems were price fluctuations in the world sugar market and uneven demand for sugar from developed countries. A major employer of sugar cane workers in this nation is a multinational business firm. There is a great temptation to castigate the "evil multinational" for causing the plight of poor workers. Further research indicates, however, that this particular multinational has done more than most of the major institutions in the Third World nation to help the poor — both their own employees and others as well.[43] To overcome the poverty of these workers in the Third World, there will have to be concerted action by many groups in the First World — trade unions, large farm owners in the U.S. who seek protective legislation limiting foreign sugar, and so on. To use the term of Pope John Paul II in *Laborem Exercens*, these First World interest groups are the "indirect employers" of Third World sugar cane workers — they are part of a web of structural injustice.[44] To correct the situation, there is a need for much discussion, for creating a "broad consensus" that the First World may have to have a more simple life style in order that the basic needs of the Third World might be met. This will not happen because of some fiat by the U.S. bishops or the pope — or even by a major multinational business. What the bishops can provide is a forum for discussion and some guidance on the priorities that should govern the difficult trade-offs involved in public policy as well as business decisions.

The Teaching Authority of a Conference of Bishops

The Roman Catholic Church with its doctrine of apostolic succession understands its bishops to be endowed with a special charism both when teaching alone and collegially. By virtue of ordination and collegiality, a bishop is a collaborator with fellow bishops in teaching and pastoral guidance. Although a conference of bishops does not have the extraordinary magisterium associated with an ecumenical council or the pope under clearly defined conditions, an episcopal conference does have doctrinal authority. The faithful are enjoined to take very seriously pastoral letters from a national conference of bishops. Canon 753 of the new code of canon law summarized this teaching:

> Although they do not enjoy infallible teaching authority, the bishops in communion with the head and members of the college, whether as individuals or gathered in conferences of bishops or in particular councils, are authentic teachers and instructors of the faith for the faithful entrusted to their care; the faithful must adhere to the authentic teaching of their own bishops with a sense of religious respect.[45]

Conclusion

Whatever the teaching, it must be communicated properly. Jesus communicated his understanding of God and God's will in masterful fashion. Unfortunately, the church is often poor in communication skills. Once the bishops decide *what* they want to say on the economy, the task that remains is *how* best to communicate that position. This latter task is, in my judgment, the crucial one. This pastoral letter could have an impact for years to come if it is heard and understood. The essays that follow will have a lasting value in aiding the understanding of the complex issues of the pastoral. As for aiding the communication, much remains to be done!

Notes

1. For collections of Catholic social teaching of the recent past, see the following: J. Gremillion, ed., *The Gospel of Peace and Justice: Catholic Social Teaching Since Pope John* (Maryknoll, NY: Orbis Books, 1976); and J. B. Benestad and F. J. Butler, eds., *Quest for Justice: A Compendium of Statements of the United States Catholic Bishops on the Political and Social Order, 1966-1980* (Washington, D.C.: United States Catholic Conference, 1981).

2. "Pastoral Letter on Marxist Communism," *Origins* 10 (1980), pp. 435-445.

3. For a discussion of the origin and development of the pastoral letter, see Archbishop Rembert Weakland, "Where Does the Economic Pastoral Stand?", *Origins* 13 (1984), pp. 753-759.

4. For a biographic sketch of the five bishops on the Committee and an analysis of the task of writing a pastoral letter on the economy, see Thomas J. Murray, "The Bishops Start a New Controversy," *Duns Business Month*, March 1984, pp. 31-35.

5. Daniel Seligman, "Keeping Up," *Fortune*, December 26, 1983, p. 32.

6. "Letters," *Fortune*, February 6, 1984, p. 20. For an interview with one of the authors of the letters, see Arthur Jones, "Capitalism Seen Through 'Teilhard's Prism'," *National Catholic Reporter*, April 27, 1984, pp. 11-13; 17-18.

7. "The Bishops Take on Conservative Economics," *Business Week*, December 19, 1983, pp. 79-80.

8. "The Bishops' Agenda," *The Wall Street Journal*, November 18, 1983, p. 30. See also Thomas Roeser, "Egad! The Bishops are Rewriting Adam Smith," *The Chicago Sun-Times*, July 3, 1983, p. 2.

9. Winston Williams, "Catholic Forum on Economy," *The New York Times*, December 15, 1983, p. 32. The concern for the poor is the common theme in nine articles on Religion and the Economy in *New Catholic World* 226, no. 1354 (1983).

10. Russell Chandler, "Catholic Bishops Look at Economics, Capitalism," *Los Angeles Times*, December 24, 1983, p. 24.

11. "School Prayer," *The Wall Street Journal*, March 20, 1984, p. 28.

12. See Oliver F. Williams, "Introduction," in Oliver F. Williams and John W. Houck, eds., *The Judeo-Christian Tradition and the Modern Corporation* (Notre Dame, Indiana: University of Notre Dame Press, 1982), pp. 1-21.

13. Aquinas, *Summa Contra Gentiles*, III, 37.

14. The Second Vatican Council decree, "The Church in the Modern World," reiterates this important point for the sphere of economics: ". . . economic activity is to be carried out according to its own methods and laws but within the limits of morality, so that God's plan for mankind can be realized." See Walter M. Abbott, ed., *The Documents of Vatican II* (New York: Guild Press, 1966), no. 64, p 273. All citations of Vatican II documents are to this edition.

15. The following sentence from the document of the 1971 World Synod of Bishops has been called "the most notable development to date in the history of modern social teaching": "Action on behalf of justice and participation in the transformation of the world fully appears to us as a constitutive dimension of the preaching of the gospel or, in other words, of the Church's

mission for the redemption of the human race and its liberation from every oppressive situation." See "Justice in the World," *The Gospel of Peace and Justice: Catholic Social Teaching Since Pope John*, ed. Joseph Gremillion (Maryknoll, N.Y.: Orbis Books, 1976), p. 514. For an analysis of this statement, see: Charles M. Murphy, "Action for Justice as Constitutive of the Preaching of the Gospel: What Did the 1971 Synod Mean?", *Theological Studies* 44 (1983), pp. 298-311; and Francis Schüssler Fiorenza, "The Church's Religious Identity and Its Social and Political Mission," *Theological Studies* 43 (1982), pp. 197-225.

16. *Laborem Exercens*, para. 27. All citations are to the text published by the United States Catholic Conference: Publication No. 825, Office of Publishing Services.

17. For a comprehensive study of the social dimension of the faith by twelve authors, see John W. Houck and Oliver F. Williams, eds., *Co-Creation and Capitalism: John Paul II's Laborem Exercens* (Washington, D.C.: University Press of America, 1983).

18. *Laborem Exercens*, para. 25.

19. *Ibid.*

20. *Ibid.*

21. The Vatican II document, "The Church in the Modern World," alludes to the dialectical aspect of the Kingdom. "On this earth that Kingdom is already present in mystery. When the Lord returns it will be brought into full flower" (no. 39).

22. Cf. H. Richard Niebuhr, *Christ and Culture* (New York: Harper, 1951); and Walter Kasper, *Jesus the Christ* (New York: Paulist Press, 1977).

23. Pope John Paul II, in his first encyclical letter, *Redemptor Hominis*, portrays his vision of integral humanism. See no. 14.

24. *Redemptor Hominis*, para. 14. All citations are to the text published by the United States Catholic Conference: Office of Publication Services.

25. For one attempt at formulating what it means to be a Christian in professional life, see Oliver F. Williams and John W. Houck, *Full Value: Cases in Christian Business Ethics* (San Francisco: Harper & Row, 1978).

26. *Political Responsibility: Choices for the 1980's*, A Statement of the Administrative Board: United States Catholic Conference, Office of Publishing Services, March 1984.

27. *The Challenge of Peace: God's Promise and Our Response*, para. 10. Text published by the United States Catholic Conference, Office of Publishing Services.

28. Adam Smith, *The Wealth of Nations*, ed. Edwin Cannan (Chicago: University of Chicago Press, 1976), p. 18.

29. *Laborem Exercens*, para. 20.

30. "Address to the Indians of Oaxaca and Chiapas on January 29, 1979,"

in John Eagleson and Philip Scharper, eds., trans. by John Drury, *Puebla and Beyond* (Maryknoll, New York: Orbis Books, 1979), p. 83.

31. "Remarks at Favela Vidigal on July 2, 1980," in *Addresses and Homilies Given in Brazil*, para. 4. Text published by the United States Catholic Conference, translation by National Catholic News Service, p. 44.

32. Cf. "Medellín Documents," in Joseph Gremillion, ed., *The Gospel of Peace and Justice: Catholic Social Teaching Since Pope John* (Maryknoll, NY: Orbis Books, 1976), p. 473. Also, see "Octogesima Adveniens," p. 496.

33. Cf. "Evangelization in Latin America's: Present and Future," in John Eagleson and Philip Scharper, eds., trans. by John Drury, *Puebla and Beyond* (Maryknoll, NY: Orbis Books, 1979), pp. 123-285.

34. In preaching on the beatitudes in Vidigal, the pope speaks a message to all: "The church also wants to draw out all that in the teaching of the eight beatitudes refers to each man: the poor, the one who lives in penury, the one who lives in abundance and well being and, finally the one who has an excess and has more than he needs. The same truths of the first beatitude refer to each one in a different way." See *Addresses and Homilies given in Brazil*, para. 4, p. 40.

35. The word "solidarity" is used ten times in *Laborem Exercens*, nine in paragraph 8 and once in paragraph 20.

36. *Laborem Exercens*, para. 8.

37. Some scholars have questioned whether *Laborem Exercens* is too optimistic about the possibility of the human race achieving such harmonious organic unity. Cf. David Hollenbach, "Human Work and the Story of Creation: Theology and Ethics," in John W. Houck and Oliver F. Williams, eds., *Co-Creation and Capitalism: John Paul II's Laborem Exercens* (Washington, D.C.: University Press of America, 1983), pp. 59-77.

38. *Laborem Exercens*, para. 20.

39. Cf. Archbishop Rembert Weakland, "Where Does the Economic Pastoral Stand?", *Origins* 13 (1984), pp. 753-759.

40. "The Church in the Modern World," *The Documents of Vatican II* (New York: Guild Press, 1966), no. 60, p. 289.

41. For the discussion of the images of the Church, see "Dogmatic Constitution on the Church," *The Documents of Vatican II*, pars. 6-9, pp. 18-26.

42. Gregory Baum, "Should Church Critique of Economy be Prophetic or Based on 'Consensus'?", *National Catholic Reporter*, March 16, 1984, p. 16. For another perspective, see O. Williams, "Religion: The Spirit or the Enemy of Capitalism," *Business Horizons* (Nov./Dec. 1983), pp. 6-13. For the full text of the Canadian Bishops' statement, "Ethical Reflections on the Economic Crisis," issued by the Episcopal Commission for Social Affairs of the Canadian Conference of Catholic Bishops, see *This World* 5 (Spring/Summer 1983), pp. 122-132.

43. Cf. O. Williams, "The Church and Multi-nationals: Who Cast the First Stone?", *Harvard Business Review*, Sept./Oct. 1984.

44. *Laborem Exercens*, para. 16. For a discussion of the concept of the indirect employer, see Donal Dorr, *Option for the Poor: A Hundred Years of Vatican Social Teaching* (Maryknoll, NY: Orbis Books, 1983), pp. 233-244.

45. For a good discussion of the meaning of "a mandate to teach" (*mandatum docendi*), see Avery Dulles, "The Teaching Authority of Bishops' Conferences," *America* (June, 1983), pp. 453-455.

Part I

Human Work and Employment Generation

JOHN W. HOUCK

According to comments made by some bishops, the letter is almost certain to call for the creation of jobs for the unemployed as a national moral imperative . . .

Los Angeles Times,
December 15, 1983

Factory shutdowns have become a major concern of the Catholic hierarchy . . . because "they have an immediate impact on the church, with people knocking on the door for food and help and family life being torn apart" . . . The bishops might urge the government to guarantee full employment and even act as the employer of last resort . . .

Dun's Business Month,
March 1984

"To deprive people of work is to exclude them from active participation in the communal human project of civilization . . . the human suffering of unemployment arises as much from isolation and loss of a sense of social participation that it produces as from the loss of income it brings."

National Catholic Register,
January 1, 1984

WORK IS A FUNDAMENTAL DIMENSION OF WHAT IT MEANS
to be human. Particularly in an industrial society, we place great emphasis on work and employment as means of self-determination and
social opportunity:

> A job gives hope for material and social advancement. It is a way of
> providing one's children a better start in life. It may mean the only
> honorable way of escape from the poverty of one's parents. It helps to
> overcome racial and other social barriers. In short . . . a job is the
> passport to freedom and to a better life. To deprive people of jobs is
> to read them out of our society.[1]

According to Catholic social teaching work is understood as a basic
human right. Part One of this volume considers the ethical and theological perspectives of human work, mainly in the essays of Joseph
Pichler and David Hollenbach, and the policy ramifications of employment generation in the essays of Rudy Oswald and Ray Marshall.

Surprising as it may seem, work and full employment can be viewed
as fulfilling a biblical commission — for it is through our work that we
humans share in the work of Divine Creation. The story of Genesis
is in a sense the first "gospel of work." In the story, creation is not
understood as having been completely finished by God. Rather, human beings are placed on earth as God's representatives and charged
with responsibility for making the world into a fuller and a more just
community. Work in this light has inherent dignity and the humane
values emerging in the work community are a revelation of God's will
for humankind.[2]

For some time, though, the moral and policy imperatives for employment generation have not been the focal point of our national
concern. The priority has been monetary restraint to reduce inflation.
The results of this policy have been mixed. Monetary restraint, while
successful in stopping the surge of inflation in the 1970s caused by
oil price increases and by the expansionary policies followed earlier,
has been accompanied by erratic business cycles, the most severe recession in the postwar era, and the highest unemployment level since
the Depression. According to many, disinflation in recent years and
the rise of poverty over the past decade have created a widespread and
pressing need for alternative economic policies to provide full employment for the general welfare.

How do we generate employment in America? The public policy debate is largely between those who would rely on the private sector for training programs and job opportunities, and those who would have the federal government take an activist role in reducing unemployment. For example, in chapter two Joseph Pichler analyzes some of the negative consequences that may occur when legislation is used as a shield against market forces. He emphasizes the need for careful analysis before endorsement of governmental proposals affecting employment. On the particular issue of minimum wage legislation, Pichler draws from the economic literature that the unintended but real result of such legislation is greatly reduced employment for the young and the lowest skilled workers.

An opposing set of considerations underlies Rudy Oswald's call in chapter three for renewed federal commitment to the Full Employment and Balanced Growth [Humphrey-Hawkins] Act of 1978. He focuses on the increasing job shortage in post-industrial America, the human misery of unemployment and its community costs, and the concomitant loss of opportunities for upward economic and social mobility. On this last point, after surveying changes in the industrial and occupational mix of the American economy, Oswald finds a gradual debasing of the nation's wage structure — especially the middle class of blue- and white-collar workers.[3] He foresees a two-tier work force:

> At the top will be a few executives, scientists and engineers, professionals, and managers, performing high-level, creative and fulfilling, high-paid, full-time work in a good environment. At the bottom will be low-paid workers performing relatively simple, low-skill, dull, routine, high-turnover jobs in a poor work environment, jobs often part-time and usually lacking job security and opportunities for advancement.

In chapter four Ray Marshall, Secretary of Labor in the Carter Administration, makes the case for a partnership of labor, management and government to deal with structural unemployment brought about by a lack of skills and training in youth, illiterates, minorities, people in depressed areas and the technologically displaced. He argues for a reformed and revitalized Comprehensive Employment and Training Act (CETA) to deal with those who are untouched by upturns in the economy.

Ethical and theological perspectives on employment increase our understanding of the meaning of work. Joseph Pichler questions whether "one can really accept the view that the 'specific dignity' of man's life is derived from work" and suggests, instead, the balancing of work with spiritual and social activities. Taking an opposite approach, Oswald describes unemployment as a "major psychological trauma" in terms of suicide, infant mortality and other death rates; alcoholism and mental disorders, child abuse and family breakdown, and just meeting the mortgage and medical bills are becoming crucial problems for the unemployed.

Along this same line, in chapter five David Hollenbach develops the broad notion of "marginalization," and shows how it takes an economic form when persons are denied access to the world of work. Employment is essentially a means of social participation: the pursuit of human dignity requires not simply a living wage but also that one actively engages in "the communal human project of civilization."

Overriding all of these distinct perspectives is a strong consensus among the contributors that unemployment in America is much too high. Some unemployment is unavoidable, so economists define "full employment" as something less than 100 percent of the labor force. During the 1960s, full employment was said to exist when about 96 percent of American workers were employed; hence, the inevitable minimum of frictional and structural unemployment was about 4 percent. In the 1970s and 1980s unemployment rates of 7 to 10 percent have been tolerated, apparently as the price for steadfastness in monetary restraint.

In the religious community, there are serious doubts about the whole idea of employing monetarist strategies at the expense of the unemployed. The bishops in their statement on *The Economy: Human Dimensions*, rejected sheer monetary restraint:

> There are those who insist that we must tolerate high levels of unemployment for some, in order to avoid ruinous inflation for all. Although we are deeply concerned about inflation, we reject such a policy as not grounded in justice . . . Low employment and high inflation are not inevitable partners, as history and the experience of other industrialized countries bear out. Policymakers should seek and use measures to combat inflation which do not rely upon high rates of joblessness.[4]

Policies for Employment Generation

In chapter two, Joseph Pichler reviews patterns of unemployment in the United States since 1947 and argues that—apart from all-important federal efforts to eradicate discrimination and poverty—the appropriate role of the government is to maintain a largely capitalistic framework that enables all participants (individuals and firms) to pursue their self-interest. For Pichler, self-interest includes "moral, aesthetic and social concerns," as well as the commonly understood "economic" interests. He wants to retain high employment and growth and to diffuse power throughout the economy by private ownership and competition. With reference to the forthcoming pastoral letter on Catholic Social Teaching and the U.S. Economy, Pichler advocates as religious touchstones liberty (or "self-determination") and "radical charity" toward those in poverty by the members of the church—with less reliance on governmental welfare at all levels.

In chapter three, Rudy Oswald, Director of Economic Research, AFL-CIO, calls for renewed and expanded legislative initiatives to assert the priority of labor over capital and to recast the employment process in the service of humankind. American capitalism, in Oswald's overview, requires substantial changes in the unemployment insurance system, reduction of the work-week, targeted public job programs, labor law and collective bargaining reforms, and greater labor-management cooperation in fashioning a voluntary industrial policy. Without such interventions, Oswald warns, the American economy may experience inadequate growth of consumer buying power, loss of mid-level occupations, and a significant decline of social stability.

Former Secretary of Labor F. Ray Marshall observes in chapter four that by the end of the 1960s traditional American economic institutions, particularly in the labor market, had already begun losing their effectiveness. A chief difficulty in getting the economy back on track is that "many of our problems have international origins and our policy instruments are mainly national in scope." Like Pichler, Marshall would rely on strong market forces; like Oswald, he does see a role for government: "Other than consensus-building, the government would not do anything it is not already responsible for—it would simply do things more effectively and in concert with representatives of the private sectors." Marshall then elaborates how the government might organize employment and training programs.

In the concluding article, David Hollenbach advocates "a new form of mixed economy" whose key institution would be a collaborative approach by labor, management, government and community groups "to evaluate and in some measure regulate their economic behavior in light of its impact on employment." Underlying his analysis are two chief concerns. One is whether market forces can generate full employment. In the postwar era, every economic recovery has left the United States with a higher unemployment level than in preceding recoveries.

The second concern is whether "a more compassionate policy on transfer payments" (such as a guaranteed annual income) could secure human dignity and social justice for persons involuntarily unemployed. Here, Hollenbach develops the concept of "justice-as-participation" in the employment sphere. On both theological and social psychological grounds, Hollenbach proposes that the prime function of work is communal participation, not simply making a living; otherwise, he adds, "our goal would be clear: a sort of generalized welfare-leisure system for all."

The Quality of Work Life

The main implication of "justice-as-participation" is full employment (possibly with the government acting as the employer of last resort). Having a job, however, is not always a sufficient condition for the realization of human dignity. It is a commonplace of the industrial scene that overly specialized or regimented jobs (i.e., those with a high degree of specialization of labor) are at odds with psychological well-being. In the 18th century, Adam Smith noted the increase in material output caused by an organizational development, the division of labor, and described its dehumanizing costs:

> In the progress of the division of labour, the employment of the far greater part of those who live by labour, that is, of the great body of the people, comes to be confined to a few very simple operations, frequently to one or two. But the understandings of the greater part of

men are necessarily formed by their ordinary employments. The man whose whole life is spent in performing a few simple operations has no occasion to exert his understanding . . . He naturally loses, therefore, the habit of such exertion, and generally becomes as stupid and ignorant as it is possible for a human creature to become. The torpor of his mind renders him, not only incapable of relishing or bearing a part in any rational conversation, but of conceiving any generous, noble, or tender sentiment, and consequently of forming any just judgment concerning many even of the ordinary duties of private life . . . It corrupts even the activity of his body, and renders him incapable of exerting his strength with vigour and perseverance in any other employment than that to which he has been bred.[5]

In the mid-19th century, Karl Marx adopted the pessimism of Adam Smith about the alienating conditions of the new industrial order, in which the worker "does not affirm himself but denies himself . . . does not develop freely his physical and mental energy but mortifies his body and ruins his mind."[6] Since Marx's time, concern for alienation in the workplace has been overridden, for the most part, by the drive for organizational efficiency and conformity.

As we continue to place a primary emphasis on efficiency and productivity within business, we live with the reality that the great number of jobs will be intrinsically inhumane in their capacity to provide personal growth and social development. It is increasingly important, as America shifts to post-industrial structures, to face this issue and to explore ways to improve the quality of work life.

Since the 1950s, there has grown a rich literature on the quality of work life, including individual choice of flexible work schedules and compensation plans; the broadening of job variety and employee-group control over engineering and evaluating job performance; and legitimization of new managerial roles, away from the sheer exercise of authority and toward the democratization of the workplace.[7] In these and other ways, we will be providing men and women with workplaces which can be the cornerstones for a higher quality of life.

> Discovering creative ways to help others develop their humanity in the business world is often a formidable challenge. . . . Yet this may be one challenge of the Gospel. The person, understood as created for union and friendship with God, possesses a dignity that has its full flowering only in community.[8]

Summary of Principles

The chairperson and commentator of this panel of essayists was Gerald Cavanagh, S.J., author of *American Business Values* and management professor at the University of Detroit. He presented several principles which he believed could serve as themes for the Bishops' Pastoral, especially as it explored the values and attitudes of the men and women in our economy.

First, unemployment is much too high for an industrial society which places great emphasis on work and employment for personal identity and purpose in life. A high unemployment level breeds human and social injustice. Not having a job means idleness, loss of skills, plummeting of morale, even family disintegration and societal decay, but having a job can mean personal worth and a chance to succeed.

Second, racial, sexual and ethnic discrimination in employment is not only unjust, it is also bad economics. The economic costs of discrimination are not widely recognized, but they are substantial. Although we cannot determine with assured accuracy the costs, the Council of Economic Advisors has estimated that if educational and employment opportunities were made equal so that the average productivity of minority labor became equal to that of white workers, the gross national product would rise by about 4 percent.[9]

Third, we must encourage more jobs in the private sector. Entrepreneurialship is critical here because most new jobs come from small firms. If we are to deal with unemployment and hiring discrimination, we obviously must establish conditions which encourage growth in small firms.

Fourth, consensus building amongst management, labor and government is essential. We spend too much time, money and moral energy in adversarial disputes between these groups. Cooperation would seem to be especially appropriate to lessen some of the rigidities of wage-bargaining patterns and to emphasize the broad range of shared interests.

Fifth, we tend to emphasize freedom and liberty at the expense of community and the common good. Freedom is not unimportant, but we need a better balance of personal and communal values in order to further greater cooperation and consensus about what needs to be done for society.

Sixth, we put too much importance on competition and ignore community-building. Individualism and competition, that is, *my* job, *my* advancement, *my* career, has won out over the needs of the broader perspective.

Seventh, shorter term considerations like the quarterly statement and next year's wage hike receive too much attention at the expense of the longer vision.

Vatican Statements

Pius XI, *Quadragesimo Anno* — 1931

74. But another point, scarcely less important, and especially vital in our times, must not be overlooked; namely, that the opportunity to work be provided for those who are able and willing to work.[10]

Pius XI, *On Atheistic Communism* — 1937

52. But social justice cannot be said to have been satisfied as long as workingmen are denied a salary that will enable them to secure proper sustenance for themselves and for their families; as long as they are denied the opportunity of acquiring a modest fortune and forestalling the plague of universal pauperism; as long as they cannot make suitable provision through public or private insurance for old age, for periods of illness and unemployment.[11]

Pius XII, *Sertum Laetitiae* — 1939

1466. May it also be brought about that each and every able-bodied man may receive an equal opportunity for work in order to earn the daily bread for himself and his own. We deeply lament the lot of those — and their number in the United States is large indeed — who, though robust, capable, and willing, cannot have the work for which they are anxiously searching.[12]

John XXIII, *Pacem in Terris* — 1963

18. When we turn to the economic sphere, it is clear that human

beings have the natural right to free initiative in the economic field and the right to work.[13]

Second Vatican Council, *Gaudium et Spes* — 1965

67. . . . It is the duty of society, moreover, according to the circumstances prevailing in it, and in keeping with its proper role, to help its citizens find opportunities for adequate employment.[14]

Paul VI. *Octogesima Adveniens* — 1971

14. . . . Every man has the right to work, to a chance to develop his qualities and his personality in the exercise of his profession . . .[15]

John Paul II, *Laborem Exercens* — 1981

18. . . . we must first direct our attention to a fundamental issue: the question of finding work or, in other words, the issue of suitable employment for all who are capable of it. The opposite of a just and right situation in this field is unemployment, that is to say, the lack of work for those who are capable of it . . . unemployment, which in all cases is an evil and which, when it reaches a certain level, can become a real social disaster.[16]

American Catholic Bishops' Statements

Unemployment — 1930

This unemployment returning again to plague us after so many repetitions during the century past is a sign of deep failure in our country. Unemployment is the great peacetime physical tragedy of the nineteenth and twentieth centuries, and both in its cause and in the imprint it leaves upon those who inflict it, those who permit it, and those who are its victims, it is one of the great moral tragedies of our time.[17]

The Church and Social Order — 1940

35. We do not wish to imply that individual employers as a class are willfully responsible for this present state of insecurity, but we do

claim that a system which tolerates such insecurity is both economically unsound and also inconsistent with the demands of social justice and social charity. Security of the workingmen, therefore, as against unemployment, old age, sickness, accident, and death, must be frankly accepted as a social responsibility of industry jointly with society. The distribution of the burden justly between the various groups must be determined, first, through mutual council and honest agreement between the employers and the employees, and, secondly, through the regulation of government acting in its sovereign capacity as promoter of the common good.[18]

The Economy: Human Dimensions — 1975

12. . . . In our society, persons without a job lose a key measure of their place in society and a source of individual fulfillment; they often feel that there is no productive role for them. Many minority youth may grow up without meaningful job experiences and come to accept a life of dependency. Unemployment frequently leads to higher rates of crime, drug addiction, and alcoholism. It is reflected in higher rates of mental illness as well as rising social tensions. The idleness, fear and financial insecurity resulting from unemployment can undermine confidence, erode family relationships, dull the spirit and destroy dreams and hopes. One can hardly bear to contemplate the disappointment of a family which has made the slow and painful climb up the economic ladder and has been pushed down once again into poverty and dependence by the loss of a job.

13. The current levels of unemployment are unacceptable and their tremendous human costs are intolerable. Unemployment represents a vast and tragic waste of our human and material resources . . . As a society, we cannot accept the notion that some will have jobs and income while others will be told to wait a few years and to subsist on welfare in the interim. For work is more than a way to earn a living. It represents a deep human need, desired not only for income but also from the sense of worth which it provides the individual.[19]

To Live in Christ Jesus: A Pastoral Reflection on the Moral Life — 1976

Chronic unemployment is a strong factor paralyzing some groups in our nation. "Minorities" are not its only victims. Women and young workers suffer disproportionately.

Behind the statistics of joblessness lie human tragedies. For example, the father who cannot feed his family, in desperation often lapses into a pattern of life whose effects spread in an ever widening circle: crime, the use of drugs, alcoholism, mental illness, family breakdown—all increase along with unemployment.

Blessed with God-given gifts that include creativity and imagination, the people of this affluent nation can and must find means by which everyone who is able to work can have gainful, productive employment. If we settle for less we are allowing ourselves to be ruled by our economy instead of ruling it.[20]

Notes

1. Henry Reuss, *The Critical Decade* (New York: McGraw-Hill, 1964), p. 133.

2. Oliver F. Williams and John W. Houck, *Full Value: Cases in Christian Business Ethics* (San Francisco, CA: Harper and Row, 1978), pp. 16-19 and 41-42.

3. See Victor F. Zonana, "Is the U.S. Middle Class Shrinking Alarmingly? Economists Are Split," *The Wall Street Journal*, June 20, 1984, p. 1.

4. National Conference of Catholic Bishops, *Quest for Justice: A Compendium of Statements of the United States Catholic Bishops on the Political and Social Order 1966-1980*, ed. J. Brian Benestad and Francis J. Butler. (Washington, D.C.: United States Catholic Conference, 1981), p. 267.

5. Adam Smith, *The Wealth of Nations* (New York: Modern Library, 1937), p. 734.

6. Karl Marx, *Economic and Philosophic Manuscripts of 1844*, trans. Martin Milligan (Moscow: Foreign Languages Publishing House, 1961), p. 72.

7. For a discussion of the quality of work life literature, see the essays by William P. Sexton, David G. Bowers and Irving Bluestone in *A Matter of Dignity: Inquiries Into the Humanization of Work*, ed. W. J. Heisler and

John W. Houck (Notre Dame, IN: University of Notre Dame Press, 1977). Also for the development of John Paul II's theme in *Laborem Exercens* that "in the final analysis, both those who work and those who manage must in some way be united . . . ," see George C. Lodge, "Managers and Managed: Problems of Ambivalence," in *Co-Creation and Capitalism: John Paul II's Laborem Exercens*, ed. John W. Houck and Oliver F. Williams (Washington, D.C.: University Press of America, 1983), pp. 229-253.

8. *Full Value*, p. 26.

9. Editors' note: Council of Economic Advisors, Office of the President, *Economic Report of the President*, 1966 (Washington: Government Printing Office, 1966), p. 110.

10. John F. Cronin, *Catholic Social Principles: The Social Teaching of the Catholic Church Applied to American Economic Life*. (Milwaukee, Wis.: Bruce Publishing Company, 1950), p. 348.

11. *Ibid.*, p. 349.

12. *Ibid.*, p. 349.

13. *The Gospel of Peace and Justice: Catholic Social Teaching Since Pope John*, ed. Joseph Gremillion (Maryknoll, N.Y.: Orbis Books, 1976), p. 205.

14. *Ibid.*, p. 303.

15. *Ibid.*, p. 492.

16. John Paul II, *Laborem Exercens* (On Human Work), *Origins* 11 (Sept. 24, 1981) para. 18.

17. *Quest for Justice*, p. 263.

18. *Catholic Social Principles*, p. 349-350.

19. *Quest for Justice*, p. 266.

20. *Ibid.*, p. 39.

Two

Capitalism and Employment: A Policy Perspective

JOSEPH A. PICHLER*

THE CHURCH'S OFFICIAL WRITINGS HAVE EMPHASIZED the dignity and theological significance of work from the earliest times into the present decade.[1] In the ninety years between *Rerum Novarum* and *Laborem Exercens*, papal statements applied Christian principles to a world that was experiencing rapid industrialization. The forthcoming pastoral letter continues this tradition and provides our bishops an opportunity to consider the implications of Catholic teaching for employment in contemporary American society.

The authors of "Catholic Social Teaching and the American Economy" must be informed by economic as well as theological principles in order to identify significant issues and address them competently. This paper presents an economic perspective on employment and related topics that might be addressed in the pastoral letter. The first three sections consider the employment record of the United States since 1947, review various dimensions of unemployment during that period, and analyze factors that are related to poverty. The fourth and fifth sections summarize government programs that address unemployment

*Joseph A. Pichler is President and Chief Operating Officer of Dillon Companies, Inc. He is a Director of The Kroger Co. and Honorary Director of Cities Service Company. This paper's content and expression are his own.

and pose several propositions regarding economic policy in a capitalist system. The purpose is to provide a background for analyzing employment strategies which might be considered for discussion in the pastoral letter. The final portion suggests perspectives that might be adopted in drafting the letter.

The Postwar Employment Record

Labor force statistics are estimated from census data collected each month in a sampling of 60,000 households. The sample is representative of the U.S. population sixteen years of age and older.

1. Persons are classified as *employed* if they worked for pay during the sample week, worked at least 15 hours in a family business, or were temporarily absent from a job because of illness, vacation, etc.

2. Persons are classified as *unemployed* if they did not work during the sample week, but were available for work, and *either* looked for a job within the preceding four weeks *or* had not looked because they were laid off or waiting to start a new job within the next 30 days.

3. The *labor force* consists of all persons who are either employed or unemployed. The civilian labor force excludes persons who are in the Armed Forces.

4. The *unemployment rate* is calculated by dividing the number of unemployed persons by the number of persons in the labor force.

5. Persons are counted as *not in the labor force* if they are classified as neither "employed" nor "unemployed."

The civilian labor force has undergone substantial increases in size and changes in composition in the postwar period. The number of participants has grown from 59.4 million in 1947 to 110.2 million in 1982, an increase of 86%.[2] The civilian labor force increased every year except 1950-51 when the Korean War drew men into the armed forces. It has grown 53% since 1963, reflecting the impact of the "baby boom" and the influx of women.

Civilian employment has also grown rapidly, from 57.0 million in 1947 to 99.5 million in 1982, an increase of 74%. Thus, the American economy has expanded at a rate sufficient to provide employment for most job seekers even though the labor force expanded at an average (uncompounded) rate of 2.5% per year.

Changes in the composition of the labor force have been even more dramatic. The number of women participants rose from 16.7 million in 1947 to 47.8 million in 1982, an increase of 186%. The number of employed women grew 157% during the same period to a total of 41.3 million. By 1982, women accounted for 43% of all employed persons as compared to 27% in 1947. The entry of women into the labor force was particularly rapid between 1970 and 1980. The increase during that decade was almost as great as the number who entered in the twenty-three year period between 1947 and 1970.[3] The explanations are: the change in women's personal interests and aspirations, new employment opportunities from developing industries, a decline in the birth rate, changes in marital status, and a greater consciousness of discrimination.

Labor force composition was also affected by the growth in the population of teenagers. The number of persons between the ages of sixteen and nineteen participating in the labor force rose 114%, from 4.3 million in 1947 to 9.2 million in 1980. The number of employed teenagers increased 94% from 3.9 million to 7.6 million during the same period. The difference between the rates of increase for the teenage labor force and employment reflects the high incidence of unemployment for this group.

The labor force activity of minority races has increased well above the total population average since 1954, the first year in which statistics for this demographic group became available. The number of minority participants classified as "black and other races" rose from 6.8 million in 1954 to 12.5 million in 1980, a change of 83%; the number who were employed increased from 6.2 million to 10.9 million, a change of 76%. The number of "black and other" teenagers in the labor force increased 112% during this period from 474,000 to 1.0 million. The number who were employed increased only 63%, from 396,000 to 648,000. Again, the difference in labor force and employment growth rates reflects the particularly high incidence of unemployment for minorities, especially teenagers.

The increase in the number of "blacks and others" either working or seeking work is largely a result of the above average population increase for this demographic group. The fraction of "black and other" males over 16 years old participating in the labor force actually declined from 85% to 71% between 1954 and 1980 as an increasing number completed high school before employment.[4] The fraction of "black

and other" women involved in labor force activity increased from 46.1%
to 53.4% in the same period.

There have been major changes in the industrial structure of employment since World War II. The number of persons employed in the agricultural sector declined 57%, from 7.9 million to 3.4 million. This reduction was caused by an extraordinary increase in agricultural productivity resulting from improvements in hybrid seeds, fertilizer, and irrigation techniques; technological change in equipment; and larger average size of farms. Table I shows the increase in civilian employment for nonagricultural industries between 1947 and 1980.* The bottom line indicates that total payroll employment in nonagricultural industries increased 107% during the postwar period. Although all nonagricultural industries experienced growth, there were marked differences among them in rate of change. Employment in construction, wholesale and retail trade, finance/insurance/real estate, services, and state/local government all increased at rates substantially above the average. Mining, durable and nondurable goods manufacturing, transportation/utilities, and federal government employment increased at rates well below the average. By comparing the changes that occured between 1947 and 1963 with those that occurred between 1963 and 1980, one can observe that employment in mining and transportation/public utilities declined during the first sixteen years of the postwar period and then expanded during the latter seventeen years. This was probably caused, respectively, by the oil shortage in the mid-70s and by the decline of railroads followed by the increase of trucking. All other industries showed a secular increase for both periods but it is apparent that growth in trade, finance/insurance/real estate, services, and state government was especially great between 1963 and 1980.

The nature of occupations has undergone substantial adjustments. In the mid 50s, the number of white collar workers first exceeded the number of blue collar employees.[5] This shift toward white collar work has continued during the past 20 years. Table II presents the change in occupational distribution between 1960 and 1980. The fraction of white collar workers increased from 43% to 52% while the fraction of blue collar workers declined from 37% to 32%. The fraction of employed persons working as private household workers and farm

*All Tables are contained in the Appendix.

workers declined substantially while other service workers increased.

The last two columns of Table II indicate that the change in the occupational distribution of "black and other races" has been especially great. The fraction of minority white collar workers increased from 16% to 39% while blue collar declined slightly. The fraction working as private household workers plummeted from 14% to 3%, and farm employment showed a comparable decline. Detailed census data, not reproduced in Table II, reveal major shifts of minority employment within the broad occupational categories. The fraction of "black and other races" classified within the white collar categories of professional, technical, managerial, or administrative workers increased from 7% to 18%. Within the blue collar category, the fraction of high-skilled craft employees increased from 6% to 10% while the fraction of non-farm laborers declined from 15% to 7%.[6] These changes suggest that there was a substantial improvement in the quality of employment for minority employees during the 20-year period. This improvement is correlated with the increased educational attainment of the minority population.[7] In 1962, only 32% of "black and other" labor force participants had completed high school and 5% had completed college. By 1980, 64% had completed high school and 9.1% had completed college. As of 1980, the median school years completed by "blacks and others" was almost equal to that of whites, 12.4 years as compared to 12.7 years.

The average weekly earnings of production and non-supervisory workers rose sharply during the postwar period. Table III indicates that earnings in current dollars increased from $45.58 to $266.92. After adjustment for inflation, the increase was from $63.30 to $92.48, an improvement of 46% in purchasing power. (Both figures are stated in terms of 1967 dollars.) The decline between 1963 and 1982 reflects, in part, the destructive effects of inflation. The Consumer Price Index rose 188% during this 15-year period; about half of this increase occurred after 1976.

In summary the labor force and the nature of employment have changed significantly in the postwar period. The economy absorbed substantial increases in the number of women, teenagers, and minority participants. Employment in agriculture dropped sharply. All other industries grew, but the rates of increase were much lower for the goods-producing sector than for others. The financial, service, and state/local government sectors increased at a very rapid rate and the occupational structure shifted away from blue collar toward white collar employment. The employment structure of minority workers changed in the same directions as the total labor force, but proceeded at a much more rapid rate. The earnings of employees in non-supervisory position rose 46% in real terms despite the record inflation rate in the late 70s.

The shifts in employment patterns that have occured since World War II are indicative of a highly dynamic economy with a labor market that is responsive to shifts in demand and technology. They occurred in the context of rapid technological change, the advent of computerization, two tragic wars, extraordinary population growth, and an international energy crisis. Amidst these shifts the nation prospered. Gross National Product (GNP), adjusted for inflation, grew from $489.8 billion in 1948 to $1,480.7 billion in 1980, an increase of 202%.

Not everyone participated in prosperity. The nation's economic performance was not sufficient to provide employment for all who sought it or to provide everyone with adequate earnings. The next sections analyze the record of unemployment and poverty and review the public policies that addressed these problems.

The Unemployment Record

Unemployment is frequently categorized by four general causes:
1. *Frictional Unemployment* is of short duration caused by job (re) entry into the labor force.
2. *Cyclical Unemployment* is caused by a decline in business activity or an expansion that is slower than the growth of the labor force. This form of unemployment is also referred to as demand-deficiency unemployment.[8]
3. *Structural Unemployment* is caused by a mismatch in labor supply and demand. Employment opportunities are available at the same time that there are unemployed people who lack the skills needed for the available jobs, are the subjects of discrimination, or live in geographic areas distant from the job opportunities.
4. *Secular Unemployment* is caused by a long-term decline in an industry, e.g. farming, resulting from shifts in consumer taste, technological change, or foreign trade. Secular unemployment is often considered as a special case of structural unemployment.

Unemployment rates are not reported by these classsifications. Careful research would be required to estimate each type at any time. However, the categories provide a useful framework for evaluating the general causes of unemployment and for designing strategies to treat each type.

Annual unemployment rates have fluctuated between 2.9% (in 1953) and 9.5% (in 1982) during the postwar period. The highest monthly figure (10.8%) occured in December, 1982 when 12 million persons were without jobs. Since that date, improved business conditions have reduced the number of unemployed to 9.9 million persons for a rate of 8.8%. The unemployment rate has not fallen below 4% since 1969, during the war in Vietnam. In that year there were 2.2 million resident members of the armed forces counted as employed, compared to the current level of 1.7 million. Table V indicates that the unemployment rate has fluctuated substantially within the past decade. It rose from 4.8% in 1973 to 8.3% in 1975, dipped to 5.8% in 1979, and reached 9.5% in 1982.

The average rates between 1970 to 1982 were substantially above those between 1960 and 1970. The rates ranged between 4.8% and 9.5% in the first period as compared to a range of 3.4% to 5.7% in the second. A part of this differential was caused by the differences in labor force growth between these periods. A total of 13.4 million persons entered the labor force betwen 1960 and 1970 for an increase of 19%. In contrast, 23 million persons entered the labor force between 1970 and 1982 for an increase of 32%. About two-thirds of this latter growth was caused by the increased participation of women. The rapid growth in the labor force size and change in its composition placed an unusual burden upon the economy. Unemployment rates showed a general increase during the last 12 years even though 21 million jobs were created between 1970 and 1982 as compared with only 13 million between 1960 and 1970. The participation rate of women in the labor force has now reached a level of 53%, and the civilian labor force growth has begun to stabilize.

Table IV shows the correlation between the rate of economic growth and the rate of expansion in employment. The columns compare the annual changes in GNP, adjusted for inflation, with changes in total employment. Real GNP expanded at a rate above 4% in fourteen of the postwar years. In nine of those same years employment expanded 3% or more. There were only two years (1969 and 1979) in which employment expanded at a 3% rate without an increase in real GNP of at least 4%. On the other hand, real GNP declined or showed no increase in seven years; in five of those years, employment either declined or was stable.

Employment opportunities are not equally distributed across the population. Certain demographic groups experience unemployment that is persistently above the national average. The unemployment rate for Hispanics is generally 4% to 5% above the national average. The rate for persons classified as "black and other races" has been at least double the national unemployment rate in twenty-one of the years between 1947 and 1982, and was at least one and a half times the average in the other thirteen years. Black unemployment rates have ranged from 8.9% to 18.9% in the past decade. The persistence of these high rates reflects a complex of structural factors including discrimination, the lack of training opportunities, family structure, the exodus of entry level employment opportunities from central cities, and the change in occupational structure toward white collar jobs.

Teenagers have consistently experienced high unemployment rates even during expansionary phases of the business cycle. The rates for individuals sixteen to nineteen years old have been in double digits since 1954 and reached a peak of 23.2% in 1982. The rate for teenage blacks has been above 20% since the mid-50s and reached 48% in 1982.

Women between the age of thirty-five and fifty-five experience consistently higher unemployment rates than their male counterparts. Among other factors, this differential reflects the historical pattern of labor force participation by women over their life cycle. In the past many women left the labor force during their twenties and thirties in order to remain home with children, and then re-entered job activity in their mid-thirties. This pattern has changed markedly during the 1970s, and labor force participation rates for women age thirty-five to fifty-five are now comparable to other age groups.

Certain occupational and industrial employees show persistently high unemployment rates throughout the cycle. Rates for persons classified as "nonfarm laborers" and "service workers" generally run twice the national average. Workers in the construction and durable goods industries are especially vulnerable to recession. In addition, about 4% of the persons classified as "employed" are on part-time schedules because of slack work, material shortages, inability to find full-time work, etc. This ratio remains relatively stable over the business cycle.

Unemployment and Poverty

In 1962, Michael Harrington published *The Other America*, and the nation was shocked into recognition that substantial poverty continued to exist within a nation that had enjoyed unparalleled economic prosperity.[9] Three years later the Johnson Administration launched a war on poverty and introduced a broad spectrum of programs designed to improve the economic employability and welfare of the poor. Several of those programs will be discussed in the next section.

Initial estimates of the poverty population varied somewhat depending upon the definition that was used. In 1964, the Social Security Administration adopted a standardized procedure for defining poverty. Revisions were made in 1969 and again in 1980. This procedure is now used by all federal agencies, including the Bureau of the Census, to estimate the poverty population. The approach is based upon a Department of Agriculture finding that families of three or more persons spend approximately one-third of their income on food. Therefore, estimates of the "poverty threshold" for four-person families are made by tripling the cost of the Department's economy food plan. Different multiples are used for families of other sizes and for unrelated individuals. The poverty threshold for each size of family unit is adjusted annually in accordance with the Consumer Price Index.

Individuals are counted within the poverty population if the total money income of their household unit falls below the poverty threshold appropriate to their family size. Money income includes all wages, interest, dividends, social security payments, public assistance, and alimony or child support. Receipts from the sale of property, withdrawals of bank deposits, inheritances and insurance payments, food stamps, health benefits, and subsidized housing are not counted as income. In 1981, single persons living alone were considered to be in poverty if their money income was below $4,620. The poverty threshold for families ranged from $5,498 for a two-person family with the householder under sixty-five years of age to $18,572 for families of nine or more persons.[10]

Table V indicates that the number of persons living in poverty has declined from 39.8 million in 1960 to 34.3 million in 1982. The fraction of the population living in poverty has declined from 22.2% to 15.0% in the same period. Comparisons within the table indicate that poverty and unemployment are related. Between 1964 and 1969 the unemployment rate fell from 5.2% to 3.4% and the poverty rate fell from 19.0% to 12.1%. This period of economic expansion brought about the sharpest decline in poverty rates during the past twenty years. Between 1973 and 1975 unemployment and poverty rates both increased. The same pattern ocurred between 1968 and 1982 as the unemployment rate rose from 6.0% to 9.5% and the poverty rate increased from 11.4% to 15%. During this four-year period, inflation caused the poverty income threshold for a four person family to rise from $6,662 to its present level of $9,862.[11]

Table V also reveals that factors other than unemployment exert a strong influence on the size of the poverty population. At no time during the past twenty-two years has the poverty rate fallen below 11.1%, even though the unemployment rate fell below 5% on seven occasions. This suggests that a significant portion of the poverty population is outside the mainstream of employment in any year because of demographic or skill-related characteristics.

Table VI categorizes the 1981 poverty population by race, age, and marital status. The bottom row indicates that of the 31.8 million persons in poverty, 67.7% are white and 28.9% are black. This statistic must be interpreted carefully. Persons classified as "white" constitute 86% of the nation's population, but only 68% of the poverty population. Persons classified as "black" constitute only 12% of the population, but account for 29% of the poverty population. The higher incidence of poverty among blacks than whites may be stated in more forceful terms: In 1981, only 11% of all white persons were poor while 34% of all black persons were poor.

The "Total" column at the far right of Table VI indicates that marital status is related to poverty. Of the total persons in poverty, 34.7% reside in families who have a female householder with no husband present. The relationship is particularly strong for blacks. There are 9.17 million black persons living in poverty, of which 5.22 million (57%) reside in a family with no husband present. The needs of young children, the complexities of arranging babysitting services and care for sick children, sex discrimination, and related factors make it difficult for many female householders to form stable labor force attachments. These problems are exacerbated by racial discrimination in the case of black females.

There is also a relationship between age and poverty. As indicated in the "Total" column, 37.9% of the poverty population are under eighteen years of age (19.8% in female household families and 18.1% in all other families). Another 12.1% are over sixty-five years of age.[12] Thus, 50.0% of the poverty population are either under eighteen or in their late sixties. A substantial portion of both groups are unable to work because of school attendance, retirement, illness, etc. Those who do participate in the labor force face substantial structural barriers to employment.

About 17% of the poor fifteen years of age or older worked at least forty weeks at part-time or full-time jobs in 1981. Another 24% worked a fewer number of weeks. Thus, 41% of the poor had some attachment to the labor force. Another 5% looked for work but were unable to find it. Fully 54% of the poor population over age fifteen were out of the labor force because of housekeeping duties (20%), school attendance (10%), illness or disability (14%), retirement (9%), or other reasons (1%).[13] In summary, over one-half of the poverty population in employable age groups were not available for employment in 1981. Thus, poverty cannot be solved solely by expanding employment opportunities.

Public Policy Toward Unemployment

Government labor market policies may be roughly divided according to the type of unemployment that each addresses. Table VII lists the major components of current policy according to the four classifications of unemployment. Monetary and fiscal policy are the principal tools for expanding employment opportunities and controlling cyclical unemployment. The Federal Reserve System determines the amount of money available in the economy. During periods of recession the "Fed" expands the money supply, primarily through open market purchases of government securities that are held by financial institutions, businesses, and individuals. The receipt of new funds enables banks to expand loans, induces investment on the part of businesses, and allows individuals to expand consumption expenditures. Inflation occurs if the rate of increase in the money supply persistently exceeds the rate of growth in national output.

Fiscal policy refers to the use of taxing and expenditure practices of government. Some level of receipts and expenditures is necessary at all times to maintain government functions. Countercyclical fiscal policy calls for a reduction in tax rates and an expansion of expenditures for public works, employment training, unemployment compensation, etc. during a recession. Government deficits are financed either by borrowing from the public or by the sale of bonds through the Federal Reserve System. The latter case, called monetizing the deficit, increases the nation's money supply as a means of financing government expenditures.[14]

There are important philosphical implications to both monetary and fiscal policy. Monetary policy that proceeds by open market purchases and sales of bonds to the public stimulates or retards economic activity through voluntary means. Individuals, businesses, and financial institutions make a choice as to whether it is in their interest to buy or sell government securities. The effects are widely dispersed through the economy by private transactions. Fiscal expenditures financed by borrowing from the public are similar in one respect: The buyers of bonds decide to purchase government securities rather than consume their funds or invest them elsewhere. However, the borrowing is used to finance public rather than private projects. Government expenditures that are financed by direct sale of treasury bonds to the Federal Reserve System do not have an element of private choice. Both the expansion of the money supply and the direction of expenditure are determined solely by public officials.

An earlier section indicated that between 1947 and 1980 federal employment expanded 52%, state employment expanded 271%, and national employment expanded 107%. A significant number of state and local employees work on programs that are financed by the federal government. During the same period federal expenditures, adjusted for inflation, increased from $42.8 billion to $108.1 billion while state and local purchases increased from $41.9 billion to $181.9 billion. Total expenditures by all government bodies increased from 17% of real GNP in 1948 to 19.6% in 1980.

A third category of public programs shown in Table VII improves the functioning of the labor market. The Job Service is a joint federal-state system that matches job applicants-employment opportunities in a wide variety of industries and locations. The Service also provides applicants and firms with a wide range of assessment counseling and related activities. All Job Service functions are performed without charge to the clients.

In a market economy individuals should be considered for employment solely on the basis of their productive capability. Discrimination based upon race, sex, age, religion, or nationality is antithetical to this principle. The Civil Rights and Age Discrimination Acts outlaw such activities and thereby reduce immoral, structural barriers that impede the functioning of labor markets.

Some public programs enhance the skills of participants. The level of formal education and its quality are among the most important determinants of a nation's productivity and prosperity. Publicly funded institutions provide a large portion of the nation's general educational activities. Other public programs provide targeted groups with the specific job skills necessary to enhance their employment opportunities. These approaches are common:

1. *On-the-job-training* activities represent a partnership between government and business. Private firms are provided with public funds to offset the unusually high training costs associated with employing individuals from disadvantaged or other targeted populations. The recently enacted Job Training Partnership Act is one example of such programs. Targeted Job Tax Credits achieve the same goal as on-the-job training by reducing employer income taxes by an amount equal to 50% of the wages earned by new employees hired from disadvantaged groups.
2. *Institutional training* consists of classroom education in job skills. The programs are provided by vocational and technical schools, community based organizations, the Job Service, unions, etc.
3. *Residential training* is the most comprehensive form of skill enhancement. It provides housing and a broad range of support services—in addition to job training—for individuals who live in personal circumstances that otherwise prevent the acquisition of skills. Job Corps is a primary example.

A variety of programs maintain the income for individuals who are unemployed or out of the labor force. Unemployment compensation is directed toward temporary unemployment and generally provides income for a period of thirteen weeks.[15] The program is financed by an employer tax that is based partly on the firm's employment stability. In 1982 and 1983, the number of persons receiving unemployment compensation ranged from 3.0 million to 4.9 million. Weekly payments average $124.00 per person. Social security and welfare payments provide longer term income supplements for individuals who are unemployed, disabled, retired, or otherwise unable to work.

Some federal programs are designed to enhance employment in targeted areas. The Model Cities and Enterprise Zone strategies are examples of strategies designed to revitalize the inner-city and expand employment opportunities.

Tariff and immigration policy directly affect employment as broader aspects of international relations. Tariffs are often imposed for the benefit of firms, unions, and employees who are experiencing significant foreign competition. Informal "anti-dumping" understandings are directed to the same end. The steel, electronics, textile, and footwear industries have all recently been the beneficiaries of government policies designed to reduce imports. Immigration policy also reflects structural unemployment and skill shortage within the nation. Individuals with certain skills that are in high demand and short supply receive immigration preference over others.

Finally, in recent years, the government has been called upon to act as an employer of last resort. Under the Comprehensive Employment and Training Act, public employment opportunities were made available as a means of providing jobs to individuals who were unable to find private employment. These public sector opportunities are also intended to provide some level of job experience and work habits.

Capitalism and Employment Policy

Thoughtful consideration of employment issues requires an understanding of the nation's economic structure and the forces that inevitably affect the implementation of policy. This section considers economic propositions and corollaries that might be of value in drafting the forthcoming pastoral letter. These propositions are drawn from economic theory, empirical evidence, and public policy experience. Each is followed by a discussion and, where appropriate, by examples. We begin by defining terms in order to facilitate unambiguous discussion.

Capitalism is a form of economic organization that is grounded in the philosophical principle of liberty and implemented by the following preconditions:

— Individuals, singly and in combination, may freely acquire and use private property.

— Money or some other generally recognized medium is utilized for exchange.

— Voluntary agreements may be entered to exchange labor, property, and money; these agreements are enforceable at law. Coercive agreements are unlawful.

— Competition is the dominant industrial structure.

The Liberty Principle requires that individuals be free to pursue their self-interest without restraint, provided that they do not restrict the freedom of others to do the same.

Self-interest includes the entire spectrum of religious, aesthetic, social, economic, and personal goals that individuals set for themselves.

Competition is the structure of economic exchange and activity that exists when:

— There are no legal restrictions placed upon relative prices, the generation and flow of information, or the mobility of labor and property.

— No single economic entity is large enough, relative to the size of its industry, to control the prices of goods or resources. Individuals and organizations are forbidden by law to control prices by agreement.[16]

These definitions are well known to economists.[17] Unfortunately, the terms are sometimes used in public policy discussion without reference to their precise meaning. Several observations on each concept might serve to reduce misunderstanding.

Liberty is clearly distinguishable from license because it permits the pursuit of self-interest only to the point at which there is encroachment on the freedom of others to pursue their own goals. Thus, liberty is inconsistent with the pursuit of self-interest through such coercive means as slavery, fraud, or collusion. Capitalism constrains license both by public policy and by economic structure. Public policy forbids involuntary agreements, enforces those that are voluntary, outlaws monopoly and collusion, and implements the competitive form of industrial structure.

"Competition" has several meanings in the English language. The term has a precise definition in economic literature that is different from its definition in other forms of activity. Economic competition does *not* mean the untrammelled pursuit of economic gain or the subjugation of the weak by the powerful. Rather it is defined, as above, to designate a specific form of industrial organization. This structure protects liberty by diffusing the economic power of individuals or organizations through the actual or potential entry of alternative partners for exchange. The absence of constraints upon the fluctuation of prices, the flow of information, and the mobility of both labor and property encourages new actors to enter product and labor markets in response to unusually high profits or wages. These same forces protect labor from exploitive conditions through profit incentives that induce employers to bid labor away from low wage firms and by attracting new firms to the market. Finally, competition encourages the conservation of privately held resources by offering higher profits to firms that utilize efficient techniques.[18]

With these definitions clarified, we turn to several propositions for public polices relating to employment.

1. The economy is a web of systematic relationships. Policy interventions in one relationship generally cause adjustments in others. These secondary reactions are often unforeseen and unintended.

There are complex interactions among the markets for labor, capital, goods, services, and resources. The economic fortunes of one geographic area often produce secondary effects in others. The actions of one party within any given market, e.g. a union within a labor market, produce effects upon other parties. This web of relationships requires that careful analysis be given to the second order effects of proposed public policies in order that benefits and costs may be accurately estimated.

Minimum wage legislation is an excellent example of well-intentioned public policy that produces negative results through secondary effects. The intended result of such legislation is to increase the wages earned by the lowest skilled persons in the labor force. The unintended but real result is a reduction in employment opportunities for those same persons. Economic theory predicts that an increase in the cost of any resource, good, or service will generally bring about a reduction in its usage.[19] Thus, theory predicts that an increase in labor costs above the market wage rate will reduce employment and that the greatest reduction will be experienced by the least productive and lowest skilled employees. A careful study by Finis Welch confirms those predictions:

If there is a general theme to the empirical literature, it is that the simple theoretical predictions are confirmed. I believe that almost every serious scholar of minimum wages would argue on the basis of available evidence that they have reduced employment of those, particularly teenagers, who would otherwise earn low wages.[20]

Welch estimates that each one percent increase in the cost of hiring teenagers reduces employment by 1.3% for persons 18-19 years old and by 2.4% for persons 16-17 years old.[21] His statistical estimates also show that the minimum wage increases the cyclical as well as the structural unemployment rates for teenagers.[22] An earlier section of this paper indicated that unemployment rates for teenagers were well above the average and that the problem was especially severe for blacks. By setting wage rates above the market, minimum wage legislation destroys the incentive for firms to provide employment experience and training for disadvantaged youth.

The price controls that were imposed upon crude oil and petroleum products during the 70s are another example of well-intentioned policy that produced negative results because of systematic secondary effects. The program was adopted, ostensibly, to move the nation toward energy independence and to reduce the burden placed upon consumers by OPEC's cartel prices. In fact, the results were exactly the opposite. By holding gasoline prices at levels below the market equilibrium, the policy discouraged both the conservation of energy and the search for new sources of supply. A maze of regulations was adopted to enforce the policy, some of which constituted serious impositions upon personal liberty. A program of entitlement payments was adopted to prevent "windfall profits" for firms that had access to cheaper domestic rather than expensive foreign crude oil. The actual effect of the entitlement payments was to subsidize OPEC and increase the nation's dependence upon foreign energy sources. Under price controls, imports of crude oil doubled between 1973 and 1979. A dramatic reversal occurred when market forces were restored, beginning in 1979. Imports plummeted 19% in that year and consumption of gasoline declined 7%.[23]

The imposition of tariffs and "anti-dumping" agreements are a third example of public policy that produces unintended, negative results. The restriction of imports is often proposed as a means of protecting domestic employment. It is a very appealing cure for visible unemployment in industries that are exposed to foreign competition. Unfortunately, the cure produces unemployment in other industries and other countries, reduces consumer welfare, and wastes natural resources. When foreign goods are banned, some consumers will pay the higher price for domestic products and they have less money to spend on other goods and services. This reduces the demand for those goods and causes a decline in employment opportunities in those industries. Other consumers may not be able to afford the domestic product and will suffer a loss in well-being. Tariffs constitute a subsidy to domestic producers who are less efficient than foreign firms and result in the waste of natural resources. It is estimated that tariff and quota restrictions cost American consumers about $70 billion a year.[24]

Numerous other examples could be cited of public policies that produce negative consequences through secondary effects. Some are initiated with the best intentions by all parties. Others, however, result from the pursuit of economic self-interest in the political realm because some are willing to benefit themselves by restricting the freedom of others. This topic is the subject of the next principle.

2. The pursuit of economic self-interest is not limited to capitalist economies. It is manifested under all forms of economic organization. The predatory drive for economic gain may be curbed by a combination of moral restraint and an economic structure that diffuses power. It is difficult to control by direct legislation without infringing upon liberty, destroying favorable incentives, and/or generating negative secondary consequences. Economic self-interest is sometimes sought through "protective" legislation that benefits some parties by imposing a cost upon others.

Individuals vary widely in the strength of their desire for economic gain. Some choose to pursue self-interest through charitable, aesthetic, or public-service activities at the cost of higher financial returns. Some prefer secure, lower income occupations to those that entail potentially higher incomes at greater risk. Despite these variations, the desire for economic gain motivates some persons in all economies, as evidenced by the fact that every economic system utilizes some form of incentive to allocate resources and distribute income. In capitalist economies these incentives take the form of prices, costs, and wages that respond to consumer desires. Planned economies, such as those organized according to Socialist and Communist principles, utilize "shadow prices" that are set by a central agency to allocate resources and labor in accordance with national goals.

When the pursuit of economic self-interest is combined with economic power based upon legislation or monopoly, the stage is set for exploitation. Capitalism is designed to retain the salutary effects of economic self-interest while diffusing power throughout the economy.

Antitrust legislation forbids monopolies and cartels. The competitive dynamic draws firms and labor toward highly profitable activities by allowing prices and wages to fluctuate without legal restraint, safeguarding the free flow of information throughout the economy and allowing the free mobility of persons, goods, and resources. All forms of economic power are based upon the ability of an individual or organization to develop valuable resources and/or restrict the alternatives that are available to other.[25] Capitalism retains the motivation to develop valued resources and, at the same time, encourages alternative suppliers of those resources to enter the market in response to income opportunities.

The pursuit of economic self-interest may lead individuals and organizations to seek a means for insulating themselves from competition. Some have chosen illegal means, as evidenced by antitrust convictions. A safer and more subtle approach utilizes public policy itself as a shield. Import restrictions have already been cited as one method of restricting foreign competition. Federal regulation of trucking and airlines, recently reduced, contained elaborate barriers against the entry of new firms. Such barriers protected both the profits of employers and the high wages of employees. Numerous states have passed laws that require retailers to sell food at a price that is above some minimum markup over cost. The tobacco industry has successfully maintained federal laws that set strict acreage allotments and limit production.

Restrictions on competition have also been implemented in the labor market. Construction unions actively sought the passage of the Davis-Bacon Act and have succeeded in maintaining its requirement that all federal construction in excess of $2,000 pay the "prevailing wage" in the relevant geographic area. In an "overwhelming number of cases" the wage has been set at union scale regardless of area or type of construction.[26] Non-union operators and employees are thereby prevented from making their most favorable bid for the work. Practitioners and unions have successfully sought state legislation that limits entry into certain occupations by requiring entrants to meet stringent licensure requirements. These restrictions are generally justified in terms of public welfare. In fact, they often damage the public by reducing services and employment.[27]

Such restrictions in the product and labor markets are certainly consistent with the self-interest of the beneficiaries. They are not consistent with capitalism. Pursuit of economic gain within the constraints of competition produces benefits for consumers as well as for firms and employees. Pursuit of self-interest through legislative or regulatory means often benefits certain firms and employee groups to the detriment of consumers, other firms, and workers who are "locked out" of the market.

Opportunities to seek self-interest are especially tempting in centrally planned economies. Prices, wages, and the allocation of both human and physical resources are determined by processes that are essentially political. To the extent that market mechanisms are set aside, economic power is centralized in government. Hedrick Smith has documented the effects of the centralization in the Soviet Union.[28] The absence of market-determined economic rewards also has a stultifying effect upon incentives. This is clearly evident in modern Russia. State farms account for over 99% of the total agricultural land in use, but their productivity per acre is far below that of the small, private farms:

> Covering less than 1% of the USSR's cultivated area, the (private) plots supplies more than 25% of total farm output and 30% of all livestock products.[29]

Soviet farms are also far less efficient than their American counterparts:

> In 1975, it was estimated that 37 million agricultural workers produced 5.3 tons of grain per head and 0.63 tons per acre, whereas 4.3 million American farmers produced 50.8 tons per head and 1.41 tons per acre.[30]

It is not public policy's role to establish conditions that favor certain companies, unions, or any other group at the expense of others. Rather, the appropriate role is to establish a framework that enables all consumers, workers, and firms to fully pursue their self-interest. Having said this, it is important to identify the specific economic role of government in a capitalist economy:

3. Economic policy is responsible for:
   — maintaining the security of persons and property from internal and external coercion;
   — enforcing voluntary agreements;
   — establishing a recognized medium of exchange;
   — implementing conditions of economic competition;
   — solving a set of economic problems that the market cannot address;
   — providing for those who are unable to earn a livable income;

—pursuing monetary and fiscal policies that will produce full employment without inflation.

The need for government to secure the safety of persons and property is well established and needs no comment. Previous sections have defined the requirements of capitalism and the framework of competition in a manner that makes government's role apparent. I have discussed the remainder of the proposition elsewhere in some detail, and I will make only limited comments here.[31] Certain industries, such as public utilities, require a major fixed investment and exhibit declining marginal costs over a wide range of output. As a result, resources would be wasted if more than one firm operated in a given area. Therefore, it is appropriate for government to allow such "natural monopolies" to exist, but to regulate their prices and profits. Government must also intervene to regulate the usage of certain resources, such as air and water, that must necessarily be held "in common." Because private transactions for such resources are impossible, government must intervene to set a price on their usage (generally in the form of a tax or reclamation requirement) in order to prevent the waste of resources. The reverse policy must be followed for certain goods and services, such as education and highways, that produce significantly positive "neighborhood effects." Here it is appropriate for government to supply the goods and services directly or to subsidize them, e.g. through tax credits. A third group of industries utilizes processes or produces products that are so dangerous that the normal forms of indemnification for the injured are insufficient. It is appropriate for government to enhance the normal market flow of information about such products by requiring prior testing.

There are two economic problems which impose especially serious human suffering if left unresolved. Public policy intervention is necessary because moral and market forces have been unable to solve these alone. In capitalist systems, personal income is earned by the productive utilization of talents and resources for activities that are desired by the market. If competitive preconditions could be perfectly implemented, income would be solely dependent on productivity rather than extraneous factors such as race and sex. Unfortunately, no system can achieve this ideal. The failure of market and moral forces to eradicate discrimination of all kinds has imposed tragic costs on a substantial number of our citizens. It is entirely appropriate for public policy to outlaw all forms of discrimination and to require redress for those who have been injured.

It is also necessary for government to provide income to those who, through no fault of their own, are unable to earn a living. Funds should be provided through tax-supported transfer payments and services that are based upon need, to provide a living standard that is adequate or at least commensurate with societal wealth, and retain incentives for those who are able to work.

Finally, public policy must be directed to minimizing unemployment while avoiding inflation. The failure to achieve *either* of these goals results in hardship through the loss of purchasing power, destruction of incentives, and social instability.

Government purchases, public payrolls, and income transfers are financed ultimately by taxes. The intrinsic nature of taxes, their level, and their structure pose certain philosophical and economic issues that deserve careful consideration.

4. Citizens have a serious obligation to support the lawful and moral activities of their government through the payment of taxes. Legislators and citizens are obliged to consider that taxes impose an involuntary exchange, grounded in the coercive power of the state, on some citizens. For this reason, legislative bodies must thoughtfully weigh the rights, obligations, and incentives of affected parties before taxes are imposed or increased. Proposals for expanding government programs should include a careful consideration of fiscal consequences and interpersonal equity.

Government expenditures for goods, services, and payrolls reduce the resources available in the private sector in order that they may be used for public purposes. In so doing they generally affect the distribution of income among persons. Government transfer payments redistribute income and also change the allocation of resources within the private sector to the extent that transfer recipients spend the funds differently from those who are taxed to finance the transfers.

As indicated under point 3 above, public policy in a capitalist system must make careful distinction between the activities that are appropriate to government and those which properly reside in the private sector. The shifting of resources from private to public use imposes involuntary costs upon some, and liberty requires that those costs be justifiable as appropriate to government. The redistibution effects of both public expenditures and transfer payments raise questions of justice as well as economic efficiency. Care must be taken to constrain the exercise of economic self-interest in the development of the tax, public expenditure, and transfer structure in order that some citizens not benefit through an unjust cost placed upon others. High tax rates may reduce the incentive of citizens to utilize their talents and resources productively and thereby reduce the national income that is available for all. Such taxes also generate incentives to underreport income, participate in the "underground" economy, and engage in avoidance activities that waste resources.

Many government programs provide direct benefits to certain identifiable individuals. Others may be shaped to produce such benefits.

5. The beneficiaries of government programs often develop powerful political constituencies that attempt to shape those programs for their own economic self-interest at the expense of other citizens.

Examples of this proposition abound. The government dairy program supports the prices by buying surplus milk at a cost to American taxpayers of $2.5 billion per year, that is, about $300,000 per hour. The storage costs of cheese and butter from current and previous years adds another $50 million per year.[32] Subsidies are increased regularly despite the fact that production of milk products far exceeds the demand with the result that the nation is now storing one billion pounds of cheese and 700 million pounds of butter. Direct subsidies are only part of the cost, however. Consumer pay a substantially higher retail price for milk and milk products because of the supports. Thus, dairy farmers' incomes are enhanced through a government program that imposes a substantial burden on other citizens. The same conclusions can be reached about virtually every government subsidized firm and industry.

National defense purchases represent another fruitful area for pursuit of self-interest. Recent revelations about the exorbitant prices exacted for parts produced at trivial cost provide a ready example of this process.[33] Opportunities for economic gain are particularly great when government purchases are based upon sole source contacts rather than competitive bids that must be responsive to market forces.

Social welfare programs are not immune from the effects of powerful political constituencies. The Comprehensive Employment and Training Act (CETA) was originally designed to improve flexibility in delivering employability services by shifting the locus of authority from the federal government to state/local governments and by replacing rigid categorical programs with services tailored to the needs of individual participants.[34] The program was launched in 1974 with a budget of $2.3 billion. Of this total 45% was allocated to training and work experience, 27% supported public sector employment, and the remaining 28% was distributed among various other programs.[35] By 1978, the program had been dramatically altered. The budget had grown to $8.1 billion, of which only 23% was devoted to training and work experience while 58% was used to fund public service employment. This shift in allocation occurred, in part, because rising unemployment reduced private employment opportunities. However, some portion of this shift was caused by political expediency: State and local governments found it possible to expand public payrolls, without increasing local taxes, by substituting federal funds for state and local taxes. In the words of a report prepared for the National Academy of Sciences: "One of the major shortcomings of the PSE (Public Service Employment) program is the degree to which its job creation objective is subverted by the substitution of federal for local funds."[36] The same report also found that there was a "markedly lower" proportion of disadvantaged persons in the Public Service Employment programs than in the private sector training programs.[37]

Earlier discussion has indicated that well-intentioned public policies may yield negative results if they conflict with market forces; the converse is also true.

6. Government programs are generally more effective when they augment or coincide with market forces rather than conflict with them.

This proposition has important implications for employment programs. For example, the operation of Job Service is entirely consistent with market forces because it improves the flow of information regarding available jobs and employees. Similarly, on-the-job training programs in the private sector consistently result in higher placement rates for trainees than institutional training or public sector work experience. It is also less costly. For example, the 1976 average man-year costs were $4,209 for on-the-job training, $4,861 for private sector institutional training, and $8,236 for public service employment.[38] Such training works in harmony with market forces because it coincides with an employer's economic interest in filling available positions. On-the-job training is especially efficient during periods of low unemployment when firms are recruiting new workers. When unemployment rises, however, these opportunities are reduced and institutional forms of training are more consistent with market forces. Targeted Job Tax Credits exhibit characteristics that are very similar to on-the-job training in that the tax incentive complements market processes to expand employment and reduces the cost of hiring disadvantaged persons.

No economic system generates equal incomes for all. The matter of income distribution poses philosophical issues of justice and economic issues of incentives.

7. Equality of opportunity does not generally yield equality of results. Income differentials are not a simple arithmetic measure of injustice. Some differentials provide incentives that are necessary to induce productive activity for the benefit of all segments of society, including the very poor.

There is a wide variation among individuals in such personal characteristics as intelligence, creativity, manual dexterity, health, etc. One would expect this distribution to produce corresponding differences in the degree to which individuals may contribute to the productivity of a society. Inequality of personal traits may be offset or enhanced by inherited social position, wealth, and luck. The task of all economies is to combine human talents and natural resources into productive endeavors that will create the goods and services needed by society. Equality of opportunity requires that all be free to utilize their talents as they see fit, free from such arbitrary obstacles as discrimination and legal barriers to social mobility. No society possesses sufficient resources or knowledge to make all individuals strictly equal in terms of personal resources.[39] It is also necessary to construct an incentive system that will draw available talent to productive ends. Thus, some income differentials are justified on economic efficiency grounds. John Rawls has argued that differentials are also morally justifiable when they induce recipients to engage in activities that produce benefits for the poorest persons in society.[40] High incomes are also morally justifiable if they do not worsen the condition of the poor.

This is not to argue that all income differentials are either just or economically efficient. Those resulting from collusion, protective legislation, and other restrictions on personal liberty must be criticized on both moral and economic grounds. Other differentials pose complex issues of conflicting rights. For example, there is strong empirical evidence that the economic gains for unionized employees are won at some cost to nonunion workers. A careful study by H. G. Lewis estimated that labor unions have increased the relative wages of organized workers by 7-11% but have lowered those in the unorganized sector by 3-4%[41]

The institution of collective bargaining must also be evaluated in terms broader than its impact of unions upon wages:

8. Collective bargaining is an important manifestation of freedom in our society. It has proven to be a versatile and creative institution for producing voluntary agreements over a wide range of employment conditions. The joint determination of wages, hours, and working conditions has reduced industrial strife, provided workers with an important degree of self-determination, and limited state intervention in employment relations.

Modern collective bargaining contracts are often complex documents that address issues of monetary compensation, fringe benefits, job assignment and promotion, discipline, work pace, industrial safety, and so on. Most contain grievance procedures that resolve disputes during the life of the contract either by arbitration or some other peaceful means. There are wide variations in negotiated terms of employment among and within occupations, industries, and geographic areas. The historical record verifies that collective bargaining is a peaceful process for joint determination of working conditions. The Bureau of Labor Statistics maintained a careful record of strikes involving six or more workers from 1948 through 1979. In only one year (1959) did the working time lost to strikes reach .005 of the total work time available. In eighteen of the thirty-one years, the fraction was less than .002.[42]

Federal law provides workers in interstate commerce with a legally protected right to self-organize and bargain collectively without interference or restraint from employers. The law is enforced by the National Labor Relations Board and by the courts. Many states have adopted parallel laws for public employees and for those few workers in private firms that are outside interstate commerce.

The fraction of workers who are unionized has declined substantially during the postwar period. At the present time less than 20%

of all employees are members of a union. This decline reflects the change in industrial and occupational structure and the failure of unions to attract new members in growth sectors other than state/local employment.

Union activities affect the welfare of unorganized workers in a variety of ways. I have already noted the impact of unions on the relative wages of both groups. In addition, there is widespread agreement that workers have the right to engage in peaceful strikes for economic gains. Such concerted action must be conducted in a manner that respects the liberty of employees who choose not to strike and of job seekers who find the offered terms of employment to be attractive. Coercive measures that inhibit operations during a strike can be morally justified only in exceptional cases.

SUMMARY: This section has discussed economic propositons that pertain to employment within an imperfect capitalist economy. Several were presented in order to address misconceptions about this form of economic organization. Some discussed the interaction between market forces and employment programs. Others analyzed negative consequences that occur when legislation is used as a shield against competition. All of the propositions indicate the complexity of our system and the need for careful analysis before endorsement of public policy proposals affecting employment.

The Pastoral Letter and Capitalism: Some Reflections

In an earlier commentary on *Laborem Exercens*, I discussed the agreement between capitalism and Church teaching on the subjects of self-determination, the relationship between labor and capital, and the appropriate role of public policy:

> Conceptual capitalism and *Laborem Exercens* are in fundamental agreement on the primacy of self-determination as the goal of economic activity. The capitalist view is based upon a philosophical commitment to liberty. The encyclical's position is grounded on the theological premise that man is the subject of work:
>
> > Man has to subdue the earth and dominate it because as the "image of God" he is a person, that is to say, a subjective being capable of

acting in a planned and rational way, capable of deciding about himself and with a tendency to self-realization.

They also agree that the relationship between labor and capital is cooperative rather than antagonistic, that production is a joint product, that public policy plays a key role in establishing an economic framework, and that there should be national commitment to full employment.[43]

The same article stated that the encyclical's views on free trade unions and tranfer payments for the involuntarily unemployed were generally consistent with capitalism.[44]

There are several areas in which the relationship between *Laborem Exercens* and conceptual capitalism is ambiguous and, possibly, in conflict. Some involve employment-related issues that might be considered in drafting the pastoral letter.[45] These comments will not be repeated here except for a brief extension of the discussion regarding the nature and meaning of work. The encyclical places great emphasis on the process of work as a humanizing action: "Man's life is built up every day from work, from work it derives its specific dignity, but at the same time work contains the unceasing measure of human toil and suffering and also of the harm and injustice which penetrate deeply into social life within individual nations and on the international level."[46] The document forcefully states that man is the "subject of work" in the sense that his total personhood is involved in this process through which the earth is subdued.[47] This vision of human work as participation in divine creation beautifully expresses the inherent dignity of work. However, the encyclical may have gone too far in stressing the significance of work as a process and not far enough in considering its objective importance. First, can one really accept the view that the "specific dignity" of man's life is derived from work? An unqualified affirmation could lead to an overemphasis on work as compared to spiritual and social activities. Second, the encyclical fails to address the idea that man is the "subject of work" in a second sense. We are consumers as well as producers; we eat the bread produced by the sweat of our brow. The nature of the goods that we produce and the use we make of them are certainly as important to our personhood as the actions by which we fashion them.

No economic system can be perfectly established. No nation has suceeded in implementing conceptual socialism or communism or capitalism. Nevertheless, an understanding of conceptual systems is important for those who develop public policy or comment upon it. The reasons are several. First, conceptual systems lay bare the philosophical basis of an economy and the structual preconditions necessary for implementation. They permit us to examine the system's moral implications and form judgments about the feasibility of implementation. Second, conceptual models help us predict the general direction in which the economy will move as a result of public policy interventions or other exogenous forces. This is important for evaluating both the primary effects of policy and the secondary—and perhaps unintended—effects. Third, a clear understanding of the model enables us to distinguish between those moral and economic problems that are inherent in the system and those that result from imperfect implementation. The distinction is *crucial* for forming policy choices. Problems (and evils) that result from imperfect implementation may be effectively addressed by legislation that perfects a precondition or complements the conceptual system's dynamic. Problems that are inherent in the conceptual system may require solutions which are outside of, or even contradictory to, basic preconditions. I have commented on the importance of this difference elsewhere and will give only two examples here to illustrate the difference.[48] Antitrust legislation was necessary to perfect the implementation of capitalism and reestablish its preconditions in the light of monopolies that began to develop in the late 19th century. In contrast, government regulations that set a price on the use of resources that must be "held in common," e.g. air, are necessary because market forces are inherently unable to allocate these resources.

As noted in the opening paragraph of this section, liberty is a touchstone of both capitalism and *Laborem Exercens*. In its fullest meaning the pursuit of self-interest, which I define as encompassing moral, aesthetic and social concerns, is synonymous with self-determination. The terms express the nature of man as pilgrim who both finds and reveals himself through the exercise of free choice. The concept of liberty might be suggested as a central theme of the forthcoming pastoral letter. This theme would provide direction to the Church in its roles as prophet, witness, and minister in matters within the realm of economics and employment.

Christians have been called to be a "leaven" in society: to interpret, teach, and apply the law of love. The Church as prophet has the duty to inform its members of their obligations to respect the liberty of all and to exercise their own in accordance with Christian principles. Those principles require that all forms of discrimination be condemned and that positive action be taken to remove their effects from society. They also oblige Christians to exercise moral and religious values as they make decisions within the markets for labor, capital, and products. This is especially important in a capitalist system because consumer choice determines the nature of the goods/services that are produced, the allocation of resources among alternative uses, and the distribution of income. The market responds with equal efficiency to moral and immoral choices. The law of love binds all Christians to share their wealth, voluntarily, with those who are in need. Church teaching has always shown a "preference for the poor," and it is appropriate that Church members be called upon to show the same preference in the disposition of their wealth. Thus, the pastoral letter might invite readers to practice radical charity toward those in poverty. A call for voluntarism in addressing poverty is consistent with the Church's historical position and with the nature of morality as the practice of virtue through free choice.

In this age the Church has a particular responsibility and opportunity to serve as a minister through which the charity of its members can assist the poor. The earlier discussion of unemployment and poverty analyzed the structural factors that prevent some members of society from earning a livable income. Some portion of the resulting distress has been reduced by tax financed programs administered by public agencies. There remains broad scope for responsible and efficient private agents who can channel voluntary contributions of money and talent to the needy. The Church might serve this ministerial role by providing disadvantaged youth with educational opportunities of high quality: offering shelter, food, and medical services to the indigent; establishing low cost day care centers for the children of working mothers; offering alternative adult education for those who have "dropped out" of the formal system; and distributing financial assistance to the unemployed and needy in a manner that respects human dignity. The activities should be offered to all without regard to race or religious creed, but special efforts should be directed toward the black, Hispanic, and immigrant communities. Many dioceses have already undertaken laudable programs to meet these needs. Nevertheless, an expansion of effort would, itself, induce further responses from those who are seeking means through which they might share their wealth.

The Church must witness its commitment to self-determination and voluntarism through its own actions as employer, educator, and minister. Church-related institutions must be a sign to all of managerial behavior that respects the dignity of work and of workers. This entails multiple obligations to: avoid all forms of discrimination based upon race, sex, and other arbitrary dimensions; provide employees with full information regarding their performance and status; recognize the right of collective bargaining; limit restraint placed upon employees to those which are necessary for the effective performance of duties; hear and accomodate the personal needs of employees insofar as they are consistent with the task at hand; and avoid actions that would foreclose the freedom of others to seek self-improvement. Finally, those in authority have an obligation to bring joy to their organizations through " . . . celebration of achievement, enthusiasm for others, and grace in times of hardship."[49] This obligation, and the opportunity to exercise it, are especially great within the Church.

TABLE I

CIVILIAN PAYROLL EMPLOYMENT IN
NONAGRICULTURAL INDUSTRIES & PERCENT CHANGE:
1947, 1963, 1980 (NUMBERS IN 000)

	1947	1963	Chg. From 1947	1980	Chg. From 1947	Chg. From 1963
Mining	955	635	(34)%	1,025	7%	61%
Construction	2,009	3,010	50%	4,469	122%	48%
Durable Goods Mfg.	8,385	9,616	15%	12,216	46%	27%
Nondurable Goods Mfg.	7,159	7,380	3%	8,147	14%	10%
Transportation/ Public Utilities	4,166	3,903	(6)%	5,155	24%	32%
Wholesale Trade	2,471	3,248	31%	5,281	114%	63%
Retail Trade	6,482	8,530	32%	15,292	136%	79%
Finance/Insurance/ Real Estate	1,728	2,850	64%	5,162	199%	82%
Services	5,025	8,277	65%	17,740	253%	114%
Federal Government	1,892	2,358	25%	2,867	52%	22%
State Government	3,582	6,868	92%	13,304	271%	94%
Total	43,857*	56,658	29%	90,656	107%	60%

*(Totals vary less than .001 as the result of rounding.)

Source: Table C-1 Employment & Training Report of the President, 1981.

TABLE II

OCCUPATIONAL DISTRIBUTION OF EMPLOYED PERSONS
1960 and 1980

	All Employed		Black & Other Races	
	1960	1980	1960	1980
White Collar Workers	43%	52%	16%	39%
Blue Collar Workers	37%	32%	40%	36%
Private Household Workers	3%	1%	14%	3%
Other Service Workers	9%	12%	18%	20%
Farmworkers	8%	3%	12%	2%
Total	100%	100%	100%	100%

Source: Tables A-19 and A-21 *Employment and Training Report of the President*, 1981.

TABLE III

AVERAGE WEEKLY EARNINGS OF PRODUCTION AND
NON-SUPERVISORY WORKERS ON PRIVATE PAYROLLS:
1947, 1963, 1980

	Current Dollars	Inflation-Adjusted Dollars*
1947	$ 45.58	$ 63.30
1967	101.84	101.84
1982	266.92	92.48

*(1967 = 100)

Source: Tables C-5 and G-6. *Employment and Training Report of the President*, 1981, and *Monthly Labor Review*, September, 1983.

TABLE IV

CHANGES IN REAL GNP & EMPLOYMENT (1948-1980)

	% Change In Real GNP	% Change In Employment
1980	0	0
1979	3	3
1978	5	4
1977	5	3
1976	5	3
1975	(1)	(1)
1974	(1)	2
1973	6	3
1972	6	3
1971	3	1
1970	0	1
1969	3	3
1968	5	2
1967	3	2
1966	6	3
1965	6	3
1964	5	2
1963	4	2
1962	6	1
1961	3	0
1960	2	2
1959	6	3
1958	0	(2)
1957	2	0
1956	2	2
1955	7	3
1954	(1)	(2)
1953	4	1
1952	4	0
1951	8	2
1950	9	2
1949	0	(1)

Source: Tables G-3 and A-1, *Employment and Training Report of the President*, 1981.

TABLE V

POVERTY AND UNEMPLOYMENT BY YEAR

Year	Number of Persons Below Poverty Level (000)	% of the Population Below Poverty Level	Unemployment Rate
1982[a]	34,300	15.0	9.5
1981	31,822	14.0	7.5
1980	29,640[b]	13.2[b]	7.0
1979	26,072	11.7	5.8
1978	24,497	11.4	6.0
1977	24,720	11.6	6.9
1976	24,975	11.8	7.6
1975	25,877	12.3	8.3
1974	23,370	11.2	5.5
1973	22,973	11.1	4.8
1972	24,460	11.9	5.5
1971	25,559	12.5	5.8
1970	25,420	12.6	4.8
1969	24,147	12.1	3.4
1968	25,389	12.8	3.5
1967	27,769	14.2	3.7
1966	28,510	14.7	3.7
1965	33,185	15.7	4.4
1964	36,055	19.0	5.2
1963	36,436	19.5	5.7
1962	38,625	21.0	5.5
1961	39,628	21.9	6.7
1960	39,851	22.2	5.5

(a) Reported in *The Wall Street Journal*; August 8, 1983

(b) Revised

Source: Current Population Report Series P-60, No. 138, *Character-istics of the Population Below the Poverty Level*: 1981 and *Employment & Training Report of the President*: 1981.

TABLE VI

Poverty Population by Race, Age, & Marital Status 1981

(000)

	WHITE		BLACK		OTHER RACES		TOTAL	
	NUMBER	%	NUMBER	%	NUMBER	%	NUMBER	%
Family Members: Female Householder No Husband Present:								
Householder Under 65 Years	1,693	5.3	1,304	4.1	59	.2	3,056	9.6
Children Under 18 Years	3,120	9.8	3,051	9.6	134	.4	6,305	19.8
Other Family Members	666	2.1	794	2.5	35	.1	1,495	4.7
Householder Over 65 Years	121	.4	73	.2	2	-	196	.6
Total	5,600	17.6	5,222	16.4	229	.7	11,051	34.7
All Other Families:								
Householder Under 65 Years	2,367	7.4	441	1.4	137	.4	2,945	9.2
Spouse of Householder	2,719	8.6	537	1.7	138	.4	3,394	10.7
Children Under 18 Years	4,309	13.5	1,119	3.5	336	1.1	5,764	18.1
Other Family Members	642	2.0	306	1.0	94	.3	1,042	3.3
Householder Over 65 Years	490	1.6	154	.5	10	-	654	2.1
Total	10,527	33.1	2,557	8.1	715	2.2	13,799	43.4
Unrelated Subfamilies:	365	1.1	98	.3	19	.1	482	1.5
Unrelated Individuals:								
Under 65 Years	3,132	9.8	830	2.6	107	.3	4,069	12.8
Over 65 Years	1,929	6.1	466	1.5	26	.1	2,421	7.6
Total	5,061	15.9	1,296	4.1	133	.4	6,490	20.4
Total	21,553	67.7	9,173	28.9	1,096	3.4	31,822	100.0

Source: Current Population Report Series P-60, No. 138, *Characteristics of the Population Below the Poverty Level: 1981*, Table 9, Page 33.

TABLE VII

PUBLIC POLICY BY TYPE OF UNEMPLOYMENT ADDRESSED

	Frictional	Cyclical	Structural	Secular
Monetary Policy		X		
General Fiscal Policy		X		
Labor Market Efficiency				
Job Service	X		X	X
Civil Rights/EEOC			X	
Age Discrimination Act			X	
Skills Enhancement				
General Education Policy			X	
On-the-Job Training			X	
Institutional Training			X	
Residential Training			X	
Targeted Job Tax Credit			X	X
Income Maintenance				
Unemployment Compensation	X	X	X	X
Social Security			X	
Trade Adjustment Act				X
Welfare (AFDC, Disability, etc.)	X	X	X	X
Directed Expenditures/ Credits				
Model Cities/Enterprise Zones			X	
Area Redevelopment				X
International Relations				
Tariff Policy			X	X
Immigration Policy		X	X	
Government as Employer of Last Resort		X	X	X

Notes

1. I Thessalonians 4:11.

2. Unless otherwise indicated, all employment statistics for 1947-1980 are taken from the *Employment and Training Report of the President*, 1981 and all statistics for 1981 and 1982 are taken from the *Monthly Labor Review*.

3. The number of women who entered the labor force between 1947 and 1970 was 14.9 million; between 1970 and 1980 it was 13.1 million.

4. See note 6 below.

5. White collar employees are defined by the Census Bureau as: professional and technical workers, managers and administrators, sales workers, and clerical workers. Blue collar workers are defined as: craft and kindred workers, operators, and nonfarm laborers.

6. Table A-21, *Employment and Training Report of the President*, 1981.

7. The decline in minority farm employment also reflects the increased urbanization of this demographic group.

8. Albert Rees, *The Economics of Work and Pay* (New York: Harper & Row Publishers, 1973), p. 113.

9. Michael Harrington, *The Other American* (New York: Macmillan, 1962).

10. For a complete explanation of the definition and estimation of poverty see: Current Populations Reports, Series P-60, No. 138, *Characteristics of the Population Below the Poverty Level*, 1981, U.S. Department of Commerce, Bureau of the Census.

11. Reported in *The Wall Street Journal*, August 8, 1983.

12. Table VI indicates that .6% of the poverty population are female householders over 65; 2.1% are male householders over 65; and 7.6% are unrelated individuals over 65. This totals 10.3% of the poverty population. An additional 1.8% of the poverty population is over 65 and classified in the Table either as "other family members" or members of "unrelated subfamilies."

13. Bureau of the Census *Current Populations Reports*, Series P-60, No. 138, Table 14, p. 52.

14. Milton Friedman and Rose Friedman, *Free to Choose* (New York: Harcourt Brace Jovanovich, 1979), pp. 264-5.

15. During periods of extremely high unemployment, the period of payment has been extended to 26 weeks under certain circumstances.

16. Definitions and the discussion of terms are adopted from Joseph A. Pichler, "Business Competence and Religious Values—A Trade Off?," *Co-*

*Creation and Capitalism: John Paul II's Laborem Exercens,*ed. John W. Houck and Oliver F. Williams (Washington, D.C.: University Press of America, 1983).

17. George J. Stigler, *The Theory of Price* (New York: Macmillan Company, 1952), Chapters 1 & 2 and Lloyd G. Reynolds, *Economics, A General Introduction* (Homewood, Ill: Richard D. Irwin, Inc., 1973), Chapters 16-19.

18. For a more complete discussion of the effects of competition see: Joseph A. Pichler, "Capitalism in America: Moral Issues and Public Policy," *Ethics, Free Enterprise, and Public Policy*, co-edited with Richard T. De George (Oxford University Press, 1978).

19. The exception to this theory is the case of monopsony, *provided* that the increase falls precisely within the area of the marginal cost curves discontinuity.

20. Finis Welch, *Minimum Wages Issues and Evidence* (Washington, D.C.: American Enterprise Institute for Public Policy Research, 1978), p. 33.

21. *Ibid.*, p. 38.

22. *Ibid.*, p. 41.

23. For a more extensive discussion of the impact of energy controls see: Joseph A. Pichler, "Capitalism, Efficiency and Morality," *Private Enterprise: Meeting the Challenges of the 80's*(Institute for Entrepreneurship, Benedictine College, Atchison, Kansas, 1981).

24. Herbert Stein, "Don't Fall for Industrial Policy." *Fortune Magazine*, November 14, 1983, p. 70.

25. Joseph A. Pichler, "Power, Influence, and Authority," *Contemporary Management Issues and Viewpoints*, ed. Joseph W. McGuire (Englewood Cliffs, New Jersey: Prentice-Hall, 1974).

26. John P. Gould, Davis-Bacon Act, *Special Analysis No. 15* (Washington, D.C.: American Enterprise Institute, November, 1971), p. 10.

27. Joseph A. Pichler, "An Economic Analysis of Accounting Power," *Institutional Issues in Public Accounting*, ed. Robert R. Sterling (Scholar Books, 1974) and Simon Rottenburg, "The Economics of Occupational Licensing," *National Bureau of Economic Research, Aspects of Labor Economics* (Princeton, New Jersey: Prentice Hall, 1962).

28. Hedrick Smith, *The Russians* (New York: Quadrangle/New York Times Book Co., 1976), especially Chapter 1.

29. Peter Mooney, *The Soviet Superpower* (Heineniann Educational Books (Labor & Exeter), 1982), p. 59. Parentheses added.

30. *Ibid.*, p. 54.

31. Joseph A. Pichler, *Co-Creation and Capitalism*, pp 101-123.

32. Lyle Everingham, "Letter to Shareholders," *The Kroger Co.* (Cincin-

nati, Ohio, June 1, 1983).

33. UPI Story in *Hutchinson News* (November 15, 1983), p. 2.

34. *CETA: Manpower Program Under Local Control* (Washington, D.C.: National Academy of Sciences, 1978), p. 2.

35. *Ibid.*, p. 18.

36. *Ibid.*, p. 11.

37. *Ibid.*, p. 10.

38. *Ibid.*, pp. 228, 229, and 237. Also see: Sar A. Levitan, Garth L. Mangum, Ray Marshall, *Human Resources and Labor Markets* (New York: Harper & Row, Publishers, 1972), especially p. 216.

39. Milton Friedman, *Free to Choose*, pp. 267-70.

40. John Rawls, *The Theory of Justice* (Cambridge, Mass: Belknap Press of Harvard University Press, 1971), pp. 276-7.

41. H. G. Lewis, *Unionism and Relative Wages in the United States* (Chicago: The Univerty of Chicago Press, 1963), p. 194.

42. Table G-8, *Employment and Training Report of the President*, 1981.

43. Joseph A. Pichler, *Co-Creation and Capitalism*, p. 113. The internal quote is from *John Paul II, Laborem Exercens* (Washington, D.C.: Office of Publishing Services, United States Catholic Conference, September 14, 1981), paragraph 6.

44. Joseph A. Pichler, *Ibid.*, p. 114.

45. *Ibid.*, especially pp. 114-121.

46. John Paul II, *Laborem Exercens*, p. 3.

47. *Ibid.*, p. 13.

48. Joseph A. Pichler, *Co-Creation and Capitalism* . . . pp. 111-113 and Joseph A. Pichler, "Is Profit Without Honor? The Case for Capitalism," *National Forum* (Summer, 1978, Abstracted *Philosophers Index*, 1979).

49. Joseph A. Pichler, *Co-Creation and Capitalism*, p. 121.

Three

The Economy and Workers' Jobs, The Living Wage and a Voice

RUDY OSWALD

IN *LABOREM EXERCENS* POPE JOHN PAUL II FORTHRIGHTLY states that the principle of the priority of labor over capital must be respected and that the employment process must be recast in the service of man. This encyclical lays out the fundamental thought that "human work is a key, probably the essential key to the whole social question" and notes that "the principle of the priority of labor over capital is a postulate of the order of social morality."

The themes of the dignity of labor and of worker rights, of the need for a just wage, and of the duty of the state to protect the worker's natural right to enter into working people's associations are all carried forward from *Rerum Novarum* (Pope Leo XIII, 1891).

They were echoed in *Quadragesimo Anno* (Pope Pius XI, 1931) in its treatment of the claims of capital and labor, the principle of just distribution of wealth and property, and the need for a just wage. The same themes, of course, reappeared in that part of *Mater and Magistra* (Pope John XXIII, 1961) which dealt with the subject of labor, where we found the reaffirmation of the right of workers to organize with the extension to the view that organization of workers is not only desirable but necessary, that unions are absolutely indispensable in modern society.

Unemployment

Workers in American society depend upon jobs for dignity and income, for status in society. A worker without a job is considered a failure and looks on himself (for convenience I use "himself" but I refer to both male and female workers) as a failure because society seems to be telling him "We don't need you. We don't want you."

Few of us can grasp the implications of the nation's unemployment problems when measured in millions of people and billions of dollars worth of lost production. These millions and billions numb the mind and erase the fact that these huge numbers represent real flesh-and-blood people who need the dignity and fulfillment of their human nature which come from employment. To these people and to their families and communities in which they live, unemployment is a tragedy, a major psychological trauma.

It is not only the question of how to put bread on the table that worries the unemployed worker, it is mortgage payments on the home, medical and dental bills for the children, and all the other bills that are coming in. Most workers are in debt for their homes, cars, refrigerators, television sets, and other appliances; so the fear of unpaid bills haunts jobless workers and their families. The human costs and the misery from unemployment are startling. High unemployment raises death rates and infant mortality, cardio-vascular and kidney disease, alcoholism and cirrhosis of the liver, suicides and homicide, admissions to mental hospitals, child abuse, family breakdowns, drug addiction, crime and imprisonment. Social and community problems as well as personal and family problems are clearly direct results of high and persistent unemployment. All jobless workers and their families suffer from the effects of unemployment, but when unemployment is concentrated in a community or a region, the problems are intensified.

Who Are the Unemployed?

In early 1984, after more than a year of expansion in the U.S. economy and a 2.7 million reduction in the ranks of the unemployed, there were still 8.8 million people included in the official unemployment statistics—but there were also some 1.4 million discouraged workers who were not included in the official statistics because they had given up a vain search for a job, and there were in addition 5.8 million people who could find only part-time work when they wanted a full-time job. Thus, we have 16 million workers who must believe that society does not grant them full or adequate opportunity for dignity, self-respect, self-fulfillment, and self-support from productive labor.

Black, Hispanic, and teenage workers have particularly serious job problems. One out of every six black workers is jobless and one out of every nine Hispanic workers is unemployed. Over the course of a year one out of every three black workers and one out of every four Hispanic workers experiences some unemployment. Among teenagers, one out of every five teenagers in the labor force and one out of every two black teenagers is unemployed.

In early 1984 there were 6.6 million white workers, 1.9 million black workers, and 640,000 Hispanic workers in the under-stated official unemployment statistics. Unemployed men, 20 years and over, number 4.1 million. Unemployed women aged 20 and over numbered 3.1 million. There were 1.5 million jobless young people aged 16 to 19 years. Holding a blue-collar job is more likely to put a worker out of a job than is a white-collar job. One out of eight blue-collar factory workers was jobless in early 1984. Blue-collar workers make up 30 percent of the workforce but 45 percent of the unemployed. The lowest unemployment occupations were white-collar manager and professional specialty jobs (2.7 percent) and white-collar technical, sales, and administrative support jobs (5.6 percent).

In addition, employment varies widely by industry. The contruction industry consistently has high unemployment. In early 1984 unemployment was 15 percent in construction. Unemployment in manufacturing is more cyclical. In February, 1983 unemployment among workers in manufacturing was 13 percent; a year later it was 7.5 percent. Wholesale and retail trade unemployment was 8.3 percent in early 1984. In finance and service industries it was 6.3 percent. In transportation and public utilities it was 5.9 percent. Among government workers unemployment was 4.5 percent, and among farm workers it was 14 percent.

Unemployment during the same period also varies by state and region. In Michigan the unemployment rate was 11.4 percent; Pennsylvania, 9.8 percent; Illinois, 9.5 percent; California 8 percent; and Florida, 6 percent. Massachusetts and Texas had unemployment rates of 5.7 percent.

Help for the Jobless

The biggest and most certain protection against the ravages of unemployment is a healthy, expanding, full employment economy. Economic growth opens up new jobs for workers who lose their jobs in our rapidly changing economy. There is an unfulfilled national commitment to full employment and balanced economic growth in the Humphrey-Hawkins Act of 1978.

It is possible to make a distincion between "cyclical" unemployment of workers who lose their jobs because of the ups and downs of the business cycle and "structural" unemployment of workers who are unemployed because of age, race, or sex discrimination, lack of education or marketable skills, geographic location, or structural changes in the economy. This is a useful distinction, but in practice these distinctions merge and overlap. Workers who may seem to be severely disadvantaged in time of depression-recession "loose" labor markets often become more attractive to employers in boom-time "tight" labor markets when hiring is followed by on-the-job training.

Unfortunately, recession-depression and slow economic growth have raised the number of jobless Americans to levels that would have been considered unthinkable less than 10 years ago. The simple fact is that the job shortage in America is getting bigger and bigger. Unemployment is getting a firm hold on a substantial part of the American work force. The AFL-CIO has projected a job shortage which will keep 4 to 6 million workers unnecessarily unemployed through the 1980s.

The first line of defense for jobless workers is the unemployment insurance system. This federal-state insurance system was originally intended to replace half of lost earnings of unemployed workers. But over time the system has been eroded. Unemployment compensation benefits now go to only one out of three unemployed workers. Severe cutbacks in eligibility, in size of benefits and duration of benefits have made the unemployment insurance system a poor defense against poverty and privation for workers and their families. Millions of workers have exhausted their unemployment benefits before finding a job.

Some of these workers and their families get food stamps or welfare assistance, but many simply drop out of the economic mainstream into a culture of poverty.

The nation's unemployment insurance system must be drastically reformed and improved to meet the basic income needs of jobless workers. This means setting federal minimum benefit standards, increasing weekly benefit amounts and benefit duration periods, and eliminating harsh and excessive eligibility and disqualification requirements.

Two more key issues for unemployed workers and their families are health care and home mortgage or rent payments. Most workers get health insurance protection for themselves and their families through their place of work. When the job is lost, health insurance is lost. Only 20 percent get continued coverage for three months or more. Since the average duration of unemployment is over four months, most jobless workers can expect to be completely without health insurance protection. Unfortunately, many unemployed workers are denied Medicaid coverage because they have not been poor long enough to meet state eligibility criteria. Legislation and adequate funds are needed to assure health insurance coverage and health services for unemployed workers and their families. Likewise, there is an urgent need for a mortgage and rent-payment relief program to protect jobless workers from the loss of their homes through mortgage foreclosures and evictions from rental housing.

Hours of Work

Hours of work need to be reduced to provide more job opportunities. The standard 40-hour workweek of the 1930s should be brought in line with the historic downward trend in hours of work. There is nothing sacred about the 40-hour workweek, just as there was nothing sacred about the 84-hour or the 60-hour workweek. In the first 40 years of this century the average workweek fell from 60 hours to 40 hours. But the standard workweek has been unchanged now for almost 50 years. Past and future gains from rising productivity make the reduced workweek affordable and justifiable and indeed necessary. To create more jobs and to increase leisure and to strengthen family life a reduction of the workweek is in order.

Existing overtime pay requirements do not sufficiently deter employers from requiring frequent and continuing overtime work. This puts an excessive and unhealthy strain on currently employed workers and deprives unemployed workers of jobs. Raising the overtime penalty can produce more leisure, more health, and more jobs.

Government Responsibility for Jobs and Training

To move America faster toward full employment and balanced economic growth, jobs must be created in the private sector and in the public sector for the millions of men and women who cannot find jobs. It is clearly in the economic and social interest of the nation to put Americans who are able and willing to work in jobs that produce useful goods and services, generate taxes, and stimulate the economy, particularly in communities with especially high unemployment.

Direct, targeted, and adequately funded public job programs are needed on a large scale when, as now, the private sector fails to create enough jobs. Needed community services should be expanded, planned community facilities should be constructed, and low-and moderate-cost housing should be built and rehabilitated.

Jobless workers should have the opportunity for training in skills that lead directly to jobs. The Job Training Partnership Act of 1982 with its lack of income support during training, its business-dominated structure, and its abysmal underfunding is totally inadequate to the nation's employment and training needs. Private and public sector training, including on-the-job training and upgrading and apprenticeship programs, needs to be broadened. Training allowances and income support should be available for workers in training programs.

Employment guidance and counseling, job search assistance, and training should be available for all unemployed workers. The existing federal-state employment service system simply does not have the resources to do an effective job in helping the nation's millions of unemployed workers. The Job Training Partnership Act of 1982 restructured and decentralized the nation's training efforts for jobless workers, but funding is far from adequate and training allowances are not available so many workers simply cannot afford to take training when they need immediate earnings to put bread on the table for their families. Job and training programs for displaced workers and youths should be greatly expanded and training allowances should be provided. There should be more targeted job training opportunities for adult workers, including women and minorities, and other groups with special needs.

Legislation is needed to protect workers and local communities against serious injury from plant closings. Such legislation should stop tax incentives for plant closings, require advance notice, protect workers' health and pension rights, provide training for dislocated workers, and provide other protections and assistance for workers and communities hit by plant closings.

Government—Employer of Last Resort

In a democratic society we have a obligation to insist that our national government accept responsibility for assuring that every worker has an opportunity to make a productive contribution, to be a part of a productive community. This social responsibility requires a renewed activist role for government to stimulate job creation and to reduce unemployment.

The commitment to full employment set forth in the Humphrey-Hawkins Full Employment and Balanced Economic Growth Act of 1978 must be fulfilled. Full employment is a moral, social, political, and economic imperative. Furthermore, economic efficiency and productivity improve at higher levels of output.

Government's legitimate activist role must be directed toward helping the unemployed, the needy, and the poor. To help the unemployed, there must be social support and income support for those who lose jobs and those who need jobs, as well as education and training for those who need to improve their skills and competencies to get and to hold jobs. And finally there must be direct job creation in the public sector for those workers who cannot find jobs in the private sector.

America has already endorsed the concept of government as the employer of last resort. The Humphrey-Hawkins law permits the President to set up a "last resort" jobs programs if he finds that other policies are failing to achieve the full employment goals set forth in the law.

The Humphrey-Hawkins law affirms the basic human right of every American to full opportunity for useful paid employment at fair rates of compensation. It sets specific numerical goals and timetables for reducing unemployment to 3 percent for adults and 4 percent overall. Unfortunately, this blueprint for economic progress is being disregarded by our government.

If the private, profit-seeking sector cannot provide enough jobs for everyone who wants and needs a job, then clearly the national government must be the employer of last resort.

A Decent Living-Wage

Workers should earn enough to achieve a decent minimum level of living for themselves and their families. This principle was advocated in the famous American Catholic Bishops' statement, *Bishops' Program of Social Reconstruction*, published in 1919:

> Since our industrial resources and instrumentalities are sufficient to provide more than a living wage for a very large proportion of the workers, why should we acquiesce in a theory which denies them the measure of the comforts of life? . . . [wages] should be ultimately high enough to make possible that amount of saving which is necessary to protect the worker and his family against sickness, accidents, invalidity, and old age.

The decline of jobs in manufacturing and the increase of jobs in the service sector have significant implications for earnings and income and decent levels of family life. In 1982 average weekly earnings in manufacturing were $331. By contrast, weekly earnings were $245 in finance, insurance, and real estate, $225 in personal and business services, and $198 in wholesale and retail trade. Thus, the shift of employment from the goods-producing sector to the services-producing sector of the U.S. economy is shifting the distribution of employment from higher-paying jobs to lower-paying jobs.

In the 1970s about 90 percent of all new jobs added to the economy were in predominantly lower-paying service occupations. By 1990 service industries will employ 72 percent of the labor force, about 90 million workers. And job growth in the 1980s will be biggest in traditionally low-pay, high-turnover jobs in sales, clerical, janitorial, and food service work. Too often these jobs do not have career ladders leading to higher skill, higher pay jobs.

Thus the changing industrial and occupational mix will bring a relative lowering of the overall wage base and a debasing of the nation's wage structure. Under the current wage system for valuing workers' contributions there are going to be a lot of poor working people. Society must accept the idea that the people in these traditionally low-pay jobs must get decent living-wages. To restore the buying power of the minimum wage to the last time the minimum wage was changed by Congress would require a $4.20 minimum wage, rather than the $3.35 an hour that has remained frozen for nearly three years. It is time to remedy that situation.

Until about 1960 most people thought a worker's wage or salary should be adequate to support a family. But that condition has disappeared. Real wages, the buying power of the worker's paycheck, have fallen. The average worker earning $280 a week has only $14,600 for 52 weeks of work—far below the $16,000 a year required for an austere life for a family of four. Even with two earners, families have problems reaching the $26,000 income required for moderate, non-luxury living for a family of four. Ten thousand dollars a year just-above-poverty level of living for an urban family of four would require full-time, year-round work at $5 an hour, which is 50 percent above the present federal minimum wage.

As computers and robots take over more functions in the office and the factory, a two-tier work force is developing. At the top will be a few executives, scientists and engineers, professionals, and managers performing high-level, creative and fulfilling, high-paid, full-time work in a good environment. At the bottom will be low-paid workers performing relatively simple, low-skill, dull, routine, high-turnover jobs in a poor work environment, jobs often part-time and usually lacking job security and opportunities for advancement.

Between these two major tiers will be fewer and fewer permanent, well-paid, full-time, skilled, semi-skilled, and craft production and maintenance jobs which in the past offered hope and opportunity and upward mobility to workers who start in low-paid entry-level jobs. Many middle-level management jobs will also be gone. The loss of middle-level, good-paying jobs raises serious questions about inadequate growth of consumer buying power in the future and about loss of opportunities for upward economic and social mobility. It also raises serious questions about social stability if middle-class America becomes relatively smaller and has less job security and lowered income expectations.

One key answer is to raise the minimum wage to a decent living-wage and to enforce the Fair Labor Standards Act so as to better protect workers at the bottom of the economic ladder — the working poor and those who suffer most from various forms of discrimination in the labor market. Another key answer I will argue is recognition and support for unions and collective bargaining as an essential part of achieving fairness in income distribution by pressing for better wages and salaries and other job-related benefits for America's working people.

Unions and Collective Bargaining

We in the American labor movement believe unions are indispensable in giving an effective voice to workers as they exercise their right of association. We welcome the support for this view from Pope John Paul II in *Laborem Exercens*:

> . . . there is affirmed the natural right to enter corporately into associations . . . workers themselves have the right to act freely and on their own initiative within the above-mentioned associations, without hindrance and as their needs dictate (22).

And this view is consistent with the nation's basic labor law which states that it is the policy of the United States to encourage the practice and procedure of collective bargaining and protect the exercise by workers of full freedom of association, self-organization, and designation of representatives of their own choosing for the purpose of negotiating the terms and conditions of their employment or other mutual aid or protection.

Unfortunately, workers and their unions, too often, face extraordinary challenges and attacks by employers, frequently aided by "labor-management consultants," who use intimidation and coercion to prevent workers from making a free choice of association and to forestall any effective participation by workers in fixing the conditions under which they will labor.

Labor law reform is needed to give substance to the theoretical right of workers to join unions. In 1980 there were 18,000 workers fired from their jobs for asserting their right to associate themselves in a labor union. Many more thousands whose names will never be known were too frightened, too intimidated, to assert this right. Employers' resistance to workers' organizing is very effective in delaying union representation elections until workers have been propagandized and intimidated by anti-union "labor-management consultants." And remedies for unfair labor practices by employers against workers are delayed by lengthy legal maneuvers. Justice delayed is justice denied. This applies also to the frequent lack of "good faith" bargaining when a union, having finally achieved recognition as the workers' representative, finds employers unwilling to negotiate the first contract.

The labor movement in America has long insisted on a written collective bargaining agreement with each employer as the fundamental protection of workers on the job and has always regarded our collective bargaining system as the cornerstone of labor-management relations and, we hope, as the basis for labor-management cooperation.

There is in fact a great deal of labor-management cooperation in many establishments, in many industries, and even at the national level where leaders from labor and leaders from business wrestle with national problems of common concern. We would like to see more of this, but it is often difficult to engage in cooperation when significant segments of industry are attacking the right of workers to organize and to bargain collectively.

In this connection, the Catholic Church should be a model employer. In Catholic schools and hospitals and other non-profit institutions, the right of workers to seek legitimate union affiliation and representation should be recognized and accepted, and the right of workers in these institutions to legitimate participation in management, based on collective bargaining agreement, should be recognized and accepted. Three months after *Laborem Exercens* appeared, the American Bishops' pastoral letter on health care included a statement on the moral obligation of Catholic health care facilities to recognize the right of their workers to organize and to bargain collectively "without unjust pressures." We hope managers of all Catholic, and indeed all religious, institutions would adopt the same policies and at least observe neutrality when their workers consider union representation.

One fruitful area for labor-management cooperation to take place is what has been labeled "industrial policy." Employment policy must be a matter of concern not only to public policy makers but also to private business leaders. The private sector must share in the serious responsibility for job creation, job opportunities, and job security and not restrict itself simply to short-run profit maximization. We support "industrial policy" proposals nurturing new institutional arrangements for business, labor, and government to work toward consensus in order to grapple with specific company, industry, regional, and national problems. Such an institutional consensus-building instrumentality should be based on solid fiscal, monetary, and labor market policies aimed at full employment, balanced economic growth, and social justice.

Social Justice

We believe that social justice and economic progress go hand in hand. Fairness and compassion are not in conflict with economic efficiency. On those occasions when short-run efficiency efforts might appear to conflict with basic standards of fairness and compassion and humanity, we insist on priority for humane values so that economic and social adjustments can be reached with a minimum of hardship to those who are least able to protect themselves against the adverse effects of change.

Fair and reasonable income distribution must be a major concern of general economic policy, government spending and tax policy, and general social policy. In practical terms this means a level of wages and income and a tax structure that provides a firm basis for workers to share in the fruits of their labor. It means that basic income support programs and assistance for the unemployed, the poor, the needy, and the elderly must be maintained and improved. The basic social programs that help the weak and the helpless are fundamental to economic progress as well as to the achievement of a humane society. These programs maintain income and consumer buying power and thus give stability and resilience and humanity to American society.

Discrimination on account of age, race, sex, religion, color, or national origin must be eliminated from all aspects of society. In the field of civil rights, as in the general pursuit of social justice, private action is necessary but it must be re-enforced by public policy.

In brief summary, we urge recognition and action on the principle that workers depend upon a job with a decent living-wage for dignity and income, for status and self-fulfillment, for physical and mental health, for family support and family stability. To give substance to this principle, government should assure training and jobs for those who cannot find jobs and government should be the employer of last resort. For those who are in need — the unemployed, the poor, the dependent, the elderly, the weak, and the helpless — the nation's basic income support and assistance programs must be maintained and strengthened. And we urge action to give substance to the principle that workers have the right to organize themselves in labor unions and to bargain collectively, that unions are indispensable in giving an effective voice to workers as they exercise their right of association.

Four

Full Employment and Selective Labor Market Policies

F. RAY MARSHALL

THE AMERICAN ECONOMY, LIKE THE ECONOMICS OF OTHER industrial market countries (IMECs), is in considerable ferment. A combination of demand management, market forces, the Bretton Woods international financial arrangements, GATT trading agreements, and traditional labor market institutions achieved relative economic stability and growth for the years between World War II and 1965. But by the late 1960s, there were obvious problems with these traditional economic and labor market institutions.

The economic manifestations of these problem were rising inflation and unemployment (or stagflation), intensified international trade problems, reduced rates of growth in productivity and total output, the reduced effectiveness of demand management (monetary and fiscal) policies, and disagreement and uncertainity over the causes of and cures for our economic problems.

The trends which contributed to the change in the effectiveness of traditional policies include:

1) the growing internationalization of the American economy and greater vulnerability to foreign price changes;
2) the influx of immigrants and refugees;
3) the changing composition of the American economy—with greater decentralization of economic activity and the shift of

economic activity and the shift of employment growth to smaller producing units;

4) the changing composition of the work force, especially the greater labor force participation of women, young people, minorities, immigrants and refugees;

5) the decline of employment in manufacturing and the increase in services, especially information technology and its accompanying employment changes which have had a particularly revolutionary impact on economic and labor market activity.

These changes, especially the internationalization of world economies, have altered our economic policy context. It is very clear that we cannot solve our economic problems without a broader view of the international economic context within which we operate. A major policy difficulty is created by the fact that many of our problems have international origins and our policy instruments are mainly national in scope. The Third World debt problem, the flow of illegal immigrants from Mexico and other countries, and the huge wage differentials between U.S. and Third World workers make it necessary for us to take a broader view of our own self-interest and attempt to develop better international cooperation towards more effective international trade, investment, financial, and labor standards mechanisms.

The diminished effectiveness of traditional macroeconomic policies has led also to a growing awareness that economic policies alone could not solve the labor problems confronting the U.S. and other industrial market economies. Selective labor market policies consequently were developed to deal with the unique problems of particular groups, regions, or sectors. These newer instruments supplemented such traditional programs as vocational and technical schools, apprenticeship and training systems, industrial relations practices, labor market activities, and the U.S. Employment Service. The selective measures include training, labor market information and mobility, job creation, measures to combat discrimination and to rationalize labor markets causing them to function more efficiently, job search and counseling services, and education and other supportive services to help people benefit from training and employment activities.

These newer labor market policies grew during the 1960s and 1970s, but have been phased down by Congress and the Reagan Administration. Paradoxically, the newer programs were reduced at the very time their need would appear to be greatest because of a sustained period of high unemployment and mounting empirical evidence that the economic returns to investments in human resources are at least as great as the returns to physical assets. Moreover, this phase-down is taking place when there is growing evidence that the newer employment and training programs were *largely successful* in improving the economic conditions of their participants and were good public investments, despite their relative newness and the incredibly difficult conditions under which they were forced to operate (see Appendix).

Logic, along with the results of these programs, makes it clear that the national objective of achieving full employment cannot be accomplished very effectively without selective employment policies, which are necessary but not sufficient to the achievement of full employment. These must be part of a comprehensive economic policy that would include balanced monetary-fiscal actions, selective anti-inflation (or "incomes") program and selective industrial policy. Although it is beyond the scope of this paper, I am convinced that the arguments for explicit industrial policies to strengthen the competitiveness of American industry far outweigh the problems such polices might cause. Moreover, industrial policy is based on the same rationale as selective labor market policies: namely, to deal with *specific* problems that are beyond the effective reach of macroeconomic policies alone. The component of industrial policy should be coordinated with the other elements of economic policy and include:

1) consensus building mechanisms;
2) international trade encouragement;
3) positive adjustment policies to achieve a more equitable sharing of the benefits and costs of change by facilitating the adjustment of labor and other resources out of non-competitive industries;
4) measures to make credit available to desirable activities on competitive terms;
5) support for research and development activities not likely to be undertaken by private enterprises;
6) selective use of tax and other government actions to strengthen the competitiveness of American industry.

As I define the term, industrial policy does not require government to plan the economy and is not incompatible with reliance on strong market forces—indeed, it would strengthen market forces. Moreover, the government would not "pick winners and losers"—public and private officials would work together to *predict* activities with the greatest and poorest competitive chances. Other than consensus building, the government would not do anything for which it is not already responsible. It would simply do things more effectively and in concert with representatives of the private sector. Similarly, private parties would not be *coerced* into participating: Incentives would be provided, and labor and management would be required to formulate acceptable plans with shared sacrifices if they wanted government help in strengthening their competitive positions.

There are, of course, many different conceptions of industrial policy, but a consensus seems to be emerging for the type I have outlined.

As noted, however, my purpose here is to outline the relationship of different components of a comprehensive economic policy and to discuss selective labor market policies in greater detail, not to discuss selective anti-inflation, industrial, or macroeconomic policy.

One other point should be noted: I assume the country is serious about the commitment to full employment and balanced growth outlined in the Full Employment and Balanced Growth Act of 1978. I make this assumption explicit because the commitment to full employment receives almost no attention from the Reagan Administration or most mainstream economists, despite the fact that unemployment causes ever greater material losses and human suffering. It is inconceivable to me that we will have a just and humane economy without a commitment to full employment. Indeed, there is scarcely a social or economic problem that would not be greatly improved by full employment. Of course, the fear of inflation is one reason for the lack of emphasis on full employment. That is the reason we must develop a less barbaric anti-inflation policy than the massive unemployment implied by monetarism. Another reason for this lack of commitment is the relative powerlessness of the unemployed and their advocates. Moreover, an industrial policy is essential to improve the *quality* of jobs, not just the number. I believe strongly that the Bishops will do the country a great service if they focus national attention on the full employment objective.

Selective Labor Market Programs

The main purposes of this paper are (1) to review the evidence with respect to the effectiveness of selective labor market programs and (2) to suggest some of the future directions these programs might take. The principles underlying selective employment policies include:

1) Macroeconomic policy alone is less effective than selective measures in treating particular labor market problems because general policies generate inflation in tight labor markets before reducing pockets of unemployment to acceptable levels. Moreover, it is generally agreed that the budget costs of reducing unemployment by selective labor market policies was considerably less than through tax cuts or general spending increases. In other words, selective labor market policies have the ability to shift the pattern of aggregate demand without shifting its level.

2) Selective labor market policies have the ability to shift the burden of unemployment from the weak to the strong, whether or not they reduce the aggregate level of unemployment. It is assumed to be equitable as well as efficient to reduce the level of unemployment by concentrating on reducing unemployment of those with the highest unemployment rates.

3) By changing the operation of labor markets, selective labor market policies improve the trade-off between unemployment and inflation in the long run and to put the unemployed to work providing useful goods and services.

The results of detailed evaluations provide no reason to question the validity of these roles for selective employment policies, even though there have been no systematic tests of all of these assumptions in the U.S. However, the results here and in other countries which make greater use of selective labor market policies are rarely unambiguous and actual program implementation has been much more complicated than a simple statement of the rationale for these programs would imply.

Program implementation in any area is always difficult and must proceed by trial and error in response to changing conditions and experiences. For example, experiences with the Manpower Development and Training Act of 1962 led to the realization that large-scale employment and training programs could not be administered effectively from Washington, leading to decentralization of most programs to state and local governments through the Comprehensive Employment and Training Act of 1973 (CETA). There was strong support for decentralization, despite some skepticism — based on historical experience — that local political institutions had either the political necessity or will to meet the labor market needs of the disadvantaged. After decentralization, participation by minorities, young people, and the private sector all declined. Moreover, one of the main early criticisms of the decentralized system was the tendency for local units of government to substitute CETA funds for regular personnel costs, diminishing CETA's ability to reduce unemployment.

CETA's passage coincided with a deep recession, during which unemployment reached 9%. Since it was generally understood that public service employment (PSE) would be the most cost-effective way to reduce unemployment, it became a higher priority to increase these programs as rapidly as the delivery system would permit. It was generally agreed that the limitations of the CETA delivery system would place the main burden of counteracting the recession on more expensive macroeconomic policies. The Carter Administration's stimulus program demonstrated that PSE could be used as a countercyclical program, but that rapid build-up (from about 290,000 to 753,000 within one year) greatly taxed the system and revealed some fundamental weaknesses in CETA's management and monitoring system. Unfortunately, some of these weaknesses in both the complex Congressional budget and legislative processes and federal, state, and local relationships were inherent, which could not be changed very quickly. For example, it was difficult to operate a system as complex as CETA on a one-year funding cycle (which produced a budget at the beginning of the fiscal year only once between 1977 and 1981). Moreover, the complicated political process required to get legislation through the Congress created timing problems, exaggerated expectations, and a proliferation of program objectives, making it very hard to achieve the managerial objectives of simplifying and concentrating national policies.

The stimulus process also made it clear that PSE could be used more effectively as a countercyclical program with (1) some automatic triggering process to avoid delay; (2) sufficient financial stability through forward funding, entitlements, or earmarked funds to permit program stability, planning, and continuity; and (3) sufficient flexibility to make it possible for local program administrators to develop an array of instruments to meet their unique labor market needs. Clearly, however, national objectives such as increasing participation by minorities, women, and the disadvantaged were not compatible with the greatest flexibility by local program administrators.

Similarly, it was very hard to simultaneously mount a large-scale PSE program and improve its management and information system.

A major problem for CETA before 1978 was the inadequate power of the federal management system to prevent fraud and abuse by local program administrators. In order to develop a better monitoring system the Carter Administration created an Office of Special Investigations in 1977 (which later became the Office of the Inspector General) and attempted to improve the management information system. Congress sought to reduce substitution in the PSE build-up by a 1976 amendment and reduced substitution still further in the CETA reauthorization of 1978. This limited the duration of participation in CETA programs, put a relatively low cap on wages paid to participants, and strengthened the penalties on local administrators for violation of the law. Unfortunately, these changes went too far toward restricting local flexibility, made PSE less useful as a countercyclical program, and reduced political support by local elected officials who were content to use CETA to administer local services—or to enhance their political support—but were less interested in employing and training the disadvantaged and less willing to risk the legal liabilities for violating a tougher law.

As a consequence of these developments and problems, as well as the decline of the general level of unemployment to less than 6 percent, the Carter Administration phased down the countercyclical PSE program and shifted greater attention to some other objectives, especially the private sector initiative, youth employment programs, welfare reform, and economic dislocation projects.

Private Sector

Despite the clear need to involve the private sector this has been controversial, partly because private sector involvement during the 1960s was considered by many critics to be ineffective. Private profit-making enterprises have not displayed much enthusiasm for employing and training the hardcore disadvantaged, which some experts consider to be incompatible with profit maximization. These critics therefore emphasize the need for continuing only public programs.

Unfortunately, much of this controversy is over extreme and unrealistic positions. Clearly, private businesses are not prepared to assume *full* responsibility because business is not very effective at reaching, providing supporting services to, or training the hardcore unemployed.

It is just as clear, however, that the private sector *must* play an important part in the delivery of employment and training services. The employment problems of the disadvantaged are not likely to be solved by public employment programs alone, especially during periods of severe public budget constraints. Moreover, placement in regular public or private jobs must be the main objective of employment and training programs. Private labor market representatives must therefore play an important role in helping design training programs and in providing employment opportunities. This is one of the main reasons the Carter Administration shifted emphasis toward greater private sector involvement. A very successful Skills Training Improvement Program (STIP) was part of the 1977 economic stimulus program and a Private Sector Initiative Program (PSIP) was made one of the most important new initiatives in the 1978 CETA reauthorization. The PSIP consisted of two parts: (1) a targeted jobs tax credit (TJTC) to provide a tax credit of 50 percent of the wages up to $6000 of eligible employees the first year and 25 percent the second, and (2) the formation of local private industry councils, or PICs, made up mainly of business, but also of labor, community-based organizations (CBOs), and other labor market representatives. The TJTC has not been noticeably popular with most employers who have not used this program as much as might have been expected from such a large tax subsidy. Experience with the TJTC casts considerable doubt on the efficacy of tax credits and on such measures as youth differentials for the minimum wage as means of meeting the employment and training needs of the disadvantaged.

The local private industry councils have received mixed reviews, but are still evolving. It was hoped that these councils would be a means whereby local labor market actors could come together to improve local employment and training systems. The objective was to help change the CETA system's main success criterion from getting people into the system to getting them out of it and into the regular economy. The targeting and wage and duration limitations imposed by the 1978 CETA reauthorization also were designed to achieve that objective.

Skeptics who point to the lackluster performance of past private sector employment and training programs ignore the essential difference between the PICs as local labor market instrumentalities and earlier national systems. It was hoped that, however limited initially, the PICs would evolve into effective local labor market organizations, which ultimately would include education, labor, and other major actors in each local labor market. While it is true that profit-maximizing firms are not likely to give high priority to the disadvantaged, tax subsidies can make businesses more willing to expand employment during upswings in the business cycle and to retain more workers during downswings. Moreover, direct public training and employment programs can prepare workers for entry-level private sector jobs.

It would, however, not be appropriate to equate all private sector organizations with profit-maximizing businesses. The PICs, for example, are not private profit-maximizing organizations. Similarly, unions and community-based organizations (CBOs) have an important role to play in employment and training systems. Some of the very best labor market programs have been conducted by unions or jointly by unions and employers, both under the traditional employment and training systems (like apprenticeship and on-the-job training) and the newer programs under Manpower Development and Training Act of 1962 (MDTA) and CETA. Indeed, a major limitation of business training programs is that their profit-maximizing motives cause them to give less attention to good training that might not increase profits (because some employers might incur the costs while workers or other employers receive the benefits). The most effective training is likely to be under conditions where the interests of workers and employers are represented and where workers receive academic along with well-rounded, on-the-job training. This kind of general training is good for workers and society, but might not be profitable for particular employers. Moreover, labor market information is a public good and cannot be efficiently supplied by private profit-making institutions.

Similarly, CBOs have an important role to play. These organizations are likely to be able to reach and serve people with labor market needs much better than employers, the Employment Service, or other traditional institutions. Outreach programs and the CBOs are among the most important and effective labor market developments of the 1960s and 1970s. It is unfortunate that budget cuts associated with the Job Training Partnership Act (JTPA), which replaced CETA in 1983, threaten the survival of many of these organizations.

In conclusion, while private organizations are not likely to be able to undertake the entire job of providing employment and training services, they have an important role to play in conjunction with other labor market institutions. A major challenge of the future is to bring disparate education, business, labor, employment service, economic development, and job development activities into closer coordination to deliver services geared to the realities in local labor markets. Perhaps the private industry councils which were given greater responsibility for the federal training system under the JTPA will evolve into effective local labor market committees.

Youth

Another major problem created by the CETA decentralization was a decline in the participation of young people, who had particularly high unemployment rates and whose early unemployment causes permanent labor market problems. While some analysts thought the aging of the baby boom generation would eliminate the youth employment problem, this idea was based on a serious misconception of its nature. The real problem was never the total youth population, but hard-core unemployment among youngsters with multiple disadvantages, whose numbers are increasing despite the fact that four million fewer 16-24 year-olds will enter the work force during the 1980s than during the 1970s. As a consequence, Congress and the Carter Administration passed the Youth Employment and Demonstration Projects Act (YEDPA) in 1977. At the same time, the Job Corps, which had demonstrated its effectiveness in helping young people with serious disadvantages, was doubled in size. The basic approach was to expand successful programs, like the Job Corps, as rapidly as consistent with good management, to enrich and improve the performance of other employment and training programs, and to undertake rigorous experiments to determine the effectiveness of different approaches to youth employment problems.

YEDPA also created four major new youth employment and training programs which were fully underway within six months of the signing of the Act. These programs played an important part in increasing youth employment and reducing unemployment. Employment in the work components of YEDPA in December 1979 accounted for one-fourth of the measured employment growth of all teenagers since December 1977 and approximately three-fourths of the growth for black teenagers—the first gains for black teenage males in the 1970s. The unemployment rate for black youth declined from about 43 percent in the spring of 1977 to 30 percent 18 months after the stimulus program was inaugurated. Moreover, careful evaluations show the youth entitlement program to have been relatively successful in providing part-time jobs to keep disadvantaged young people in school. This is very important in view of the fact that school dropouts have serious permanent labor market disadvantages. It is therefore unfortunate that the JTPA phased out the public service employment programs which had been very successful under YEDPA.

Welfare Reform

Another unfinished employment and training activity is reforming the welfare system by simplifying and rationalizing public assistance and providing paying jobs to the welfare eligibles who could not find jobs in the private sector. Unlike the Reagan "workfare" approach (which places an average 95 percent tax on the earnings of welfare recipients who work and forces those who cannot find jobs to work off their grants in specially created public jobs), the Carter Administration's proposal stressed cash incentives to work and provided paid public service jobs if an intensive search did not find jobs for those expected to work.

The Labor Department launched an Employment Opportunities Pilot Project as a carefully controlled test of the jobs component of President Carter's welfare reform proposals. The pilot program provided (1) an intensive job search program providing initial and recurring assistance in finding private sector employment together with supportive services, and (2) a job and training component for those who could not find private sector employment initially, preparatory to additional private sector job placement activities. The program had enrolled about ten thousand participants in fourteen job sites by July 1980. All AFDC recipients were required to participate if they had work requirements and all AFDC eligible adults could participate voluntarily; about half of the participants were volunteers. Under this pilot project, those who were unable to find jobs after eight weeks of job searching were placed in federally-assisted work or training positions, and efforts were made to provide skills and work experience leading to jobs in the regular economy.

After one year, this pilot project demonstrated that a surprisingly large proportion of participants had been placed. After intensive job search through a job club, the average placement was about 50 percent, and was 70 percent in Lowell, Massachusetts. If this placement rate held up, it would have made a welfare reform job program much less expensive than originally assumed.

However, the Reagan Administration did not continue the welfare reform pilot project, electing instead for workfare. This is a curious inconsistency in the Administration's approach to incentives. The rich are given financial encouragement through a large reduction in marginal tax rates, while the poor are forced to work by the threat of being made even worse off. Able-bodied parents of AFDC children would be required to "work off" their grants in specially created jobs. Recipients would not be paid wages, but would be given credit for hours worked. Their grants would be cut if they failed to work the necessary hours.

The surprising thing about this approach is not only its conflict with the Administration's emphasis on market incentives, but also because such programs have not been effective ways to promote productive work. One of the most notable failures was in California when Mr. Reagan was governor. In 1971, California began experimenting with workfare programs. According to a study by the State of California, during the peak year, 1974, only about 5,760 people participated—less than 1 percent of the California AFDC cases that year. The state's study found no difference in trends in welfare and cases costs between counties with work projects and those without them. Recipients enrolled in a Massachusetts work-relief project actually stayed on welfare longer than a comparable group not required to participate.

The reason for the greater success of the type of pilot project launched by the Carter Administration should come as no surprise to people familiar with secondary labor markets. Most welfare recipients want to work and will do so if they see employment as a dignified way to a better life, but the poor, like the rich, are unwilling to work for little or no economic gain. Forcing unwilling people into "make-work" jobs will not save welfare money and is not compatible with a system based on market incentives.

Relation to Other Programs

Federal employment and training programs are most effective when they are coordinated with other programs. The relationship to macroeconomic policies is relatively clear. Employment and training programs cannot substitute for macroeconomic policies to reduce unemployment, but they can complement those policies and reach certain targeted groups more effectively and at lower cost.

Employment and training programs also must be coordinated with the Employment Service which plays an important labor market role, despite the fact that it has been underfunded and understaffed and has been criticized by some labor market experts for being inefficient and insensitive to the needs of the disadvantaged. Nevertheless, competition with the CETA system, the requirements of anti-discrimination legislation, and the use of CETA funds to provide services to CETA participants by traditional public programs has caused these institutions to be more responsive to the needs of the poor. The Employment Service is therefore no longer the institution it was in the 1950s. Moreover, despite criticism for lack of coordination between CETA and the Employment Service, experience shows these labor market institutions were establishing closer working relationships in 1981 when funding for both was curtailed.

Public employment and training programs have also helped meet other national objectives by putting the unemployed to work providing such useful services as energy and environmental conservation, health care, public safety, day care, and recreation that otherwise would not be provided. Demonstration projects during the Carter Administration also revealed the potential of public employment and training programs as components of positive adjustment activities to help provide job opportunities for workers and communities during major economic dislocation and structural changes like those in the automobile, steel, and other industries heavily impacted by international trade and technological changes. However, in order to be most effective, adjustment programs cannot be as narrowly targeted on low-income groups as most of CETA was, because many higher-income workers would not be eligible. While budget constraints force targeting to low-income groups, labor market services available to all workers would be a good public investment and would remove some of the stigma from employment and training programs and provide broader support.

Shifting Responsibility to the States

In the Job Training Partnership Act (JTPA), passed in 1983, the Administration and Congress assigned more responsiblity for a limited and scaled-down employment and training program to the states. In some ways this is logical because the states have major responsibility for education, economic development, and other human resource development programs, all of which should be coordinated with employment and training activities. Critics point out, however, that the failure of the states to meet the employment and training needs of the disadvantaged is what led to the federal employment and training programs in the first place. They also point out that the disadvantaged do not have as much political influence in most state capitals as they do in Washington, that there is a danger of competitive devaluation of human resource development programs as states compete for scarce job-creating industries, that state and local governments rely more heavily than the federal government on regressive sales and property taxes, and that the states did not do a particularly good job with their responsibilities under CETA and have demonstrated little interest in developing innovative employment and training programs for young people and welfare recipients.

On the other hand, the states have an opportunity to make the most of the employment and training needs of their people and to build the base for a more effective federal employment and training system in the future. States and state institutions are not the same as they were in the 1950s and 1960s when they acquired their reputation for being apathetic to the interests of the disadvantaged; indeed, some states have developed exemplary employment and training programs. Moreover, the bias against states caused their role and resources to be limited in the past. Given the political atmosphere and scarce employment and training resources, governors and state legislatures could perform an outstanding national service by developing imaginative employment, training, and education programs.

Another problem for the nation's employment and training system is the Reagan Administration's budget cuts for labor market statistics. This is particularly troublesome in a time when better and more accurate labor market information systems are necessary to evaluate the impact of the Administration's radical program changes and to improve the operation of labor markets.

The Negative Image of Jobs Programs?

There are several explanations for the negative image for selective employment programs. Ideological biases against government have always caused some people to denigrate public programs. This was done with the WPA, the CCC, as well as with CETA, and is equally wrong.

Many academics, especially those trained in neoclassical and macro-economics, are biased against selective labor market interventions and therefore have done "simulation" studies where they "predict" failure — as when simulations "proved" erroneously in the 1970s that "substitution" was between 50 and 95% in the CETA program. Economists — even those in the Carter Administration's CEA and OMB — were predisposed to believe these outrageous "studies" that built their conclusions into the way they set up the problem. Moreover, academics tend to have a critical temper which causes them to compare public programs with ideal models, concentrating on the departures from perfection rather than positive achievements relative to realistic alternatives.

Some aspects of CETA had serious programmatic and organizational shortcomings. CETA was a complex system with multiple, conflicting objectives, 50,000 subcontractors, inadequate management information systems and ridiculously short funding cycles, constantly changing legal requirements, and local political and programmatic interests. Despite these problems, hard work and dedication by the overwhelming majority of the people in the system made it work. Unfortunately, public attention tends to focus more on fraud and abuse than on program successes, and ignorance of the benefits by the media and many public officials caused the media accounts of fraud and abuse to become reality for them. Moreover, economists who should know better and editorial writers (who are not always expected to) undermined support for employment and training programs by creating the false impression that increased funding for these programs played a major role in the increased inflation of 1979-80, despite the fact that the total was less than the overrun on forty weapons systems during the last three months of 1980! By reducing transfer payments, providing useful public services, and improving the productivity of people in training programs, these activities served to reduce inflationary pressures. In short, the CETA system was so unstable and complicated that it was hard for even the experts to keep things in perspective.

State and local communities that were quite willing to accept employment and training funds which they could substitute for local resources, and for which accounting was not very strict, were much less interested in the targeted programs with stricter accountability introduced in the CETA reauthorization of 1978. The popularity of CETA was further reduced by constant funding uncertainties that plagued the program throughout its existence.

In order to provide for a more adequate employment and training system in the future, the program must not be as tightly targeted as CETA, must have greater funding stability, and must be regarded as a major public investment that will yield substantial social dividends.

Conclusions

Conceptually, selective employment and training programs have an important role to play in economic and social policy, but these programs have not realized their potential. There are many inherent problems in making selective labor market policies approximate their potential:

1) Complicated and fragmented government structures which cause policy making to be more complicated and coordination more difficult than is the case in other countries. There is little coordination or continuity in economic policy, which is divided between the Congress, the White House, the Federal Reserve, and state and local governments, and no mechanism to build consensus, coordination, or cooperation between these public agencies and the private sector. Indeed, there is not even an effective mechanism to develop agreement on the facts about whether or not the programs "worked".

2) There is no coherent economic policy to which selective employment and training measures can be related. Our economy is fragmented and contradictory with little effort to promote economic stability, relatively full use of resources, and long run growth of key industries; or to provide for more equitable sharing of the costs and benefits of economic change; or to facilitate adjustments; or to sort out the logical division of labor between public, private, and public-private institutions; or to develop coherent long run international economic strategies. Selective employment policies could play important roles in overall economic and social policies, but they cannot do that very effectively if those policies are misguided, as they are in this administration, or lack coherence, as they have in most past administrations.

3) The immediate outlook for selective employment and training programs is not bright, but those of us who believe in them should work to make the most of the opportunities that do ex-

ist to improve public understanding and continue to improve the employment and training system so that it will be more responsive to national and international needs. Those of us who believe in democratic processes must have faith in the power of public education and in Abraham Lincoln's declaration: "I will get ready and my time will come."

APPENDIX

Accomplishments of CETA

Before its recent elimination, CETA was a relatively new program with a mix of successes, problems, and failures, but the overwhelming evidence from independent evaluations suggests far more successes than failures. There also is general agreement that it was improving and problems were being overcome before the Reagan Administration and Congress replaced it with a much smaller training program, The Job Training Partnership Act (JTPA).

For example, when CETA was first decentralized from the Manpower Development and Training Act (MDTA), there was lower participation by the private sector, minorities, and young people, which limited the net impact on employment and unemployment. Successive changes, especially the CETA reauthorization of 1978 and administrative changes, improved performance and overcame some of these problems. The National Association of Counties reported that, despite a very sluggish economy, CETA had a 54 percent placement ratio between October 1979 and June 1980 — 43.6 percent were placed in jobs and the others returned to schools or other successful placements.

A 1982 study by the Urban Institute (Laurie J. Bassi, "CETA: Is it a Cost-Effective Method for Increasing the Earnings of Disadvantaged Workers?") concluded:

1) Since the 1978 reauthorization, CETA had served the intended target group almost exclusively.
2) CETA had been responsible for significant post-program increases in the employability and earnings of participants. The groups that benefited most from CETA participation were women and the economically disadvantaged.

3) Before the 1978 changes in CETA's eligiblility criteria, it was not a cost-effective means of increasing workers' earnings. This was because the program was much less targeted to the economically disadvantaged—the group that benefits the most from participation in CETA.

4) Every dollar eliminated from the federal budget by cutting CETA will be offset by at least 22-45 cents because of the increased expenditures on programs such as welfare, food stamps, unemployment insurance, and decreased receipts from payroll and income taxes.

5) The elimination of PSE will result in a substantial reduction in services provided by many local governments and non-profit organizations.

In January 1981 the National Council on Employment Policy ("Management of Remedial Employment and Training Programs in the 1980s") concluded after an exhaustive evaluation:

> The desire for a major overhaul often stems from the notion that CETA has failed. However, the most current longitudinal data, backed up by other sources, indicate that almost all of the major CETA components have been a good investment for society, and have returned benefits well in excess of costs.

These and many other positive evaluations relate primarily to the improvements made as a consequence of CETA reauthorization which strengthened the program's effectiveness. The evidence suggests that even those who entered before these 1978 improvements benefited from the program. The first longitudinal study (by Westat, Inc.) of the long-term post-program experience of terminees who entered CETA during January to June 1975 concluded that CETA terminees' employment and earnings increased in the second post-program year over the first and the pre-entry years. Westat estimates found that the 1976 CETA terminees earned $300 more in 1977 than comparable non-participants. On the job training (OJT) had the largest impact, followed by classroom training and PSE. Work experience programs had no statistically significant impact. The largest gains were made by participants who had the lowest pre-program earnings (less than $2,000 gained $550 over non-participant counterparts), women ($500-600), men ($200), and the one-third of participants who were placed in jobs by the programs and who registered net gains of $1,250 in 1977.

Eli Ginzberg, a long-time student of employment and training programs, concluded: "There is no way of reading the experience with decentralization after 1973 as anything other than a success" (*Employing the Unemployed*, McGraw-Hill, 1980). Assessing the impact on minorities and youth, Bernard Anderson concluded: "What is clear is that employment and training programs as a whole provide returns to society that exceed their cost" (*Ibid*, p. 59). Richard Nathan of Princeton University conducted detailed field studies for the Brookings Institution and concluded:

> The most striking conclusion from the Brookings monitoring research to date is the degree to which the balancing of the goal at all government levels has produced a workable bargain, one that allowed the PSE program to function reasonably smoothly and to build up rapidly in 1977-78. A total of 425,000 jobs were added nationally between May 1977 and 1978. Overall, we found a large stimulus effect. (*Ibid*, p. 65).

A 1981 study for the Department of Labor by Vernon Briggs, Brian Rungeling, and R. Smith (*Public Service Employment in the Rural South*) based on extensive and detailed field work, concluded:

> Whether the objective of PSE is countercyclical or counterstructural . . . PSE is a viable and positive program in the rural South. As a countercyclical program, PSE demonstrated that it was possible to create a large number of jobs in a relatively short period of time. It allowed local governments in a relatively impoverished region to expand their basic services and in a number of instances, to add 'new services' that were not previously available.
>
> PSE benefited both the participants and the communities . . . [and] was found to be especially beneficial to the rural South due to the fact that it provided access to types of public service jobs to which they had traditionally been excluded.

The CETA youth program also produced impressive results. By the end of 1979 the Youth Employment and Demonstration Projects Act of 1978 accounted for one-fourth of the measured growth in teenage employment and three-fourths of black teenage employment; this was the first gain for black teenage males in the 1970s.

The Brookings study found that the quality of services performed by PSE workers was consistently at least equal to that of regular public employees in each occupation. When CETA's focus shifted more to serving the disadvantaged, the jobs were not as politically attractive, but they were still socially useful work that otherwise would not have been done: weatherization, home health care, conservation, repair of public buildings, law enforcement aides, etc.

Similarly, localized studies showed generally favorable results. A 1981 Johns Hopkins study of the Baltimore experience (Report to the National Center for Health Services Research, under contract #HS93046) found that real wages were 16 percent higher for CETA participants the first year out of the program compared with pre-CETA, and that the post-program employment rate increased dramatically over time: The immediate transition rate was 48 percent, 59 percent one month later, 66 percent at six months, 70 percent at one year, and 74-80 percent for three to five years.

There also were a large number of very successful programs targeted at particular groups. For example, the supported work program greatly improved the economic conditions of welfare recipients, helped welfare mothers who earned 50 percent more and worked 35 percent more hours than a comparison group one year after leaving the program. Results were also most favorable for those who had been on welfare the longest and were the most disadvantaged.

CETA has a minimal inflationary impact because it is targeted on the unemployed and statistically disadvantaged and because wages paid are subject to strict limitations. This means workers who take PSE jobs are not in short supply and therefore do not create bottlenecks nor add to inflationary pressures.

Five

Unemployment and Jobs:
A Theological and Ethical Perspective

DAVID HOLLENBACH, S.J.

AS THE AMERICAN BISHOPS MOVE FORWARD IN DRAFTING a pastoral letter on Catholic Social Teaching and the American Economy, the question of employment and unemployment will surely be of central concern. The history of modern Catholic social teaching is customarily marked as beginning in 1891 with Leo XIII's encyclical on the condition of labor, *Rerum Novarum*. From this early social encyclical right down to the most recent such document from John Paul II, *Laborem Exercens*, papal social teaching has consistently addressed the questions of work, wages, working conditions, and unemployment. Moral and theological analysis of work has been one of the main themes of papal social teaching. It has also occupied a major place in the past social teaching and in the engagement of the American Catholic hierarchy in the life of our country. Similarly, the problems of employment and unemployment have been and continue to be central in the general public discussion of social morality and justice in United States economic life. So it is certainly fitting that the bishops' efforts to throw some light on the current problems of our economy from the resources of Catholic tradition should give significant attention to employment and unemployment.

This essay attempts to assist the bishops in their difficult and important task by situating the contemporary problems of unemployment and job-generation in a theological and ethical context. The argument has three phases. First, the multiple dimensions of the problem of unemployment in present-day American society will be sketched and the challenges they pose for citizens and policy-makers will be outlined. Second, a theological assessment of the significance and importance of work in the lives of human beings will be proposed, relying on both the biblical foundations of the Christian faith and the development of these foundations in Christian tradition. Third, several ethical norms will be highlighted which can help shape the responses of both the Christian community and secular society to the problem of unemployment, namely the right to employment and the standard of justice as a norm for guiding the effort to implement this right. This final section will also make a number of proposals about how the bishops might address specific issues of public policy from a Christian theological perspective.

As the argument of the essay unfolds, it will become clear that no single branch of knowledge — whether it be economics, theology, ethics or policy studies — has a definitive or exhaustive understanding of either the problems or the solutions in this exceedingly complex area. Anyone who undertakes a project such as that which this symposium is addressing needs a large measure of the virtue of humility. The need for humility, of course, applies not only to the bishops, but also to citizens and secular policy analysts. Therefore, the bishops should be careful not to affirm as certain or obligatory what is doubtful or possible. By the same token, they should also recognize that they have a most important contribution to make to the public debate. Though the church clearly does not have all the answers, neither do the economists or the business schools. The appropriate tone for a church response to the problem of unemployment should be that of a dialogue — a form of conversation and discourse in which the bishops are sure enough of their own proper role both to listen and to speak. This essay itself tries to follow this advice.

Dimensions of the Problem

One can distinguish at least four different kinds of unemployment on the basis of their causes. The first is the "frictional unemployment," which is the consequence of the fact that in an economy like ours where people change jobs periodically some of them will be out of work at any given moment. There are, of course, serious disputes about how much of this frictional unemployment is a necessity in our economy.

Second is the cyclical unemployment which increases as the economy contracts and decreases as the economy expands through the business cycle. Here again there are disputes about how to respond to this kind of unemployment. New Deal style approaches call for a variety of job-creating initiatives such as government expenditures to stimulate the demand for work and direct public works projects. Supply-side policies favored by the present administration seek to generate jobs by encouraging private investment through reduced taxes. The experience of recent years suggests that neither of these theories provides an all-purpose panacea for cyclical unemployment.

A third sort of unemployment has been called chronic or structural unemployment. In Paul Samuelson's textbook definition, it is that form of unemployment "which cannot be cured by expansion of over-all monetary demand, but which is attributable to lack of proper skills, location and attitudes among youth, the aged, the illiterate, minorities, the residents of depressed areas, and the technologically displaced."[1] This is the unemployment of people whose chances of finding a job are slim or non-existent in any phase of the business cycle because they lack the skills or other prerequisites for finding work in our kind of economy. Various responses to chronic unemployment have been attempted since the 1960s, most notably those created by the passage of the Comprehensive Employment and Training Act (CETA). These programs have generated considerable controversy. However, there is evidence that, despite notable weaknesses, they did accomplish at least part of their purpose.[2] They are presently being dismantled by the Reagan administration and replaced with programs which rely more heavily on the private sector in line with goals of reduced government intervention in the economy and decreased public expenditure. As the Brookings Institution study of the 1983 budget points out, the burdens of these CETA reductions fall most heavily on low income families with a potential earner.[3] Also, these burdens will weigh especially heavily on those at the very bottom of our society, for the new Reagan programs are targeted to assist unemployed persons with higher skill levels in order to increase the efficiency and success rate of the effort.

All three of these forms of unemployment have been the subject of considerable reflection and analysis for many years. We have built up a body of theories—both economic and moral—on how to deal with them. Pluralism reigns, but at least people have some sense of what the issues are, and the church has some experience in reflecting upon them from an ethical point of view. In recent years, however, a fourth type of unemployment has become a central topic of discussion in the United States. Something like a consensus appears to be developing that the United States stands at a moment of basic transition in the way its economy works. Those with less optimistic dispositions or a greater sense of the dramatic are inclined to see it as a moment of crisis. Whether transition or crisis, something seems to be happening to the United States job market as a result of very complex interactions between the processes of technological change and the shifting patterns of the international division of labor.

It seems certain that the present high rate of unemployment in the United States is in part caused by these technological and international shifts that some refer to as "the deindustrialization of America." Though it is equally clear that very high rates of unemployment have been brought about in part by the fiscal and monetary policies of the Reagan government, this does not appear to be the whole story.[4] Each of the economic recoveries of recent years has left the United States with a higher unemployment rate than the recovery which preceded it. Thus it is likely that a considerable number of the jobs which were lost in the most recent recession will not be regained even if we succeed in moving back to the top of the business cycle curve. This suggests that we are faced with a new and more threatening form of structural unemployment which is caused by a combination of the effects of the exporting of jobs to countries with lower wage demand, the transfer of sophisticated and efficient technology to these countries, and the displacement of industrial jobs by a smaller number of jobs in the high-tech and service sectors within the United States itself.

Conclusions on how to deal with unemployment in the United States are therefore dependent on an understanding of these new technological and international dynamics. And here there is even less agreement than on the remedies prescribed by theories developed in response to the three other more traditional types of unemployment. This puts the bishops in a difficult position as they attempt to offer moral guidance and contribute to the formation of public opinion.

A few examples will illustrate the problem. In their study of plant closings and the unemployment which necessarily accompanies them,

Barry Bluestone and Bennett Harrison call for greater governmental limits on the mobility and export of capital in the interest of protecting American jobs.[5] This view is opposed by Lester Thurow, who argues that locking up capital and workers in low productivity industries insures economic decline and ultimately greater job loss.[6] Therefore he argues in favor of shutting down low-productivity "sunset" plants more rapidly and relocating workers in growing "sunrise" industries as the best way to protect jobs — exactly the opposite conclusion from that reached by Bluestone and Harrison. This debate also has international dimensions. Insuring jobs in America's aging smokestack industries against competition from products produced abroad in more modern plants with cheaper labor will require protectionist legislation. Bluestone calls for a limited amount of such protectionism. Thurow sees this as a formula for saving American jobs only in the short run, at the cost of keeping "the rest of the world poor."[7]

There are further issues in the discussion of the present economic transition that also complicate the bishops' task. Groups as diverse as a team of editors from *Business Week*, in their study on *The Reindustrialization of America*,[8] and the United Auto Workers, in their "Blueprint for a Working America,"[9] have called for a new form of public planning in the economy in the interest of improving productivity and saving jobs. Both groups call for a partnership of labor, management, and government in planning how to target credit for investment that will enhance productivity and preserve jobs. The *Business Week* team notes that such cooperation depends on whether or not the three groups "can break out of their ideological shells to adopt a program that appears to rub, at certain seams, against the idea of a free market."[10] The UAW plan resembles the *Business Week* proposal in urging the institution of a limited amount of collaborative planning to guide investment into job-producing sectors. However, in a characteristic difference of vocabulary, the UAW plan speaks of getting labor, management, and government together "to bargain" on the direction this targeted investment should take, while *Business Week* speaks of "cooperation" between the three groups. The *Business Week* group is concerned over labor's adversarial relationship to management. The UAW, on the other hand, fears that since the funds for investment must come from somewhere they are quite likely to come from the salaries of the working class. Thus the UAW blueprint insists that "not only is top-down planning by a private or public elite undemocratic, but it won't work well. We need democratic decision making."[12] The *Business Week* team acknowledges that the burdens of reinvestment costs must be distributed fairly and that the success of any planning effort will depend on the degree to which it reaches out to include chronically unemployed minorities and avoids exacting sacrifice from those least able to bear it, that is, from the poor.[11] Though the concern for fairness is evident in both these proposals, they reveal a conflict among the interests of the industrial working class, of the poor and minorities, of management, and of local communities which are significantly dependent on an aging heavy industry base.

In addition, most of these proposals for "reindustrialization" have included calls for programs to retrain significant numbers of workers for new jobs. The reason such retraining is needed is that many of the new jobs to replace those lost in basic industry and manufacturing will be in high technology areas such as microelectronics, robotics and other fields dependent on a highly skilled work force. Robert Reich has argued forcefully that production which depends on the assembly line and relatively unskilled labor "can be accomplished more cheaply in developing nations."[13] The problem with these proposals for retraining industrial workers for high-tech jobs is that such high-tech training programs are the ones that the chronically unemployed are least prepared to enter, because of the low level of basic verbal and quantitative skills among this group. Retraining for high-tech jobs, if pursued alone, threatens to increase class differences within the United States. It could lead us to a divided society where, as someone has remarked, one class operates computers and manufactures silicon chips and the other class cooks Big Macs. The *Business Week* team rightly concluded that "the country's economic health is increasingly determined by 'invisible' investment in human capital," i.e., in the education of a skilled work force.[14] But the skills needed are not only in the high-tech area, but also on more basic levels. Bluestone and Harrison have argued that there are significant needs for new investment and output in the United States in the areas of housing, energy, mass transit, freight rail transit, and health. Publicly guided investment in these areas could fill social needs and generate a significant number of jobs with diverse skill requirements.[15] Training on a diversity of skill levels thus seems called for if the unemployment problem is to be dealt with adequately.

Finally, all of these proposals for guided investment, collaborative planning by management, labor, and government, and programmed retraining are criticized as unworkable by the neo-conservative right. Authors such as George Gilder and Amitai Etzioni oppose such steps as excessive politicization of the market. Gilder believes that the solution lies in reliance on the entrepreneurship of innovative small companies and a tax structure that will make them viable. Etzioni argues that planned reindustrialization is impossible because we have no way of knowing what sectors of the economy are sunrise sectors until they have already risen, and because the Japanese model of guided change is incompatible with American culture.[16] It should come as no surprise that these views are shared by the Reagan administration.

In short, the current reality of unemployment has multiple causes diagnosed in a variety of ways. The efforts to generate new jobs must be on a variety of levels and no single initiative will serve as a panacea. Indeed, there are serious conflicts between steps that would relieve the problem of unemployment in one segment of society and those which would relieve it in another. For example, high-tech investment may generate jobs for the more highly skilled, but eliminate jobs for the less skilled. Policies to protect American jobs will threaten jobs in other countries, including the poor countries of the Third World. Proposed solutions to the unemployment problem in the United States will also have a significant impact on the employment picture in other industrialized nations and on the possibilities for economic diversification and development in less developed countries. It is within this complex context that the bishops must seek to develop their pastoral letter providing theological and ethical guidance for policy.

The Theological Significance of Work

Before turning to the task of examining how Christian moral principles can be of help in reaching decisions about where the bishops should place their priorities in the face of these tensions and trade-offs, it will be useful to address the question of why unemployment is a matter of such concern in the first place. In the light of the economic considerations just sketched and the mounting evidence that there is a longterm trend toward increasing unemployment in industrialized societies, Gregory Baum has raised this fundamental question:

Should the Church in the face of a society with chronic unemployment demand full employment and continue to promote a piety that leads to dedication and diligence, or should the Church recognize that there is no return to full employment and hence produce a spiritual outlook that enables people to remain humanly and psychically well even if they do not work? Has the time come when the Church must transcend the work ethic?[17]

Baum's question suggests that we might be faced with the need to develop a whole new approach to unemployment by moving toward a spiritual and cultural stance which gives increasing significance to leisure and decreasing significance to work. He implies that we might address the problem by focusing on the virtues of leisure rather than the vices of unemployment.

This same question has been raised in a radical way and answered positively by some social philosophers who synthesize Marxist and Freudian perspectives on labor. Herbert Marcuse, for example, quoting C. B. Chisholm, maintains that

the true spirit of psychoanalytic theory lives in the uncompromising efforts to reveal the anti-humanistic forces behind the philosophy of productiveness: 'Of all things, hard work has become a virtue instead of the curse it was always advertised to be by our remote ancestors. . . . Our children should be prepared to bring their children up so they won't have to work as a neurotic necessity. The necessity to work is a neurotic symptom. It is a crutch. It is an attempt to make oneself feel valuable even though there is no particular need for one's working.'[18]

In dealing with this issue let me indicate at the outset that I believe that Baum's question should be answered with a strong negative and that Marcuse's conclusions are quite thoroughly wrong. Their challenges to the work ethic, however, have the value of pressing the issue at hand to the foundations of our understanding of the meaning and value of work in human life. In dealing with the issue of unemployment and jobs, the bishops will be playing on their own turf if they give careful attention to such questions of fundamental meaning and value. And they will do so by appealing to the understanding of the significance of work contained in the bible and Christian tradition and by showing the relationship between these Christian theological warrants and contemporary social experience.

Examination of these theological resources reveals that the Christian tradition contains two quite different valuations of work, one of which views work as a very positive expression of human creativity and the other which sees it as a burdensome toil and punishment for sin. Both of these valuations can be found in the opening pages of the bible, chapters 1 to 11 of the book of Genesis.

The narrative account of creation in Genesis portrays work, economic life and the development of technology as expressions of the creativity of human beings. Persons are created in the image of God. Their creative work together in society can be an image of the action of God the creator. Pope John Paul II has emphasized this high theological valuation of human work. In his encyclical *Laborem Exercens* the pope states, "The human person is the image of God partly through the mandate received from the creator to subdue, to dominate the earth. In carrying out this mandate, humankind, every human being, reflects the very action of the creator of the universe."[19] At the same time, the biblical accounts also portray the burdensome, sometimes sterile, and conflict-ridden quality of work and economic activity. In the biblical vision, this aspect of work is presented as the result of sin: a rebellion against God which is inseparable from an attempt by human beings to deny their limits through domination of each other. Conflict and alienation are part of the bible's view of the domain of labor and economic life.

Both of these themes are present through the history of Christian theological reflection on the meaning and value of work. Francis Schüssler Fiorenza has summarized this history succintly and has shown that it has clear parallels in contemporary social experience.

> In the religious tradition, work has both a positive and a negative evalua-
> tion. It is seen as creative, as a service to community, and as a divine
> vocation. Yet it is also negatively evaluated as a punishment for sin.
> In contemporary society, a similar ambivalence exists. On the one hand
> work is seen as important for the individual's self-concept, sense of fulfill-
> ment, and integration into society. On the other hand, there is an in-
> creasingly instrumentalistic attitude toward work: persons work not so
> much for the sake of the work itself, but for the rewards of work.[20]

These two different views of work, however, are not simply juxtaposed as contradictory elements within the Christian tradition. Both in the bible and in subsequent theological tradition the positive, creative potential of human work is regarded as more fundamental in the sense that it is the intention of the Creator that human labor itself be a creative expression of human dignity. Like human beings, work and economic activity were created "good, . . . very good." The conflict and alienation that distort the world of work are seen as the consequences of human sin and therefore as counter to the structures of human existence as created by God. This sinfulness, moreover, is not simply the result of individual choice. It has become embedded in the economic and social institutions of human communities. As Fiorenza points out, both Christian tradition and contemporary human experience reveal that the value of work is ambiguous and unstable precisely because it is deeply shot through with the tension between God's creative purposes for humanity and humanity's sinful distortion of these purposes which Christians perceive in all human activity. Nevertheless, work is also a sphere of human existence which is open to the healing, redeeming, and emancipating action of the redemption offered by Christ. The negative evaluation of work, therefore, is not to be accepted as a co-equal with the positive interpretation of its meaning in Christian theology. These negative dimensions of the world of work are realities to be resisted and overcome, even though Christians believe that this final overcoming of conflict and alienation will occur fully only in the Kingodm of God.

From these theological considerations it should be clear what the response of Christian theology to Baum's question ought to be. The Marxist-Freudian perspective of a Marcuse echoes a *part* of the Christian tradition's valuation of work, but only a part of it. Alienated labor, drudgery and servile toil are not discoveries of the disciples of Marx and Freud. They were well known to Moses and to the prophets and sages of Hebrew tradition. These biblical authors, however, did not propose a "rationality of gratification," a "libidinous morality" or an ethic of leisure and play as the alternative to the alienation and frustration of the work world.[21] Rather, they saw *work in its created wholeness and healed redemption as an energetic contribution to the common life of society, an active form of human participation in human community*. From a biblical and Christian theological point of view the overcoming of sin is not simply the result of the de-repression of human instinct but rather the creation of authentic channels by which persons can contribute their energies to the creation and maintenance of the human community itself. Through such contributions individual persons in turn are enabled to discover the meaning and value of their own lives as images of God the creator. While avoiding any overly romantic view of the creative capacities of the vast majority of human beings, a Christian theology of work should insist that work's primary meaning is the bonding to community which it can foster. *This* kind of work ethic is close to the heart of Christian faith.

Biblical and theological perspectives such as these have strong echoes in the conclusions reached by social psychologists and anthropologists who have studied patterns of employment and unemployment in contemporary industrial societies. It is clear that forms of work can change significantly from one historical period to another. Nevertheless, there can be no human civilization apart from the continual creation and maintenance of that civilization by human agents. Though human work may become more "knowledge intensive" and less "muscle intensive" in post-industrial societies, to deprive people of work is to thwart their exercise of creativity and to exclude them from active participation in the communal human project of civilization. Work in our society is partly an instrumental means to the income which is necessary if one's basic human needs are to be met and one's leisure-time possibilities are to be broadened. Were this instrumental function of work its primary meaning, however, then our goal would be clear: a sort of generalized welfare-leisure system for all. Not only is such a proposal an affront to the actual experience of most of the unemployed in the United States and the world today, but it also flies in the face of the conclusions of recent systematic analyses of this experience. It is clear from social psychological research that the human suffering of unemployment arises as much from the isolation and loss of a sense of social participation which it produces as from the loss of income it brings.[22] This research confirms the biblical picture which portrays work as having the dual purpose of fulfilling physical human needs and creating community, civilization and culture.[23] On these theological and social-psychological grounds, therefore, the bishops should rest their case that persons are harmed and society is distorted by unemployment. These perspectives imply that even though unemployment insurance and transfer payments in the form of welfare are clearly demanded to meet the basic needs of the unemployed, the more basic issue is that of overcoming unemployment.

In preparing their pastoral letter, the American bishops should appeal *both* to these theological perspectives *and* to the social-psychological research which shows the congruence between theology and contemporary reality. Without the appeal to bible and theology the bishops will risk failing to show why they, as *bishops*, are concerned with these questions in the first place. Without the evidence from present experience and its systematic interpretation in the social sciences they will be subject to the charge that their theological message is irrelevant to the contemporary situation. Though the bishops clearly need not fear that many will challenge the assertion that unemployment is a serious social problem, they do need to be concerned that the assessment of why it is a problem gets properly framed. For the way the question is asked will have much to do with the way it is answered. This will likely be their most important contribution to the current debate.

Ethical Principles: Justice and the Right to Employment

Recent church teachings on the ethical principles which should shape both the Christian and secular response to issues of social policy have increasingly been set down in the language of human rights. This use of "rights language" has been just as characteristic of discussions of unemployment and jobs as it has of other moral issues that arise in the trajectory of human life from womb to tomb. Indeed papal, conciliar and episcopal teachings have repeatedly affirmed that human persons have a right to employment which makes an urgent and imperative demand on society in all its parts. For example, *Pacem in Terris* stated, "When we turn to the economic sphere, it is clear that human beings have the natural right to free initiative in the economic field and the right to work."[24] *Gaudium et Spes* affirmed "every person's duty to labor faithfully and also his right to work."[25] Both of these statements were referred to by the U.S. Catholic bishops in their 1975 statement, "The Economy: Human Dimensions." The bishops stated, "Opportunities to work must be provided for those who are able and willing to work. Every person has the right to useful employment, to just wages and to adequate assistance in the case of real need."[26] This statement was repeated a number of times by individual bishops testifying before congressional committees on behalf of the USCC in favor of the Humphrey-Hawkins full employment bill.[27] This indicates a firm commitment in Catholic social teaching to a policy that would guarantee a job for everyone able to work. This commitment is a practical implication of the theological and social-psychological perspectives outlined in section II of this essay.

However, the matter is not quite this simple. Immediately following the sentence in which *Gaudium et Spes* sets forth the duty and right of every person to work, the Council qualified its meaning somewhat: "It is the duty of society, moreover, *according to the circumstances prevailing in it, and in keeping with its proper role*, to help its citizens find opportunities for adequate employment."[28] The qualifying phrases in this sentence suggest that there may be different ways of implementing the right to employment in different social circumstances. But the Council did not elaborate on what these might be. In *Laborem Exercens* there is a similar ambiguity. Though Pope John Paul II does not refer explicitly to a right to employment in this letter, he does state forcefully that unemployment "in all cases is an evil" and "the opposite of a just and right situation." He also states, "the question of finding work or . . . suitable employment for all who are capable of it" is a fundamental issue. John Paul II introduces the notion of the "indirect employer" into Catholic social teaching in discussing the employment question, a notion which includes "all the agents at the national and international level that are responsible for the whole orientation of labor policy." This is a very broad concept. It is made somewhat more precise by the pope's statement that "in the final analysis this overall concern weighs on the shoulders of the state," provided this is not interpreted as a call for "one-sided centralization by the public authorities." Finally he specifies what the content of this responsibility is: "to act against unemployment."[29]

Recent church teachings, then, clearly argue for the presence of an obligation that society make efforts to provide employment for all. At the same time, the means for fulfilling this obligation are left unspecified. Similarly unspecified are the agents responsible, though governments have a special role provided they avoid statist approaches. Because of this hesitancy in offering detailed plans for implementing the right to employment, recent church teachings might be open to the charge of timidity or inconsistency. Before the American bishops plead guilty to this charge on behalf of the authors of previous church documents and seek to make amends by adopting a simple and prophetic alternative, they would do well to remember these words of Dietrich Bonhoeffer:

> What then . . . is an "ethic" which by definition makes a theme of the ethical? And what is an ethicist? We can begin more easily by saying what, in any case, an ethic and an ethicist cannot be. An ethic cannot

be a book in which there is set out how everything in the world actually ought to be but unfortunately is not, and an ethicist cannot be a man who always knows better than others what is to be done and how it is to be done.[30]

Bonhoeffer's words put us on guard against an approach which would suggest that an adequate ethical perspective on employment will be one which simply *declares* that there should be work for all. This is inadequate because neither Christian ethicists nor bishops nor the church as a whole are in a position to create employment by fiat. And neither is anybody else. A Christian ethical approach to the right to employment must be concerned with providing guidance on the priorities we should adopt as we confront the hard choices and trade-offs that are necessarily present in the formation of social policy. A Christian ethical approach to employment and job generation must recognize that we are dealing with a multiplicity of values in dynamic relation and tension with each other. It will then go on to try to discern which balance between these values seems most in harmony with human dignity and a Christian vision of the fullness of human community.

The task, then, is to move beyond moral proclamation to careful analysis of modes of implementing the right to employment. Concern with implementation is itself a genuinely moral concern, not simply a technical or political one. It is therefore both a proper and necessary part of the bishops' concern. The moral content of the concern for implementation becomes evident if we examine the right to employment more carefully from the viewpoint of moral philosophy and political theory.

The right to work belongs to that class of rights known in normative political theory as social-economic rights. Social-economic rights, which also include the right to food, to adequate housing, to health care and to social security, are contrasted with civil-political rights such as freedom of religion, expression, assembly and due process of law. One of the keys to the distinction between the two sets of rights is the difference in what must be done to implement them. The right to religious freedom is implemented by a combination of constitutional law and judicial action that restrains the state or other persons from interfering with religious belief and expression. It is a negative right, an immunity from coercion, guaranteed juridically. Implementation of a social right such as the right to work is a considerably more complex task in our society. An interlocking series of positive steps by the society as a whole must be taken if this right is to be secured in action. It is a positive right, an entitlement or empowerment that demands action rather than restraint on the part of both society and the state.[31]

It should be noted, however, that the difference between the two types of rights is partly a matter of the kinds of institutions which *already* exist within a society. The creation of institutions for the protection of civil-political rights in the West, such as constitutional government, involved a whole series of vigorous positive steps from the time of the Magna Carta down to the present, including revolution and the development of an immensely complex judicial system. The institutional machinery for the protection of civil-political rights is in place in the West, and therefore their implementation is a relatively easy task compared to the implementation of social-economic rights. The securing of the right to work is more difficult because the implementing institutions are not so fully developed and because we do not have clear and convincing ideas on how to bring them into existence in fully functional form. In a highly interdependent world economy the implementation of the right to work involves not only economic and political issues of great complexity within the United States, but similar issues of even greater complexity on a world scale. So when past church documents stop short of specifying detailed methods for the implementation of the right to work, this is in large part because we are much less clear about the institutions needed than we are for the implementation of civil and political rights.

From a theological point of view, a second aspect of the problem of implementing the right to employment comes into view. As noted above, the Christian tradition contains a two-fold understanding of work. Work is understood primarily as a positively valued sphere for the expression of human participation in community. But the world of work is also a sphere in which human sinfulness in the form of arrogance, greed or sloth can lead to alienation, oppression and domination. The consequences of this sinfulness are present not only in toilsome burdens and alienating patterns in some forms of industrial labor. They are also powerfully present in the exclusion from community and denial of creativity which is an important dimension of the reality of unemployment.

Unemployment is not *simply* a result of our limited understanding of the appropriate institutional means for overcoming it. It is also the consequence of human perversity on both the levels of the economic choices made by individuals and of the economic patterns which institutionalize the dominance of some groups over others. The primal sin, according to the book of Genesis, is the foolish attempt of human beings to deny the limits of their creaturelilness by breaking free from their dependence on God and on each other. It is their attempt to become "like God" (Gen 3:5) and to avoid being their brother's keeper. The human consequences of such a denial are portrayed on the individual level in Cain's murder of his brother Abel (Gen 4:8ff). And on the social level, this denial of limits in the story of the tower of Babel—the construction of a city and a tower with its top in the heavens in order that the builders might "make a name" for themselves—led to the confusion of languages and the breakdown of community (Gen 11:1-9). In an elegantly compressed literary mode, these stories explain the origins of the toil, struggle and conflict that run through human history, including economic history. This origin is the human denial of limits and interdependence. From a theological point of view, unemployment must in part be regarded as the result of such a denial by society and by the powerful groups within it. And Christians who are true to the belief that sin will only be fully eliminated from the human heart in the final coming of the Kingdom of God must be prepared to face the reality of the brokenness of human community in the economic sphere. We will not eliminate unemployment by the declaration of the existence of the right to a job, but by participation in the sustained struggle to overcome the distortions of human community and work introduced by human duplicity and selfishness.

Does this mean, then, that the bishops should abandon any effort to present clear ethical guidance on the problem of overcoming unemployment and generating jobs in the American economy? Do the limits of our knowledge of the institutions which are needed to implement the right to work and the regretful acknowledgment of the presence of sin in our economic activity mean that we should be resigned to the continuing reality of high unemployment rates? I think the answer to this question is a resounding *no*. It is precisely the acknowledgment of these limits which will enable the bishops to make an important contribution to this debate by focusing their teaching on the real problem in all of its apparent intractability. The powerful biblical and theological vision of the positive function of work in the lives of all human beings must remain a central focus of a Christian economic ethic. Also, the healing of human brokenness which will be fulfilled in the Kingdom proclaimed by Jesus has already begun among us, and we must look for signs of its presence in the evolving economic order. Finally, we must formulate clear moral guidelines which will direct social life in the direction of this healing and which will rule out those policies and patterns of economic activity which we can see as clear impediments to employment for all.

What I am proposing is quite parallel to the method of theological and ethical analysis followed in the bishops' pastoral letter on war and peace. In that document the section on "The Kingdom and History" pointed out that there is a tension between the full justice and peace of the Kingdom of God and the realities of a world which was created good but which has a history marked by both achievement and failure in the pursuit of justice and peace. The document then went on to elaborate moral norms which can guide both individuals and nations in the pursuit of justice and peace in the nuclear age. The letter acknowledged that the causes of war are multiple, that peace is possible but precarious, and that it must be constantly protected. The bishops stated that this perspective "accounts in large measure for the complexity of Catholic teaching on warfare."[32] The same sort of complex moral argument about the norms which can shape our economy in a way which acknowledges the multiple causes of unemployment, which recognizes that full employment is possible but precarious, and which sets limits on economic behavior which will protect jobs against forces which destroy them is called for in the pastoral letter presently being drafted. Just as the war and peace pastoral sought to translate Paul VI's cry "no more war" into concrete norms capable of guiding action in a conflict-ridden world, so this pastoral letter should attempt to translate John Paul II's call to society to "act against unemployment" into such similarly detailed action guides.

The fundamental framework for moving from the affirmation of the human importance of work and the conviction that unemployment is an evil to moral action guides for dealing with this evil is the theory of justice which has been elaborated within the Catholic social tradition. Reinhold Neibuhr has described justice as the moral norm governing "the claims and counter-claims of historical existence."[33] In the discussion of the problem of unemployment, the American bishops are faced with more than a few claims and counter-claims, such as unemployment vs. inflation, jobs in the United States vs. jobs abroad, the role of the market vs. the role of planning, the distribution of jobs and income vs. the enhancement of productivity through capital investment. A satisfactory approach to these conflicts will not result from simply choosing sides in each of the debates. Nor will it come by saying all the claims are important and should be granted equal moral status. What is needed is a way of determining the proper ordering of these claims and the priorities which should exist among them as we seek to structure the economic system in a way that respects human dignity, resists human sinfulness and responds to the call to the Kingdom of God. In *Rerum Novarum* Leo XIII described justice as the principle which helps define "the relative rights and mutual duties of the rich and the poor, of capital and labor."[34] This is what is needed in the discussion of unemployment: a description of relative rights and mutual duties which can help us discern which elements of the many proposals for dealing with the present transition in the American economy are more satisfactory from a Christian ethical point of view.

The Meaning of Justice

It is not my purpose to lay out the entire teaching of modern Catholic tradition on the meaning of justice in order to show how all these economic proposals for dealing with unemployment should be evaluated.[35] Rather, for present purposes it will be enough to take note of some of the key aspects of this understanding of justice that are relevant to the most pressing issues in the current debate as it touches the employment question. I think that the pastoral letter should also limit itself to some such approach.

First, the most fundamental thing to be said about justice in Roman Catholic thought is that it is concerned to establish the minimum conditions for the participation of all persons in the life of the human community. The ultimate injustice is to be actively treated or passively abandoned as a non-member of the moral community which is the human race. This is another way of saying that justice demands respect for the dignity of all persons. But it highlights the fact that human dignity is not a quality that persons simply possess provided nobody else takes it away from them. The realization of human dignity requires that one participate in social life. The dignity of the person is the dignity of a social being. Therefore both the possibility and the actuality of social participation are crucial to human dignity.

The injustice of being effectively rendered a non-member of the human community can take many forms. Murder is the most atrocious and obvious example. But recent Catholic teaching has spoken of a variety of other forms of greater or lesser severity which result from the patterns of organization of contemporary society. These it groups under the broad notion of "marginalization."[36] Marginalization can take a political form, as when a person or group is denied access to influence on public decision-making through denial of free speech, through outright repression by the state, or through an inordinate concentration of political power in the hands of a few. It can also take an economic form, as when persons face hunger and have no way to overcome it, or when they are denied access to the world of work and employment. In the phrase of Joan Costello, the marginalized are those who have "no voice and no choice." The suffering which befalls such persons is not only physical. It has a quality which is more specifically human or even distinctively spiritual about it. It is the suffering of being told that they do not count as part of the human community. Thus, in recent Catholic teaching, the overcoming of injustice is closely identified with the enhancement of social patterns of active participation in the political, economic and cultural life of society and the overcoming of all forms of discriminatory exclusion on the basis of race, sex, national origin or other arbitrary standard. Though it is clear that some persons will be more active participants than others in each of these spheres, there is a minimum level of access which must be made possible for all: "Participation constitutes a right which is to be applied in the economic and in the social and political field."[37] In discussing the implementation of the right to employment the bishops both can and should insist that the creation of institutions for the enhancement of economic participation is of the highest priority and that racial or sexual discrimination in employment can never be justified.

In relating the notion of justice-as-participation to the jobs question several more specific points are important. First, justice in the employment sphere means that persons should have the opportunity to contribute to society through economic activity in concert with others. Employment justice is not just a matter of seeing to it that people's private needs are fulfilled. Work—especially work in an industrial or post-industrial society—is for the community as well as for oneself. The charge has been heard frequently of late that Catholic social thought has stressed the distribution of wealth and ignored the production of wealth. While there is a measure of truth in this charge, it is not the whole story. The notion of "social justice," which has a technical meaning in Catholic moral theology, refers to the obligation of all persons to contribute to the production and protection of the common good of society. In the words of Pius XI, "It is of the very essence of social justice to demand from each individual all that is necessary for the common good."[38] This statement assumes that the common or public good needs to be created and protected. In all but hunter-gatherer societies this is clearly true in the economic sphere. It is especially evident in an advanced industrial economy. Social justice, as understood by Pius XI, would, in my opinion, be better designated "aggregative justice" — that form of moral obligation which calls on persons to contribute to the generation of the public good by aggregating their activity, to the extent they are able, with that of others in a productive way. This is the active meaning of justice as participation. It helps us see that justice in employment is as much a matter of creating the public good of a society as it is a matter of distributing it.

It should also be noted that the public good which aggregative justice calls on us to create in the economic sphere must be measured by indices more complex than that of the gross national product. The GNP measures one element of the public economic good. But there are other highly important public goods or evils which result from the way the productive side of the economy is organized, including full employment, equal opportunity, environmental quality, or the lack of all these goods. The conditions of aggregative or productive justice are not limited to the generation of the GNP, but involve these other important public concerns as well. In measuring whether the economy is productive, these other values must be taken into account.

The norm of aggregative justice, therefore, implies that the bishops should stress that the public good to which all are obliged to contribute is a social as well as a narrowly defined economic one. The justice of the productive side of the economy cannot be measured solely by its output in goods and services, important as these surely are. The organization of production also has very important effects on employment levels, patterns of discrimination and environmental quality. Economists are fond of calling these effects "externalities." But if we are honest in evaluating what the economy is "producing," these effects must be regarded as integral to economic activity and subject to scrutiny in the light of the overarching norm of justice-as-participation.

Just as enterprises which damage environmental quality or whose products are potentially threatening to human health are legitimately subject to governmental regulation, so is the structure of the productive side of the economy a legitimate governmental concern from the standpoint of its impact on employment levels.

Recent debates have made it clear that there are intense disagreements about when governmental regulation in the interest of environmental quality begins to become counterproductive for the overall well-being of the community. Such disputes are inevitable in this domain as well. But I believe the bishops are in a position to make a forceful point here without stifling debate and smothering pluralism: It is the responsibility of our society—jointly through management, labor, government and community groups—to evaluate and in some measure regulate their economic behavior in light of its impact on employment. To fail to do so would be to say that some people simply do not count as members of the human community, namely those who are unemployed. Such a failure would also be a way of saying that the actual productive capacity of unemployed skilled workers or the potential capacity of those with lower skills are of little or no value as we seek to negotiate the present economic transition. Such would be marginalization with a vengeance: You just do not count.

The notion of justice-as-participation also has important implications for our understanding of the distributive side of the economy. The image most commonly used in discussions of distributive justice is that of slicing up a pie and handing out the pieces. While this may be an adequate image for discussing the distribution of incomes, it gives a false picture of the distribution side as a whole. A job, for example, is not like a piece of pie that someone gives me, or like a paycheck that I take home with me. A job is not a consumer good. It is something I go to, something I engage in with many others in highly complex, structured activity that is linked with a vast interlocking system. From this point of view it is really more accurate to speak of participating in the work of society than of having a job. The distribution of jobs, therefore, concerns the way that participation in the economic process is structured—how it provides access to work for all or just for some, whom it excludes and whom it includes. Though it is clear that the kind of participation open to different persons can and should be different, the notion of justice-as-participation on the distributive side demands that the same kind of structural concerns with patterns of active participation in the economic life of society be brought to bear here as were discussed above in considering the aggregative side. This parallel is no accident, for it is an illusion to think that the process of production and the process of distribution operate independently of each other. In fact they are closely interconnected and mutually reinforcing.[39]

This means that the demands of distributive justice will not be met simply by proposing some form of income policy such as a negative income tax, guaranteed annual income or other welfare proposals, admirable as these may be from my point of view. Distributive justice will not be realized simply by a more compassionate policy on transfer payments. Such transfers are called for in justice in the cases of those with special needs such as the ill, the aged and the handicapped. These economic disadvantages are in some sense beyond the control of both the persons affected and society at large. However, in the case of persons who through no fault of their own have been placed in a seriously disadvantaged position through socially correctible maldistribution of opportunity and power, transfers are at best a palliative for injustice. They do not represent distributive justice in any full sense. Therefore, the bishops should be in a position to argue that any debate about income policy in our society should be placed in the context of this larger question of employment. The argument will not be likely to please either labor or management. It may displease labor, for it suggests that the preservation of existing industrial jobs at high hourly wage rates is not the be-all and end-all of distributive justice. At the same time it is likely to disgruntle management for it implies that the bottom line on the quarterly report is hardly an adequate index of their performance. If the bishops could make a forceful and persuasive appeal to these two groups in our society to recognize the larger dimensions of the problem they will have done quite a lot.

These considerations provide a few indications of what it means to recognize that the right to employment is a social right whose implementation depends on a moral analysis of the responsibilities of diverse actors in a complex social system. By situating this right in the context of the structures of participation on both the aggregative and distributive sides of the economy, we are in a position to get some insight on how to move from declaring the existence of this right toward implementing it. Such implementation will depend on how the patterns of capital investment are taking place, what levels of employment and unemployment are present in the United States, and how employment and unemployment distributed among different demographic groups are inseparable from each other. When the jobs question is looked at from an ethical point of view, these issues must be looked at in their interconnectedness rather than separately.

A political consideration will bring what I am prepared to propose to a tentative conclusion. There is a strong tendency for aspects of this interconnected whole to become identified with the agendum of particular groups in society. The business and financial communities place strong emphasis on capital investment in the interests of increased productivity leading to profit maximization. Organized labor has the protection of existing jobs, wages and benefits as its prime focus. Minority groups and advocates of the poor press for new job creation, including public works and training programs. As both the UAW and *Business Week* studies mentioned above have noted, a continued fragmentation of these groups along ideological lines carries us away from rather than toward a solution to major problems besetting the economy today. While it would be naive to think that these groups either can or should adopt a common perspective, it is certain that all of these perspectives must contribute to finding a just solution to the problem of unemployment.

Government also has an important role to play in balancing the competing claims of these diverse groups. It has long been a tenet of Catholic social thinking that the government has as one of its prime tasks the coordination of the activities of diverse groups in society in a way that is productive of the common good. As Paul VI put it, "As a social being man builds up his destiny within a series of groupings which demand, as their completion and as the necessary condition for their development, a vaster society, one of a universal character, the political society."[40] At the same time, however, it is clear that "statist" solutions are excluded by the principle of subsidiarity which insists that the government "should supply help (*subsidium*) to the members of the social body, but may never destroy or absorb them."[41] This principle defends institutional pluralism while also granting a limited role to the government in the economic sphere. It implies that job generation is a task for all the relevant institutionalized groups of American economic life: labor, management and government working together.

There will, without doubt, be conflict among the interests of these groups. The recent appeals for more collaborative relations between labor and management are in line with the main thrust of Catholic social thought[42] and with the interpretation of justice-as-participation advanced here. But the cooperation envisioned must be based on a distribution of real power which enables the diverse groups to make their legitimate perspectives part of the formula on which compromise is reached. A number of the recent critics of the adversarial relationship between labor and management seem to expect labor to do all the cooperating in the form of reduced demands. Though "give backs" may be needed in some cases and plant closings may be the only solution in others, such decisions should not rest solely in the hands of management. The interests of the workers involved, the long term health of the firm or industry as represented by management, the effects on local communities, and the common good of the society as a whole which is the concern of government should all have an influence on decisions which affect the generation and distribution of jobs. Though the adversarial relationship must be reduced, a condition for *just* cooperative relations is a *genuine* influence for the cooperating partners. Paternalism, whether by the government or by management, must be avoided. Also implied here is the need for advance notice when plants are to be closed and for adequate plans for retraining and relocating workers when such closings are necessary. All the partners in the collaborative relationship have responsibilities to help provide for this retraining and relocation when it is necessary. It is not the responsibility of management, labor, local or national government alone, but neither are any of these groups free to wash their hands of this problem which is likely to become more prevalent in the years ahead.

This generalized call for a new collaborative and participatory approach to our economic problems should not be confused with socialism or state capitalism. It is rather a "mixed" economy model, which seeks to institutionalize the representation of the diverse interests of a pluralist society in the investment and job generation process. The key to this kind of development of a *new form* of mixed economy, it seems to me, lies in giving each of the sectors of labor, management and the several levels of government some say in the structure of the production and distribution of jobs. It will embody a new form of justice-as-participation, a form which is called for by the transition which our economy is undergoing.

This new form of collaboration in shaping investment policy is probably the central implication of the application of the principles of justice to the dynamics of employment and unemployment today. It is not likely, however, to be able to eliminate unemployment entirely. The encouragement of innovative entrepreneurship will also be important. The bishops should recognize and encourage such entrepreneurship and not suggest that it is somehow contrary to the Christian vocation when it takes place with a sense of social responsibility, a commitment to racial equality, and a sense of its importance for society as well as for self. Indeed, I would suggest that any statements the bishops make on this entrepreneurial component in the overall effort to generate jobs should include a commitment by the church to use its leverage of persuasion, organization and limited resources to help small businesses get off the ground in depressed inner-city areas. In the city where I live, the churches have played a small but important catalytic role in initiating a potentially significant effort to direct venture capital into job-starved sections of Boston. Without significant leadership from lay members of the Archdiocesan Justice and Peace Commission such a project might have begun, but it is not likely that it would have. This suggests that the bishops should examine ways that the church itself—especially its lay members—can play an important and direct role in addressing the problem of unemployment. The pastoral letter should speak not only on behalf of the victims in our society, but also should address invitation, encouragement and challenge to those of its members who are in a position to make a difference in direct and fairly immediate projects.

From a broader perspective, the pastoral letter should also address the question of direct governmental involvement in the effort to generate jobs through appropriately designed programs of publicly financed reconstruction of the basic infrastructure of American society.[43] Such projects have been challenged of late as wasteful and fruitless. If government has any responsibility at all for the economic life of the nation, however, this responsibility surely extends to the maintenance of public highways, bridges, and systems of transportation, transport, and communication. Without these the basic conditions of social interaction and economic exchange will deteriorate. They are public goods and thus deserve public support. Jobs generated by such publicly financed projects are not "make work" or "dead-end jobs." They are a genuine and necessary contribution to the common good of society as a whole. One can even argue plausibly that such jobs have a particular worth because of their direct contribution to the common good of society as a whole.

These reflections are far from an adequate response to the employment and unemployment problems of American society. Much more needs to be said about them as well as about a host of other questions. They do, however, indicate some of the directions the American bishops should go in their pastoral letter. These suggestions are based on a theological valuation which sees work as a fundamental value and necessity in human life, but also as a value threatened by the limits on our knowledge and our sinful condition. They seek not only to proclaim that all have a right to work, but also to find ways to implement this right in a way that respects the pluralism of American society. They acknowledge that productivity is central in the challenge we face, but also insist that patterns of production are governed by basic norms of justice — justice-as-participation in both the production and distribution sides of our complex economic system. Finally, they emphasize that the problem of unemployment is a *public* problem. It is a *social* harm and demands a *social* form of relief, to which all segments of economic society contribute. They provide no panacea. They are incomplete. The primary lacuna is no minor matter, for these proposals say far too little about the international dimension of the issues. I suspect, however, that the goal of the proposed pastoral letter will be best served by keeping this international dimension on the agenda and arguing that no group in American society has the right to assert its interests in an exclusive way through protectionist legislation. A fuller exploration of these international questions should be undertaken at another time. For the present, I suggest that movement and experimentation along the lines sketched here are called for if we are to move beyond declaring "how everything in the world actually ought to be but unfortunately is not."

Notes

1. Paul A. Samuelson, *Economics: An Introductory Analysis*, sixth edition (New York: McGraw-Hill, 1964), p. 572.
2. See Paul Bullock, *CETA at the Crossroads: Employment Policy and Politics* (Los Angeles: Institute of Industrial Relations, University of California at Los Angeles, 1981).

3. Joseph A. Pechman, ed., *Setting National Priorities: The 1983 Budget* (Washington, D.C.: The Brookings Institution, 1982), p. 149.

4. Even as strong a defender of the Reagan policies as Michael Novak is willing to acknowledge that these policies are most open to criticism on the grounds of their effects on the employment picture. See his "Helping the Poor," *Center Journal* 2 (1983), p. 44 and "The Rich, the Poor and the Reagan Administration," *Commentary* 76 (August, 1983), pp. 27-31.

5. See Barry Bluestone and Bennett Harison, *The Deindustrialization of America: Plant Closings, Community Abandonment and the Dismantling of Basic Industry* (New York: Basic Books, 1982), pp. 233-240, and *passim*.

6. Lester C. Thurow, *The Zero-Sum Society: Distribution and the Possibilities for Economic Change* (New York: Penguin Books, 1981). pp. 77-82.

7. See the very interesting debate on this issue between Thurow Bluestone and Harley Shaiken, "Reindustrialization and Jobs," *Working Papers* 7 (Nov./Dec., 1980). pp. 47-59.

8. The *Business Week* Team (Seymour Zucker *et al.*), *The Reindustrialization of America* (New York: McGraw Hill, 1982).

9. "Blueprint for a Working American," *Solidarity* (May 16-31, 1983).

10. *The Reindustialization of America*, p. 185.

11. "Blueprint," p. 11.

12. *The Reindustrialization of America*, p. 77.

13. Robert B. Reich, "The Next American Frontier," *The Atlantic Monthly* (March 1983), p. 46.

14. *The Reindustrialization of America*, p. 160.

15. Barry Bluestone and Bennett Harrison, "Economic Development, the Public Sector, and Full Employment: An Outline for a Plan," in Marcus Raskin, ed., *The Federal Budget and Social Reconstruction: The People and the State* (Washington, D.C.: Institute for Policy Studies, 1978), pp. 416ff.

16. See George Gilder, "A Supply-Side Economics of the Left," and Amitai Etzioni, "The MITIzation of America?," *The Public Interest* 72 (1983), pp. 29-43 and 44-51.

17. Gregory Baum, ed., *Work and Religion* (New York: Seabury, 1980), pp. vii-viii.

18. Herbert Marcuse, *Eros and Civilization: A Philosophical Inquiry into Freud* (New York: Vintage, 1961). The internal quotation is from C. B. Chisholm, "The Psychiatry of Enduring Peace and Social Progress," *Psychiatry* IX, no. 1 (1946), p. 31.

19. John Paul II, *Laborem Exercens*, no. 4. For a discussion of John Paul II's theology of work and a critique of the way it uses the Genesis stories, see my essay, "Human Work and the Story of Creation: Theology and Ethics in *Laborem Exercens*," in John W. Houck and Oliver F. Williams eds., *Co-Creation and Capitalism: John Paul II's Laborem Exercens* (Washington, D.C.:

University Press of America, 1983), pp. 59-77.

20. Francis Schüssler Fiorenza, "Religious Beliefs and Praxis: Reflections on Catholic Theological Views of Work," in Baum, ed., *Work and Religion* p. 98. See also his essay, "Work and Critical Theology," in W. J. Heisler and John W. Houck, eds., *A Matter of Dignity: Inquiries into the Humanization of Work* (Notre Dame, Ind.: University of Notre Dame Press, 1977), pp. 23-44. For a fuller discussion of recent analyses and interpretations of the contemporary Western experience of work, see Marie Jahoda, *Employment and Unemployment: A Social-Psychological Analysis* (Cambridge: Cambridge University Press, 1982).

21. *Contra* Marcuse, *Eros and Civilization*, chap. 11.

22. See Jahoda, *Employment and Unemployment*, pp. 58-61.

23. See Claus Westermann, "Work, Civilization and Culture in the Bible," in Baum, ed., *Religion and Work*, pp. 81-91.

24. *Pacem in Terris*, no. 18.

25. *Gaudium et Spes*, no. 67.

26. United States Catholic Conference, "The Economy: Human Dimensions," statement of November 20, 1975 in J. Brian Benestad and Francis J. Butler, eds., *Quest for Justice: A Compendium of Statements of the United States Catholic Bishops on the Political and Social Order 1966-1980* (Washington, D.C.: United States Catholic Conference, 1981), pp. 264-65.

27. Three examples of this testimony are the interventions of Bishops James S. Rausch, Eugene A. Marino, and Archbishop Thomas A. Donnellan, published in John Carr, ed., *Full Employment and Economic Justice: Resources for Education and Action* (Washington, D.C.: United States Catholic Conference, 1977), pp. 19-38. See the commentary on these church initiatives by Ronald Krietemeyer, "The Genesis and Development of the Right to Work," in Jacques Pohier and Dietmar Mieth, eds., *Unemployment and the Right to Work* (New York: Seabury, 1982), pp. 27-33. A detailed discussion of the evolution of the Humphrey-Hawkins bill can be found in Helen Ginsburg, *Full Employment and Public Policy: The United States and Sweden* (Toronto: D. C. Heath, 1983), chap. 3.

28. *Gaudium et Spes*, no. 60.

29. *Laborem Exercens*, no. 18.

30. Dietrich Bonhoeffer, *Ethics*, ed. by Eberhard Bethge, trans. N. H. Smith (New York: Macmillan Paper Edition, 1965), p. 269.

31. Henry Shue has argued cogently that the distinction between the two types of rights should not be interpreted as an opposition. I fully agree. But the distinction does have its usefulness. See Henry Shue, *Basic Rights: Subsistence, Affluence and U. S. Foreign Policy* (Princeton: Princeton University Press, 1980), esp. pp. 35-40. A helpful discussion of the evolution of the understanding of the right to work as a social right within Catholic social

thought can be found in Friedhelm Hengsbach, "The Church and the Right to Work," in Pohier and Mieth, *Unemployment and the Right to Work*, pp. 40-49.

32. National Conference of Catholic Bishops, "The Challenge of Peace: God's Promise and Our Response," *Origins* 13 (1983), p. 7, col. 3.

33. Reinhold Niebuhr, *The Nature and Destiny of Man*, vol. 2 (New York: Scribner's, 1964), p. 72.

34. Leo XIII, *Rerum Novarum*, no. 2.

35. I have tried to present a synthetic summary of the theory of justice contained in modern Catholic social teaching elsewhere. See my "Modern Catholic Teachings Concerning Justice" in John C. Haughey, ed., *The Faith that Does Justice* (New York: Paulist, 1977), pp. 207-31, and *Claims in Conflict: Retrieving and Renewing the Catholic Human Rights Tradition* (New York: Paulist, 1979), esp. chap. 4.

36. See 1971 Synod of Bishops, *Justice in the World*, nos. 10 and 16, and *Octogesima Adveniens*, no. 15.

37. *Justice in the World*, no. 18.

38. Pius XI, *Divini Redemptoris*, no. 52.

39. See Nicholas Rescher, *Distributive Justice* (Indianapolis, Ind.: Bobbs-Merrill, 1966), pp. 12-18.

40. *Octogesima Adveniens*, no. 24. See also *Gaudium et Spes*, no. 74.

41. *Quadragesimo Anno*, no. 79.

42. See the proposals from the UAW and from the *Business Week* team referred to in notes 8 and 9 above. See also Felix Rohatyn, "Time for a Change," *New York Review of Books* XXX (August 18, 1983), pp. 46-49.

43. See "Infrastructure: A National Need to Build and Repair," in *State and Local Government in Trouble*, Special Report, *Business Week*, October 26, 1981, pp. 138-41.

Part II

The Poor and the Disadvantaged

JOHN W. HOUCK

"I have a feeling we haven't captured the sense of urgency among the poor," Bishop William K. Weigand of Salt Lake City said at one point.

New York Times,
December 15, 1983

". . . U.S. Catholics have to get a handle on consumerism, and get in touch with people who are poor. The church has a duty, when it sees people suffering and struggling to speak to the consciences of Catholics and others."

Chicago Tribune,
December 15, 1983.

"We must provide in our own household a model of how we treat the disadvantaged and the poor . . . the church itself is called not only to be the body of Christ but to look like the body of Christ."

National Catholic Reporter,
December 23, 1983

POVERTY IN AFFLUENT SOCIETY IS AN ENDURING BUT largely hidden problem. The poor and disadvantaged are, as a group, isolated from economic life and political participation. Americans tend to ignore poverty because we share with all societies the capacity for not seeing what we do not wish to see. Since antiquity, this capacity has allowed those with power and position to enjoy their dinner while remaining oblivious to the beggar at the door. Consider the story of "The Rich Man and Lazarus" (Luke 16:19-31), in which living in luxury while poverty is near is an obstacle to salvation. Sin is portrayed in the parable not as the commission of deliberate harm but as the omission of compassion and action to remedy the situation of the poor.

The account of the Gospel in Luke, sometimes called the "Gospel of the Poor," emphasizes that Jesus' life work was centered on the needy and disadvantaged. To describe His mission of service, Jesus reads from Isaiah 61:1-2: "He has sent me to bring the good news to the poor, to proclaim liberty to captives and to the blind new sight, to set the downtrodden free . . . " (Luke 4:18). Because of Jesus' life and teaching, a new community was formed to follow after him and stand as witness to his sustaining mission.[1]

In American society, there is a general consensus that all citizens should be enabled to maintain some minimum standard of living and that it is appropriate for government to redistribute income toward that goal. Michael Novak contends in chapter seven that these two propositions are nonnegotiable:

> In American politics, there is no longer any argument of principle between the major parties concerning two propositions: (1) every citizen of the United States is entitled to the opportunity to improve his or her condition; and (2) there must be a floor or safety net providing at least the rudiments of decent living conditions under every citizen.

Public Debate About the Poor

However, there is considerable controversy over three basic approaches to the design of welfare programs. One is the rising-tide-lifts-all-boats approach, which relies on employment generation and the production of goods to stimulate a general advance in income. Although, granting that a growing economy and employment is socially desirable, some experts point out that the poor are often too young or too old, or lacking in health or job-related skills, to be affected by the business cycle. Another approach is an elaborate system of transfer payments and government programs, like the War on Poverty, to reach the poor. The last approach is a form of negative tax, which would empower the federal government to provide a guaranteed income to individuals and families living below the poverty line. Resolution of this controversy requires striking a balance between (1) an income redistribution that ensures a decent and adequate life for all citizens, (2) a welfare system that has effective work incentives for able-bodied recipients, and (3) public policies that do not undermine the social fabric, especially the family.

Part II examines this public policy debate and focuses on certain issues that weigh in the balance. These issues include the breakdown of the two-parent household and concomitant feminization of poverty;[2] the corrupting effects of unearned income on the human spirit; and the respective roles of government, business, and the church in eradicating poverty. The three chapters include historical trends and measurements of poverty, a description of the characteristics of the poor and near-poor, an analysis of factors underlying the steady rise of poverty in the United States, and theological and ethical considerations for policy-making.

In chapter six, Graciela Olivarez recalls the heyday of the war on poverty under Lyndon Johnson and traces the political demise of the Office of Economic Opportunity (OEO) under later administrations. OEO had developed a fairly comprehensive set of programs in meeting human needs and was "perhaps indispensable in fostering political awareness and leadership among the poor and minorities." By the early 1980s, however, welfare programs were badly off track after economic recessions, anti-welfare sloganeering, and the problem of budget deficits.

Olivarez surveys patterns of poverty in the United States for 1982 (the lastest count):

- 34.4 million Americans live below the poverty line;
- This count represents 15 percent of the population, the highest poverty rate since 1965;
- Large differences in poverty rates persist among races — 12.0 percent for white persons, 35.6 percent for black persons, 29.9 percent for persons of Spanish origin, and 27.5 percent for native American Indians;
- Both the absolute and relative numbers of the poor have increased every year since 1978 for all geographical regions;

• The number of children growing up in poverty — 13.5 million — is the greastest increase since poverty statistics have been collected;

• The poverty rate for families headed by a lone female (35.2 percent) is far higher than the rate for two-parent families (8.1 percent).

For policy-making purposes, Olivarez would include among the poor the working- or near-poor, who comprise one in five American families who require non-cash subsidies to subsist at a low standard of living. In the next few years, the poverty rate will likely increase as large numbers of the working poor, facing decreases in government subsidies, fall below the official poverty threshold; and as growing numbers of mothers, mostly teenagers, fail to form families.

In chapter six, Graciela Olivarez, the former director of the U.S. Community Services Administration, advocates income redistribution through a simple, expedient negative tax. The material and nutritional well-being of the poor is the primary task at hand. (There will be occasion later for considering ways to achieve full employment for workers of low productivity.) Overall, a negative tax would end irresolute growth in the number of welfare programs, smooth income and non-cash benefit inequalities among the states, and reestablish federal activism in the war on poverty. With regard to the breakdown of traditional family life, Olivarez proposes that welfare programs enable lone parents to be self-reliant through training and child-care programs. In the long run, solutions to teenage pregnancies, particularly among minorities, may require sustained economic growth and fair opportunity in the American mainstream.

Toward A National Family Policy

Michael Novak in chapter seven generally accepts the idea of a negative tax but recognizes another area of human potential requisite for curtailing poverty: the preservation of the two-parent family. To Novak, Resident Scholar in Religion and Public Policy at the American Enterprise Institute, "strong families provide the surest and most direct path out of poverty."

Novak makes two essential arguments for reorienting our system of welfare payments around a national family policy. First, existing welfare programs, by encouraging single mothers to be dependent on the state rather that on the fathers of their children, have contributed significantly to the disintegration of the two-parent household. Second, monetary grants and other material assistance cannot alone solve the problem of poverty, which has a "moral-cultural dimension." This dimension, on the negative side, constitutes "disadvantage" in health, skills, and attitudes; on the positive side, it connotes "self-reliance" and associated abilities in literacy, applying for and holding a job, and governing and conducting oneself.

The national family policy put forth by Novak may be briefly outlined:

1) child allowances would be paid by the federal government on a monthly basis directly to husband-wife intact families;

2) for heads of non-formed and broken families who are below 20 years of age, federal and state assistance would not be paid directly to the needy but to sponsoring local organizations, which would provide instruction in self-reliance and in child care.

It is in step two, which addresses the moral-cultural dimension of poverty among young unwed mothers, where Novak envisions "leagues of female-headed households" being formed under the auspices of local churches, neighborhood associations, and voluntary organizations. These leagues, through personalized counseling and educational programs, could empower the needy to care for themselves. In this way, federal monetary assistance need not lead to dependency upon the state; and the intergenerational cycle of poverty would be ameliorated.

It should be noted that Michael Novak and Dennis McCann, the final essayist in Part II, offer different perspectives on a national family policy. While Novak regards the building of intact families as all-important, McCann suggests that, in some instances, welfare programs enable "suffering people, mainly women, with the opportunity to liberate themselves from an oppressive union that should not be called a marriage anyway." During the Symposium, McCann also argued that Novak's plan had a paternalistic ring "because the permanent, male-dominant, monogamous norm for the family is under serious question." Archbishop Rembert Weakland of Milwaukee objected that the family, however understood, is not an absolute in the New Testament. Jesus focuses on the relationship of the individual with God. For all these reasons, McCann cautions against uncritical acceptance of a family assistance program which would "have the effect of discriminating against single-parent families."

In chapter eight, Dennis McCann, the author of *Christian Realism* and Liberation Theology and a religious ethicist at DePaul University, shows how two overarching values of Catholic social teaching, the dignity of labor and the integrity of the family, constitute an agenda for reform in the area of welfare policy. Drawing on the works *Distributive Justice* by John Ryan and *A Theory of Justice* by John Rawls, McCann demonstrates that "the right to meaningful employment is one of the necessary preconditions of self-respect."

Although McCann corroborates Novak's finding that the current level of spending on welfare exceeds what would be needed to guarantee every poor family an income above the poverty level, he rejects primary reliance on a negative income tax. A guaranteed income cannot account for the "spiritual and cultural deprivation [of poverty] and all the behavioral disabilities implied by those." Moreover, McCann fears that a guaranteed income would "become the instrument for creating a permanent 'underclass'."

McCann concludes that, "Jobs, not handouts, are the first priority for welfare reform" and calls for employment generation, strong work incentives within income maintenance programs, and job training by the church and private sector.

Despite some policy differences, it is fair to say the three authors agree on a triad of welfare measures. One is minimum income maintenance for the poor. Olivarez advocates a negative income tax, in part to allow the poor the dignity of managing their own incomes. The second leg of the triad is special attention to poverty in female-headed families. Progress in eliminating poverty will depend greatly on the extent to which lone mothers can be given sustained help. The last leg is employment generation, that is, the hope is for general prosperity to provide avenues of upward mobility for minorities and to narrow the income gap between the races *and* between the sexes.

Ecclesiological Principles and Our Response to Poverty

The chairperson and commentator of this panel of essayists was Father Richard McBrien, the author of *Catholicism* and the Chairman of Notre Dame's Department of Theology. He spoke from his background in the field of ecclesiology which he defined as "that area of theology which is concerned with the church's self-understanding of its nature and mission."

I have argued elsewhere and repeat here that the ecclesiological dimension of the bishops' pastoral on *The Challenge of Peace* will still be significant long after events and circumstances have rendered much of its ethical content out of date, which is not meant to be derogatory. But there are some extremely important lessons to be learned from that bishop's pastoral, lessons that we ought to see applied to the proposed pastoral, but with one additional point.

First of all, I want to talk about the process. The bishops' pastoral on *The Challenge of Peace* moved along a line that presupposed two basic ecclesiological principles. One is that the church is the whole people of God, or another way of saying it, that the spirit is present in the whole community of faith. And two is that the church must be open to the world, indeed, that the church is part of the world, the world as created by God and as providentially sustained by God. God continues to be active in the world, and in the words of *Gaudium et Spes* of Vatican II, the church must always be alert to read "the signs of the times" by discerning the ever-present activity of God in the world and responding to it according to the dictates of the Gospel.[3] In writing *The Challege of Peace* the bishops held hearings (as this committee is doing). It invited expert opinion from a whole wide spectrum of views in society; it distributed its drafts and welcomed reactions, suggestions, criticisms and amendments. That process has ecclesiological significance, and it is now the teaching style of The American bishops. And we like to think that our pastoral leaders generally have been unalterably reshaped by the process of that bishops' pastoral. *The Challenge of Peace* is perhaps the first significant teaching document that really reflects those important ecclesiological principles of Vatican II that the church is the whole people of God and that the church must be always open to dialogue with the world of which it is itself a part.

The second aspect of that bishops' pastoral which is relevent to this one is audience. Precisely because the bishops perceive that the church is the whole people of God and that God is present in the whole world and in the church, the bishops understood their audience to be not only the faith community itself, but also the wider society.

The third point has to do with levels of teaching authority. The bishops' pastoral letter on war and peace is remarkable because it is one of the few documents (one could even say it is probably the first major document since Vatican II) that explicitly takes care to identify levels of teaching authority. In other words, it nuances the whole concept of a magisterial document. It deliberately disengages itself from the assumption that the authority of a document is determined solely by the authors of the document, which is an extrinsic norm. Who wrote it? The Pope wrote it, therefore it has papal authority. Who wrote it? The bishops wrote it, therefore it has bishops' authority. But in *The Challenge of Peace*, the bishops took care to say that there are different levels of authority. There are certain principles which are part of the core of the Christian tradition, whether biblically or dogmatically formulated. There are other principles which are articulated in papal encyclicals and other authoritative documents but do not have the same sort of dogmatic status that others have. And then there are many applications of principles, and here, of course, we are in the realm of prudential judgment. And the bishops not only admitted that they were making prudential judgments, but they actually invited their readers (even following the final draft) to submit criticisms. This contributed to making the pastoral a *living* document; it became a focus for dialogue and debate in the church and in the wider society.

Now what I am urging here is that the same ecclesiological process will be at work in the writing of the present pastoral letter on the U.S. economy. The process is the same because the same ecclesiological principles are at work; the church is the whole people of God, the spirit is in the whole church, the church is in dialogue with the world, "the signs of the time," and so forth. Secondly, the audience is also twofold, both within and without the faith community, following directly from that ecclesiological principle. And thirdly, I predict that the bishops will take great care to distinguish among levels of authority and to invite criticism, suggestions and amendments so that this pastoral will also be a living document. Hopefully it will become a focus of a lively debate which will contribute to a better, more enlightened social policy.

There is still a fourth ecclesiological element that must be added in this pastoral which could not have been added in the other document. And it is that the church is called upon, particularly in this document, to be a model of a just community. It is one thing for us to applaud the Nobel prize for Lech Walesa and to cheer from the sidelines the Solidarity Movement in Poland, but to be indifferent to the repression of a legitimate movement for unionization in Catholic hospitals, colleges, universities and elementary schools. Or as Dennis McCann states it in his essay:

If, for example, Catholic social teaching advocates the worker's right to a family living wage and his or her right of association in labor unions, these rights must first of all be fulfilled in the policies and practices of Catholic institutions.

In my reading, the only document in recent Catholic social teaching which makes this connection is the document *Justice in the World* of the Synod of Bishops, Second General Assembly:

> 40. While the Church is bound to give witness to justice, she recognizes that anyone who ventures to speak to people about justice must first be just in their eyes.[4]

This proposition is so because the church itself is a sacrament, that is, it is a sign, an instrument of our intimate union with God and with one another. And because the church is a sacrament, it has to practice what it preaches. It has a missionary responsibility, not only to be the body of Christ, but to look like the body of Christ. Not only to be the people of God, but to look like the people of God. And so it is the ecclesiological concept, the church is a sacrament, which challenges the church to practice what it preaches to the U.S. economy.

Vatican Statements

Leo XIII, *Rerum Novarum* — 1891

83. Certainly, the well-being which is so longed for is chiefly to be expected from an abundant outpouring of charity; of Christian charity, We mean, which is in epitome the law of the Gospel, and which, always ready to sacrifice itself for the benefit of others, is man's surest antidote against the insolence of the world and immoderate love of self; the divine office and features of this virtue being described by the Apostle Paul in these words: "Charity is patient, is kind . . . is not self-seeking . . . bears with all things . . . endures all things."[5]

Leo XIII, *Graves de Communi* — 1901

II. By the law of mutual charity, which, as it were, completes the law of justice, we are bidden not only to give their due to all and interfere with the rights of none, but also to practice kindnesses one to another "not in word nor in tongue, but in deed and in truth" (I John iii, 18), remembering what Christ most lovingly said to His disciples: "A new commandment I give unto you, that you love one another, as I have loved you, that you also love one another. By this shall all men know that you are my disciples, if you have love for one another" (John xiii, 34, 35). Such zeal in the performance of deeds of charity, though it ought to be first of all solicitous about the eternal good of souls, should nevertheless not neglect what is good and useful for this life.[6]

Pius XI, *Quadragesimo Anno* — 1931

4. Quite agreeable, of course, was this state of things to those who thought it in their abundant riches the result of inevitable economic laws and accordingly, as if it were for charity to veil the violation of justice which lawmakers not only tolerated but at times sanctioned, wanted the whole care of supporting the poor committed to charity alone.[7]

Pius XI, *On Atheistic Communism* — 1937

47. But when on the one hand We see thousands of the needy, victims of real misery for various reasons beyond their control, and on the other so many round about them who spend huge sums of money on useless things and frivolous amusement, We cannot fail to remark with sorrow not only that justice is poorly observed, but that the precept of charity also is not sufficiently appreciated, is not a vital thing in daily life.[8]

Unitatis Redintergratio (2nd Vatican Decree on Ecumenism) — 1964

12. . . . Christians should also work together in the use of every possible means to relieve the afflictions of our times, such as famine and natural disasters, illiteracy and poverty, lack of housing, and the unequal distribution of wealth.[9]

Paul VI, *Populorum Progressio* — 1967

47. . . . It is not just a matter of eliminating hunger, nor even of reducing poverty. The struggle against destitution, though urgent and necessary, is not enough. It is a question, rather, of building a world where every man, no matter what his race, religion or nationality,

can live a fully human life, freed from servitude imposed on him by other men or by natural forces over which he has not sufficient control; a world where freedom is not an empty word and where the poor man Lazarus can sit down at the same table with the rich man. This demands great generosity, much sacrifice and unceasing effort on the part of the rich man. Let each one examine his conscience, a conscience that conveys a new message for our times. Is he prepared to support out of his own pocket works and undertakings organised in favour of the most destitute? Is he ready to pay higher taxes so that the public authorities can intensify their efforts in favour of development?[10]

American Catholic Bishops' Statements

The Church and Social Order — 1940

63. Unfortuantely there has been a tendency among too many to dissociate the virtue of justice from the virtue of charity, with the result that life has been made even more selfish and heartless. Charity is no substitute for justice, but it cannot be ignored or derided without failing utterly to comprehend its meaning and its potent influence in regulating and sublimating our social relations and responsibilities. We need justice without doubt or equivocation, but we also need charity if we are to put our lives in harmony with God's plan and promote that spirit of benevolence which will lift the burdens not only from the backs but also from the souls of men.[11]

U.S. Catholic Conference, Department of Development and World Peace, "Welfare Reform in the 1970s" — 1977

Principles

In view of the problems of the present welfare system, we believe that there is an immediate need for change. Our heritage of Catholic social teachings and long experience in providing services to the poor, provide us with a sound basis from which to address the problem of poverty in our society. Based on these traditions, we believe that there are certain principles which should be reflected in any approach to welfare reform. We will evaluate proposed reforms in light of the following norms:

I. —Every human person has the right to an income, sufficient to insure a decent and dignified life for one's self and one's family.

II. —Welfare reform should be developed in conjunction with broader economic policies directed toward the development of a genuine full employment economy that serves all our people.

III. —Our nation must provide jobs at a decent wage for those who can work and a decent income for those who cannot work.

IV. —The maintenance and revitalization of family life should be a primary concern.

V. —Income assistance should be available to those who are employed but who do not receive an adequate income.

VI. —Income assistance should be determined solely on the basis of need.

VII. —Any income assistance program should permit the poor to manage their own income and personal needs.

VIII. —The processes through which welfare policies and regulations and standards are formulated should involve the poor as participants.

IX. —The administration of Welfare assistance should be improved and simplified.[12]

Notes

1. John R. Donahue, "Biblical Perspectives on Justice," in *The Faith That Does Justice: Examining the Christian Sources for Social Change,* ed. John C. Haughey (New York: Paulist Press, 1977), pp. 68-112. See also Oliver F. Williams and John W. Houck, *Full Value: Cases in Christian Business Ethics* (San Francisco, CA.: Harper & Row, 1978), pp. 29-30.

2. See Andrea Lee, IHM, and Amata Miller, IHM, "Women in the Workplace: Challenges and Opportunities," in *Co-Creation and Capitalism: John Paul's Laborem Exercens,* ed. John W. Houck and Oliver F. Williams (Washington, D.C.: University Press of America, 1983), pp. 199-228.

3. *The Gospel of Peace and Justice,* ed. Joseph Gremillion (Maryknoll, N.Y.: Orbis Books, 1976), pp. 243-335, especially p. 246.

4. *Ibid.,* p. 522.

5. John F. Cronin, *Catholic Social Principles: The Social Teaching of the Catholic Church Applied to American Economic Life* (Milwaukee, Wis.: The Bruce Publishing Company, 1950), p. 100.

6. *Ibid.*, p. 99.

7. *Ibid.*, p. 100.

8. *Ibid.*, p. 102.

9. *The Gospel of Peace and Justice*, p. 364.

10. *Ibid.*, p. 401.

11. *Catholic Social Principles*, p. 102.

12. National Conference of Catholic Bishops, *Quest for Justice: A Compendium of Statements of the United States Catholic Bishops on the Political and Social Order 1966-1980*, ed. J. Brian Benestad and Francis J. Butler (Washington, D.C.: United States Catholic Conference, 1981), pp. 274-276.

Six

The Poor in the United States

GRACIELA OLIVAREZ[*]

AMERICANS OVER THIRTY COMMONLY REFER TO THE 1960S AS the "good old days," when we were confident that we could eradicate poverty, expand political and civil rights, and put a man on the moon. Although expansion of democratic norms and the space program have remained national priorities, few of us have kept the same commitment to the war on poverty. Indeed, in the 1980s poverty seems less and less a subject of serious discussion, as if the adage about our learning to walk on the moon but failing to feed our children reflects a natural course of events.

As it has declined as a political and social topic, poverty has grown as a national problem. For 1982 (the last count), one in seven Americans lived below the official poverty level and one in five relied on federal assistance to supplement incomes too small to meet even their basic needs. These rates for the truly needy and for the working- or near-poor are the highest since 1965. In the current difficult economy and with greatly tightened eligibility rules for welfare programs, poverty is on the rise in the United States.

A fundamental remedy would be to provide the poor the minimum income essential for material and nutritional well-being as a matter of national policy. This paper discusses one type of guaranteed income, a negative income tax, and some associated issues.

[*]Special thanks are due to Charles A. Schwartz, Ph.D. for his editorial assistance.

The War on Poverty

During the years 1964 to 1969 Americans rightfully believed that we could effectively reduce the numbers of poor. The poverty rate for the total population declined steadily from 17.3 to 12.1 percent in that period (see Appendix). The Office of Economic Opportunity (OEO), created by Lyndon Johnson, started with about 33 million Americans living below the poverty threshold. By 1978, following a decade of erratic fluctuations in the poverty rate, the number of poor had been reduced to 25 million and their rate to 11.4 percent of the population. Since then, the poverty population and rate have increased every year.

OEO was a broad effort to fulfill human needs and widen opportunity through the creation of community development corporations and such programs as Head Start, Legal Services, VISTA, Job Corps, Community Action, housing weatherization, aid to migrant farm workers and their families, and the like. Complementing OEO, in 1965 amendments to the Social Security Act formed Medicaid for the poor and Medicare for the elderly. The Food Stamp Program began in 1967 and was joined by supplemental programs to provide basic nutritional items to low-income children and pregnant women. The school lunch program, federally subsidized housing, and the Elementary and Secondary Education Act all followed in this period of national commitment to disadvantaged groups. The Equal Employment Opportunity Commission, primarily a civil rights agency, provided additional impetus to the war on poverty by establishing employment rights for minorities, who represent a disproportionate number of the poor.

These early poverty programs were indispensable in fostering political awareness and leadership among the poor and minorities. For example, when OEO began, there were some 70 blacks in elected or appointed positions of political significance. By 1977 their number had increased to 1700 and included mayors, county commissioners, city counselors and judges. Without the opportunity afforded poor and minority groups to sit on boards of local poverty agencies and to get experience working with the political system, such participation would have been slowed or blocked.

There are countless cases of low-income Americans who were given their first opportunity to work full-time as a result of OEO, which required welfare agencies to hire the poor. Who better than the poor should initiate and assess programs for human need and opportunity? These workers did not all remain in entry-level positions; a large share have advanced to the managerial level.

For example, during hearings in 1977 by the Community Services Administration (the name given OEO by Richard Nixon), success stories by formerly unemployed poor from region after region emerged. Former teacher aides in Head Start, clerk-typists in community action programs, cooks in school lunch programs are now small business owners, high school or college teachers, public administrators, bank tellers—the list goes on.

Unlike the majority of welfare programs it developed, OEO did not survive. With the advent of the Nixon administration in 1969, the war on poverty was replaced by a "get tough" campaign against the "undeserving poor." Nixon's attempt to dismantle OEO was resisted by Congress but, in the process, OEO was whittled down severely and finally reorganized as the Community Services Administration.

The Carter administration designed or supported a number of initiatives to get the war on poverty back on track, but encountered Congressional and conservative resistance. A 1978 plan that would have standardized certain welfare requirements (thereby removing some of the awful disparities among state programs) and expanded by $19 billion basic nutritional programs died in Congressional committee. By then, the nation had been racked by two recessions, growing inflation and unemployment, an apparent energy shortage, and much anti-government sloganeering.

The spirit of Proposition 13 (which advocated balancing the budget for the state of California) engulfed the land and encouraged widespread political and media attacks on unemployed youths in Community Education and Training (CETA) programs, elderly people on fixed incomes, handicapped people with special needs, welfare recipients, mental patients, and workers who could not afford soaring medical costs.

The irony of such negative attitudes toward the poor and toward basic human and social services lies in our uncertain economy. Among the millions currently unemployed are some former citizen-critics of governmental "giveaway programs" whose automobiles sported "I fight poverty, I work!" bumper stickers. Now, many of these Americans have lost their jobs through no fault of their own and must make do with appallingly low standards of welfare support. In a special report *Business*

Week recently found no real prospects for additional savings in welfare expenditures to reduce the budget deficit: "Current programs are very close to the minimum level of support that a wealthy society has decided it must provide to its poorest citizens."[1]

Poverty and the National Population

Both the absolute and relative numbers of Americans living below the poverty level have increased every year since 1978 (see Appendix). In the latest count—for 1982—34.4 million, 15.0 percent of the population, live in poverty. This is the highest rate since 1965 and does not include undocumented workers (variously estimated at 4 to 14 million). The threshold below which poverty officially begins is now $9,862 for a family of four but ranges from $4,901 for a one-person household to $19,698 for a family of nine or more.[2]

Many groups have poverty rates well above or below the national average. In the 1978-82 period, the rate for white persons (8.7 percent in 1978, increasing to 12.0 percent or 23.5 million in 1982) was much lower than for black persons (30.6 percent in 1978, 35.6 percent or 9.7 million in 1982) or for persons of Spanish origin (21.6 percent in 1978, 29.9 percent or 4.3 million in 1982). Poverty among persons of Asian and Pacific Island descent for 1980 (the last year reported) was 13.1 percent, and among native American Indians 27.5 percent.[3]

All major geographical regions have experienced rising poverty rates since 1978: the Northeast rate climbed from 11.2 to 13.0 percent, the North Central rate from 10.5 to 13.3 percent, the Southern rate from 15.4 to 18.1 percent, the West 11.3 to 14.1 percent. Also for 1982, the highest poverty rate for metropolitan areas was in central cities (16.7 percent), the lowest rate was in the suburbs (7.5 percent).[4]

The rate of poor persons sixty-five years old or over has been cut in half over the past quarter-century (from 35.2 percent in 1959) but has remained at about 15 percent during the past five years with wide and persistent differences among races: 13.1 percent poverty among elderly whites, 39.0 percent among elderly blacks, and 25.7 percent among the elderly of Spanish origin.[5]

The sharpest rises in poverty have been among children and among households headed by a female with no husband present. A report by the Children's Defense Fund concluded that the number of children growing up in poverty in 1982 — 13.5 million — was 31 percent higher than in 1978. This is the greatest increase in the number of poor children since poverty statistics have been collected. On average today, one in five children grow up in poverty and minority children are three times more likely than white children to be poor. In all races, over half the children in poverty are raised in female-headed households.[6]

The poverty level for families headed by female (35.2 percent in 1981) is far higher than the rate for married-couple families (8.1 percent).[7] The majority of white families below the poverty level are married-couple families (59 percent in 1979); by contrast, most poor black families are maintained by women with no husband present (72 percent).[8] Generally, 47 percent of all (poverty level and higher income) black families are headed by females, as against 14 percent of all white families. In both races, the proportion of poor families headed by a female has increased 53 percent since 1970.[9]

Breakdown of traditional family structure is an important and growing cause of poverty, in part because a lone female parent often cannot or should not work. Problems of single mothers, black and white, are compounded by the relatively low salaries women earn. The median earnings of working black women in 1982 ($7,802) were slightly higher than earnings for working white women ($7,640), but the average working male earned about twice as much ($15,373).

Child care is another special problem for lone parents. There are 1.2 million licensed day-care center slots but 13 million children whose mothers work full-time. Consequently, about 2 million children between the ages of seven and thirteen — "latchkey kids" — must care for themselves after school. At least 20 thousand preschoolers are left alone.

If not for means-tested, non-cash benefits from Aid to Families with Dependent Children (AFDC), poor families and their children would encounter great difficulty surviving. As the Children's Defense Fund report confirms, poor nutrition, substandard housing, and a lack of regular health care pose very serious obstacles to family life.[10]

Many analysts now include among the poor the working or near-poor, those with incomes below 125 percent of the poverty level. In 1982, this larger poverty indicator was $12,328 for a non-farm family of four. 46.5 million, 20 percent of the population, comprise the poor and near-poor class (see Appendix).

This broader category makes sense on a number of counts. The

Department of Labor estimates that it costs a family of four more than $12,328 to get by at a low standard of living.[11] The income shortfall has been met, in part, by federal non-cash subsidies: medical care, food stamps, school lunches, and housing. Such subsidies now go to one American family in six, and they account for two of every three federal dollars spent on welfare programs.[12]

The material well-being of the near-poor has declined sharply this decade with a prolonged recession, the deterioration of old-line industries, and severe tightening of eligibility rules and benefit formulas for welfare benefits. As one indicator, the Congressional Budget Office balanced the loss of cash and in-kind benefits against the gains from 1981 tax cuts and reported that average households at opposite ends of the income scale would be affected as follows:[13]

	Less than $10,000	$80,000 and over
Cash benefits lost	$ -270	$ -70
Tax Cuts	120	15,250
NET	-150	15,180
In-kind benefits lost	-90	-50
Net including in-kind benefits	$ -240	$15,130

Despite the growth in the overall poverty rate this decade from 11.7 to 15.0 percent, spending for welfare programs is no higher in fiscal 1984 than in 1980; excluding medicaid, it was 5 percent lower: 24.9 billion in 1984, 26.1 billion in 1980. Under the new eligibility standards, the federal government will pay less this year for welfare (adjusted for inflation) than in 1980.[14] As a result, large numbers of the 12.1 million near-poor will probably fall down into the poverty level for years to come.

Redirecting the War

When he launched the war on poverty in 1964, Lyndon Johnson said that he wanted "to offer the forgotten fifth of our people opportunity and not doles." Give the poor the tools to lift themselves out of poverty, he reasoned, and working Americans would no longer have to provide them relief. But Johnson's inclusion of food stamps and minimum wages implied an opposite idea as well: That some groups are chronically poor and require income transfers and other entitlements to survive.[15]

The evidence now is that at least 70 percent of America's poor are chronically poor: the elderly, the disabled, and families headed by a female. For these groups the whole net gain against poverty over the past two decades can be attributed to transfer payments.[16]

This is not to say that national economic growth has been without effect. Also among the poor are temporary fellow-travelers of that class; they dislike welfare and get off of it as quickly as they can find employment. But the market mechanism and even general prosperity cannot safeguard the material well-being and health of those who cannot be expected to work regularly.

Long before the war on poverty, economists generally recognized the practicality of providing a regular source of income to the poor as a matter of national policy.[17] In the latest plan, the contention is that the entire patchwork of welfare programs should be replaced by a negative income tax, whereby the federal government would subsidize households when their incomes fall below a given level.[18] This plan would include a benefit-loss ratio at which benefits are reduced as a consequence of earned income.

A notable feature of a negative income tax has been the absence of widespread political appeal for it. In the past, Americans have clung to the obsolete supposition that the only cure for poverty lies in remedies that allow people to look after themselves. In preparing the war on poverty, the Council of Economic Advisors in 1964 decided that a negative tax would not be a proper solution because "Americans want to *earn* the American standard of living by their own efforts and contributions."[19]

This notion grossly exaggerates any adverse effect of unearned income on the poor and ignores the special handicaps of chronically poor groups who cannot participate in the economy.

The negative income tax, of course, is no panacea for policy-making. Adjusting the benefit-loss ratio for earned income, for example, would involve the same trade-offs among conflicting goals inherent in any welfare program: policies should be effective in reducing poverty, they should provide adequate incentives to work, and they should keep the cost reasonable.

The current set of welfare programs, designed with a low schedule of benefits and a high benefit-loss rate, keeps costs down. But the low benefits mean the programs are not effective in coping with poverty and the high benefit-loss rate weakens work incentives. A negative income tax, by contrast, should entail a higher guaranteed minimum income to help eliminate poverty, and stronger work incentives to allow beneficiaries to keep a greater proportion of benefits relative to earned income.

At present, the average benefit reduction in the Aid to Families with Dependent Children is 40 percent for every dollar of earned income. Because AFDC beneficiaries also receive food stamps (with their 30 percent benefit-loss rate) and often reside in public housing (where rent subsidies decrease as earnings increase), their cumulative tax rate is nearly 70 percent, higher than for any other group in the country. An income maintenance experiment in Seattle and Denver in 1979 found that reduced tax rates, which allowed working beneficiaries to keep a greater portion of their welfare benefits, *increased* the amount of paid work they did.[20]

Under a negative tax system, adjustments in benefits-coverage levels to eliminate poverty and in benefit-loss rates to encourage employment would be ongoing issues and trade-offs. But the establishment of a negative income tax would be a long-term solution to at least three worrisome trends in poverty programs. First, it would end willy-nilly growth in the number of major and minor programs. Second, a negative income tax would remedy the notoriously uneven distribution of in-kind benefits within federal programs and the income inequalities among the poor in different states. Most important, a negative income tax would nail down federal responsibility for eradicating poverty in America.

Recent efforts to decentralize control over poverty programs raise serious concerns about the will or ability of the fifty states to regulate and fund the programs. The federal government has always shown more feeling for the poor than the states; indeed, the war on poverty was developed because many states were not doing the job. Equality in the distribution of income and satisfactory progress against poverty can be effectively accomplished only by national resources and agenda.

For many people, there would be additional desire to work if the benefit-loss rates (or the marginal tax rates) applicable to welfare recipients were significantly reduced. However, given the low education, skill level, and work experience of most beneficiaries, an increased job search would probably not secure employment. Even if the nation eventually achieved "full employment," structural unemployment would remain a serious problem.

Two kinds of policies may be necessary to increase the demand for workers of low productivity: targeted public service job programs and employment subsidies.[21] So-called work-fare, which requires able-bodied and unemployed beneficiaries to perform public service jobs, has not been very successful in providing real job training or other employment prospects in the private sector. Nevertheless, some work opportunity should be afforded the unemployed for these reasons: being unemployed is so demoralizing that work is often recognized as a basic right;[22] this nation's public infrastructure is in serious disrepair; there are bound to be workers who will not find jobs but who can rebuild worn and unsafe roads, bridges, and other facilities.

Expanded employment subsidies along the lines of the current Targeted Jobs Tax Credit program would enable low-skilled workers to be paid a higher wage than appropriate for their level of productivity. A broadened program would thereby offset the adverse effects of the minimum wage, which reduces the demand for low-skilled labor. The combination of a negative income tax and these employment programs are a necessary but insufficient step toward eliminating poverty.

Fundamental to eradicating poverty is the problem of family breakdown. Whether being poor causes family breakdown or divorce, separation and abandonment lead to poverty, the correlation between the two is clear. In all races, families headed by women have twice the poverty rate of two-parent families; half of all families headed by minorities are below the poverty level; increasingly, the mothers are teenagers. The failure to form families is now a greater problem than family breakup.[23]

In the short run, welfare programs should be refocused to include job training and child care for young mothers so that they can become self-supporting. In the longer run, solutions to teenage pregnancies and family breakdown may require sustained economic growth and fair opportunity, so that minority as well as white, female as well as male, can participate effectively in the economic mainstream.

Conclusions

None of the foregoing patterns of poverty or proposals to remedy them is particularly new. The limiting factor in the war on poverty is not knowledge. It is overwhelmingly a shortage of national will to provide, as an ordinary governmental function, an income to those without.

Some of our national indifference can be traced to old notions about the corrupting effect of unearned income on the undeserving poor. Another part comes from blind reliance on the market mechanism as the best way to allocate incomes. Still another part is benign neglect of the one in seven truly needy Americans who is politically invisible. Poverty in the United States is increasingly isolated in central cities and in chronically depressed areas off the beaten path of the middle and upper classes. The poor do not, in the main, join social or political organizations; they have no lobbies and fewer and fewer leaders.

A negative income tax would provide decency and comfort to the poor, who are mainly old, disabled, or single parents. It would protect the able-bodied poor from erratic business cycles, prolonged recession, and politics as usual. It would help ensure that the misfortunes of parents are not heaped on their children, that poverty is not self-perpetuating. Provision of such a basic source of welfare assistance must henceforth be the next strategic step in the war on poverty. To continue to do little is to permit real deprivation among the truly needy and unfairly low economic security for one in five of us.

Appendix

Persons Below Poverty Level and Below 125 Percent of Poverty Level: 1959 to 1982

YEAR	NUMBER BELOW POVERTY LEVEL (mil.)				PERCENT BELOW POVERTY LEVEL				BELOW 125 PERCENT OF POVERTY LEVEL		AVERAGE INCOME CUTOFFS FOR NON-FARM FAMILY OF 4[3]	
	All races[1]	White	Black	Spanish origin[2]	All races[1]	White	Black	Spanish origin[2]	Number (mil.)	Percent of total population	At poverty level	At 125 percent of poverty level
1959	39.5	28.5	9.9	(NA)	22.4	18.1	55.1	(NA)	54.9	31.1	$2,973	$3,716
1960	39.9	28.3	(NA)	(NA)	22.2	17.8	(NA)	(NA)	54.6	30.4	3,022	3,778
1965	33.2	22.5	(NA)	(NA)	17.3	13.3	(NA)	(NA)	46.2	24.1	3,223	4,029
1966	28.5	20.8	8.9	(NA)	14.7	12.2	41.8	(NA)	41.3	21.3	3,317	4,146
1968	25.4	17.4	7.6	(NA)	12.8	10.0	34.7	(NA)	35.9	18.2	3,553	4,441
1969	24.1	16.7	7.1	(NA)	12.1	9.5	32.2	(NA)	34.7	17.4	3,743	4,679
1970	25.4	17.5	7.5	(NA)	12.6	9.9	33.5	(NA)	35.6	17.6	3,968	4,960
1971	25.6	17.8	7.4	(NA)	12.5	9.9	32.5	(NA)	36.5	17.8	4,137	5,171
1972	24.5	16.2	7.7	2.4	11.9	9.0	33.3	22.8	34.7	16.8	4,275	5,344
1973	23.0	15.1	7.4	2.4	11.1	8.4	31.4	21.9	32.8	15.8	4,540	5,675
1974	23.4	15.7	7.2	2.6	11.2	8.6	30.3	23.0	33.7	16.1	5,038	6,298
1975	25.9	17.8	7.5	3.0	12.3	9.7	31.3	26.9	37.2	17.6	5,500	6,875
1976	25.0	16.7	7.6	2.8	11.8	9.1	31.1	24.7	35.5	16.7	5,815	7,269
1977	24.7	16.4	7.7	2.7	11.6	8.9	31.3	22.4	35.7	16.7	6,191	7,739
1978	24.5	16.3	7.6	2.6	11.4	8.7	30.6	21.6	34.2	15.8	6,662	8,328
1979[4]	25.3	16.8	7.8	2.9	11.6	8.9	30.9	21.6	35.6	16.3	7,412	9,265
1979[5]	26.1	17.2	8.1	2.9	11.7	9.0	31.0	21.8	36.6	16.4	7,412	9,265
1980	29.3	19.7	8.6	3.5	13.0	10.2	32.5	25.7	40.7	18.1	8,414	10,518
1981[6]	31.8	21.6	9.2	3.7	14.0	11.1	34.2	26.5	43.7	19.3	9,287	11,609
1982[6]	34.4	23.5	9.7	4.3	15.0	12.0	35.6	29.9	46.5	20.3	9,862	12,328

(NA) Not available.   [1]Includes other races not shown separately.   [2]Persons of Spanish origin may be of any race.   [3]Beginning 1981, income cutoffs for nonfarm families are applied to all families, both farm and nonfarm.   [4]Population controls based on 1970 census; see text, pp. 2 and 446.   [5]Population controls based on 1980 census; see text, pp. 2 and 446.   [6]Data based on revised poverty definition; see text, p. 447 for explanation.

Source: *Statistical Abstract of the United States 1984*, 104th edition, U.S. Department of Commerce, 1983, 471.

Notes

1. "How to Cut the Deficit," *Business Week*, March 26, 1984, p. 84.
2. *Statistical Abstract of the United States 1984*, 104th edition, U.S. Department of Commerce, 1983, p.447.

3. Children's Defense Fund, *America's Children and Their Families: Key Facts*, Washington, D.C., 1983.

4. *Statistical Abstract of the United States 1984*, p. 475 and p. 476.

5. *Ibid.*, p. 474.

6. Children's Defense Fund, *op. cit.*

7. *Statistical Abstract of the United States 1984*, p. 473.

8. "An Overview of the Population Below the Poverty Line," *Monthly Labor Review* 105, August 1982, p. 53.

9. Judith Cummings, "Breakup of Black Family Imperils Gains of Decades," *The New York Times*, November 20, 1983, p. 1.

10. Children's Defense Fund, *op. cit.*

11. "How the Poor Will Be Hurt," *Newsweek*, March 23, 1981, p. 23.

12. "Has Reagan Hurt the Poor?," *Fortune*, January 24, 1983, p. 78.

13. *Ibid.*

14. "How to Cut the Deficit," p. 81.

15. Carl M. Brauer, "Kennedy, Johnson, and the War on Poverty,"*The Journal of American History* 69, 1 (June 1982), p. 108.

16. "Has Reagan Hurt the Poor?," p. 80.

17. John Kenneth Galbraith, *The Affluent Society*, second edition (New York: New American Library, 1959), p. 250.

18. See, for example, Sheldon Danziger *et al.*, "Poverty, Welfare, and Earnings: A New Approach," *Challenge*, September-October 1979 p. 28-34; Milton Friedman, "Newsweek on Poverty," *Newsweek*, April 19, 1982, 80, citing his *Capitalism and Freedom* (Chicago: University of Chicago Press, 1952), p. 192ff.

19. Brauer, p. 108.

20. Danziger, p. 30.

21. Danziger, *op cit.*

22. Editorial, "Recognizing Work As a Human Right," *National Catholic Reporter*, December 10, 1982, p. 36.

23. Cummings, p. 1.

Seven

To Promote the General Welfare: Catholic Principles for Welfare Policy

MICHAEL NOVAK

> The goals of our public welfare program must be positive and construc-
> tive. . . . It must stress the integrity and preservation of the family unit.
> It must contribute to the attack on dependency, juvenile delinquency,
> family breakdown, illegitimacy, ill health, and disability. It must reduce
> the incidence of these problems, prevent their occurrence and recur-
> rence, and strengthen and protect the vulnerable in a highly competi-
> tive world.
>
> > John F. Kennedy
> > Budget Message
> > February 1, 1962

IN AMERICAN POLITICS THERE IS NO LONGER ANY ARGU-
ment of principle between the major parties concerning two propositions: (1) Every citizen of the United States is entitled to the opportunity to improve his or her condition; and (2) There must be a floor
or safety net providing at least the rudiments of decent living conditions under every citizen.

In this respect basic Catholic social teaching has been in principle
vindicated within the American system. This is not to say that important debates do not remain or that the agenda for action has been fulfilled. It is only to say that, on these two propositions at least, agreement in principle has been reached. Debate now centers on the *de-*

sign of actual programs and the probable consequences of alternative designs, not on the matter of principle.

Furthermore, a capitalist economy, a democratic political system, and a pluralistic Jewish-Christian moral-cultural system — the three-systems-in-one which constitutes democratic capitalism — properly provides for the welfare of dependent and needy persons. It is not only consistent with, but incumbent upon, a democratic capitalist society to "promote the general welfare" through care for the less fortunate. Those on the left tend to turn for such care to the state; those on the right tend to turn for such care to the private sector. Such differences afford much controversy and political struggle. But the disputes center on the means, not on the goal. The view is almost universal that something is desperately wrong with the present design. For example the so-called Tarrytown Group of black scholars recently declared that welfare programs for poor mothers particularly "need to be completely reconceptualized and redesigned."[1]

The Catholic bishops of the United States, therefore, have an opportunity to help imagine a better future. Which principles of the Catholic tradition offer light to guide future public welfare policy? Three such principles seem especially promising: the building of intact families; what the Vatican calls "self-reliance;" and subsidiarity. Such principles could establish a new course for U.S. public policy.

A new course is surely needed. In 1959, 23 percent of poor families were headed by females. In 1982, after billions of dollars of welfare programs and the massive efforts of the War on Poverty (with welfare expenditures in 1980 *twenty-one times* the levels of expenditures in 1950),[2] the proportion of female-headed households in poverty had increased to 48 percent.[3] This destruction of families is unprecedented. The Catholic tradition cannot possibly be used to defend it. What is wrong? What needs to be changed in the *design* of public policy?

Furthermore, despite immense and unprecedented expenditures to eliminate poverty, the poverty level in the U.S. hit its lowest historical plateau at 11 percent in 1973, climbed back up to 13 percent in 1980, and to 15 percent in 1982.[4] The sums of money being spent to eliminate poverty exceed by far the sums necessary to lift every man, woman and child in the U.S. above the poverty line. Something clearly absurd is going on.

It might be well, then, to look closely at the official description of the poor in the United States to gauge the nature and the dimensions of the problem. Then we shall turn to the Catholic traditions to shed light on how problems of need and dependency might be susceptible to social solution. It is my intention, above all, to stress the importance of *family* welfare policy. This primary strength of Catholic social teaching has never, so far, been utilized in U.S. social policy.

The Poor and the Disadvantaged in the U.S.

According to the Census Bureau Report for 1982, some 34 million persons in the United States have an income below $9,862 for a non-farm family of four. This figure does not include any of the non-cash benefits (food stamps, housing assistance, medicare, etc.) received by such persons. Not counting non-cash benefits, the total *cash* income reported by the poor—not enough to lift them out of poverty—comes to $55 billion.[5] Half of all poor households received at least $6,477 in 1982 as cash; half received less.[6] Put another way, the *poverty short-fall*, the amount that would have been needed to raise the cash income of all over the poverty line, came to approximately $45 billion dollars.[7] Viewed in itself this is not an insuperable amount. It may be compared to annual expenditures for social services in the federal budget (not counting social service expenditures by the states and not counting assistance from private sources) of $390 billion in 1982.[8]

As these figures show, an annual grant totaling about $45 billion would suffice to eliminate poverty as a monetary matter. Yet significantly more than this amount is already being *targeted* for the poor. Consider the following estimated expenditures in FY 1983 (ending September 30, 1983) for programs targeted for the poor.[9]

Food stamps	$12.0 billion
Housing assistance	9.3 billion
AFDC	7.8 billion
Women, infants and children	1.1 billion
Low Income Energy Assistance	1.8 billion
Child nutrition	3.2 billion
Supplemental Security Income	8.8 billion
Medicaid (federal; does not count state)	19.3 billion
Unemployment benefits	36.9 billion
Earned income tax credit	1.2 billion
Total	$101.4 billion

One may not conclude from these figures that the poor in the United States are adequately cared for. What one must conclude is that sufficient federal funds are being expended to have lifted every man, woman and child in the United States above the basic poverty level of $9,862 for a non-farm family of four.

It is clear from these figures that if poverty were merely a matter of dollars, the actual cash earnings of the 34 million poor plus the amounts already expended by the federal government in their assistance would have already eliminated poverty in the United States. Our eyes tell us this is not the case. But before delving deeper into the problems of the poor, it is well to see from the Census Bureau reports just who they are. The following table illustrates their profile (numbers in thousands).

Profile of the Poor in the U.S. (Dec. 1982)[10]

Total poverty population, 1982:	34,398
Children under 15:	11,587
Persons over 65:	3,751
Young singles (16-24):	1,349
Other adults (25-64):	18,012
Persons living alone:	6,458
White:	23,517
Black:	9,697
Hispanic:	4,301
Single female head of households (number of households):	3,434
— Same, including children:	11,286
Ill or disabled:	2,809
Looking for work:	1,327
Located in Northeastern states:	6,364
North Central states:	7,772
Southern states:	13,967
Western states:	6,296
Outside metropolitan areas:	13,152
Inside metropolitan areas:	21,247
Inside central cities:	12,696

These figures illustrate that only 19.4 million of the poor are between the ages of sixteen and sixty-four. Of these, nearly 3.4 million are living at home with small children. Another 3 million of the poor are ill or disabled. Thus, only about 13 million of the poor are potentially able to work. Of these, 9 million worked for pay during at least part of 1982.[11]

This brief survey shows that the vast majority of the poor are truly dependent. Through no fault of their own most are not, and cannot be, self-reliant. Other studies show that *individuals* typically move into and out of the poverty ranks with considerable volatility. A study by the University of Michigan showed that only 17 percent of the poor (in the ten years surveyed) had been in poverty for as long as two years running. Poverty for most, the researchers conclude, tends not to be a permanent condition. Individuals in vast numbers fall into it temporarily and rise again. (Many graduate students, numbering 1.6 million nationwide, can testify to that).[12] This is important in countering the myth of "a permanent underclass."[13] Many of the poor are temporarily down on their luck and help received can start them on an upward path again.

There are two schools of thought on the problem of poverty. One argues chiefly in dollar terms. The point is simply to give money to the poor and stop worrying. The second is that poverty is not primarily a money problem but a problem dollars alone cannot solve. It is a problem of human potential (the economists say "human capital"). Many of the poor, especially among the young, need help in learning skills and attitudes: how to read, how to apply for and hold a job, how to govern and conduct themselves. Self-reliance is a virtue of many parts, according to this view, and it can be taught. This is especially true of youths currently unprepared for employment, the so-called "unemployables" who even if they get a job do not hold it long.[14] Modern society demands skills in nutrition, child care, literacy, and technique of many kinds (driving a car, making purchases, preparing a resume, expressing oneself clearly) which are not given automatically but must be learned. Indeed, the term "disadvantaged" points in part to this aspect, suggesting that not all persons start out with the same advantages.

It is crucial to note here that some persons even of an earlier aristocracy or proper middle class may now be as financially poor as church mice, without being "poor" in social class, while some financially poor persons are "bourgeois" in their virtues and attitudes.[15] In this sense the "advantages" of a certain culture are not coincidental with financial status. The problem of poverty is, therefore, quite different when it is only a question of income and when it is a question of skills. Many Americans can well remember being very poor, in the sense of having a very low income, without ever having felt "poor," in the sense of being culturally disadvantaged.

This is an important point. For church bodies can do a great deal about the moral-cultural dimension of poverty which mere money cannot do. It would be naive to believe that money is always an incentive to "lifting oneself out of poverty." Money can subsidize habits which lead to demoralization. This assertion is subject to empirical testing. In a section of downtown Albany, persons today classified as poor have financial resources of families who lived there in preceding generations; simultaneously, they suffer from far higher levels of violence, demoralization and despair than were ever known there before.[16]

We are accustomed to talking about poverty in pious tones which are blind to its awful reality. For often what we are talking about is not the relative absence of money but the psychological destructiveness felt by individuals. These feelings may not arise from free will; indeed, those possessed of them feel victimized. This is a spiritual, not an economic disease. Some share it who — as dope dealers, thieves, prostitutes or pimps — have income far above the national median. There is a moral dimension to poverty — what Kenneth Clark has described as its "pathology"[17] — of which churchmen, above all, are aware.

The vast majority of the poor, as Census Bureau figures show, are white. Many such persons (like many in all races) do not "feel" poor. Some live largely outside the cash economy, needing to purchase only those things they do not produce for themselves. Some live as they do in order to be self-reliant. A cash income of $9,862 a year in 1982 did not seem to many in the small towns of America a "poverty income" or a cause for desperation.

It may be well to sum up the analysis so far.

First Thesis: In every society a certain percentage of persons (the too young, the too old, the disabled, mothers with small children) are not capable of economic independence but are dependent on others. In a good society such persons must be cared for.

Second Thesis: In the United States the poverty short-fall (1982) amounted to between $43-45 billion; this represents the cash income needed to lift all persons above the official poverty line of $9,862 for a non-farm family of four. This is not a socially insuperable amount;

in fact, more than that amount is already being spent in federal assistance alone (not counting state, local, and private efforts).

Third Thesis: Clearly, the mere supplying of "the poverty shortfall" through monetary grants would not solve the problem of poverty, since poverty is not merely a matter of dollars only but also has a moral-cultural dimension, usually captured by the modifier "disadvantaged." Economic sufficiency and independence depend on health, skills and attitudes; lack of these constitutes "disadvantaged."

From these three thesis two social policy decisions seem to follow: (1) Those of the poor (especially the young) who possess the health, skills and attitudes necessary to achieve self-reliance need to be assisted by programs which *empower* them but *do not generate dependency*. (2) Those of the poor who lack the skills and attitudes necessary for self-reliance require special assistance. In this second arena the churches can make a unique contribution.

Beyond finite limits the church cannot give dollars or provide more than modest material assistance: food lines, used clothing and the like. Some forms of poverty are not psychologically destructive; many persons have been poor without pathology. Yet the evidence is overwhelming that some portion of the poor is suffering from demoralization and self-destructive behavior.[18] Unless church leaders address this core problem, a problem of the moral-cultural dimension, they turn away from their proper task. For this is a problem in which the state has no special competence and in which great expenditures by the state appear, by the evidence, to be making matters worse.

Consider the devastation to the family which appears to accompany federal expenditures. The integrity of the family is a primary issue of social justice. It is one of the main justifications for the concern of the churches about poverty. If poverty made no spiritual difference, especially to families, the churches would have little cause to be concerned with it. What can the Catholic church do for poor families?

A National Family Policy?

One of the deepest and best of all Catholic social traditions is its concern for the integrity of the family. The family, in Catholic social thought (and in virtually universal judgment), is the basic social unit. Modern Anglo-American thought has tended, however, to pay disproportionate attention to "the individual" (the conservative pole) and "the state" (since 1935 the liberal pole[19]). The individual and the state were the two novel realities of modern times. For the rise in individual opportunity liberated the human person from the fixed status of birth and family heritage, which had governed feudalism. And the rise of the modern nation state overrode the social forms of the feudal era. In this shift of attention to the individual and the state, the fundamental importance of family was typically not so much denied as ignored, although not so in Catholic social thought.

It may not at all have been an accident, then, that President John F. Kennedy in his budget message of 1962 laid down as the first principle of a sound welfare policy (the first step toward President Lyndon Johnson's "War on Poverty") that "It must stress the integrity and preservation of the family unit." Similarly, concentration on the family has been a preoccupation of Senator Daniel Patrick Moynihan.[20] Recent publications of the NAACP and the Civil Rights Commission have also begun to pay close attention to the deterioration in the families of those parts of the population most affected by welfare programs since 1962.[21]

The irony is clear. Welfare programs whose first criterion in 1962 was to "stress the integrity and presentation of the family unit" seem to be correlated with precisely the reverse results. Devastating results have been experienced in white and Hispanic welfare families; even more devastating results in black families.

In 1960, before the federal government became involved in the "War on Poverty," white mothers with dependent children constituted 6.0 percent of all poor families with children, while the equivalent figure for black families was 20.7 percent. By 1970, these percentages had grown 7.8 percent and 30.6 percent, respectively. By 1980 they had leapt again to 13.4 percent and 46.9 percent.[22] Clearly, each time these mothers have another child, the poverty figures will rise. Each poor young girl aged fifteen to nineteen who has a child will also add to the figures. The birth rate among poor teenagers keeps growing.[23]

In 1982 the percentage of poor persons was 15 percent. But if single mothers with dependent children had remained at the same rate as in 1960, the percentage of poor persons would fall to 13.0 percent (from 34.4 million to 29.9 million).[24] This is in part because intact husband-wife families among blacks between the ages of 25-34 have income levels at 89 percent of similar white couples.[25] Of the 9.6 million blacks who are poor, almost half (4.6 million) are in female-headed households. This portion of the poverty population continues to grow at a rapid pace. The following table illustrates the composition of the black poor.[26]

Poverty Status of Blacks in the U.S. (1982)

(in thousands)	TOTAL	Below Poverty Level	
		Number	Percent
ALL BLACKS	27,216	9,697	35.6
Under 18 years	9,401	4,472	47.6
22-64 years	13,458	3,578	26.6
Over 65	2,124	811	38.2
Black families	6,530	2,158	33.0
Married Couple Families	3,481	543	15.6
Female householder, no husband present	2,734	1,535	56.2

These figures show clearly that the presence of both a mother and a father in the home is the most certain road out of poverty. Only 15.6 percent of such black families are poor. On the other hand 56.2 percent of black female-headed families are poor. In short, the "integrity and preservation of the family unit" of which President Kennedy spoke in 1962 does seem to work as a way out of poverty. But whatever is causing the growth in female-headed households is slowly multiplying the numbers of the black poor: 1,535,000 female heads of households and approximately 3 million children, nearly half the black poor, fall in this growing class.[27] This is a human-made tragedy, caused by neither nature nor nature's God. It should not be beyond the wit of humans to halt what they have set in motion.

Catholic social teaching offers no pat remedy for this problem. It does command the Catholic conscience to attend to it. To assert merely that the federal government should distribute more benefits to single mothers with dependent children is not likely to lead to a decrease in the number of single-parent mothers and their dependent children. On the contrary the number seems to be increasing from decade to decade in correlation with the advent of social welfare programs designed, purportedly, for the opposite effect. Something seems wrong in the design.

It seems worth pausing to mention that a similar deterioration is taking place in white and Hispanic welfare families. Of the 5,118,000 white families who are poor, 1,813,000 (35 percent) are headed by a female householder, no husband present.[28] Of the 916,000 Spanish-origin families who are poor, 425,000 (46 percent) are headed by a female householder, no husband present.[29] These numbers, too, keep growing.

Unless welfare programs arrest the growth in female-headed families, no husbands present, it seems certain that the numbers of the poor will continue to grow in future years. In 1980 the largest single category of the poor were single mothers and their dependent children. Their total number came to 13 million, or 30 percent of all poor persons.[30]

It must be added that a growing percentage of single mothers are not abandoned by their *husbands*; a growing percentage of children every year is being born illegitimate. In 1970, for example, the percentages of illegitimate births were as follows: among whites 5.7 percent; among blacks 37.6 percent. By 1980 these percentages had climbed to 11 percent and 55.2 percent respectively.[31] Worse still, the *ages* of young women giving birth also declined. Between 1970 and 1980 the proportion of illegitimate births among women aged 15-19 rose from 17 percent to 33 percent among whites and from 63 percent to 85 percent among blacks.[32]

Questions of poverty, therefore, are today inextricable from questions of family life. The so-called "feminization of poverty" is, as the figures show, mostly a problem of abandoned single women, many of whom have never formed families.

Moreover, this deterioration in the struggle against poverty is growing just as progress is being made in other areas. In 1959, 22 percent of the U.S. population was officially classified as poor. Of these, 13.8 percent was comprised of persons over 65.[33] By 1982 advances in social security (especially in indexing payments to inflation) had lowered these numbers to 10.9 percent of those over 65, and non-cash programs like food stamps, housing assistance and medicare had ameliorated the lot even of these.[34] Similarly, poverty rates for intact husband-wife families had been lowered considerably, although much remains to be done. Finally, the numbers of adult poor persons living alone had been lowered to 6,458 thousand.[35]

The great disappointment has been with regard to family life. There welfare programs have seemed to have perverse effects, exactly opposite to those intended. Since so many children are involved, and since a sizeable proportion of their young mothers are not much more than children, the problem is heart-rending and acute.

What is to be done? There can be no doubt that assistance must be provided. Assistance for Families with Dependent Children (AFDC) is a relatively small portion of the welfare budget. In 1982 it came to $8.2 billion.[36] Typically AFDC checks are paid directly to the young mother. So are other forms of assistance, including food stamps, housing assistance, medicaid and the like. These grants paid directly to the woman make her dependent upon them rather than upon the father of her children. The incentive for males to take responsibility for their own children is bypassed. The state, feeling no requirement to intervene in matters of morality, may simply mail a check. But this act seems counter to all known systems of social morality and social accountability, and counter to family morality as well. So what is to be done?

Imaginative social philosophy is clearly called for. The United States remains virtually the only welfare state not to have in place a family welfare policy. No doubt the received intellectual tradition of concentrating either on the individual or on the state, while ignoring the family, has had a profound effect upon public policy. Yet the Catholic tradition clearly teaches that the welfare of families — Kennedy's "integrity and preservation of the family unit" — is paramount in all schemes of social justice. What would be a fresh Catholic response to the existing problems of care for the needy and dependent in American social policy?

A Fresh Start: A Family Welfare Policy.

The 1919 statement by the U.S. Catholic bishops was far in advance of its time. It is the same sort of imaginative leap that seems called for in our present circumstances. The criteria for a new social welfare policy issued by the bishops should be threefold: that it be distinctively Catholic; that it meet an urgent social need; and that it be, in the long run — if not the short run, workable or at least worth working towards.

Reflection on the current "poverty" population of the U.S. reveals that the vast majority of the needy — some 28 million — live in families. Thus, a welfare policy designed explicitly for families would go a very long way toward ending (or seriously alleviating) poverty in the the United States. Secondly, reflection on "the poverty shortfall" in 1982 shows that the *financial cost* of a family welfare policy ought not be prohibitive. This is particularly true if the new policy were to replace the present confusing, overlapping "welfare mess." Finally, from all sides, conservative and liberal, cries for welfare reform coincide with visible exhaustion concerning how to bring it about. These three factors suggest that a new design is worth working towards and, in time, may prove highly practical.

So let us begin with the children first. The best circumstance for infants and the young is an intact family, with both mother and father present. If social policy desires something as the circumstance, it should reward it. Therefore, social policy ought to provide child allowances to parents of intact families. Parents serve the common good by the care they bestow on their children. In the United States in 1982 there were 49.6 million intact families, with a total of 25.3 million children. There were 3.8 million intact poor families with a total of 13 million poor children.[37] Clearly, the latter population needs help more than the whole range of families. On the other hand, political action is often easier if its base is as inclusive as possible. So it is with social security.

Thus, two principles come into conflict: (1) To help the neediest; (2) To treat all equally. Usually, a compromise is possible. Thus, one can imagine *larger* child allowances to category (1), and *smaller* allowances above certain income levels. One way to do this would be to treat child allowances as taxable income, in such a way that those whose income is below the poverty level are exempted from taxation, and those above it are taxed at proportionate rates.

A non-farm family of four in 1982 required a cash income of $9,862 to meet the official poverty level. In 1982 all poverty families together numbered 7.5 million.[38] If such families had earned no income at all, the maximum cost of full income support would be less than $75 billion ($9,862 X 7.5 m.). This sum by itself would in that case eradicate poverty as a monetary matter. But of course no such sum would be needed, since most poor families, and especially intact families, already have considerable cash income. The short-fall as we have seen, is closer to $45 billion. It seems plausible that a child allowance of $150 per child per month or $1800 per year would suffice to raise a large majority of intact poor families above the poverty level.

It may not be wise to attach numbers to these matters at this early stage. The public policy principle is to devise a system of social welfare which stresses "the integrity and preservation of the family unit." The point is to achieve two goals at once: to alleviate (or eliminate) poverty while simultaneously rewarding intact families in the hopes of generating more of them. Perhaps one cannot solve the *whole* problem of poverty. But if one could lift out of poverty of 3.8 million intact families who were poor in 1982 (together with their approximately 7.6 million children), one would have dramatically reduced the dimensions of poverty. The total cost of such an effort in 1982 would have been $14 billion — slightly larger than the food-stamp program ($1800 X 7.6 m. children).

What about the remaining poor families, those headed by single mothers? Such persons, numbering 11.3 million mothers and children are often in desperate need; many of the mothers are teenagers themselves (often enough the daughters of mothers who began life the same way). The problem for public policy has three parts: (1) to help such women and their children in a way that they may escape from dependency; (2) to avoid having the state assume responsibilities which properly belong to the fathers of children; and (3) to avoid supplying unintentional incentives to others who might choose to follow this path. It is not easy to meet all three criteria.

The critical technical problem seems to be the mailing of the welfare check directly to the young single woman. Possibly, a distinction must be observed according to age. Above the age of twenty a single mother might be entitled to receive the check directly. Below the age of twenty the check might have to be countersigned by a legal guardian (her minister, her mother, or some other authority figure specified by law; and best of all, by the father of her child). If a sort of financial independence is a perverse incentive to a younger single woman, even at the cost of becoming a ward of the state, this proviso would help to dispel it.

But what burden can be placed upon the father? His identity is probably known to the law only in the case of legal marriage interrupted by death, divorce, desertion and the like, and what can be done when the father is unknown? Nonetheless the numbers are still growing. Despite the rapid growth in the number of abortions among the poor, by 1980 fifty-five percent of all births to black women were of fathers unknown to the law, up from 38 percent in 1970.[39] This immense flight of males from the most basic responsibility of manhood is both a social and a moral catastrophe. But what the state can do about it is unclear. Making welfare checks payable directly to a young woman, especially in the 31 states which require the absence of any male, seems clearly to be an incentive to male irresponsibility. It may be wrong to involve the state in questions of marital status, but the claim to assistance based upon marital status does so involve it. For this reason it seems important that, at least for younger women, state assistance should neither be nor seem to be an incentive to male irresponsibility.

Having a child outside of wedlock, furthermore, should be looked at as a matter not solely of morality but also of social consequences, one of which may be dependency upon the state. May the society not exact costs in return? Socially burdensome behavior must be discouraged, just as socially beneficial behavior should be rewarded. Are there devices open to a good and generous society which might meet the required criteria? Social thinkers have been hesitant in approaching this matter, as well they should be. Their hesitance is a contributing factor to the growing incidence of female-headed households in poverty.

The children in such households are already penalized by the lack of a father to guide their steps, to supply a masculine discipline and presence, and to help prepare them for the social economy. They need assistance in overcoming these disadvantages as well as those of poverty itself. This the state alone can hardly supply.

It thus becomes clear that the poverty which results from single-parent households is a problem demanding social action on a scale larger than that available to the state alone. Moral and cultural institutions must play a role; so must the media, the schools, families, neighborhood groups, and associations of every sort. The problem in its present dimensions is a social problem. While it seems clear that it is beyond the ministrations of the state, that does not acquit the rest of us of our social obligations. Having children out of wedlock places a grievous burden upon those children and upon the society at large. Society at large, frustrated by the limits of the competence of the state, must construct a solution.

This effort will require moral leadership. For having children out of wedlock, or abandoning the woman and child one has fathered, are not afflictions which fall from the skies but are consequences of voluntary human behavior. The Catholic bishops could provide significant leadership in convening a broad-based coalition of church leaders, media elites, and social workers to support poor persons in non-formed families and in families broken by widowhood or divorce. For example, on each local level leagues of female-headed househoulds could be formed under the auspices of local churches, neighborhood associations, and voluntary organizations. The idea would be to have local persons who know the heads of households personally become the administrators of social assistance. There is reason to believe that the vast majority of female-headed families are found in cities and towns in which local organizations already flourish. No new bureaucracy would have to be created. Rather, the good works of such organizations could be sharply focussed upon assistance to needy families. Such assistance would have personal as well as monetary dimensions.

Furthermore, AFDC and other forms of federal and state assistance would then be channelled through local family centers. Checks would not be distributed directly to individuals below the specified age (age 20), but only through the sponsoring organizations. It would be more useful for federal funds to be paid to urban churches, for example, to maintain day-care centers for children and learning sessions for young heads of households, including meal service, than to give the funds to individuals. The point is to use the financial power of the state to strengthen the local networks whose personnel know the needy personally, and to spend funds in such a way that the educational assistance they provide *empowers* the needy to begin, at a later stage, to care for themselves. In this way state assistance need not lead to dependency upon the state, but to personal empowerment.

The moral principle is that state power must not be used to create dependency, but rather to empower local social organizations to meet genuine social needs and to empower needy individuals to acquire the skills of self-reliance.

A summary of Catholic family welfare policy for the needy would, therefore, be as follows:

(1) Child allowances would be paid on a monthly basis to husband-wife intact families. These funds would count as taxable income. Those families below the poverty level would not, of course, pay taxes. Indeed, families up to one hundred percent above the poverty line (approximately the median income level) might be exempted.

(2) For non-formed families and families broken by abandonment, separation, divorce and death, and for heads of households below the

age of 20, federal and state assistance would not be paid directly to the needy, but rather to local family centers which would provide child care, instruction and meals.

These two steps should provide two considerable steps forward. First, a significant percentage of intact families now in poverty should be lifted out of poverty by step one. Second, the cycle of dependency would be ameliorated by personalized local assistance and educational programs aimed at self-reliance.

These programs would not alone eliminate all poverty. But by concentrating on family strengths they would significantly diminish the numbers of intact families who are poor. They would also provide, as it were, local surrogate extended families for non-formed and broken families. These alone would represent great steps forward for millions from among the poor. Immediately they should reduce the numbers of the poor from among intact families. Immediately they should reduce the impersonal dependence of non-formed and broken families on government checks, while providing significant personal and financial assistance.

The Family in Catholic Social Thought.

In 1920 John A. Ryan quoted with approval the statement of an Interdenominational Conference of Social Service Unions in Great Britain, which "points out that all social reform must take as its end and guide the maintenance of pure and wholesome family life."[40] Similarly, many years earlier, Bishop von Ketteler, whom Pope Leo XIII described as a major founder of modern Catholic social thought, held that the chief fault of Geman liberalism was its opposition to "the divine plan for the procreation and education of men by means of the family."[41] Indeed, it was concern for the family, the cradle of all human morality and spirituality, that justified for Leo XIIı papal attention to the problems of social reconstruction. This tradition is summarized very clearly by Pope John XXIII in *Pacem in Terris* (Para. 16):

> The family, grounded on marriage freely contracted, monogamous and indissoluble, must be considered the first and essential cell of human society. To it must be given, therefore, every consideration of an economic, social, cultural and moral nature which will strengthen its stability and facilitate the fulfillment of its specific mission.[42]

In *Mater et Magistra* Pope John XXIII also summarized the teaching of Pius XII. The latter, celebrating in 1941 the fiftieth anniversary of *Rerum Novarum*, calls attention to "the three principal issues of social life in economic affairs, which are mutually related and connected one with the other, and thus interdependent: namely, the use of material goods, labor, and the family."[43]

One of the very strongest texts of the Catholic tradition, however, is found in *Rerum Novarum* (Para. 10):

> For it is a most sacred law of nature that a father must provide food and all necessaries for those whom he has begotten; and similarly, nature dictates that a man's children, who carry on, as it were, and continue his own personality, should be provided by him with all that is needful to enable them honorably to keep themselves from want and misery in the uncertainties of this mortal life. Now, in no other way can a father effect this except by the ownership of profitable property, which he can transmit to his children by inheritance. A family, no less than a State, is, as we have said, a true society, governed by a power within itself, that is to say, by the father. Wherefore, provided the limits be not transgressed which are prescribed by the very purposes for which it exists, the family has, at least, equal rights with the State in the choice and pursuit of those things which are needful to its preservation and its just liberty. . . . We say, at least equal rights; for since the domestic household is anterior both in idea and in fact to the gathering of men into a commonwealth, the former must necessarily have rights and duties which are prior to those of the latter, and which rest more immediately on nature. If the citizens of a State — that is to say, the families — on entering into association and fellowship, experienced at the hands of the State hindrance instead of help, and found their rights attacked instead of being protected, such associations were rather to be repudiated than sought after.[44]

This text powerfully underlines the emphasis on families and their associations suggested in the proposal of local family centers independent of state bureaucracy mentioned above.

Allan Carlson in an important article has recently pointed out that the cultural system of democratic capitalist societies powerfully inhibits naked individualism. He writes: "The natural unplanned genius of the new order lay in the cultural forces which kept this destructive consequence of liberal-capitalism in check. *The first of these was the family*."[45] Jewish-Christian sexual and family teaching is a crucial component of the holistic liberal sensibility; emphasis on family is central to the American ethos. He continues:

> The creative social bond between morality and the modern family was particularly strong in the United States. Tocqueville noted that although European visitors to America disagreed on many points, they all concurred that moral standards were far stricter in this country than elsewhere. He attributed this to the unique balance of freedom, equality, and responsibility found in the American marriage covenant.[46]

Catholic social teaching, clearly, recognizes that the family is the essential, fundamental unit at whose integrity and fruition wise social policy should be aimed. Indeed, were there to be a conflict between the will of the state and the good of families, the Church would clearly be bound to side with the latter. Thus, U.S. social welfare policies for the poor must be scrutinized in the light of the good of families. In this respect President Kennedy's criteria for a sound welfare reform were sound: "It must stress the integrity and preservation of the family unit. It must contribute to the attack on dependency, juvenile delinquency, family breakdown, illegitimacy, ill health, and disability."

No one can correctly say that the people of the United States are not spending, through their government, enough money to have eliminated poverty. For the total sum of money needed to bring the 7.5 million poor families in the U.S. (1982) to $10,000 per year is $75 billion, far less than is currently being spent. Neither can anyone correctly say that the current *design* of the U.S. public policy for the poor is meeting the criteria President Kennedy set for it in its beginnings.

Here is where the Catholic bishops have an *opportunity*. Given the emphasis of Catholic social teaching on family welfare, they have the possibility of offering some badly needed originality. In the past conservatives faced with a problem have typically turned to the *individual*; liberals faced with a problem have turned to the *state*. Neither solution, time has shown, meets the tests of reality. In drawing the attention of the public policy community to the *family* — a mediating structure *between* the individual and the state — the Catholic bishops could propose a new public policy agenda as wide-reaching for the next fifty years as the New Deal was for the past fifty. The role of the state is to *empower* people, not to make them dependent.[47] The institution designed by nature to empower them, above all, is the family. The programs of the state should be designed to strengthen families. For strong families provide the surest and most direct path out of poverty, and are nature's own institutional means for providing adequate income to the poor and the needy.

Catholic social policy differs from traditional American conservatism (at least of the libertarian type) by holding that the state must play a role in helping the needy. It differs from traditional American liberalism by holding that state assistance which generates dependency violates the principle of subsidiarity, that the family is prior to the state, and that family is prior to the individual as the focus for social policy. In all these respects Catholic social policy has an opportunity to establish new directions, at a moment when new directions are universally desired.

Notes

1. See Judith Cummings, "Breakup of Black Family Imperils Gains of Decades," *New York Times,* November 20, 1983.

2. Charles A. Murray, *Safety Nets and the Truly Needy: Rethinking the Truly Needy* (Washington, D.C.: Heritage Foundation, 1982), p. viii.

3. David O'Neill, "Poverty and Use of Clever Slogans," *Washington Times,* November 24, 1983, p. 1C. The devastation of the black family is especially evident. The Census Bureau reports: "The number of poor Black families with a female householder rose from 834,000 in 1970 to 1.4 million in 1981. These families accounted for 70 percent of all poor Black families in 1981, substantially up from 56 percent in 1970." U.S. Bureau of the Census, *America's Black Population: 1970 to 1982*, Special Publication PIO/POP-83-1 (Washington, D.C.: 1983), pp. 4, 9.

4. U.S. Bureau of the Census, *Statistical Abstract of the United States: 1982-83*, 103d ed. (Washington, D.C.: 1983), table 727; *Money Income and Poverty Status of Families and Persons in the United States: 1982*, table B.

5. Telephone inquiry, U.S. Bureau of the Census, October 6, 1983; figure from unpublished Current Population survey.

6. See *Money Income and Poverty Status of Families and Persons in the United States: 1982*, table 20.

7. Spencer Rich, " 'Poverty Gap' Put at $45 Billion," *Washington Post,*

October 19, 1983, p. A6. Testimonies of Rudolph G. Penner, Director, Congressional Budget Office and Sheldon Danziger of the Institute for Research on Poverty, University of Wisconsin to the House Ways and Means Committee, October 18, 1983.

8. Office of Management and Budget, *Payments to Individuals*, February, 1983.

9. Office of Management and Budget, *Outlays for Social Programs*, February 1, 1983.

10. *Money Income and Poverty Status of Families and Persons in the United States: 1982*, table 14. Testimony of David A. Stockman, Director, Office of Management and Budget before the House Ways and Means Subcommittees on Oversight, and Public Assistance and Unemployment, November 3, 1983, p.4.

11. *Ibid.*, table 17.

12. National Center for Education Statistics, *Opening Fall Enrollment*, 1982 (unpublished).

13. See Ken Auletta, *The Underclass* (New York: Random House, 1982).

14. "If poverty and lower-class existence are viewed as *structural* patterns, caused by a poor distribution of skills, jobs, income, and the like, then the remedy is apparent: expand lower-class blacks' access to these resources. If, on the other hand, lower-class existence is viewed more broadly, as a function of cultural patterns, then the remedy is far more elusive and problematic. For then the difficulty becomes one of devising solutions that simultaneously correct maladaptive cultural patterns (delinquency, crime, unwed motherhood, street-corner lifestyles, drugs) and those structural deficiencies or institutional inequities (inflation, recession, unemployment, poor schools, and the like) that shrink opportunity for the poor . . . . Allies of the black lower class must devise ways and means for reducing certain cultural or societal pathologies widely prevalent among lower-class blacks. Lower-class lifestyles among young men and women that are associated with the "man-child" and "woman-child" syndrome — above all, becoming mothers and fathers while still in one's teens — must be interdicted, constrained, and reversed." Martin Kilson, "Black Social Classes and Intergenerational Poverty," *Public Interest*, LXIV (Summer, 1981), pp. 68-70.

15. "Class may (or may not) find phenomenological expression, but at root it is a mode of self-definition. There are aristocrats in England who are as poor as church mice but are definitely 'upper class.' And there are immigrants to the United States who are also as poor as church mice but are definitely 'middle class' from the moment they set foot here. The very thought that there is someone ('up there?') who knows better than we do what class we are in is as breathtaking in its intellectual presumption as it is sterile for all serious purposes of social research." Irving Kristol, *Reflections of a*

Neoconservative (New York: Basic Books, 1983), pp. 199-200. See the whole of ch. 14, "Some Personal Reflections on Economic Well-Being and Income Distribution."

16. See George Gilder, *Visible Man* (New York: Basic Books, 1978).

17. See Kenneth B. Clark, *Dark Ghetto* (New York: Harper and Row, 1965). See esp. ch. 5, "The Pathology of the Ghetto," pp. 81-110. "The dark ghetto is institutionalized pathology; it is chronic, self-perpetuating pathology; and it is the futile attempt by those with power to confine that pathology so as to prevent the spread of its contagion to the 'larger community.' Not only is the pathology of the ghetto self-perpetuating, but one kind of pathology breeds another. The child born in the ghetto is more likely to come into a world of broken homes and illegitimacy; and this family and social instability is conducive to delinquency, drug addiction, and criminal violence" (p. 81).

18. See Auletta, *op. cit.*

19. See John Dewey, *Liberalism and Social Action* (New York: Capricorn Books, 1963).

20. See Daniel Patrick Moynihan's introduction to Alva Myrdal, *Nation and Family* (Cambridge, Mass.: MIT Press, 1968).

21. See, for example, United States Commissioin on Civil Rights, *A Growing Crisis: Disadvantaged Women and Their Children*, Clearinghouse Publication 78, May 1983.

22. *Statistical Abstract of the United States: 1982-83*, table 73.

23. "Prior to 1970, women 15 to 19 years old had less than half of all illegitimate births. By 1975, as a result of decreasing illegitimacy rates at older ages and increasing rates among women 15 to 19 years old, teenage women accounted for more than half of all illegitimate births." U.S. Bureau of the Census, *Perspectives on American Fertility*, Series P-23, No. 70 (July 1978), pp. 40-41. From 1975 to 1979, the number of births to unmarried women aged 15-19 increased by 14 percent, from 222 per 1,000 to 253 per 1,000. See *Statistical Abstract of the United States: 1982-83*, table 97.

24. Calculated from *Money Income and Poverty Status of Families and Persons in the United States: 1982*, tables 14-15. As a proportion of the total poverty population, female heads of housholds with their dependent children virtually doubled between 1960 and 1982, climbing from 15 percent to 29 percent. Despite a reduction in the total number of poor children, from 17.3 million in 1960 to 13.1 million in 1982, the number of poor children in families headed by females increased from 4.1 million to 6.7 million during the same period of time. See *ibid.*, tables 14-15.

25. United States Department of Commerce News, CB 83-127, August 22, 1983.

26. *Money Income and Poverty Status of Families and Persons in the United*

States: 1982, tables 14, 17-18.

27. *Ibid.*, tables 15 and 18.

28. *Ibid.*, table 18.

29. *Ibid.*

30. *Statistical Abstract of the United States: 1982-83*, table 728.

31. National Center for Health Statistics, *Monthly Vital Statistics Report*, Advance Report of Final Natology Statistics, vol. XXXI, No. 8, (November 30, 1982).

32. *Ibid.*

33. *Money Income and Poverty Status of Families and Persons in the United States: 1982*, table 15.

34. *Ibid.*

35. *Ibid.*, table 14.

36. U.S. Executive Office of the President, Office of Management and Budget, *Budget of the United States Government, Fiscal Year 1984*, p. V-125.

37. U.S. Bureau of the Census, Current Population Reports, series P-20, No. 381, *Household and Family Characteristics: March 1982* (Washington, D.C.: 1983) table 5; *Money Income and Poverty Status of Families and Persons in the United States: 1982*, tables 14-15.

38. *Ibid.*, table 18.

39. *American's Black Population: 1970 to 1982*, p. 20.

40. John A. Ryan, *Social Reconstruction* (New York: Macmillan, 1920), p. 222.

41. L. Lenhart, "Ketteler, Wilhelm Emmanuel von," *New Catholic Encyclopedia* (New York: MacGraw Hill, 1907), VIII, 170.

42. *Seven Great Encyclicals*, (Glen Rock, N.J.: Paulist Press, 1963), p. 292.

43. *Ibid.*, p. 227.

44. *Ibid.*, p. 6.

45. Allan C. Carlson, "The Family and Liberal Capitalism," *Modern Age,* Summer/Fall, 1982, p. 366.

46. *Ibid.*, p. 369.

47. Peter L. Berger and Richard Neuhaus, *To Empower People* (Washington, D.C.: American Enterprise Institute, 1977). See also my essay, "Creation Theology," in *Co-Creation and Capitalism: John Paul II's Laborem Exerceus*, ed. John W. Houck and Oliver F. Williams (Washington, D.C.: University Press of America, 1983).

Eight

Redeeming The "City of Pigs": Catholic Principles for Welfare Justice

DENNIS P. McCANN

IN BOOK II OF PLATO'S *REPUBLIC* SOCRATES IS ENGAGED in conversation with Glaucon and Adeimantus over the nature of justice. They agree that a distinction needs to be made between the justice of one man and the justice of a whole city. Since a city is larger than a man, they find it expedient to begin there by creating an ideal model of the whole starting from its very foundation. "I think a city comes to be," says Socrates, "because not one of us is self-sufficient, but needs many things." Having secured the assent of Glaucon and Adeimantus to this principle, Socrates goes on to sketch how people make use of one another to secure these basic needs like food, clothing, shelter, and such things, through a natural division of labor regulated through some form of free market system. They conclude that the essential minimum for such a city would be four or five men and they foresee the need for trading relations with many other similarly structured cities. After drawing from Adeimantus the conjecture that justice would probably consist in the quality of the relations among these people, Socrates becomes eloquent in describing the life the citizens of such a city must enjoy:

> Obviously they will produce grain and wine and clothes and shoes. They
> will build their houses. In the summer they will strip for their work
> and go without shoes, though they will be adequately clothed and shod

in the winter. For food they will make flour from wheat and meal from barley; they will bake the former and knead the latter; they will put their excellent cakes and loaves upon reeds or clean leaves; then, reclining upon a bed of strewn byrony and mrtyle leaves, they will feast together with their children, drinking of their wine. Crowned with wreaths they will hymn the gods and enjoy each other, bearing no more children than their means allow, cautious to avoid poverty and war.[1]

This vision of peace and prosperity apparently is not to Glaucon's taste. At first egging Socrates on by pointing out that such "feasts" usually include "cooked dishes" and "seasoning," Glaucon interrupts his teacher's modest list of culinary embellishments with an immodest, if not impertinent, question: "If you were founding a city of pigs, Socrates, what else would you fatten them on?"

We must imagine Socrates pulled up short, perhaps even startled back into dialogue. Here's what follows:

> And how shall I feed them, Glaucon? said I. In the conventional way, he said. If they are not to be miserable they should recline on proper couches and dine at a table, with the cooked foods and delicacies which people have nowadays. Very well, I said, I understand. We should examine not only the birth of a city, but of a luxurious city. This may not be a bad idea, for in examining such a one we might very well see how justice and injustice grow in the cities. Yet to me the true city is that which we described, like a healthy individual. However, if you wish, let us observe the feverish city.[2]

Socrates goes on to paint what could be a picture of contemporary Athens or one of the other successful Greek city-states. He notes the multiplication of needs and the occupations intent on serving them. He emphasizes the necessity of territorial expansion and the inevitability of war among such "luxurious" and "feverish" cities, and from there he begins his discussion of the character of that class devoted to the craft of warfare, the guardians. All of which, in light of the self-destruction of the Greek city-state system in the Peloponnesian War, suggests a savage irony at work in Plato's parable of social justice, *The Republic*.

I begin my attempt to describe the moral principles that may be at stake in questions of welfare policy with this ancient story for many reasons. First, I think it conveys the right mood for this discussion, not only in the sense that the shadow of self-destruction and much worse hangs over our own international system of civic nation-states, but also in the sense that the very need to consider welfare policy itself is a thermometer recording the degree of our feverishness. Second, this story not surprisingly finds several echoes in the tradition of Catholic social teaching which we are bound to scrutinize in our search for relevant moral principles. Not only would the bulk of that tradition have commended to the laity the vision of vigorous modesty so stupidly dismissed by Glaucon, but they would have applauded Socrates' implied rebuke to his pupil that, on the contrary, it is the luxurious and feverish city that truly is a city of pigs. Pope John Paul II's encyclical, *Laborem Exercens*, as the following may suggest, owes as much to this parable of Greek realism ultimately as it does to the Creation narratives of Genesis. More specifically, when John A. Ryan, in his classic treatise, *Distributive Justice*, concludes his chapter on the moral and religious "Duty of Distributing Superfluous Wealth" by contrasting the true and the false conceptions of "Welfare," it is this same struggle over the city of pigs, over what is necessary and what is superfluous in the pursuit of human fulfillment.

There may be other insights to be gathered from this story and its echoes in our tradition, but the one with which I would hope to begin is that in this perspective the Welfare State, as we have come to know it both in theory and in practice, must be regarded as something of anomaly. In Socrates' model city everyone performs the function best suited to him by talent and disposition. There is no structural unemployment and hence no specific programs of public assistance[3] because such things would only be necessary to combat the ills of a luxurious and feverish city. Similarly, it came as a surprise to me at least that the "Right Rev. New Dealer," John A. Ryann, makes only negligible reference to anything that could be construed as welfare policy in *Distributive Justice*. Like the encyclical, *Laborem Exercens,* Ryan's treatise keeps its focus on the dignity of labor and the right to a living wage. Consistent with economic opinion of that time,[4] Ryan argues that the Great Depression resulted from distributional inequities in the national income and that, among other things, the adoption of Catholic proposals for a living wage would virtually eliminate unemployment.[5] I infer that the neglect of welfare policy by Socrates, the Pope, and the Monsignor, was not the result of inadvertence or a failure of imagination but the result of a moral vision of the just society in which programs of public assistance would not be necessary. The point of this observation is not to emphasize the usual discrepancy between the ideal and the real, but to indicate that welfare policy in this tradition must be approached systematically in terms of its role in society as a whole and its specific contribution, if any, to the common good. This inference, for me at least, provides the point of departure for what follows.

In order to pursue this insight I will proceed in the following manner. First, procedurally, I wish to explore what is involved in formulating an ethical analysis of U.S. welfare policy within the context of a National Conference of Catholic Bishops (N.C.C.B.) pastoral letter. I will investigate the mode of moral reasoning evident in the bishops' recent pastoral letter, *The Challenge of Peace: God's Promise and Our Response*, concentrating on two issues: 1) the bishops' intent to speak to both the civic community as a whole and the Catholic community as a distinctive part of this whole, and 2) the threefold distinction of levels of moral authority operative in the various conclusions outlined in that letter. I will contend that any pastoral letter on the American economy dare not fall below the standard of moral reasoning set in that recent letter on nuclear weapons policy. The other items on my agenda therefore will be organized in accordance with this standard. Thus, secondly, I will look for "universally binding moral principles" of distributive justice operative in the assessment of welfare policy by comparing selectively John A. Ryan's *Distributive Justice*, a classic at least within the Catholic community, with John Rawls's *A Theory of Justice*, a plausible candidate for similar status within the American philosophical tradition. I will try to establish the outlines of a common approach to welfare policy within which certain important perspective differences persist, differences that may be understood by narrowing in on the semantics of "Human Welfare" in Ryan and "Self-Respect" in Rawls. Thirdly, I will examine recent authoritative interpretations of Catholic faith, "the statements of recent Popes and the teachings of Vatican II," in order to situate the distinctiveness of Catholic social teaching in this area within the moral culture of pluralism. Finally, I will seek to apply the norms discovered in the previous two sections by making "prudential judgments" about the general outlines of current U.S. welfare policy. I will show how Catholic social teaching constitutes an agenda for reform in response to two overarching values: the dignity of labor and the integrity of the family. All policy recommendations, in other words, will have to be assessed in relation to these norms. In conclusion, I will argue that the whole area of welfare policy holds a position in a letter on the American economy analogous to that held by nuclear deterrence in a letter on war and peace. Both deserve only a "strictly conditioned moral acceptance" to the extent that they in morally questionable ways seek to prevent even greater catastrophes. The "strict conditions" in the case of welfare policy, of course, are implicit in the norms of the dignity of labor and the integrity of the family at stake in the Catholic vision of a just society.

Moral Reasoning in Pastoral Letters

First, what is involved in making an ethical analysis of public policy in pastoral letter? This question was raised at various stages of the drafting of the pastoral letter, *The Challenge of Peace: God's Promise and Our Response*, most notably by the inquiry of Cardinal Ratzinger concerning the *mandatum docendi* of any national bishops' conference.[6] The clarifications made at the January, 1983 meeting with Cardinal Ratzinger and others at the Vatican and the way they were implemented in the third and final drafts of that pastoral letter should serve as guidelines for any similar letters issued by the N.C.C.B. Among other things the following points were made: First, in such pastoral letters the bishops speak out of "a long tradition in the United States" of "addressing moral issues not only as a magisterium, but as a body of persons exercising a respected role in public debate." Pastoral letters in this context "are an attempt to interpret principles in light of the signs of the times." While the bishops claim that the nuclear threat in particular warrants this more specific approach to their role as "moral teachers," their argument I believe is applicable to any public policy issue that they may find it necessary to address.

The tradition to which they refer here needs further explanation. The third and final drafts of that letter exhibit an extraordinarily explicit awareness of the bishops' vocation as "moral teachers" within a pluralistic society. For they expect their teaching to be taken seriously not just by the Catholic community but also by the public at large. This necessitates "two complementary but distinct styles of teaching," one addressed to the "religious community [sharing] a specific perspective of faith," the other addressed to the "civil community" bound by the moral "law written on the human heart by God." Not surprisingly, these two "styles" overlap in a form of moral discourse that seeks to "both identify the specific contributions a community of faith can make . . . and relate these to the wider work . . . pursued by other groups and institutions in society." It is not as if the bishops speak one moral language in their own community and another when addressing the public at large; rather, it is that whatever arguments they make must be intelligible, if not persuasive, to the public at large and hence in some sense accountable to the public at large as a condition for entering into a community of moral discourse with it. America, in short, is a pluralistic society within which the bishops, as the anointed leaders of the Catholic community, accept certain responsibilities as "moral teachers" for the purpose of helping to form the consciences of Catholics while also influencing public opinion. Their authority in assuming these responsibilities was clarified by their second point in response to the Ratzinger inquiry.

Inasmuch as the pastoral letter offers a range of conclusions from very specific to general, based on a variety of moral arguments, the bishops were told that the second draft risked creating confusion about how these moral teachings are to be accepted in both the Catholic community and the public at large. Are they merely presented for policy debate or are they meant to bind in conscience? They answered this question by distinguishing three different levels of moral teaching, each with its own claim to authority: (1) universally binding moral principles, based presumably on natural law, which are matters of conscience for both the community of faith and the public at large; (2) statements of recent popes and the teachings of Vatican II, which provide an authoritative interpretation of "the signs of the times" that is binding in conscience only within the community of faith; (3) prudential moral judgments applying both of these to specific cases, about which there is room for debate and informed dissent within both the community of faith and the public at large. When the bishops teach at the first level, they engage all reasonable, morally serious persons in argument; their interpretations of this common law of conscience, however, must be taken seriously by all persons even though it is binding only upon Catholics. At the second level, of course, the bishops do bind the faithful in conscience as a matter of "doctrine" and not, in the words of the memorandum on the Ratzinger meeting, of "debate." At the third level, Catholics are obliged to take the bishops "prudential judgments" seriously in forming their consciences, but they have a right to dissent from these when their own competence and/or familiarity with the issue in question indicates that the bishops' judgments are either misinformed or imprudent. The third and final drafts of the pastoral letter not only present these distinctions systematically[7] but also appeal to them at key points in making their specific policy recommendations.[8] It would seem that the mixed style of moral discourse called for in this tradition of pastoral letters will be greatly enhanced if these distinctions are made explicit in any future policy recommendations as well.

I draw two conclusions from these procedural guidelines regarding the shape of Catholic approach to welfare policy. First, given the bishops' awareness of their complex role as "moral teachers" of a particular community of faith within a pluralistic society, their discussion of welfare policy should address two distinct but interrelated situations: 1) public assistance programs funded by and administered in the name of the civic community as a whole, and 2) the programs of welfare and human services provided by the Catholic community through its own system of private institutions. The point is that the full agenda of Catholic social teaching should be more apparent, presumably, in the Campaign for Human Development than in the U.S. Department of Health and Human Services. Whatever policy recommendations are proposed to the public at large should be seen as already being tested, revised, and implemented in the programs of our own private institutions. Especially should a new sense of the distinctively Catholic agenda in welfare policy — perhaps a spelling out of what Cardinal Joseph Bernadin referred to as a "comprehensive and consistent ethics of life"[9] — emerge in this pastoral letter; it would be appropriate to call for a systematic evaluation of the policies and practices of Catholic institutions to determine the extent to which these could provide a model for implementing the new agenda. The same would have to be true for the other areas of economic policy discussed in a pastoral letter. If, for example, Catholic social teaching advocates the worker's right to a family living wage and his or her right of association in labor unions, these rights must first of all be fulfilled in the policies and practices of Catholic institutions.

The reason for this rule is not simply that the logic of moral discourse obliges us to practice what we preach. Over and above that, it is that the system of Catholic institutions is sufficiently large and complex to provide the Church with a unique opportunity to test the policies that it advocates on religious and ethical grounds. These institutions should be structured in such a way that they can respond more flexibly to the priorities established in Catholic social teaching, that they can conduct a variety of social experiments to test the feasibility of these priorities, and thus generally provide a sense that alternatives are possible, and worth pursuing. For the new awareness of our situation within a pluralistic society should open up a new appreciation of the distinctiveness of the Catholic social agenda. If the community of faith sees itself as making "specific contributions . . . to the wider work . . . pursued by other groups and institutions in society," the institutions of this community should be the primary place where these specific contributions take shape in policies and practices.

The second procedural conclusion regards the practical implications of the threefold distinction of levels of authority in moral teaching. It is obvious that the moral questions raised in any attempt to evaluate the basic structures of the American economy are just as complex as those raised in the recent assessment of nuclear weapons policy. If anything, they may be even more complex theoretically; for there is relatively less consensus among ethicists about the appropriate paradigm of social and economic justice than there is about the traditions of just war theory and Christian pacifism. I believe that this is just as true today among Catholic theologians and ethicists as it is among the moralists who address themselves to the public at large. Despite this relative lack of consensus the bishops must not hesitate to exercise their responsibilities as "moral teachers." They must not hesitate to make "prudential judgments". Responsibility in public discourse demands only that they be as explicit as they can about the degree of consensus they seek about their specific moral judgments and the various warrants for them. In short, the final draft of the envisioned pastoral letter will probably have to be even more carefully argued than the letter on nuclear weapons policy.

Given the way in which consensus on matters of policy usually is achieved in the Catholic community, I suspect that the interpretation of the recent papal encyclical, *Laborem Exercens*, will be central to the pastoral letter as a whole and in its parts. It will cast light in both directions in the threefold process of moral reasoning outlined by the bishops. It will provide a hermeneutic key for interpreting and judging among the various competing paradigms of "universally binding moral principles" of social and economic justice. It will perform a similar function by providing an authoritative guide to "the signs of the times," so necessary for describing and evaluating the situations calling for "prudential judgments."[10] In what follows, whether I am able to make it always explicit or not, I will be assuming this encyclical as the fundamental hermeneutic presupposition in all three areas of moral reasoning.

Moral Principles: John A. Ryan's Contribution

Let us turn, then, to the search for "universally binding moral principles" for guiding the formation of welfare policy. A good place to begin is with our basic moral intuitions concerning what Frances Fox Piven and Richard Cloward have called "the ancient right of the poor to subsistence."[11] By this they mean "the complex rights to the forests and the commons and the local food supply that had guaranteed people resources for subsistence." Concretely they are thinking of the actual conditions of the peasantry of medieval Europe, which according to Catholic teaching included priority of "common use" over private property rights. Piven and Cloward argue that this system and the ethos that supported it were destroyed at the time of the Industrial Revolution through political changes that forced the creation of the modern wage labor system. Welfare rights, in short, are merely the renewed claim to this ancient right of subsistence within the context of the actual dynamics of the modern labor market system. Virtually all social philosophies this side of libertarianism in one way or another recognize some version of the moral claim at stake in this ancient right. Whether they speak, as John Rawls does, of a "social minimum,"[12] or as Milton and Rose Friedman do, of a "negative income tax,"[13] their proposals presuppose the validity of this claim.

In our pluralistic culture, however, it is not surprising that these and other authors differ greatly over precisely what policies are entailed by this claim, as well as the principles warranting this claim in the first place. Piven and Cloward are more interested in defending this "ancient right" than in explaining its moral basis. Others acknowledge the moral intuition at stake in the claim but are unsure whether the claim is really grounded in human rights, or is merely socially useful or possibly fair and just. Given our hermeneutic presuppositions, John

A. Ryan's classic, *Distributive Justice*, seems the appropriate place to look for the principles that are at stake in the claims to "'subsistence."

While it is clear that Ryan's world as yet does not include the idea of a permanent "underclass" requiring the maintenance of a welfare system, his principles of distributive justice are just as relevant to this new development as they are to the struggle between labor and capital to which he addressed himself. At the heart of his policy recommendations is a set of five "cannons of distributive justice" to which he adds a sixth canon, "the canon of human welfare," by which to adjudicate the inevitably conflicting priorities among the five.[14] The canons are as follows:

(1) *The Canon of Equality*: Ryan describes this as the "rule of arithmetical equality" in the sense that it would entitle everyone who contributes to the product to receive the same amount of remuneration.[15] He rejects it as unjust, for it treats unequals equally and would deter the more efficient from putting forth their best effort.

(2) *The Canon of Needs*: This rule "would require each person to be rewarded in accordance with his capacity to use goods reasonably." Ryan finds this inadequate for it fails to take account of the relationship between distribution and production. Furthermore, "men's needs vary so widely and so imperceptibly that no human authority could use them as the basis of even an approximately accurate distribution."[16]

(3) *The Canon of Efforts and Sacrifices*: Ryan conceives of this rule largely but not exclusively in physical terms, by referring to the "painful exertions" of laborers. He rejects it as a sufficient basis for compensation because "human welfare" demands that "needs and capacities for self-development" as well as "comparative productivity" must be taken into account.[17]

(4) *The Canon of Productivity*: This category, which rewards on the basis of contribution, also is inadequate to the extent that it "ignores the moral claims of needs and efforts." Nevertheless, Ryan insists that "superior productivity" must be taken into account, especially if it is the result of "larger effort and expense put forth in study and in other forms of industrial preparation." He is less enthusiastic about the claims of those whose productivity "is due merely to higher native qualities" and not to "personal responsibility, will-effort, or creativeness."[18]

(5) *The Canon of Scarcity*: Here the market system of supply and demand rules to the exclusion of all other criteria. Ryan would be willing to acknowledge the rough justice of this principle were it not for the

fact that much scarcity is "the result of unequal opportunities." Were opportunities unrestricted, scarcity would be determined by "varying costs of training, varying degrees of danger and unattractiveness among occupations, and inequalities in the distribution of native ability." In such situations competition would tend to distribute rewards on the basis of "efforts, sacrifices, and efficiency."[19]

(6) *The Canon of Human Welfare*: The fact that each of the five canons is inadequate in some ways does not mean that they are to be repudiated either singly or collectively. They are to be subsumed into a sixth canon, the canon of human welfare, which "requires that all human beings be treated as persons, as possessed of natural rights . . . that all industrial persons receive at least that amount of income which is necessary for decent living and reasonable self-development . . . that some consideration must be accorded to manifestations of good will by those who take part in the proceses of industry," and that "reasonable recognition" be given to the claims of productivity and scarcity. There is a set of priorities implicit in this list of canons: "When the natural rights and the essential needs of the individual have been safeguarded, all additional compensation should be determined by the rule of maximum net results, or whatever is necessary to evoke from a producer his maximum *net* product."[20]

The policy implications of the canon of human welfare may be readily grasped from Ryan's doctrine of the living wage. "Every man," he says, "who is willing to work has, therefore, an inborn right to sustenance from the earth on reasonable terms or conditions." He goes on to describe a "*decent* livelihood" in terms that may remind us of Socrates' ill-used "city of pigs":

> [H]e has a right to so much of the requisites of sustenance as will enable him to live in a manner worthy of a human being. The elements of decent livelihood may be summarily described as: Food, clothing, and housing sufficient in quantity and quality to maintain the worker in normal health, in elementary comfort, and in an environment suitable to the protection of morality and religion; sufficient provision for the future to bring elementary contentment, and security against sickness, accident, and invalidity; and sufficient opportunities of recreation, social intercourse, education, and church membership to conserve health and strength and to render possible the exercise of the higher faculties.[21]

When asked for the basis for this right, Ryan justifies it "on the same ground that validates his right to life, marriage, or any of the other

fundamental goods of human existence. On the dignity of personality."
If the killing of the innocent is wrong, he argues, so is the unjust
deprivation of the "minimum conditions" of personal development,
that is, "the quantity of goods and opportunities which fair-minded
men would regard as indispensable to humane, efficient, and reasonable
life." Lest we assume that there is something narrowly Catholic about
this right to a decent livelihood, Ryan notes that his summary description of these minimum conditions "would probably be accepted by
all men who really believe in the intrinsic worth of personality."[22]

Ryan's canon of human welfare and the right to a decent livelihood,
however, are only obliquely related to the "ancient right of the poor
to subsistence" that Piven and Cloward invoke to justify expanded programs of public assistance. For one thing Ryan explicitly states that
"in our present industrial system, the employer is society's paymaster."[23]
In other words, the moral obligation to fulfill this basic human right
falls directly upon business and not upon government. Were the state
to become "society's paymaster," the obligation would then fall upon
it. Secondly, Ryan's "decent livelihood" is more than mere subsistence.
It is a "living wage." The obligation is not met simply by transfer
payments but by the provision of sufficient employment opportunities
on reasonable terms. The key, of course, is the notion of human dignity
at the heart of Ryan's ideal of personal development. Meaningful
employment, in short, is an indispensable precondition of human
welfare.

Three basic ethical principles determine Ryan's labor-oriented approach to human welfare:

(1) "God created the earth for the sustenance of *all* His children;
therefore, all persons are equal in their inherent claims upon the bounty
of nature."[24]

(2) "The inherent right of access to the earth is conditioned upon,
and becomes actually valid through, the expenditure of useful labor."[25]
Important for our purposes is Ryan's discussion of exceptions to the
general rule that "if a man will not work neither shall he eat." Of these,
the very young and the infirm "have claims to a livelihood through
piety and charity", while "the possessors of a sufficient amount of property" have "at least a presumptive claim of justice to rent and interest,
and a certain claim of justice to the money value of their goods."[26]
The elderly, remember, will have been able to make "sufficient provision for the future" out of the savings made possible by a "decent
livelihood." As for those unable to work Ryan insists that all of us are

under a serious moral obligation, based on justice as well as charity, to distribute our "superfluous goods" to the needy. He envisions the needy neither as beggars dependent upon the occasional charitable dispositions of the wealthy nor as wards of the State; rather, they are the clients of a vast network of "religious and benevolent institutions and enterprises."[27] These private institutions, in his view, constitute "the best objects of effective distribution." Nevertheless, it is clear from the less than systematic treatment given to these "exceptions" that Ryan's primary focus remains on what justice demands for useful labor.

(3) Consequently, the practical corollary to the first two principles takes the form of a demand for meaningful employment: "The men who are in present control of the opportunities of the earth are obliged to permit reasonable access to these opportunities by persons who are willing to work."[28] This demand goes beyond what is currently referred to as equality of opportunity. The point is not just that businesses must be fair in their personnel policies but that the owners and managers within the present system must organize their resources so that "non-owners will not find it unreasonably difficult to get a livelihood." At the very least, it seems, Ryan is pointing in the direction of full employment and a fair minimum wage.

There is one other dimension to the doctrine of the living wage that is of crucial importance here. Given the ideal of personal development, Ryan goes on to define a decent livelihood concretely as a "family living wage." Since "family life is among the essential needs of a normal and reasonable existence," a living wage must be sufficient to allow "the average adult male" to make "provision for his family."[29] Ryan thus recommends a "family allowance system" according to which "married male wage earners are remunerated in proportion to the number of their children." Here, too, Ryan conceives of this as some sort of private social insurance system, and not as a form of government-administered public assistance program. Lest Ryan's notion of a "family living wage" be dismissed as sexist, the following observation made in the spirit of equity is worth quoting:

> In view of the very large number of women wage earners who have to support dependents, they ought to be included in any family allowance system. The objections drawn from the integrity of the family, the normal place of the mother, and the responsibility of the father, seem insufficient to outweigh the actual human needs of so many thousands of working women and their children. At any rate, it is not probable

that the number of husbands who desert or die would be materially increased through this arrangement.[30]

Although Ryan's principles of distributive justice were worked out in a context that did not yet know the modern Welfare State, it should not be too difficult to derive the outlines of an approach to welfare policy from them. At this point I will make but two observations: First, even allowing for the different circumstances in which Ryan wrote, I am convinced that for him the question of public welfare would have to be regarded as an anomaly. The remarks that I have quoted about the exceptions to the principle of the necessity of labor and the moral obligations of business to provide meaningful employment opportunities suggest that the question of public welfare could only arise if the market system proved itself generally unable to implement the proposal for a family living wage, for either moral or technical reasons. Public welfare is at best redundant, and at worst usurpatious, when private corporations and private benevolent institutions are capable of institutionalizing "the canon of human welfare" without further ado. Had Ryan lived to see the full flowering of the New Deal after World War II and its apotheosis in the Great Society programs of the 1960's, he may have concluded, as so many have, that as a matter of historical fact the Great Depression demonstrated the massive moral and technical failure of the market system. Only in light of that historical presupposition would the moral necessity of the Welfare State override the Catholic principle of subsidiarity tacitly operative in Ryan's doctrine of the family living wage. Second, assuming the moral legitimacy of the Welfare State provisionally, I see no reason not to think that Ryan's basic conception of a "decent livelihood" would govern his evaluation of the policies and programs of the Welfare State. The two basic values operative in the conception, namely the dignity of labor and the integrity of the family, would be used to assess the moral validity of these policies and programs. They would be criticized as morally dubious, in short, to the extent that they tended to undermine either or both of these basic values.

John Rawls's Contribution

I want to turn to John Rawls's recent work, A Theory of Justice. Can he do any better than Ryan in providing us with a coherent set of universal moral principles for judging welfare policy?

The problems with Ryan's formulations arise typically in any attempt to develop "universally binding moral principles" within a particular historical tradition. Those familiar with the fundamentals of Catholic social teaching and its distinctiveness vis-à-vis other social philosphies no doubt will be impressed by the irrepressibly Catholic quality of Ryan's thought. True enough, throughout his argument it is clear that he intends to formulate a position that would be persuasive to all morally serious persons without the aid of any religious authority; nevertheless, in a pluralistic society it would not be surprising if many morally serious persons were to question Ryan's success in making good on that intention. The problem of universality seems implicit in any attempt to give even a basic description of "the elements of a decent livelihood." As Frederick Olafson reminds us, such descriptions involve us in "the problem of achieving evaluative objectivity in history."[31] In Olafson's terms Ryan can be understood as making the "classic move" of defining the "telos" or "the supremely worthwhile goal which alone qualifies for this status." Most obviously, the policy of a family living wage presupposes a normative model of family life that Ryan did not question as "supremely worthwhile." This classic move may be met, as Olafson remarks, with an "equally classic riposte": "There are other goals that rank as high or higher than the one thus established; and in the absence of any generally accepted decision-procedure for determining which of these goals is the truly authoritative one the whole matter . . . is consigned to the status of . . . unarbitrable opinion."[32] In other words, since the culture of pluralism seems to be incapable of transcending moral relativism, policy questions cannot be resolved in principle but only in the pragmatic processes of special interest politics. To be specific, Ryan's principles may be plausibly universal in some sectors of the American Catholic community; but in the absence of consensus within the civic community as a whole, Catholics must be prepared to sacrifice matters of principle for some sort of piecemeal compromise. Neither Ryan nor Olafson would be very happy, however, with this result.

Is there any way out of the impasse of moral relativism at the level of "universally binding moral principles?" Olafson, in light of his reading of Kant, Hegel, and Habermas,[33] suggests a partial answer. "It is just this sequence of moves that is avoided by the writers discussed above . . . because it has been internalized and . . . in effect [lifted] . . . to a new level." What Olafson has in mind is a reinter-pretation of value conflicts that redefines the "supremely worthwhile goal" itself "in such a way as to make the resolution of these conflicts a necessary condition for qualifying some postulated goal as the com-mon telos of mankind's development."[34] This, I would contend, is precisely what is at stake in John Rawls's A *Theory of Justice* and thus why it deserves serious consideration in any attempt to retrieve the prin-ciples defended in the tradition of Catholic social teaching.

Rawls's two principles of justice for institutions are probably already familiar:

> *First principle*: Each person is to have an equal right to the most ex-tensive total system of basic liberties compatible with a similar system of liberty for all.
> *Second principle*: Social and economic equalities are to be arranged so that they are both:
> (a) to the greatest benefit of the least advantaged, consistent with the just savings principle, and
> (b) attached to offices and positions open to all under conditions of fair equality of opportunity.[35]

After working out priority rules for interpreting these two principles, rules which establish a lexical ordering between the principles and the priority of fair equality of opportunity (2b) over "the difference prin-ciple" (2a), Rawls offers this statement of his general conception:

> All social primary goods — liberty and opportunity, income and wealth, and the bases of self-respect — are to be distributed equally unless an unequal distribution of any or all of these goods is to the advantage of the least favored.[36]

While it is heartening that Rawls and Ryan appear to agree on many points, the mere fact of that agreement is not what Olafson had in mind when he called for lifting the discussion to a new level.

Rawls's theory, in short, is less interesting for its conclusions than for the "decision-procedure" it proposes for arriving at these conclu-sions. This procedure, according to Rawls, depends neither on our un-tutored moral intuitions nor on the classics of any particular religious and moral traditions, but on a hypothetical situation in which rationally self-interested persons must decide the overall shape of the society in which they are to live. This hypothetical situation, of course, is Rawls's "original position."[37] It is characterized by general knowledge about the conditions that obtain in the world, but also by a "veil of ignorance" hiding the particular facts about their individual circumstances there.[38] Given this situation of choice, Rawls claims that the "maximin" rule is appropriate, that is, that rationally self-interested persons under uncertainty will "rank alternatives by their worst possible outcomes . . . and adopt the alternative the worst outcome of which is superior to the worst outcomes of the others."[39] To be concrete, Rawls argues that you and I, being ignorant about our particular sex, race, religious loyalty, and socio-economic status as well as our particular talents and dispositions, yet possessing general knowledge about the world and its vicissitudes, will choose that set of principles that will leave us least worse off regardless of however advantaged or disadvanted we might turn out to be. We would regard this set of principles as both fair and maximally in our rational self-interest, and so regarding them we would be willing to bind ourselves and our descendants to live by them faithfully. The burden of proof in Rawls's treatise is to show convincingly that with this procedure we would, in fact, choose his two principles of justice, their lexical ordering, and the policy consequences that follow from them.

Despite the fact that both the procedure and the principles in Rawls's theory remain controversial on various grounds, let us assume that they do take the discussion to the new level that Olafson calls for. Given our purposes here, we can confine ourselves to two questions: (1) What, in comparison with Ryan, does Rawls have to offer by way of principles for evaluating welfare policy? (2) How might Rawls contribute to our clarification of the distinctive perspective of Catholic social teaching in our pluralistic society?

Any serious comparison of Ryan and Rawls apparently must yield mixed results. For when one gets beyond Rawls's "general conception" and into his more detailed remarks on the "background institutions" for distributive justice and their moral justification, one senses an abyss of difference opening up between the two positions. The first hint of the problem occurs when Rawls announces that "the government guarantees a social minimum either by family allowances and special payments for sickness and employment, or more systematically by such devices as a graded income supplement (a so-called negative income tax.)"[40] While there is some overlap here between Rawls's "social minimum" and Ryan's notion of "human welfare," the question is why is this a government function and not primarily a moral obligation of employers and secondarily the concern of private benevolent institutions? Rawls's answer is implicit in his discussion of "the precepts of justice."[41] Here he defends the idea that "income and wages will be just once a (workably) competitive price system is properly organized and embedded in a just basic structure."[42] Indeed, he specifically rejects any other principle of wage justice by pointing out the indeterminacy and/or irrelevance of various "common sense" precepts of distributive justice. His argument easily could be read as a critique of Ryan's six canons of distributive justice. Since justice is an attribute of the social system as a whole, he sees no reason to interfere with the labor market specifically in order to achieve human welfare: "Thus the precept of need is left to the transfer branch [of government]; it does not serve as a precept of wages at all."[43]

In light of this important difference, a closer comparison of Rawls's discussion of "social primary goods" and Ryan's ideal of a "decent livelihood" is in order. Consistent with the procedures of the "original position", Rawls defines these as "things which it is supposed a rational man wants whatever else he wants.[44] His list, as we have seen, includes "liberty and opportunity, income and wealth, and the bases of self-respect." It does not explicitly include a right to meaningful employment, such as Ryan describes it as the concrete basis of a decent livelihood. Rawls's social primary goods, however, are to be distributed equally unless an unequal distribution is to the advantage of the least advantaged group. Two observations may be in order here: First, it is clear why Rawls restricts himself to this "thin" theory of primary goods; he is convinced that any thicker description may dissolve the consensus achieved through the "original position." His "thin" theory implies no disparagement of these other goods; only that they are not what every "man wants whatever else he wants." Thus he assumes nothing about the intrinsic dignity of labor or the normative validity of the father-oriented monogamous family.

Nevertheless, as Frank Michelman has pointed out,[45] there is one ambiguous category in Rawls's list of social primary goods that fairly cries out for thicker description, namely, "the bases of self-respect." To his credit Rawls admits that this is "perhaps the most important primary good."[46] For "without it nothing may seem worth doing, or if some things have value for us, we lack the will to strive for them." All the same Rawls's account of self-respect remains strictly formal: It involves (1) "having a rational plan of life, and in particular one that satisfies the Aristotelian Principle; and (2) finding our person and deeds appreciated and confirmed by others who are likewise esteemed and their association enjoyed."[47] But this "Aristotelian Principle" gives only the faintest echo of Socrates's "city of pigs", for it too is strictly formal: "other things equal, human beings enjoy the exercise of their realized capacities (their innate or trained abilities), and this enjoyment increases the more the capacity is realized, or the greater its complexity."[48] Although Rawls claims the status of a "psychological law" for this Aristotelian Principle, nowhere does he mention the fact that for the majority of persons in our society "the exercise of their realized capacities" occurs through meaningful employment. It is here, in short, at the core of his notion of "self-respect" that I find Rawls to be near and yet so far from Ryan's idea of "human welfare."

In the light of these theoretical differences Rawls's off-hand identification of the "social minimum" and a "negative income tax" should come as no surprise. If justice as fairness can be done to the "legitimate expectations" of the disadvantaged sufficiently through a government administered transfer of wealth, then in a "just basic structure" our collective obligations to the poor and disadvantaged could simply be met through the negative income tax. Michelman, however, has criticized this application of Rawls's "difference principles" because it, in turn, is unfair. People's needs are so particular and so various that a guaranteed income itself may not meet their actual social minimum requirements. The point is not that the minimum levels should be raised but that they cannot be aggregated and averaged in an income guarantee without doing some needy people an injustice. Michelman shows that Rawls's offhand endorsement of the negative income tax can be reconsidered without calling the whole theory of justice into question. He uses that ambiguous category of primary goods, "the bases of self-respect," in order to argue for a "hybrid" program that includes "an array of standard minimum service levels respecting various needs" as well as "a residual minimum income guaranty."[49] Nevertheless, this comprehensive "welfare rights" proposal represents a revision of Rawls's position, not something that Rawls himself was willing to advocate.

In light of these comparisons we turn to our second question, "How might Rawls contribute to our clarification of the distinctive perspective of Catholic social teaching in our pluralistic society?" From Rawls's own perspective Catholic social teaching, despite its internal coherence and practical relevance, must be regarded as "intuition guided by lower-order standards."[50] It remains locked into what Olafson calls "the classic move" insofar as it does not provide a rational "decision-procedure" for resolving the value conflicts between itself and alternative social philosphies. While the Catholic perspective, as outlined by Ryan, may strike many of us as intuitively correct, Rawls's chief contribution may be to challenge us to reformulate these intuitions and common sense principles at the new level of formal "decision-procedures." The procedural argument, rather than the substantive implications of Rawls's own "lower-order" disagreements with Catholic social teaching,[51] should be the focus of response. Is Rawls's "original position" and the other assumptions built into it, the appropriately procedural equivalent to the Catholic intention of formulating "universally binding moral principles" within the tradition of natural law? If it is, can the Catholic principles be shown to be the rational choice in the "original position"? If that procedural move can be validated, can the perspective of Catholic social teaching explain why Rawls failed to make these choices himself?

Without pausing to give my reasons why I simply record my opinion here that the Catholic perspective can be so reformulated. Furthermore, lest this be dismissed as fruitless, let me point out that it is the bishops' sense of their vocation as "moral teachers" in a pluralistic society that requires something like the exercise I have just outlined. If they expect to be taken seriously by the public at large in a pluralistic society that by definition does not share a consensus about the appropriate precepts of distributive justice, they must show the public at large how they could decide to adopt the Catholic social teaching as their own. Whatever his shortcomings, Rawls provides a promising procedure for doing precisely that.

Papal Social Teaching: *Laborem Exercens*

In order to carry this discussion further it is necessary now to proceed to the second level of moral teaching, "the statements of recent Popes and the teachings of Vatican II." For reasons already given I will confine my remarks to the recent encyclical, *Laborem Exercens*. Contrary to those who see the encyclical as a dramatic "shift to the left" in Catholic social teaching, I read it as a timely summary of the tradition that began with *Rerum Novarum*. The encyclical's contribution is not so much in the area of policy as in the area of basic principles.

Equally critical of both Marxist socialism and laissez-faire capitalism, it sketches the theoretical foundation for a critique of "economism" that could lead to the moral reform of either or both. In the context of this discussion it provides a firmer foundation for the moral intuitions about distributive justice that we discovered in Ryan and reinforces our contention that the two fundamental values at stake in any distinctively Catholic approach to welfare policy are the dignity of labor and the integrity of the family.

The critique of "economism" is a most opportune discernment of the "signs of the times." By economism the Pope means the error of "considering human labor solely according to its economic purpose," that is, as a factor of production. Although the Pope does not make this point explicitly, this error has two forms: one possibly benign the other probably malignant. The benign form is the methodological abstraction, *homo economicus*, operative in virtually all forms of modern economic thought; the malignant form is metaphysical materialism, the world-view of those who think that human persons really are nothing more than what the methodological abstraction takes them to be.[52] This basic error has both theoretical and practical consequences. Theoretically it blinds us to a necessary distinction between "work in an objective sense" and "work in a subjective sense." Economism blinds us to the meaning of work in a subjective sense for it reduces human labor to the status of a technology. The subjective sense, by contrast, is fully disclosed by reflecting on "man's" vocation on earth as sharing in the Divine activity of Creation.[53] The point of this theology of work is minimally evident in every person's experience of himself as "a subjective being capable of acting in a planned and rational way, capable of deciding about himself and with a tendency to self-realization."[54] Economism, in theory, is overcome by recognizing that work ultimately falls in the category of human interaction.

The practical consequences of this categorical insight are enormous. The Pope dramatizes them by asserting "a principle that has always been taught by the Church: the principle of the priority of labor over capital."[55] This statement is categorical; it does not mean that the Pope is taking sides in what some prefer to describe as "the class struggle." Instead, as the Pope himself says, it means that "in this process [of production] labor is always the primary efficient cause, while capital, the whole collection of means of production, remain a mere instrument or instrumental cause." This reversal of the priorities implied by most forms of modern economic theory rests on an inclusive vision of "labor" encompassing all forms of productive activity: managers, college professors, homemakers, service personnel, as well as blue collar workers, in this vision are "labor." By the same token "capital" can no longer be regarded as an inanimate object, say, an "investment portfolio," but itself "the historical heritage of human labor:" "The concept of capital includes not only the natural resources placed at man's disposal, but also the whole collection of means by which man appropriates natural resources and transforms them in accordance with his needs (and thus in a sense humanizes them)."[56] In light of this inclusive vision of labor and capital, two perennial issues are clarified: the nature of ownership and the basis of the rights of workers. Both of these are crucial for a Catholic approach to welfare policy.

If capital is "the historical heritage of human labor," the only legitimate basis for private ownership of the means of production is that private ownership fulfills "the right common to all to use the goods of the whole of creation:"

> [The means of production] cannot be possessed against labor, they cannot even be possessed for possession's sake, because the only legitimate title to their possesion — whether in the form of private ownership or in the form of public or collective ownership — is that they should serve labor and thus by serving labor that they should make possible the achievement of the first principle of this order, namely the universal destination of goods and the right to common use of them.[57]

The right of common use, however, does not require the elimination of private ownership, but the "satisfactory socialization" of the means of production. Such socialization requires a reform of either capitalism or socialism or both. Specifically the Pope mentions "associating labor with the ownership of capital, as far as possible, and by producing a wide range of intermediate bodies with economic, social, and cultural purposes." Socialization, in short, means creating relations of production which will allow "each person . . . to consider himself a part owner of the great workbench at which he is working with everyone else" in a manner consistent with the principle of subsidiarity. Nothing more and nothing less.

The basic rights of workers rest on this principle of ownership. If each person, insofar as he is human, has partial title to "the historical heritage of human labor," each person has a right and moral obligation to work. Otherwise the process of co-creation stops and the "historical heritage" cannot be enhanced and bequeathed to our descendants. Given this inclusive view of labor and capital, the Pope calls for a crucially important distinction between the "direct and indirect employer."[58] The "direct" employer is "the person or institution with whom the worker enters directly into a work contract," while "the indirect employer" refers to the basic institutional matrix of society which is responsible for an "ethically correct labor policy." Usually, and in the first place, notes the Pope, the indirect employer is the state.[59] It is not to usurp the role of the direct employer but to regulate it with "a just labor policy." If the basic right is a right to meaningful employment, then a "just labor policy" is obliged to act against unemployment, to provide adequate unemployment benefits, to ensure that direct employers give "just remuneration for work done," to protect the workers' right of association, and to ensure adequate health and safety standards at the "workbench."

Let us consider, then, what the priority of labor over capital means for welfare policy. I find two places where the encyclical addresses our question directly. First, in describing what is entailed by "just remuneration for work done," the Pope reiterates the traditional Catholic position on a family living wage. This can be accomplished in two ways: Either the direct employer provides "a single salary given to the head of the family for his work, sufficient for the needs of the family without the other spouse having to take up gainful employment outside the home;" or the indirect employer takes responsibility for "social measures such as family allowances or grants to mothers devoting themselves exclusively to their families."[60] Second, the Pope's remarks on "the disabled person and work" indicate that such persons should not be excluded from meaningful employment. "The disabled person is one of us and participates fully in the same humanity that we possess. It would be radically unworthy of man and a denial of our common humanity to admit to the life of the community, and thus admit to work, only those who are fully functional."[61] Specifically, the Pope calls for each community to "set up suitable structures for finding or creating jobs for such people both in the usual public or private enterprises, by offering them ordinary or suitably adapted jobs, and in what are called 'protected' enterprises and surroundings."[62] The principle at stake here is that if we recognize the meaning of "work in the subjective sense," we must create "a situation which will make it possible for disabled people to feel that they are not cut off from the working world or dependent upon society. . . . "[63] From these two places I infer that the priority of labor over capital requires us to evaluate welfare policy in terms of the dignity of labor and the integrity of the family.

It is clear, then, that this authoritative interpretation of "the signs of the times" reiterates conclusions already evident in John A. Ryan's universal principles of distributive justice. But does it provide us with a basis for further dialogue with John Rawls in terms of his own formally universal "decision-procedure?" I think that it does in two important ways. Negatively, the critique of economism must be directed against certain tendencies evident throughout Rawls's theory of justice to assume the axiomatic status of *homo economicus* in his conception of the rationally self-interested persons who would choose his principles and the primary goods that all of them would want whatever else they want. I do not believe that economism can be used to overturn the "maximin" rule that governs the actual decisions made in the "original position," for I regard this as a basic rule of prudence, though hardly the only rule. I do find economism, however, in his puzzling reluctance to tamper with the mechanisms of the free market system, thus leaving scope for the "difference principle" primarily, if not exclusively, in the government's "transfer branch."[64] Similarly, economism is probably to be found in his offhand identification of the social minimum was a negative income tax as if some sort of transfer based on an abstract statistical norm were sufficient to do justice to the particular needs of particular persons. Economism, in short, is the patronizing and demeaning assumption that people's basic needs can be met with a handout and not with a job. If we assume the Pope's critique of economism, we must confront this popular fallacy head-on. Positively, I take the Pope's discussion of "work in the subjective sense" to be sufficiently self-evident to call for a concrete revision of Rawls's primary good of "self-respect." What the Pope's phenomenology of work implies is that neither a rational plan of life, nor the mutual recognition that stems from fruitful human association, nor the Aristotelian Principle that is operative in them both, can be implemented—all other things being equal—without meaningful employment. If this is so, then the right to meaningful employment is one of the necessary preconditions of self-respect. It would be included in the primary goods that any rationally self-interested person would choose to distribute equally under the rubric of the "original position." The point, in short, is that the encyclical's argument is suitably theoretical to be developed at the "new level" called for by Olafson and procedurally developed by Rawls. Thus, I conclude that a coherent and relevant approach to welfare policy is implicit in Catholic social teaching, one that is warranted both at the level of "universally binding moral principles" and at the level of the particular community's "authoritative interpretation of 'the signs of the times.' " It remains for us to consider what sorts of "prudential judgments" may be entailed by our reaffirmation of the dignity of labor and the integrity of the family.

The Dignity of Labor and the Integrity of the Family

I approach this ultimate level of ethical analysis with some hesitation because I can neither claim to be nor do I have any desire to become an expert on U.S. welfare policy. I know even less about the actual operations of the various welfare programs sponsored by private benevolent institutions, including the Church. What I know of the welfare problem stems from two years' experience during the mid-1960's as a volunteer staff person in a Welfare Rights Organization affiliated with the movement of that name organized by Dr. George Wiley. That experience, of course, has shaped my reading and reflections over the years; but I do not believe it gives me any privileged perspective on the dilemmas of welfare policy.

Since my days as a social activist, then, it is clear that public expenditures for social welfare programs have increased significantly. Neil Gilbert, whose important recent book, *Capitalism and the Welfare State: Dilemmas of Social Benevolence*, will serve as the "data base" for the judgments I intend to make, reports that between 1960 and 1978 "per capita social welfare expenditures [under all public auspices] climbed from 38% of the poverty index for an urban family of four in 1960 to 107% in 1978."[65] Even after making allowance for the controversial Reagan budget cuts in "income maintenance programs"[66] and for the fact that Gilbert's statistics include expenditures for public education, we must admit that the current level of spending is far in excess of what would be needed to guarantee every family in the country an income at or slightly above the poverty level, were it necessary to do so. Indeed, clearly it would be less expensive to institute even the most generous proposals for a guaranteed annual income or "social minimum" via a "negative income tax" than it would be to continue to finance the Welfare State. The first policy question, then, is why not simply support this form of guaranteed annual income, and then proceed to dismantle the Welfare State?

This proposal, which is essentially what Milton and Rose Friedman advocate, is not a sufficient answer to the problem of poverty because that problem is not reducible to economics. Whatever else it is, poverty is surely the lack of the primary goods mentioned by Rawls. It is spiritual and cultural deprivation, and all the behavioral disabilities implied by these[67] as well as economic disadvantage. In the absence of any attempt to address these other disabilities, the economic panacea of a "negative income tax" may well become the instrument for creating a permanent "underclass." There is an empirical basis for this fear. Among other things Gilbert discusses the Seattle and Denver Income Maintenance Experiments (SIME/DIME) which began in 1970 and 1971 and ran from three to five years. Two disturbing trends were reported in those experiments. First, the guaranteed minimum income seems to have resulted in a 29% reduction in the work effort of low-income workers.[68] Second, the programs seem to have had a significant effect on family stability: "Overall the rate of marital dissolution for experimental families was approximately twice that of control group families."[69] If welfare policy is to be assessed by the twofold criteria of the dignity of labor and the integrity of the family, these results have to place the guaranteed annual income proposals in a highly unfavorable light. Something like a guaranteed income may be a necessary element in a package of just and humane welfare policies, but it alone clearly is not sufficient.

In order to be more constructive it is necessary to add a few key facts about who the people are whose needs are served by welfare programs and what programs there are to serve them. According to studies cited by Ken Auletta, in 1980 there were 29.3 million Americans living in poverty: "19.7 million were white, 8.6 million black, and 3.5 million were Hispanic." Yet of these perhaps only a third may be considered "long-term poor," that is, the 9 million or so who "are poor at least five years out of every seven."[70] In this group, commonly referred to as the "underclass," seventy percent is nonwhite, about half live in female-headed households, about seventy percent are children under the age of eighteen.[71] As Auletta amply documents, these people suffer a variety of behavioral as well as income deficiencies. Besides persons with various physical and mental disabilities, they include approximately 1.2 million "discouraged workers," that is, those who have ceased looking for work since they could not find a job and 2.6 million "hard core unemployed," that is, persons who worked not at all during the past year. What these figures suggest is that the "underclass" is at the core of the welfare problem; they are the neediest of the needy, those most likely to require forms of assistance beyond an income guarantee.

The statistics on "social welfare expenditures under public programs," cited by Gilbert, list seven basic categories of aid: (1) social insurance, which includes social security, medicare, various public pension plans, unemployment, and various workers' compensation plans; (2) public aid, which includes various forms of public assistance, such as aid to dependent children and food stamps; (3) health and medical programs, which includes medicaid, and other public health programs; (4) veterans programs; (5) public education; (6) housing; and (7) other programs, including various OEO and ACTION programs. In 1978 total social welfare expenditure for these seven areas was $394.3 billion or 19.3 percent of U.S. GNP. Of this roughly two-thirds went to social insurance, education, and veterans benefits, or in other words, to social welfare programs not specifically targeted toward the "long-term poor." Approximately $70 billion, or 3.4 percent of the 1978 U.S. G.N.P., went to programs that were directed to this "hard core." While each of these programs would have to be developed in terms of the twofold criteria of Catholic social teaching, the most vexing "prudential judgments" will concern whether or not the circumstances of the "long-term poor" can be improved by these programs or any plausible alternative to them.

In light of the Pope's inclusive vision of "the priority of labor," it is clear that his recommendations concerning disabled persons would be applicable to what we have described here as the "underclass." We must "set suitable structures for finding or creating jobs for such people both in the usual public or private enterprises, by offering them ordinary or suitably adapted jobs, and in what are called 'protected' enterprises and surroundings." Given the Pope's distinction between the "direct" and the "indirect" employers and their moral responsibilities, a welfare program responsive to this recommendation would do everything possible either to ensure employment for heads of households or to make them employable as soon as possible. Jobs, not handouts, are the first priority for welfare reform. Such a program would include income guarantees, but transfer payments to individuals would be made only as a last resort. To be specific, whatever income maintenance programs are established should be designed in such a way that they encourage welfare recipients to work up to the full level of their capacities. It should not be all that difficult for social scientists to design programs in which rational self-interest favors work rather than dependence. Rather than penalizing recipients for work, the system should reward them with bonuses and/or tax credits.[72] For those heads of household whose responsibilities preclude them from seeking or accepting employment outside the home, for example single mothers of small children, the income maintenance program should be designed so that the dignity of homemaking is recognized as a form of meaningful employment for which just compensation is due. In short, what the Pope says about the "disabled" should be understood to apply to all welfare recipients. We must create "a situation which will make it possible for disabled people to feel that they are not cut off from the working world or dependent upon society." But this involves, of course, more than just a change of perceptions on the part of welfare recipients.

If welfare programs are to be reformed so that positive work incentives are provided, then the labor market itself may have to be restructured in ways that will guarantee meaningful employment to those who are willing and able to work. Full employment, once again, must become a national priority. In the context of welfare policy resources must be focused on viable job training programs. The government, or perhaps an alliance of private foundations and other benevolent institutions, should reassess the history of the C.E.T.A. (Comprehensive Employment and Training Act) programs, with an emphasis on what can be learned from those that were successful. While success necessarily must be judged in terms of what percentage of participants actually found meaningful employment, the standards of success should be realistically geared to the actual situation of the "underclass." I believe that the possibilities for such programs have yet to be pursued as they might be. Given the often adversarial situation obtaining between business and government, the churches and other private benevolent institutions should focus more of their own resources on coordinating training programs with the actual needs of employers. They can provide a climate of collaboration and mutual understanding that is usually missing in the routine relationships between government bureaucrats and business executives. Here too it should not be all that difficult for social scientists to design positive incentives, say in the form of tax credits and/or other subsidies, to encourage businesses to work for rather than against full employment. If the opportunities are there, and if the appropriate training is there, and if the income maintenance programs are designed to encourage employment, there is no reason to think that the "underclass" need be permanent. Not to resign ourselves to that fate is the biggest challenge facing our attempt to implement the norm of the dignity of labor.

The integrity of the family also implies a far-reaching reform of current welfare programs. The values honored by the Catholic tradition are well-known in this area, but they may be more dificult to apply to policy in pluralistic society. In upholding the integrity of the family Catholic social teaching concretely has had in mind the ideal of a permanent, monogamous, male-dominant marriage. Give the increasingly accepted pluralism of "life-styles" in our society and the intense controversy over sexism within both the Catholic community and the public at large, how can this traditional norm still be used to guide policy questions? The statistic previously reported on the SIME/DIME programs, for example, can be interpreted in at least two ways: Either the welfare programs are encouraging marital dissolution, or they are simply providing suffering people, mainly women, with the opportunity to liberate themselves from an oppressive union that should not be called a marriage anyway. In the current state of controversy family stability can be both a problem and a solution. In such a situation prudence would seem to dictate policies that do nothing to encourage marital breakdown, but not policies which enjoin a particular community's ideal upon the public at large. To be specific: Any income maintenance program that has the effect of breaking up stable family units, for example, aid to dependent children programs which often are contingent upon the father's absence from the home, should be sharply repudiated; on the other hand family assistance programs which would have the effect of discriminating against single-parent families are also problematic. If the one sins against dignity, the other surely sins against compassion. Between these two extremes there may be many innovations in family policy worth considering. Neil Gilbert's proposals "in support of domesticity" seem to point in the direction of an appropriately non-discriminatory approach for public assistance in a pluralistic society.[73] By the same token, however, the Catholic community should have no hesitation about enjoining its own ideals upon its own institutions. Indeed, as I pointed out earlier, it is precisely as a witness to the particular values of our community's particular traditions that these institutions fulfill their distinctive purpose.

Redeeming the "City of Pigs"

Let me conclude this paper by returning to Socrates and Glaucon and their sharp little dispute over the "city of pigs." Socrates commends to us an ideal in which the inhabitants of this city will find satisfaction in their work, in their families, and in their religious festivals. They will be, he said, "cautious to avoid poverty and war." Like Glaucon, the modern world has found this ideal a little too boring, or a little too confining, or both and has chosen instead to create a "luxurious" and "feverish city", or at least to yearn ardently for it. And, as Socrates promised, we have managed to have our "delicacies" but only by unwittingly contracting the miasma of perpetual war. The plague has become so virulent that it threatens not only to curtail our enjoyment of these delicacies but to make any sort of civic life impossible.

The American bishops have responded to our growing awareness of this plague by summoning the resources of a religious and moral transition that goes back at least as far as Jesus and Socrates. Their attempt to avert the ultimate consequences of war and poverty amounts, perhaps, to one last attempt to redeem the "city of pigs." They know that such a city cannot be regained simply by wishing it; instead, fully aware of the complex necessities of life in a "luxurious" and "feverish city," they have sketched out a path by which the thing might slowly but surely be turned around. Just as war cannot be wished away by unilaterally renouncing the necessity of deterrence, so poverty cannot be made to vanish by dismantling the Welfare State. Although both ultimately must be understood as the expediencies of a "luxurious" and "feverish city," both must be slowly and carefully transformed in our attempt to rebuild the old city.

If this parable is relevant, and if the analogy I draw from it is valid, then there is a coherent direction for welfare policy implicit in it. If deterrence can be given a "strictly conditioned moral acceptance" insofar as it provides us with the time and the space in which to work for disarmament and world peace, so the programs of the Welfare State deserve a similarly "strictly conditioned moral acceptance." Criticized and transformed in light of our true priorities—the dignity of labor and the integrity of the family—such policies may give us the time and the space necessary to work for the economic justice which ultimately contributes to peace. From the perspective of the "city of pigs," of course, both deterrence and welfare are curious anomalies. But then, the "city of pigs" remains the place where people are "cautious to avoid poverty and war."

Notes

1. Plato, *Plato's Republic*, translated by G. M. A. Grube. (Indianapolis, Indiana: Hackett Publishing Company, 1974), p. 42.

2. *Ibid.*, pp. 42-3

3. One could argue that Plato's "republic" contains such, insofar as the State in Book V usurps the role of the family in the education of children. But there is little evidence to support the thesis that Plato's "republic" is the same as Socrates' own model city. Nor can we be sure that the *Republic* as a whole is meant to be taken seriously as a model for the social order.

4. John A. Ryan, *Distributive Justice, Third Edition* (New York: The Macmillan Company, 1942), p. 330.

5. *Ibid.*, pp. 331-2.

6. Jan Schotte, "A Vatican Synthesis: Rome Consultation on Peace and Disarmament," *Origns: N. C. Documentary Service*, 12, No. 43 (April 7, 1983), p. 692.

7. N.C.C.B., "The Challenge of Peace: God's Promise and Our Response." In *National Catholic Reporter*, June 17, 1983, p. 7.

8. *Ibid.*, pp. 17-20.

9. Barbara Brotman, "Cardinal hits nuclear war, death penalty." *The Chicago Tribune*, December 7, 1983, p. 1.

10. On the interrelationship between interpreting the signs of the times and making moral judgments, see James M. Gustafson, *Can Ethics be Christian?* Chicago: University of Chicago Press, 1975. Chapter five, "Theological Interpretation of the Significance of Circumstances," has been especially influential in my own thinking.

11. Frances F. Piven and Richard A. Coward, *The New Class War: Reagan's Attack on the Welfare State and its Consequences* (New York: Pantheon Books, 1982), p. 50.

12. John Rawls, *A Theory of Justice* (Cambridge: Harvard University Press, 1971), p.275.

13. Milton and Rose Friedman, *Free to Choose* (New York: Avon Books, 1980), pp. 110-17.

14. Ryan, *op. cit.*, pp. 180-8.

15. *Ibid.*, p. 180.

16. *Ibid.*, p. 182.

17. *Ibid.*, pp. 182-3.

18. *Ibid.*, p. 184.

19. *Ibid.*, p. 187.

20. *Ibid.*, p. 188.

21. *Ibid.*, p. 273.

22. *Ibid.*, p. 274.

23. *Ibid.*, p. 275.

24. *Ibid.*, p. 270. Lest this be dismissed as a particular theological judgment, Ryan argues that the "second part of the proposition" can be acknowledged by anyone who understands "the personal dignity of the individual, and the equal dignity of all persons."

25. *Ibid.*, p. 271. This second principle, of course, is the most explicit point of connection between Ryan's universal principles and the authoritative interpretation outlined in Pope John Paul's encyclical, *Laborem Exercens*.

26. *Ibid.*

27. *Ibid.*, p. 241.

28. *Ibid.*, p. 272.

29. *Ibid.*, p. 283.

30. *Ibid.*, p. 285.

31. Fredrick A. Olafson, *The Dialectic of Action: A Philosophical Interpretation of History and the Humanities* (Chicago: University of Chicago Press, 1979), P. 247.

32. *Ibid.*

33. My own assesment of the importance of Habermas's work for theology and ethics is available in an essay, "Habermas and the Theologians," *Religious Studies Review*, 7, No. 1 (January, 1981), pp. 14-21.

34. Olafson, *op. cit.*, p. 247.

35. Rawls, *op. cit.*, p. 302.

36. *Ibid.*

37. *Ibid.*, pp. 17-21.

38. *Ibid.*, pp. 136-142.

39. *Ibid.*, pp. 152-3.

40. *Ibid.*, p. 275.
41. *Ibid.*, pp. 303-310.
42. *Ibid.*, p. 304.
43. *Ibid.*, p. 309.
44. *Ibid.*, p. 92.
45. Frank I. Michelman "Constitutional Welfare Rights and *A Theory of Justice," Reading Rawls: Critical Studies of A Theory of Justice.* ed. Norman Daniels (New York: Basic Books, 1974), pp. 319-347.
46. Rawls, *op. cit.*, p. 440.
47. *Ibid.*
48. *Ibid.*, p. 426.
49. Michelman, *op. cit.*, p. 333.
50. Rawls, *op. cit.*, p. 318.
51. This response to Rawls is different from the substantive dialogue carried out in David Hollenbach, *Claims in Conflict: Retrieving and Renewing the Catholic Human Rights Tradition* (New York, The Paulist Press, 1979), pp. 16-20. Because Hollenbach fails to see the significance of the procedural issues in Rawls, he is not as optimistic as I am about the possibilities of dialogue.
52. Pope John Paul II, "Laborem Exercens," in Gregory Baum, *The Priority of Labor.* (New York: The Paulist Press, 1982), p. 120. See also John W. Houck and Oliver F. Williams (ed), *Co-Creation and Capitalism: John Paul's Laborem Exercens* (Washington, D.C.: University Press of America, 1983).
53. *Ibid.*, pp. 100-2, 142-4.
54. *Ibid.*, p. 104.
55. *Ibid.*, p. 117.
56. *Ibid.*, p. 118.
57. *Ibid.*, p. 122.
58. *Ibid.*, pp. 127-9.
59. *Ibid.*, p. 128.
60. *Ibid.*, p. 130.
61. *Ibid.*, p. 139.
62. *Ibid*
63. *Ibid.*, p. 140.
64. Rawls, *op. cit.*, p. 276.
65. Neil Gilbert, *Capitalism and the Welfare State: Dilemmas of Benevolence* (New Haven: Yale University Press, 1983), p. 140.
66. Piven and Cloward, *op. cit.*, pp. 16-19.
67. cf. Ken Auletta, *The Underclass* (New York: Random/Vintage Books, 1982), pp. 3-19f.
68. Gilbert, *op. cit.*, p. 39.
69. *Ibid.*, p. 99.

70. Auletta, *op. cit.*, p. 27.

71. *Ibid.*

72. cf. Charles L. Schultze, *The Public Use of Private Interest.* (Washington, D. C.: The Brookings Institution), 1977.

73. Gilbert, *op. cit.*, p. 108-114.

Part III

U.S. Trade with Developing Countries

JOHN W. HOUCK

The growing sympathy in the Catholic Church for the plight of people in developing countries could lead to recommendations for lower tariffs to spur exports rather than protectionism . . .

Business Week,
December 19, 1984

"The key is to begin to look seriously at the global economy in the same way we look at domestic economy . . . As Christians I think that is our moral obligation . . ."

South Bend Tribune,
December 15, 1983

The bishops may not have too many specific proposals for international economic policies, but they will, hopefully, contribute a most important perspective — that meeting the needs of the poor takes priority . . .

Horizons,
Spring, 1984

WORLDWIDE TRADE AND ECONOMIC DEVELOPMENT IS, for the Christian, considered in the light of Christ's ministry: "He has sent me to bring good news to the poor, to proclaim liberty to captives and to the blind new sight, to set the downtrodden free" (Luke 4:18). Keeping in mind this image of Christ's service to the poor and the weak, the Christian is disposed to examine the technical issues of trade and economic development with a strong sense of priority. Otherwise how could he or she fulfill the mandate of Psalm 72 that we should have "pity on the poor and feeble, and save the lives of those in need?" It is in this spirit that the religious leader, Theodore M. Hesburgh, C.S.C., adopts the imagery of the spaceship to dramatize the challenge of global injustice:

> To put the case for the poor most simply, imagine our Spaceship Earth with only five people aboard instead of more than 3.5 billion. Imagine that one of those five crew members represents those of us earth passengers who live in the Western world of North American and Europe — one-fifth of humanity on earth, mainly white and Christian. The person representing us has the use and control of 80 percent of the total life-sustaining resources available aboard our spacecraft. The other four crewmen, representing the other four-fifths of humanity — better than 2.5 billion people — have to get along on the 20 percent of the resources that are left, leaving them each about 5 percent to our man's 80 percent. To make it worse, our man is in the process of increasing his portion of these limited resources to 90 percent.[1]

The strength of Father Hesburgh's image is that it reminds us that the individual, whether a person or nation, is part of a larger social community. In the religious tradition individual or national self-interest should be subordinated to the common good "so that God's plan" for the passengers on the Spaceship can be realized.[2]

Further we are reminded of the real dangers and injustices stemming from a high-consumption life style. We can be blinded by the material advantages that we have as our "feverish activity" to obtain more pulls us on, while the basic needs of many are not being provided. The times would seem to require that Jews and Christians live lives of restraint and some sacrifice in order to open up possibilities, either by sharing or by leadership, for substantial reforms on board Spaceship Earth.[3]

International Trade: Analysis and Policy

Part III examines the international interdependence of the U.S. economy from three perspectives. C. Fred Bergsten, Director of the

Institute for International Economics, takes up in chapter nine the free trade position, which relies on open markets to increase international wealth and rejects protectionism as a stagnating policy. He points out that if one's ethical concerns are with the poor of the world then the best way to help them is by allowing them to sell to the U.S. This enables the poor to earn the dollars which they can use to buy essentials. But Bergsten acknowledges that a liberal trading system will leave some developing countries in losing positions and advocates (1) another round of multilateral trade liberalization negotiations in the General Agreement on Tariffs and Trade (GATT) to encourage developing-country exports to industrial-country markets, and (2) an expansion of international financial assistance to developing countries by the International Bank for Reconstruction and Development (World Bank) and the International Monetary Fund.

Bergsten recognizes that free trade can impact adversely on U.S. workers and companies who are hurt by cheaper imports, for instance, textiles, steel and shoes. To counter this negative impact, he advocates "explicit government help to workers (and perhaps firms) displaced by the resulting imports, which is better than the traditional Trade Adjustment Assistance in achieving real adjustment." He places a high priority on effective and generous assistance, otherwise the clamor for protectionism will gain further momentum.

The second perspective is presented by Ernest Bartell, C.S.C., a Notre Dame economist, who argues in chapter ten that international capitalistic competition can widen the gap between rich and poor nations: "For a variety of historical and technical reasons the distribution of gains from market activity in international markets for products and services, for labor and capital, is frequently biased against the poor countries of the world and against the poor within those countries." He fears a growing gap between the rich and poor worldwide unless positive policies are adopted quickly; otherwise Less Developed Countries (LDCs) will be locked into long-term "dependency" on the industrial powers *and* massive outlays for service of foreign debt. Bartell calls for creation of global "mediating institutions" along the lines of the United Nations Conference on Trade and Development (UNCTAD) to foster greater economic growth and equality for LDCs.

> For a long time domestic public policy in most countries, capitalist and socialist, has intervened in economic activity to achieve socially acceptable mixes of freedom, equality and growth. The tools are familiar,

ranging from tax and transfer mechanisms and public expenditures for social purposes to public ownership of productive resources and regulation of prices, incomes, and output. The international economy, however, has historically been subject to much less international public intervention of this kind.

In addition, Bartell examines the proposition that through free trade policies industrial countries not only export their products but also their cultural values. He criticizes the impact of "aggressively materialist attitudes" on traditional cultures, where frivolous consumer products are trumpeted as essentials. Therefore, the higher priority, the basic human needs of the poor and the weak, is oftentimes ignored.

Another perspective is developed in chapter eleven by Joe Holland of the Center for Concern. His analysis begins with the priority of labor — in contrast with the Capitalist priority of the market or the Socialist priority of the state. Holland adopts John Paul II's theme in *Laborem Exercens* that the priority of labor is "probably the essential key" to solving the contemporary social question. The solution "must be sought in the direction of 'making life more human,' then the key, namely human work, acquires fundamental and decisive importance." This new priority leads then to the pragmatic test of any social or economic policy: Does it contribute to or obstruct the priority of labor? Holland therefore would want governments to stop subjecting their people to low wages and poor working conditions. Instead they should concentrate on the rights of their laborers in trading policies and find ways to make multinational corporations more accountable for their social and cultural impact on host countries. Holland compares the current "national security" form of capitalism, which extols international competition over human considerations, with alternative models of economic cooperation and development based on the priority of labor.

While advocating a longer term movement away from the mechanistic civilization, Holland details an "interim ethic" which is needed in examining international trade: (1) while trade ought to be free between nations, it must also be fair, that is, relatively equal in government involvement and subsidy; (2) suppression of labor should not be tolerated as a part of competition; (3) governments and corporations must contribute to rebuilding communities injured by competition; (4) the resources of the earth are ultimately to be held in trust for all mankind; and (5) the world is evolving into a system of greater interdependence and cooperation which should be directed toward the common good.

Apart from their separate philosophical approaches to shaping a viable and just world economy, the authors tend to agree that several factors have weakened the international trading position of the LDCs and thus point toward the need for direct investment by multinational corporations (MNCs). (These factors include declining terms of trade, mounting external debt, a downturn in industrial-country growth, and slowed flows of official development assistance; thus LDCs are less able to exploit comparative trade advantages, to realize economies of scale, or to earn the foreign exchange necessary to finance imports). For their part MNCs must weigh complex considerations of profitability, political stability, local labor and resource markets, and so forth. The LDC host countries can gain scarce capital, new technology, managerial know-how, and greater economic viability. In the spirit of mutual benefit to both parties, some of the frustrations about direct aid or trade may yield to guarded optimism about the future.

While much has been said, often negative, about the power of MNCs, not enough has been made of their capacity to liberate humankind from global inefficiencies, obsolete technologies, and myopic nation-state loyalty—with attendent protectionism and belligerency. There is no doubt that MNCs can produce wealth and distribute employment worldwide.[4] But do they see themselves in the wider social and humane context proposed in the Vatican II Pastoral, *Gaudium et Spes*:

> . . . the modern world shows itself at once powerful and weak, capable of the noblest deeds or the foulest. Before it lies the path to freedom or to slavery, to progress or retreat, to brotherhood or hatred.[5]

The Moral Challenge to International Trade

The chairperson and commentator of the panel was Lee A. Tavis, C.R. Smith Professor of Business Administration at Notre Dame and the editor of *Multinational Managers and Poverty in the Third World*.

As we turn to the international segment, we reencounter all of the issues that we have discussed so far. When we talk about the poor and the disadvantaged or unemployment in the United States, we recognize that the alternatives open to the various groups, indeed, to our country itself, are strongly influenced by our position in the world political/economic system, and subject to decisions made in other countries.

Of far greater significance, however, is the fact that the U.S. Catholic Church, as the Catholic Church anywhere in the world, is universal. In Christianity, there is no "we" and "they." We cannot rely on nationalism to weight our objective functions and to make the trade-offs in our national favor. We cannot stand by while vast numbers of people in this world are trapped in abject poverty as were their parents and grandparents before them with no hope of escape. No one would disagree that the welfare of these people is a basic responsibility for us since we are in a position to ameliorate their conditions. Thus, no matter where the discussion takes us, we must continually return to this point of basic agreement.

The Northern and Southern Hemispheres of our world are not only differentiated by a disparity of consumption, but also by massive differences in the sophistication of local institutions and the ability of these institutions to represent their own members. This is also true because they have less competitive and efficient markets. These factors lead to different power balances within Third World countries and important differences in power between the United States and these countries. As Ernest Bartell points out, underdevelopment means that there will be meager economic conditions now, but also a lack of the preconditions for future economic growth.

The basic issue of our concern is how does the international economic system work and toward what ends? What groups will control the allocation of productive resources in this system, and who will determine the distribution of the fruits from this productivity? There are three pressures at work:

1. Free Markets: Efficient markets will represent the best interests of the consumer in those markets.
2. National Planning: Effective governmental regulation will constrain free markets and reallocate resources within the society. Most of this planning is a component of national, not international, planning.
3. Corporate Planning: Within the constraints set by efficient markets and effective governmental regulations, managers make

productivity decisions (committing factors to production) and decisions as to the distribution of the reward from that production. A basic issue with multinational corporations is the strength of constraints imposed by the markets and governments, which, of course, determines the freedom of choice for multinational managers.

Within the matrix of these pressures, a number of key issues have been raised in the three papers:

(1) The Desirability of Liberalizing Trade

Our speakers recognize the comparative advantage argument, at least in theory, that with free trade overall global productivity would be increased. They all recognize that, in today's world, countries do not allow it to work and that they protect their internal markets. And this is an area where management and labor in affected industries stand shoulder to shoulder. One of our speakers would dismantle such protection and move to a liberalization of trade. Joe Holland would argue for an extended, but globally enlightened, control of trade, as an offset to what he sees as the present drive of nation-states to increase their competitive stance through export support as well as import control.

Trade liberalization will lead to job dislocation in the U.S., and we must be concerned with the human as well as community costs of these dislocations. We are trading-off employment, or the availability of jobs for workers in the Third World, many of whom exist at the margin of acceptable human living conditions, against the often temporary but painful dislocation of workers in this country. At issue: Who has the right to work—Third World or U.S. laborers?

(2) The Problems Associated with Commodity Trade from the Third World

Beyond the free trade issue, we have a unique concern for commodity trade. As noted, Third World exports are to us predominately commodities (or primary products) while what we sell to them are predominately manufactured goods. There is a basic difference in the nature of these markets and thus in market power. Primary products are traded in competitive world markets where prices have been very unstable and have declined in recent decades; while markets for sophisticated manufactured products range from highly competitive to very protected. Also, the terms of trade for Third World countries have deteriorated over time. Again, the policy alternatives related to the commodity trade issues are relatively clear. They have been proposed by the United Nations and supported by our speakers. Here, again, is a clear opportunity for the United States to contribute to Third World welfare by working to stabilize these declining prices and market power.

(3) Third World Labor Subsidies To the First World

Our speakers all concentrated on employment in the Third World and the return to those laborers. Noting their low wages relative to the United States, and their productivity, our speakers suggested that these workers were paid less than their marginal product, meaning that the value they add to the product is greater than the remuneration they receive. This excess, then, acrues to someone in the First World. Consumers: If the markets are competitive, consumers will receive the benefits. Capital: The benefit may flow to investors in the form of excess returns. Labor: In the presence of strong U.S. labor unions, this subsidy could flow to them.

(4) Capital Transfer To the Third World

In the 1970s, multinational banks did a remarkable job of recycling petro dollars from surpluses in the Near East to uses in the Third World. Our speakers have commented on the current debt crisis in these countries. There is a historical question whether this debt was legitimately demanded by Third World borrowers or forced on them by international banks. In any case, much of the monies did not flow to productive uses in the Third World countries and thus did not build a basis for servicing the debt. Other major capital flows have moved through direct investment of multinational corporations. By and large, these multinational corporate flows are channeled directly to productive uses within the Third World. There is little question that the movement of this factor of production to the poorer countries has led to increases in their productivity, but these countries have a great distance to go before they can rightly be called "developed."

(5) Cultural Effects of U.S. Trade

In countries trying to develop, the culture reflects the techniques of rising productivity: specialization of labor, vigorous standards and controls, and much mobility of labor. This can be very traumatic for local cultures because the rate of "modernization" can easily be too fast and highly destructive. Yet in Third World countries the need for development too frequently pushes aside these concerns.

Vatican Statements

Pius XI, *Quadragesimo Anno* — 1931

89. Furthermore, since the various nations largely depend on one another in economic matters and need one another's help, they should strive with a united purpose and effort to promote by wisely conceived pacts and institutions a prosperous and happy international co-operation in economic life.[6]

Pius XI, *On Atheistic Communism* — 1937

76. In international trade relations let all means be sedulously employed for the removal of those artificial barriers to economic life which are the effects of distrust and hatred. All must remember that the peoples of the earth form but one family in God.[7]

John XXIII, *Mater et Magistra* — 1961

161. It is clear to everyone that some nations have surpluses in foodstuffs, particularly from farm products, while elsewhere large masses of people experience want and hunger. Now justice and humanity require that these richer countries come to the aid of those in need. Accordingly, to destroy entirely or to waste goods necessary for the lives of men, runs counter to our obligations in justice and humanity.

162. We are quite well aware that to produce surpluses, especially of farm products, in excess of the needs of a country, can occasion harm to various classes of citizens. Nevertheless, it does not therefore

follow that nations with surpluses have no obligation to aid the poor and hungry where some particular emergency arises. Rather, diligent efforts should be made that inconveniences arising from surplus goods be minimized and borne by every citizen on a fair basis.[8]

John XXIII, *Pacem in Terris* — 1963

125. It is vitally important, therefore that the wealthier states, in providing varied forms of assistance to the poorer, should respect the moral heritage and ethnic characteristics peculiar to each, and also that they should avoid any intention of political domination. If this is done, "a precious contribution will be made toward the formation of a world community, a community in which each member, while conscious of its own individual rights and duties, will work in a relationship of equality toward the attainment of the universal common good."[9]

Paul VI, *Populorum Progressio* — 1967

56. The efforts which are being made to assist developing nations on a financial and technical basis, though considerable, would be illusory if their benefits were to be partially nullified as a consequence of the trade relations existing between rich and poor countries. The confidence of these latter would be severely shaken if they had the impression that what was being given them with one hand was being taken away with the other.[10]

John Paul II, *Laborem Exercens* — 1981

The disproportionate distribution of wealth and poverty and the existence of some countries and continents that are developed and of others that are not call for a leveling out and for a search for ways to ensure just development for all. . . ."[11]

American Catholic Bishops' Statement

Development-Dependency: The Role of Multinational Corporations — 1974

Pope Paul VI in his encyclical *Populorum Progressio* praised the process of industrialization as a necessity for economic growth and human development. But he also said that, unfortunately, in industrialized society:

> A system has been constructed which considers profit as the key motive for economic progress, competition as the supreme law of economics and private ownership of the means of production as an absolute right that has no limits and carries no corresponding social obligations. This unchecked liberalism leads to dictatorship rightly denounced by Pius XI as producing "the international imperialism of money." One cannot condemn such abuses too strongly, solemnly recalling once again that the economy is at the service of man.

. . . A growing number of Catholics are beginning to share Pope Paul VI's concern about the emerging power of multinational corporations. Church people, both here and in the Third World, are becoming increasingly aware that many U.S. domestic and international policies are linked together to serve the interests of these transnational business enterprises. The time is at hand for us not only to question the enormous power wielded by so few people and institutions, but in a more fundamental way, to question the underlying motivation behind such unbridled power. For the motivation continually to increase profit emerges from values which promote excessive individualism, unnecessary consumption, and disregard for the quality of human life, all of which are contrary to the deepest values of the Judeo-Christian tradition.

. . . In the Third World, most people have the daily experience of powerlessness in the face of the relative few who own and control most of the wealth and income, land, industry, political and military power. In our country, there is a growing sense among working people as well as minority groups that power belongs only to those few who hold enormous wealth. As Catholics, we must continue to rediscover our own distinct identity as a religious, prophetic people who stand apart from the powers which possess dominant control in society. In such a process, we can learn much from the Church in the Third World. Together in our preaching and actions, we are moved to pronounce God's judgment on the side of powerless life whether of the unborn child, of the elderly without care or security, of the overtaxed citizen, or of the poor in the barrios of Latin America.[12]

Notes

1. Theodore M. Hesburgh, C.S.C., *The Humane Imperative* (New Haven: Conn.: Yale University Press, 1974), p. 101.

2. See Michael Novak's discussion of the validity of the Spaceship Earth imagery in his essay, "Can a Christian Work for a Corporation?" in *The Judeo-Christian Vision and the Modern Corporation*, ed. Oliver F. Williams and John W. Houck (Notre Dame, IN.: University of Notre Dame Press, 1982), pp. 193-194.

3. "The second ethical proposition is that Christian corporate personnel have a duty to struggle endlessly to transform the very structures of corporate life within which they operate." See Denis Goulet's essay, "Goals in Conflict: Corporate Success and Global Justice?" in *Judeo-Christian Vision and the Modern Corporation*, p. 241.

4. John Kenneth Galbraith, "The Defense of the Multinational Company," *Harvard Business Review*, March-April 1978, pp. 83-94.

5. *The Gospel of Peace and Justice: Catholic Social Teaching Since Pope John*, ed. Joseph Gremillion (Maryknoll, N.Y.: Orbis Books, 1976), p. 250.

6. John F. Cronin, *Catholic Social Principles: The Social Teaching of the Catholic Church Applied to American Economic Life* (Milwaukee, Wis.: Bruce Publishing Company, 1950), pp. 526-527.

7. *Ibid.*, p. 527.

8. *The Gospel of Peace and Justice*, pp. 178-179.

9. *Ibid.*, p. 227.

10. *Ibid.*, p. 404.

11. John Paul II, *Laborem Exercens* (On Human Work), *Origins* 11 (Sept. 24, 1981) para. 2.

12. National Conference of Catholic Bishops, *Quest for Justice: A Compendium of Statements of the United States Catholic Bishops on the Political and Social Order 1966-1980*, ed. J. Brian Benestad and Francis J. Butler. (Washington, D.C.: United States Catholic Conference, 1981), p. 105 and p. 112.

Nine

Trade Relations Between The United States and Developing Countries

C. FRED BERGSTEN*

AMERICAN TRADE POLICY TOWARD THE LESS DEVELOPED countries (LDC's)[1] raises profound and complex moral, as well as "purely economic," questions.

It is frequently argued that a liberal U.S. approach toward imports from LDC's, by promoting purchases from those countries rather than from domestic producers, trades off U.S. jobs for LDC jobs. Moreover, many of the lost U.S. jobs are likely to affect low-skilled and relatively poor Americans.

Even at this simplistic level of discourse, two central moral issues immediately emerge. First, should U.S. trade policy concern itself equally with Americans and foreigners? Second, since it is usually admitted that adversely affected American workers are substantially better off in *absolute* terms than the workers in LDC's whose incomes can be augmented (often substantially) by increased sales to the United States, is absolute or relative poverty the key standard against which ethical judgments should be made? If one's focus is cosmopolitan and on absolute levels of income, a policy of virtually free trade is clearly suggested. But at least a measure of protection seems called for if one

*I would like to thank David Johnson for his help in researching and preparing this paper. Helpful comments were received from William Cline, Howard Rosen, Jeffrey Schott and John Williamson of the Institute for International Economics.

concludes that a nation's obligation is primarily to its own citizens and that relative income *within* a country's borders is what counts.

The Issues

These apparent dilemmas can be substantially eased, however, by taking into account a series of "general equilibrium" economic effects. At least four such considerations must be mentioned.

First, liberal U.S. trade policies limit our rate of inflation by adding to the supply of available goods and maintaining competitive pressures on domestic industries. In turn, reduced inflation lessens the need to adopt restrictive macroeconomic policies which create higher levels of unemployment, notably among the poorest (last in, first out) workers. Moreover, there is some evidence that low-income consumers, in particular, benefit from freer trade because their market basket of consumed goods is relatively heavily weighted toward imported products, including those where controls are frequently deployed or threatened, such as apparel and footwear.[2]

Second, the income levels of workers in some import-competing industries which seek protection are by no means located toward the bottom of the U.S. income distribution ladder. Autos and steel, where wages range near the top of the profile, are examples. Hence import controls in some industries may have a regressive income redistribution impact.

Third, restrictive trade policies cost as well as preserve jobs. A reduction in U.S. imports inevitably leads to a reduction in U.S. exports because of the cut in income and foreign exchange earnings abroad.[3] In some cases, U.S. import restrictions produce overt retaliation against our exports. It is also the case that in some industries (such as autos) a substantial number of jobs has been created to distribute and service imported products; indeed, the wage levels of these import-related jobs may be below those of at least some of the workers in the import-competing industries, as just noted.

Fourth, the global debt crisis brings a new dimension and urgency to the issue. Debtor LDC's can resume servicing their external debts in a reasonably stable way only if they are permitted to earn the requisite foreign exchange, primarily via export expansion. The U.S. obviously has a major stake in a successful resolution of the debt crisis, due both to the direct exposure of its banking system and the indirect, but pervasive, consequences for its (and the world's) overall economy.[4]

Hence it is quite likely that the traditional case for open trading policies, which has its roots in moral (e.g., employment and income distibution) norms as well as economic theorems, applies today with regard to U.S. policy toward the LDC's. Several deviations from the assumptions underlying that case must be acknowledged:

1. Consider the substantial overvaluation of the dollar in the exchange markets, now on the order of 20-25% in terms of the underlying trade competitiveness of the United States with a number of other countries.[5] This has the same effect as placing a 20-25% tax on all U.S. exports and paying a subsidy of 20-25% on all imports into the United States, and is the primary reason why the U.S. merchandise trade deficit has already soared to record levels and will probably hit $100-120 billion in 1984. The dollar overvaluation comes primarily against the currencies of other industrial countries so it should have relatively little effect on U.S. trade policy toward the LDC's;[6] however, the existence of such massive trade imbalances obviously adds to the political pressure for restraint against imports from all quarters.

2. Witness the continuing high levels of unemployment. Though sharply reduced in recent months, high unemployment obviously adds to the desire to find additional ways to create jobs, particularly in those industries which are most depressed and most labor-intensive.

3. Consider "unfair trading practices" by other countries. It is frequently alleged, and sometimes demonstrated, that foreign governments are intervening in the trading process by subsidizing their exports and/or restricting American access to their domestic markets.

As with the currency problem, concern with the "unfairness" of such practices exists much more extensively with regard to other industrial countries (especially Japan and, especially with regard to agriculture, Europe) than to LDC's. Nevertheless, though somewhat tempered for now by the exigencies of the debt crisis, there is growing criticism of such practices in at least the more advanced LDC's (such as Brazil). The increased importance of these countries in world trade suggests that, in light of the "policy interdependence" among the important players, they too must make at least a limited and phased contribution to any general move toward further opening of world markets. In addition, of course, the widespread doubts that the United States is competing "on a level playing field" casts a large cloud over trade policy as a whole.

With respect to all three of these issues, economic analysis offers two conclusions. First, each of them can provide a justification for temporary deviation from free trade. In times of high unemployment, one may be able to justify import restraints and export subsidies. In times of currency overvaluation, one may justify an offsetting import surcharge/export subsidy. In times of demonstated (not just alleged) unfairness by foreign trading partners, tit-for-tat responses may be defensible.

Second, however, such trade controls would be decidedly "second best" (or "fourth best") responses to the problems cited. Full employment should obviously be sought through changes in overall macroeconomic policy. Exchange-rate equilibrium should also be sought through changes in macroeconomic policy (i.e., a credible prospect of lower U.S. outyear budget deficits would foster lower interest rates here and thus avoid the huge capital inflows which prop the dollar), direct intervention in the exchange market, improvements in the functioning of the international monetary system itself, and perhaps direct manipulation of capital flows.[7] Foreign barriers should, at least in the first instance, be attacked via multilateral (i.e., GATT) and bilateral negotiation, as they have been, with a large measure of success, throughout the postwar period.

Moreover, the use of trade policy instruments against these very real difficulties would be unlikely to work and would almost certainly make the U.S. situation worse, certainly in the medium and longer run, for the reasons already cited, and perhaps even in the immediate future. As noted, U.S. imposition of new import controls would disrupt U.S. exports as well; the outcome might well be no net gain in American jobs at all, or even a loss, beyond the very shortest run. An import surcharge, in an effort to offset the dollar overvaluation, would under today's regime of flexible exchange rates simply strengthen the dollar further (by reducing the U.S. trade deficit) and soon obviate any trade gain. Even U.S. retribution against objectionable foreign trade policies could simply vindicate such policies and lead to their further escalation, rather than achieve their elimination.

Indeed, *any* major U.S. retreat from its sustained, bipartisan effort of the past fifty years to lead the world toward freer trade would be extremely dangerous at this time. Despite the rapid recovery of our own economy, most of the rest of the world remains mired in stagnation or worse, partly as a result of U.S. economic policy itself.[8] Unemployment continues to grow in Europe. Latin American economic conditions are not much better than in the Great Depression; by some measures, Brazil is in worse shape now than in 1929-31. As noted, the "debt bomb" remains poised over the entire world economy. Any U.S. move to restrict trade from others would thus, even more than usually, be likely to produce retaliation from abroad and risk a total unraveling of the trading system as in the 1930s, with incalculable consequences for overall international relations as well as the economies of virtually all nations.

Even if one decisively rejects protectionism, however, the question remains as to whether additional liberalization should be sought. Two issues are central to the response. The first, with regard to the LDC's, is that there clearly remain large gains for trade, including for consumers in the United States and other industrial countries, to be exploited from further liberalization.[9] The other is that, given the less buoyant world economy now expected by most observers for the foreseeable future, such liberalization becomes critical for them to experience substantial export growth since economic growth in the industrial world alone will not be providing nearly as much opportunity as it did in the 1960s and 1970s. And, as noted above, the LDC's (and all of us) can escape the debt crisis, and thereby resume at least a modicum of economic development, only if they can expand their export earnings sharply and on a sustained basis.

Moreover, the history of trade policy reveals that steady progress toward liberalization is an essential component of any successful strategy to avoid protectionism. This "bicycle theory" posits that trade policy, like a bicycle, is dynamically unstable: it must either move forward steadily toward opening markets further, in the overall economic interest of all countries, or it will topple in the face of pressures for relief from particular sectors in individual countries.[10]

The practical issue for policy, then, is *how* to renew the process of liberalization, at least for the LDC's, in the face of the formidable hurdles outlined above. The prospects for achieving such a "positive sum" trade policy, of benefit to both the United States and the

LDC's, would certainly be enhanced by macroeconomic policies which achieved full employment—specific measures to restore currency equilibrium and inauguration of a new trade-liberalizing negotiation among all major (industrial and developing) countries. These "big picture" steps are central to satisfactory resolution of the more specific "North-South" trade issues.

In addition, the possibility that both U.S. and LDC interests can be served by a single trade policy can be enhanced by several auxiliary steps. For example, part of the consumer benefits from freer trade can be devoted to easing the adjustment costs of workers displaced by the resulting imports. Indeed, such a program of Trade Adjustment Assistance (TAA) has existed for two decades. However, that program has failed to achieve much real adjustment. For that reason, as well as for budgetary and ideological reasons, TAA has been almost totally gutted during the last two years. Thorough reform and renewal of this program could help resolve the (moral as well as "purely economic") conflicts which arise in setting trade policy toward the LDC's, assuming that ways for government to promote adjustment effectively can be developed and implemented.[11]

Another possibility is to employ a discriminatory import regime in favor of the LDC's, vis-à-vis suppliers in the other industrial countries (OIC's). Three rationales exist: an overt desire to prefer the LDC's as suppliers; greater concern with OICs than LDC's over the issues cited above as deterring trade liberalization (currency imbalances, "unfair" trade practices); and/or an overall political environment which permits free(r) imports from LDC's but not the world as a whole. Such a discriminatory program, the Generalized System of Tariff Preferences (GSP), has in fact been in existence for about a decade (although in severely restricted form), which limits its actual impact on trade flows.

The discussion so far has focussed on trade policy in general and its usual tools of tariffs and non-tariff barriers. In addition, specific measures can be and have been adopted for commodity trade in particular, which is still of major (even overwhelming) importance in the export patterns of many LDC's accounting for over one half of all their export earnings, if fuels are included, and for about one quarter of the total even when fuels are omitted.

Particularly during the early 1970s, many LDC's at least covertly espoused the negotiation of a set of international commodity agreements which would deliberately set prices above market levels and thus transfer income from consumers in richer countries to producers in poorer countries. Such proposals raise some of the same internal and international distributional questions cited above.

Two alternative approaches were more widely accepted. One set of schemes sought to stabilize the *incomes* of commodity-producing countries (rather than the prices of their commodities). The other was commodity agreements which sought to *stabilize prices* (rather than transfer income) in the presumed interest of both exporting and importing countries to avoid wide fluctuations in commodity prices and thus domestic inflation and investment responses. Analysis of these commodity issues is presented below.

The rest of this paper is divided into three sections. The first, drawing heavily (to a large extent, verbatim) on an earlier paper by Richard N. Cooper,[12] lays out the traditional analysis of trade theory hopefully in a nontechnical manner and describes the conditions which need to be met for its policy conclusions (i.e., free trade) to follow. The next section describes the US-LDC trade problem across its several dimensions: the existing situation in terms of both objective circumstances and policies, the policy options for the near and longer run, and (more briefly) the related issues of commodity trade and "North-South" financial flows. The final pages then seek to draw together the previous strands and suggest a course of action.

Economic Assumptions of the Case for Liberal Trade

The case for liberal trade is essentially the same as the case for voluntary exchange economy extended to other countries. The case for an exchange economy as opposed to individual or family self-sufficiency rests on the rise in real income that can be obtained by all individuals when each concentrates his efforts on the marketable activities he is best able to do and exchanges the production in excess of his own needs for goods and services that others can produce with relatively greater efficiency through similar concentration of effort. This basic argument does not stop at national borders. Unless exchange can take place readily between as well as within nations, the benefits from trading with foreigners having special skills or technology or location will be lost, and incomes will be lower as a result.

Foreign trade thus represents a possible extension of the production opportunities of every country. If a country's citizens desire to purchase a particular good (or service), the country can either devote its own resources — labor, capital, natural resources — to production of the good, or it can devote its resources to the production of something quite different that can in turn be exchanged for the desired good. The latter alternative often will require far fewer resources than the former. This will be true for a variety of reasons. Strong locational factors (e.g., climate, soil quality, good natural harbors), economies of scale, and substantial differences in land per worker, capital per worker, or worker skills all give rise to substantial gains from trade.

This basic proposition holds for all economies, regardless of their form of organization; it is applicable whether an economy is competitive or monopolistic, whether it is capitalist or socialist or communist.

The case for liberal trade (i.e., without impediments to making the best possible exchange) does however rest on the philosophical assumption that production is not an end in itself but only a means to the goods and services produced to satisfy human wants. It also assumes therefore that economic gains by the citizens of other countries are not losses to the citizens of our country, that is, in matters of trade the world is engaged in a positive sum game. Economists have always recognized that satisfying human wants in the form of goods and services is not the exclusive aim of mankind. In particular, they have acknowledged that "defense is more important than opulence" or, as it has been put more recently, "prosperity is not a substitute for security." They are also conscious of the dignity of honest effort. But by and large, they have assumed that labor is a means to an end, not an end in itself, and that as a means labor can be applied with equal satisfaction to any of a variety of activities and therefore should be applied to those activities where it yields, through production and exchange, the greatest rewards in terms of satisfying human wants.

There are, however, two classes of exemptions which need discussion. The first broad class of exceptions concerns the distribution of income or, more generally, of welfare among those who are affected by free exchange. The second broad class of exceptions concerns discrepancies between the market prices reached in a market economy and the true social cost of production.

If trade is allowed to take place freely between nations, *the dis-*

tribution of income will generally differ from the distribution under a regime in which trade is not allowed to take place freely. Sometimes the effect is on the distribution of income between the trading countries (on the assumption that the residents of each country can be meaningfully aggregated into "countries"). A country that has some monopoly power either as a seller or a buyer can improve its real income by restricting its trade somewhat, by in effect imposing a tax on those foreigners that are willing to pay prices above cost.

Sometimes the effect is on the distribution of income within the trading countries. Even when a liberal trade policy benefits the country as a whole by raising total GNP, for instance, or permitting greater leisure, it may still reduce the real income of certain residents who, because of their particular skills or their location, would benefit by restrictions on imported goods. In general, a policy of liberal trade will favor those elements of the economy whose efforts or resources are used relatively intensively in production for export, especially if they are keyed specifically to those industries and are relatively immobile. Cutting down trade will hurt this group for the benefit of those who compete most intensively with imported goods and services.

The theory of welfare economics suggests that liberal trade is superior to restricted trade in spite of these distributional effects, provided that income is redistributed from the prospective gainers to the prospective losers. Since total income will have been increased, it should be possible, by suitable redistribution, to make everyone better off.

When this issue arises between nations, it calls for grants from one nation to another, that is, for "foreign aid." When the distributional issue arises within countries it assumes there is a costless mechanism for achieving the required redistribution. Since virtually all taxes introduce their own distortion, however, the process of redistribution almost always itself entails a cost. It may be, therefore, that restrictions on trade are the most economical (i.e., least inefficient) way to achieve a desired distribution of income. While this is a logical possibility, however, it would be surprising indeed if our social notions about desirable distributions of income generally took the relatively few particular forms that could best be achieved by restrictions on foreign trade, although it may do so in a few countries.

The second broad class of possible qualifications for the case for liberal trade concerns *instances in which market prices convey the wrong signals* to producers and consumers from a social point of view.

This can happen in a large number of different circumstances, and only the most important of them will be reviewed here. Several of these price distortions can pervade the entire economy; the most significant distortions concern the failure to achieve full employment in a national recession and the failure to achieve balance-of-payments equilibrium because a country's exchange rate is at an inappropriate level.

The most important assumption underlying the case for liberal trade is that each country's *resources will be fully employed*. This does not mean that all resources (productive land, the capital stock, and the labor force) will be fully employed all the time, for that is neither possible nor desirable in a dynamic economy. Capital becomes obsolete, the pattern of demand changes, technology alters costs, and all of these factors will give rise to temporary unemployment associated with adjustment to the new circumstances.

But it does mean both that most resources are employed most of the time and that any unemployment of resources that does arise is of short duration. If these conditions do not obtain, then a country may be better off under certain circumstances by restricting imports from abroad and under other circumstances by subsidizing exports. In industrialized countries, however, modern techniques of macroeconomic management through monetary and fiscal policy should undercut any need to restrict or stimulate trade artificially on a lasting basis in order to maintain employment.

Modern techniques of macroeconomic management have not succeeded in avoiding economic recessions altogether, however, so this particular flaw in the price system does exist, even in advanced economies. But trade policies are sufficiently inertial in their effects that they are particularly inappropriate to deal with it. In periods of high unemployment it is understandably common to hear calls for protection against imported goods, which are seen to compete wastefully with goods and services that could be produced by unemployed domestic labor and capital and land. But appropriate monetary and fiscal policies can generally deal with that unemployment both faster and at lower cost.

A second key assumption underlying the case for liberal trade is that *international payments* will remain in balance. In this sense the case pertains to the long run, for it is recognized that in any given short period of time payments may be out of equilibrium. Any disequilibrium, however, is assumed to be corrected within a relatively short period of time. Since in the long run a country's payments must be in equilibrium, the difficult problem arises in the "medium run" of two to ten years, in which a country may be able to finance a payments disequilibrium rather than eliminate it.

Since the case for liberal trade is based on specialization and exchange, it does not encompass the case in which, say, a country maintains an overvalued currency for several years to the point at which a number of firms that compete with imports during the period of disequilibrium are driven from business, or the case in which a country artificially builds up a substantial export industry that can thrive only so long as the country's exchange rate is undervalued. These transactions involve the exchange of goods and services, not for other goods and services or even for long-term debt that represents claims on future goods and services, but for short-term IOU's or other liquid assets that cannot be considered long-term debt. It is the classic case, for a country in deficit, of living beyond its means or, for a country in surplus, of failing to enjoy the maximum possible standard of living. Under these circumstances, firms and workers may be placed under unwarranted hardship in competition from imports that cannot persist, but can persist long enough to do damage.

An undervalued exchange rate may mistakenly attract capital and labor into an industry because of its medium-term capacity to compete with foreign products, but these resources will have to leave the industry when the exchange rate is altered. Under such circumstances, some restrictions on imports by a country with an overvalued currency may be preferable to completely unimpeded trade until such time as the exchange rate is changed. This willingness of the residents of one country to subsidize consumption in another, even when it is known that the subsidy cannot last, should not, however, be considered an unmitigated detriment. The particular case must be examined closely to determine the optimal policy.

Apart from the total market for labor and capital and the market for foreign exchange, *distortions* arising in any number of particular markets may also affect the case for liberal trade, at least for the affected products. Traditionally, deviations from competition, where one or several firms influence prices by restricting supply, have been the most commonly discussed form of market distortion. Liberal trade operates directly to weaken this form of distortion, however, by increasing the degree of competition in national markets. (Liberal capital movements, in contrast, may increase the degree of oligopoly in the world economy.[13])

The kind of market imperfection most commonly discussed today concerns "external effects," such as congestion and pollution, that represent social costs but are not costs of production paid by the firm. A liberal trade policy may stimulate an export industry that is a heavy polluter, for example, and the result is more pollution under a liberal trade policy than under a restrictive one. (Of course, the effect could also go the other way. If import-competing industries are heavier polluters than export industries, liberal trade will reduce pollution; this in reality is probably the case for the United States.) Or a liberal trade policy may lead to the demise of an efficient processor whose domestic source of bulky raw material is subject to monopoly pricing but whose foreign competitors are not placed at a similar disadvantage. (Again, this effect could also go the other way, if the firm facing a monopolist is in an export industry.)

In each of these cases of market distortion the most appropriate course of action is to eliminate the distortions directly so that market prices reflect social costs. If it is infeasible to eliminate the distortion, then we are in a world of what economists have come to call "second best," in which a restrictive trade policy may lead to a higher level of welfare than would liberal trade policy. Trade restrictions may become a second-best policy for dealing with the distortions. But they may not. The analytical difficulty with a world of market imperfections is that easy generalization becomes impossible. Trade restrictions may alleviate the particular problem, but they may also aggravate it, as when they protect a national oligopoly from foreign competition. Each particular case must be examined on its merits by taking into account the ramifications of actions in one area of the economy on other, even seemingly remote, areas of the economy. For this reason also, it is preferable to attack market distortions directly rather than indirectly.

One important possible source of misunderstanding arises in the realm of market imperfections, particularly as governments engage in increasingly detailed governance of national economies. Complaints have been raised about the trade-distorting effects of "regional" policies adopted by many governments in Europe, and a similar issue has been raised with respect to the controls on pollution urged in the

United States. But if these policies are accurately aimed at correcting market imperfections, then while they may influence trade flows, they do not distort trade flows; on the contrary, they "undistort" trade flows and thus strengthen the case for liberal trade. A difficulty and a danger is that policies whose origins are to eliminate distortions or inequities may in the course of time take on a life of their own and be extended where they are not warranted.

The LDC's and Trade Policy

One of the great success stories of the postwar period has been the *rapid expansion of LDC exports*, including manufactured products. Between 1970 and 1980, these exports grew annually by 4.6% and 12.9% respectively, in real terms. This rapid progress was fostered by three factors: rapid economic growth in the industrial countries;[14] the relatively open and steadily liberalizing trade policies maintained (under U.S. leadership) by most industrial countries; and the export-oriented growth strategies of most LDC's themselves.

To be sure, not all LDC's shared equally in this export expansion. The "newly industrializing countries" (NIC's) in the Far East (especially) and Latin America showed the most progress, while South Asian and (especially) African countries lagged substantially behind. (The fortunes of the OPEC countries shifted sharply, of course, with the rise and fall in the world price of oil.) Moreover, the global recession of the early 1980s and the creeping erosion of the world trading regime as well as the huge debt burdens accumulated by many LDC's in connection with their export-oriented strategies, have led some LDC's to question again whether they can, or should, maintain the approach of the past two decades.

Despite the growth in LDC exports in the 1960s and 1970s, they still meet a very small share of final demand in most OECD countries. In the case of the United States, total manufacturing imports from all countries accounted in 1980 for about 5 percent of GNP, of which LDC suppliers provided about one quarter. For industrial countries as a group, LDC's provide about 13 percent of all imports of manufactures which, in turn, equate to about 10 percent of GNP.[15] So imports of manufactures from LDC's, in the aggregate, account for only 1 percent of final demand in the industial countries. In some sectors, however, such as steel and some electronics products as well as the traditional textiles and footwear, some NIC's have become formidable competitors and are achieving substantially higher market shares.

One of the most important developments in the world trading system in the postwar era has been the *decline in average tariff barriers*. Successive rounds of multilateral trade negotiations (MTN's) held under the auspices of the General Agreement on Tariffs and Trade (GATT) have substantially reduced tariffs on a broad range of products. The Tokyo Round tariff cuts now being implemented will reduce the weighted average of industrial country tariffs to less than 5 percent ad valorem.

The low average level of tariffs conceals some continuing problems of market access for developing countries, however. In general, tariff cuts have been less in areas where developing countries enjoy large cost advantages, such as textiles and footwear. Tariff "escalation" in industrial countries — the tendency for import duties to rise with the degree of processing — remains a deterrent to upgrading of LDC exports to enable them to achieve greater value-added. It is nevertheless true that industrial country tariffs have become less important as barriers to developing country exports in the past decade. That is due both to MTN tariff reductions and to the introduction of nonreciprocal tariff preferences for developing countries.

The Generalized System of Tariff Preferences (GSP), in which the United States participates, is based on the idea that developing countries' exports need special encouragement. Under GSP, developed countries agree to give tariff preferences to developing countries in selected product areas (primarily manufactures) for a temporary (but renewable) period of time. The duration of preferences is limited, in principle, because developing countries are expected to overcome their initial disadvantages and evolve into efficient producers — but virtually all industrial countries, with the possible exception of the United States due to Congressional hostility to the program, are likely to keep it in place indefinitely.

The developed countries exercise discretion on product coverage and the size of preferences. The United States provides duty-free treatment for a large number of manufactured and semimanufactured goods and some agricultural products; approximately 2900 products are now accorded GSP treatment. But products included in the

U.S. scheme accounted for only about a tenth of the value of U.S. imports from beneficiary countries in 1980. This is partly because many imports from LDC's, especially primary products, were already free of duty. But it is also because a number of items where LDC's can compete effectively are excluded from the outset[16] and because products are "graduated" once they hit trigger levels of actual sales (now $53 million or 50 percent of total imports in a given year).

The effectiveness of GSP is difficult to gauge. On the one hand, the proportion of total imports from developing countries covered by GSP is not very large (less than 20 percent for the eleven OECD schemes combined), and tariff reductions negotiated in the Tokyo Round have had the effect of reducing preference margins. On the other hand, imports accorded GSP treatment have grown faster than other imports from developing countries. In the United States, average annual growth for GSP imports was 23.8 percent in 1976-80, compared with 14.8 percent for other dutiable imports from developing countries (excluding oil). While some of this difference may be explained by factors other than GSP, the data suggest that tariff preferences have contributed to improved market access and trade expansion.

The principal beneficiaries of GSP have been newly industrializing countries such as South Korea, Taiwan, Hong Kong and Brazil. However, GSP has benefitted traditional resource producers that have begun to industrialize such as the Philippines, Malaysia and Thailand. As more exports from the most successful NIC's "graduate" from developing-country status, GSP will open up new oportunities for industrial exports by the "next generation" in Latin America and Asia.

One of the most immediate issues for U.S. trade policy toward the LDC's is whether to extend GSP beyond 1984 and, if so, on what terms. Many in Congress wish to terminate the program altogether or at least exclude the NIC's from it. On the other hand, as noted above, LDC export needs are greater than ever and the international environment has turned badly against them. This issue will probably be the next focal point for the debate on U.S. trade policy toward LDC's.

Several other international schemes provide tariff preferences for developing countries. Among the most important is the Lome Convention, an agreement concluded between the European Economic

Community and 63 former colonies in Asia, Africa and the Caribbean. The Convention provides duty-free entry into the EEC for all products with the exception of some agricultural goods. These benefits are more extensive than those provided under GSP, although import volumes are comparatively small. The EEC has additional trade arrangements with Mediterranean, North African and Middle Eastern countries.

The United States is now implementing additional tariff preferences for Caribbean countries. As originally proposed the Caribbean Basin Initiative (CBI) would have eliminated import duties on all products except textiles for a period of 12 years and expanded existing quotas for imports of some agricultural products. The program that finally emerged from Congress had more exceptions, however, and less than 10 percent of the region's exports will receive new duty-free treatment. Moreover, the bill levied a number of conditions on countries seeking eligibility. But the first eleven countries have just qualified and a number of others will presumably do so soon.

The United States also operates another preferential scheme: the offshore assembly provisions (OAP) of the tariff code (Sections 806 and 807), which provide special tariff exemptions for products which incorporate U.S.-made components. Tariffs are applied only to the "foreign" share of import cost, mainly labor value-added. The OAP do not explicitly favor LDC's, and in fact much of the original trade under them came from Europe. Now, however, the main beneficiaries are Mexico (especially its border plants) and several Far Eastern countries which process, e.g., U.S.-made microchips into final consumer electronic products for sale in the United States.

Tariff reductions and preferences can expand nontraditional exports from developing countries. In a number of product areas where developing countries are already competitive, however, industrial countries use *nontariff barriers* (NTB's) to limit their market access.

Textiles and apparel are a classic example. Since the early 1960s world trade in textiles has been regulated by a succession of international agreements designed to limit "market disruption" in importing countries. The Multi-Fiber Arrangement (MFA), recently extended through 1986, provides a multilateral framework within which the United States and other developed countries establish quotas for textile and apparel imports. The quotas have limited the growth of imports from developing countries and protected higher cost domestic producers while raising the average prices for textiles and apparel paid by consumers.

From the standpoint of international comparative advantage the current restrictions on textiles are extremely difficult to justify. Yet the obstacles to liberalization are formidable: The textile sector accounts for 12 percent of manufacturing employment in industrial countries, and a recent study has estimated that sectoral employment could fall by a third if import restrictions were eliminated altogether.[17] Adjustment of this magnitude would be difficult to implement except over an extended period (though, as already noted, potential gains to consumers would be substantial). For these reasons, proponents of the MFA argue that it is a less disruptive alternative to the array of national quotas which would allegedly ensue otherwise. And it should be noted that LDC textile exports have grown fairly rapidly (13.2 percent annually in real terms, 1970-1980) despite the widespread restraints.

Agriculture is a second area where there has been little progress toward trade liberalization. Although industrial countries dominate world agricultural exports, developing countries have become increasingly important suppliers of particular commodities. The United States maintains quotas for some agricultural imports (such as sugar, cotton, peanuts and dairy products), but its overall levels of protection are not high.

More serious distortions to agricultural trade arise from price supports and variable import levies in the European Community. The Common Agricultural Policy (CAP) effectively shields European producers from foreign competition; at the same time artificial price supports encourage the production of huge surpluses for export. Attention has focused recently on agricultural trade disputes between the EC and the United States, whose exports are being displaced from traditional markets. However, developing country exporters are also adversely affected by U.S. and (especially) EC trade restrictions and export subsidies. It has been estimated that if existing trade restrictions on select agricultural products in OECD countries were reduced by half, more than a third of the resulting export expansion would accrue to developing countries and their agricultural sales would rise by more than 10 percent.[18]

Within several manufacturing sectors, there has been a tendency for the United States and other industrial countries to settle trade disputes through bilateral agreements. Examples are recent U.S. "voluntary export restraints" on Japanese automobiles, on Japanese and European steel, on Brazilian specialty steel and, a few years ago, on Korean and Taiwanese shoes. To the extent that industrial countries drift toward "managed world trade," a system based on semi-permanent quantitative restrictions, the interests of developing countries are seriously threatened. Of late, particular anomalies have arisen in the erection of new trade barriers against the major debtor countries which are simultaneously receiving new infusions of financial help from the same industrial nations (and the IMF). The dangers are that developing countries will fail to realize their export potential because of new trade barriers and because the fear of encountering such barriers discourages investment in potentially successful export industries.

One attempt to check such steps centered on the negotiation of a "safeguard code" in the latest (Tokyo) round of multilateral trade negotiations, especially in 1977-79. Such a code would implant "safeguards on safeguards" by bringing *all* trade controls under agreed "rules of the game," many of which now take place outside the GATT or any other international framework. The EC insisted on the right to apply controls on a discriminatory basis, however, while the United States (and most LDC's) insisted on maintaining the traditional most-favored-nation treatment. Hence no agreement was reached on an issue which, if handled satisfactorily, could provide at least some protection for LDC market access.

Commodity Trade

Despite the increasing relative importance of manufactures, developing countries remain dependent on *primary commodities* for a substantial share of their total export earnings.[19] In 1980, primary products accounted for 46 percent of the non-fuel merchandise exports of developing countries. A number of the low income countries in Asia and Africa are dependent on primary products for a much larger share of their merchandise exports, and product concentration is extreme in some cases. Examples include Uganda (coffee, 98 percent of exports), Ghana (cocoa, 70 percent), and Zambia (copper, 89 percent).

The last two years have been particularly unfavorable to commodity producers. In 1981 and 1982, world prices for nonfuel commodities (after adjustment for inflation) reached their lowest level in the postwar period. The commodity price declines caused large export shortfalls for developing countries (cumulatively, in the range of $35 billion during 1981-82)[20] which contributed to the recent widespread interruption of normal debt servicing. Thus, while low commodity prices have helped to reduce inflationary pressures in the industrial countries, they have had severely adverse effect on LDC exporters.

Commodity prices have been depressed in the last two years for various reasons, but most important was the prolonged world recession. Demand for industrial raw materials responds to cyclical trends in the United States, Europe and Japan, and the recent recession was more severe than any since the 1930s. High real interest rates have also reduced the demand for commodities by increasing the cost of holding inventories. In addition, the strength of the dollar against other major currencies has depressed foreign willingness to buy dollar-denominated commodities while increasing the real burden of developing countries' dollar-denominated debt.

Although U.S. and world recovery should contribute to an upturn in commodity prices, the long-term problem of market instability remains. Prices of non-oil commodities were subject to larger fluctuations in the past decade than previously, largely because of a more unstable macroeconomic environment. Dramatic swings in interest rates, inflation, exchange rates and oil prices have added to uncertainty in commodity markets and increased the possibility for destabilizing speculation. Price volatility is particularly damaging to commodity producers: Apart from making export receipts less predictable, extreme price swings distort investment patterns and stimulate product substitution in importing countries. For these and other reasons, commodity stabilization has been one of the focal points of North-South negotiation.

The existing international arrangements for commodity stabilization take a variety of forms. As noted above, they reflect three different objectives: price stabilization, stabilization of export earnings, and (more controversially) improvement in long-term terms of trade.

The most ambitious scheme was the Integrated Program for Commodities (IPC) proposed by UNCTAD (the United Nations Conference on Trade and Development) in the early 1970s. The centerpiece of the Integrated Program was to be a Common Fund for financing buffer stocks in 10 core commodities (8 agricultural products and 2 metals).[21]

Despite years of discussion, implementation of the IPC has not proceeded very far, owing largely to the technical difficulties of negotiating agreements. The United States and other major industrial countries have accepted only those few agreements (coffee, cocoa, sugar, tin, rubber) where effective price stabilization appeared to be at least arguably feasible. They generally reject the idea that prices should be "stabilized" around a trend which improves the purchasing power of commodities in terms of manufactured goods as an unacceptable form of income transfer.

The existing agreements seek to keep price fluctuations within agreed limits through operation of buffer stocks or export controls. However, most of them have had little success in moderating price fluctuations. Buffer stocks are often inadequate, and export controls have become inoperable under extreme price pressures. Policies of major consuming countries (for example, sales and purchases from the US strategic stockpile) can exert a more pronounced influence on commodity prices than formal stabilization schemes.

The Stabex program of the European Community established under the Lome Convention represents a different approach. Rather than attempting to stabilize prices, Stabex focuses on the export earnings of commodity producers. Under Stabex, countries covered by the Convention (in Africa, the Caribbean and Pacific) are compensated for export shortfall due to natural disaster or unfavorable economic conditions. The shortfall must reach at least 7.5 percent of average export earnings from the previous four-year period for a covered commodity (2.5 percent in the case of least-developed countries). Repayment is expected over five years, but no repayment is required of least-developed countries and the loans carry no interest. These are extremely generous terms. However, Stabex only applies to trade with the European Comunity and many commodities (and commodity producers) are not covered. Requests for compensation under Stabex have far exceeded appropriations, and payments (equivalent to $200 million in 1981) have been small in relation to other forms of financial assistance.

The Compensatory Financing Facility (CFF) of the International Monetary Fund also protects countries against temporary export shortfalls due to factors beyond their control. The CFF is available to all members of the Fund and applies to a broader range of export earnings than does Stabex. The resources of the CFF are also considerably larger: Developing countries borrowed approximately $4 billion under this facility in the past year. Unlike some other types of financial assistance from the Fund, the CFF does not involve strong policy conditions. The CFF has been liberalized in recent years to provide compensation to countries hurt by price increases for imported cereals, as well as shorfalls in export earnings. More recently, it has been proposed that countries with other temporary difficulties such as abnormally high interest payments be made eligible for further compensatory finance.

Financial Flows to Developing Countries

Though trade is the major focus of this paper, a few words on financial flows are necessary to round out the picture.[22] Until recently, this topic could be divided reasonably clearly into two portions: market-related flows (from the multilateral development banks and national export credit agencies as well as commercial banks) to the more advanced LDC's and concessional flows (mainly bilateral aid and IDA-type multilateral credits) for the poorest.

Now, however, the situation has changed dramatically. The annual growth of bank lending to (primarily) the NIC's, which grew at average rates of over 20 percent after the first oil shock, was sharply cut in 1982. Modest lending to heavily-indebted countries has continued in 1983 under the aegis of rescheduling agreements, but few banks will agree to more than marginal increases in their exposure and countries that have hitherto avoided debt service disruptions are now facing lending cutoffs.

This problem may not be so short term. Even under a favorable world economic scenario of steady growth and lower interest rates (and with tough adjustment measures by debtor countries), the current account deficits of developing countries are likely to remain in the neighborhood of $60-75 billion for several years to come.[23] The cutback in private banks' balance-of-payments lending will impose a greater burden on other financial sources, particularly the official bilateral and multilateral lending agencies, at a time when foreign aid is encountering even more than the usual level of political resistance in donor countries for budgetary and other reasons. Indeed, concessional aid has grown very slowly in real terms over the last decade and has hardly grown at all as a share of donor countries' GNP. In the United States, aid as a share of GNP has fallen over the past decade, to the lowest level of all OECD countries except Italy.

To an even larger extent then heretofore, trade liberalization and increased lending are policy alternatives for the United States (and OIC's) in the Third World. This is not the place for a detailed exposition of the pros and cons of private and public, bilateral and multilateral, credits to LDC's. But the possibilities, and particularly the constraints, in this area must be kept very much in mind in developing an approach toward trade policy in the years ahead.

Conclusions

Few simple answers, on economic let alone moral grounds, can be provided as to the "proper" trade policy for the United States toward LDC's. However, several general propositions can fairly reliably be derived from the above analysis:

1. If the United States has any moral obligation toward the LDC's, it seems inevitable that relatively open access to our markets for their exports must play an important role in fulfilling that obligation.

2. The freer the trade among all countries, in fact, the larger the overall pie and thus total income for the world as a whole.

3. Barring some theoretically possible but pragmatically unlikely conditions, this in turn will almost certainly mean higher *total* incomes for both the United States and the LDC's (with an indeterminate sharing of benefits between them).

4. The internal income distribution effects within both exporting and importing countries are also indeterminate. In all likelihood some groups (e.g., unskilled U.S. labor) will be "losers" just as some groups will be "winners." There will almost certainly be more of the latter, though they may be more dispersed (e.g., consumers) and thus less powerful politically.

5. Given these indeterminacies, which are often little less opaque *ex post* than *ex ante*, a policy of maximum free trade is best because of its positive aggregate effects.

6. Such a policy will be much more defensible and practicable, however, if steps are taken on the macroeconomics and international monetary fronts to reduce unemployment and overvaluation of the dollar—the two key impediments to fulfilling the traditional conditions conducive to a liberal trade policy.

7. Moreover, it will be important to launch soon a new, multilateral trade-liberalizing negotiation in the GATT, both to reduce further the "unfair" trade practices of other countries and to impart new momentum to the liberalization process (the "bicycle theory"). Liberalization toward LDC's, or at least products of special interest to LDC's, should be a focal point of such an effect along with a new "safeguard code," or like device, to limit recourse by industrial countries to devices which restrain LDC market access.

8. To counter the adverse distributional effects of free(r) trade within the United States, explicit government help to workers (and perhaps firms) displaced by the resulting imports, which is better than the traditional Trade Adjustment Assistance in achieving real adjustment, needs to be developed and implemented effectively and generously.

9. If economic or political pressures in the United States preclude free(r) trade in products of importance to LDC's, a "second best" approach may be a free (or at least more liberal) regime for imports *from the LDC's*. This could be done by further liberalization of the Generalized System of Tariff Preferences and/or new steps favoring LDC exports in previously exempted sectors such as textiles/apparel and protected agricultural products.

10. Of course, the United States can also deploy a series of non-trade policies, in addition to or in lieu of more liberal trade policies, to help the LDC's. Prime candidates, in light of the budgetary constraints on concessional assistance, would be sharp expansion in the international financial intermediation role of the regional development banks, and the IMF (via authorizing it to commence borrowing directly in the private markets).

Notes

1. It must be recognized immediately that there are at least three major categories of LDC's: the newly industrializing countries (NIC's, such as Korea and Brazil) which have achieved rapid growth and become major world traders, the OPEC countries with their oil wealth, and the poorer LDC's in South Asia and Africa. Different policy approaches are needed for each, as will become apparent below.

2. Norman S. Fieleke, "The Cost of Tariffs to Consumers," *New England Economic Review,* September-October 1971, pp. 13-18, and Glenn P. Jenkins, "Costs and Consequences of the New Protectionism: The Case of Canada's Clothing Sector," Ottawa: North-South Institute, 1980.

3. The famous "Leontief paradox" reveals that the wage component of American exports tends to be higher than the wage component of American imports, because the skill level is higher in export industries than in import-competing industries, so that an equal reduction in both would tend to *reduce* labor income in the United States. This seems to be particularly true with respect to U.S. trade with the LDC's, which have been both our fastest growing markets for the past two decades (and were taking 40% of all U.S. exports in the late 1970s) and would be most likely to reduce their purchases from us if we reduced our purchases from them. See Robert Baldwin, "Determinants of the Commodity Structure of U.S. Trade," *American Economic Review*, March 1971 (esp. p. 140.)

4. For a comprehensive analysis see William R. Cline, *International Debt and the Stability of the World Economy* (Washington: Institute for International Economics, September 1983).

5. See John Williamson, *The Exchange Rate System* (Washington: Institute for International Economics, September 1983).

6. Dollar overvaluation hurts LDC exports to other countries, however, because most of them peg their currencies to the dollar and thus lose competitiveness vis-à-vis Europe and Japan. Moreover, a strong dollar depresses demand for LDC commodity exports (including oil) because most of them are sold in dollar-denominated markets. The high U.S. interest rates which are a chief cause of the dollar overvaluation also add directly to LDC debt servicing costs, by about $4 billion (net) per percentage point.

7. See C. Fred Bergsten, "What to Do About the U.S.-Japan Economic Problem," *Foreign Affairs*, Summer 1982.

8. See C. Fred Bergsten, "The Costs of Reaganomics," *Foreign Policy*, Fall 1981 and "The International Implications of Reaganomics," Kieler Vorträge, No. 96, 1982. The main problem is that the bizarre U.S. policy mix of 1981-83, combining very loose fiscal policy with basically responsible

monetary policy, has generated record real interest rates which — via the exchange markets — proscribe the possibility for other countries to stimulate their economies via the traditional tools of monetary policy. The greatest U.S. contribution to the world economy (including the LDC's) at the present would be a correction of its policy mix problem, for these macroeconomic as well as exchange-rate reasons.

9. For example, it has been estimated that the cost to U.S. consumers of the textile/apparel restraints alone totaled $18.4 billion in 1980. See Michael C. Munger, "The Costs of Protectionism: Estimates of the Hidden Tax of Trade Restraint", Working Paper No. 80, Center for Study of American Business, Washington University, St. Louis, July 1983.

10. See C. Fred Bergsten and William R. Cline, *Trade Policy in the 1980s* (Washington: Institute for International Economics, November, 1982).

11. Under a grant from the Ford Foundation, the Institute for International Economics has launched a major study of this issue, directed by Gary Clyde Hufbauer and Howard F. Rosen, which seeks to produce new policy proposals by early 1985.

12. Richard N. Cooper, "Economic Assumptions of the Case for Liberal Trade," in C. Fred Bergsten, ed., *Toward a New World Trade: The Maidenhead Papers* (Lexington, Mass.: D.C. Heath and Co., 1975).

13. For an extended analysis of the relationship between foreign direct investment and trade for the United States, see C. Fred Bergsten, Thomas O. Horst and Theodore H. Moran, *American Multinationals and American Interests* (Washington: The Brookings Institution, 1978).

14. When the OECD countries achieve real economic growth in excess of 2 percent annually, their non-oil imports have grown by three times the excess — setting up a virtuous, self-reinforcing cycle of positive growth and trade. But when OECD growth drops below 1½-2 percent, their imports decline by three times the shortfall — setting up a vicious spiral of shrinking growth and trade, in which all countries seek to export their way out of stagnation but cannot possibly do so because the total market is declining. See Bergsten and Cline, *Trade Policy in the 1980s*, p. 17.

15. IBRD, *World Development Report 1982*, p. 12.

16. Exclusions include textile and apparel articles subject to textile agreements; import-sensitive electronics, glass, and iron and steel articles; watches; most categories of footwear; and any articles subject to import relief under Section 203 of the 1974 Trade Act. See *26th Annual Report of the President on Trade Agreements Program 1981-82*, p. 214.

17. Donald Keesing and Martin Wolf, *Textile Quotas Against Developing Countries* (London: Trade Policy Research Centre, 1980, pp. 133-140).

18. Alberto Valdés and Joachim Zietz, *Agricultural Protection in OECD Countries: Its Cost to Less-Developed Countries* (Washington: International

Food Policy Research Institute, Research Report No. 21, December 1980). The United States would also experience a net increase in exports under such a scenario. The "losers" would be Japan and most of Western Europe.

19. An interesting moral question arises in the context of commodity trade. The Charter of Economic Rights and Duties of States, adopted by the United Nations in 1974, asserts that sovereign nations have the legal right to control totally natural resources within their boundaries. But, in view of the universality of mankind, why should the United States be able to limit wheat output when people in Africa are starving or Saudi Arabia be able to limit oil output when people in the United States are freezing?

20. IMF. *World Economic Outlook 1983*, p. 155.

21. The Common Fund finally negotiated in 1980, and not yet implemented, had much more modest objectives. It sought only to pool the financial resources of those commodity agreements operated through buffer stocks, on the view that the differences in price movements for each would minimize the costs of price stabilization for the agreements taken together.

22. An issue entirely omitted from this paper is immigration. In principle, of course, industrial countries could accept larger inflows of LDC workers instead of (or in addition to) larger inflows of LDC goods.

23. Cline, *International Debt and the Stability of the World Economy*.

Ten

The United States and Third World Poor In the World Economy: Some Economic and Ethical Issues

ERNEST BARTELL, C.S.C.

DESPITE THE FACT THAT VALUE QUESTIONS ARE INVARIABLY present, explicitly or implicitly, in economic decision-making, discourse between the fields of economics and ethics seems inevitably difficult. Mainstream economists, armed with the analytical tools of positive economics, are conditioned to ignore, to accept as given or to assume away virtually all value judgments except those implicit in the normative criteria of efficiency and maximization. These are the criteria that determine "optimal" solutions in much of the analysis of resource allocation and economic growth, especially through the markets for final products and services and for factors of production such as labor and capital. In the eyes of the ethicist the methodology of positive economics thus gives operational priority to one set of values, those related to efficiency and maximization, over other normative criteria, especially the human values affecting and affected by the distribution of income and wealth.

The circular flow of income that underlies positive economic analysis does in fact acknowledge the interaction between the distribution of income and wealth and the behavior of an economy with respect to resource allocation and economic growth. It recognizes the influence of markets and prices upon the determination and distributions of these benefits among the participants in the economy. It also recognizes the influence that the spending habits of those with varying shares of income have upon subsequent resource allocation and growth. The spending decisions of a single hypothetically wealthy economic participant who receives the lion's share of the income generated in an economy are likely to result in different employment opportunities and a different set of goods and services produced than the spending decisions of a population receiving more modest, relatively equal shares of income.

Most models of economic analysis, however, assume distribution to be socially given or held fixed through some hypothetical and instantaneous social mechanism for redistribution so that the analysis can isolate the operation of other normative criteria, e.g., efficiency and maximization, without concern for the interaction of distribution with those other criteria. Ethicists, on the other hand, come to economics from different premises, those based upon philosophical or theological perceptions about human equality and justice whose economic implications immediately relate to questions of distribution. So it is not surprising that those familiar with the importance of efficiency criteria in economic analysis, especially the analysis of markets, are apt to criticize the do-gooders for too much emphasis upon distribution in their evaluation of economic systems. The efficiency norm has thus come to be a potent and popular weapon for apologists of free markets as the best hope for successful economic development in the Third World.[1]

However, it is also important for those who would understand the actual possibilities and constraints for development in the Third World to attend closely to the ways in which the gains from development are actually distributed, especially in the socially unregulated international marketplace. For a variety of historical and technical reasons the distribution of gains from market activity in international markets for products and services, for labor and for capital, is frequently biased against the poor countries of the world and against the poor within those countries. Hence, for an adequate understanding of the possibilities of development in the Third World the questions of distribution cannot be assumed away as neatly as they are in conventional positive analysis.

Moreover, the questions of distribution that arise from the workings of international markets raise ethical issues for developed countries, especially the United States, whose economic policies can directly influence the markets for products, financial capital and labor upon which developing countries depend. The balance of this paper seeks to identify some of the analytical links between distribution and development in economics that have ethical implications in the context of Catholic social teaching. Special emphasis is given to the distributional biases against the poor of the Third World in international markets for products and services, for labor and for financial capital, with some attention to the role of United States economic policy and practice in shaping those markets.

Development and Distribution

The United States relates economically to the developing countries of the Third World with the same categories of two-way transactions that determine domestic and other international economic activity, e.g., the buying and selling of goods and services, financial transactions and flows of capital through direct investment, and loans and grants across both private and public sectors. Nevertheless, the scope and intensity of ethical discussion about economic relationships between developed and developing countries (perhaps especially within developing countries) is frequently greater than that concerning economic activity within or among developed nations.

Most professional economic analysis in the United States explicitly excludes from consideration all normative criteria, with the exception of the criterion of efficiency or maximization in the allocation of the world's resources, which, like the instruments of economic activity, is morally ambiguous or neutral. There is no necessary inherent relationship, positive or negative, between efficiency in the marketplace or maximization of growth rates, for example, and ethical norms of social justice.

Economic development, however, is much more than efficient economic growth. Economic development is sometimes characterized as growth with equity, where equity embraces implicit and explicit judgments about distributional inequality — inequality in the distribution of the preconditions for growth and inequality in the distribution of the benefits of growth for both private and social purposes.

The normative criteria for distributive justice in Catholic social teaching are principally based on human values, namely the possession of rights that are determined not in economic systems and economic analysis, but in the dignity and worth of all human persons as created in the image of God and united in the redemptive love of Jesus Christ.[2] It is these universally shared rights that ground ethical evaluation of both the freedoms and the inequalities generated by systems of economic production, exchange and growth. We appeal to these same rights to justify personal freedoms as well as the limitation of personal liberties by collective values embraced in such norms as the common good or human solidarity.

Also acknowledged in Catholic social teaching are distributional criteria based on principles of meritorious activity, such as individual effort or personal contribution to social well-being.[3] But merit itself can be grounded on different ethical bases. Part of the ethical appeal of competitive free markets rests on the ability to demonstrate that such markets not only allocate resources efficiently in meeting market demand, but also that the income generated is distributed according to the market value of the marginal product of workers and other suppliers of inputs. In *Laborem Exercens*, however, the claim for merit in human labor is based not on its market value but on its participation in the creative work of God.[4] Some distributional principles, such as the principle of equal pay for equal work, can be grounded in criteria of both rights and merit.

Various theories of economic distribution incorporate criteria of equality and freedom in varying proportions. Egalitarian theories of income distribution as they apply to international economics typically stress a commonality of human rights, including the minimal right to the means necessary for the satisfaction of some measure of basic human needs. Libertarian theories tend to emphasize individual rights associated with economic liberty, including ownership of property, rewards for entrepreneurial initiative and the personal and social benefits derived therefrom.

For a long time domestic public policy in most countries, capitalist and socialist, has intervened in economic activity to achieve socially acceptable mixes of freedom, equality and growth. The tools are familiar, ranging from tax and transfer mechanisms and public expenditures for social purposes to public ownership of productive resources and regulation of prices, incomes and output. The international economy, however, has historically been subject to much less international public intervention of this kind. Hence, although domestic regulations obviously impose some constraints on freedom in international transactions, it is not surprising that international inequalities are a major target of ethical scrutiny of the economic relations between the developed and the developing economies of the world.

In 1981, for example, the developing countries of the world were inhabited by over three-quarters of the world's population, but accounted for only about one-fifth of the world's gross national product (GNP).[5] Expressed differently, the 1981 average per capita GNP of $772 in 143 developing countries was less than ten percent of the $8855 average in 29 developed countries, and only six percent of the $12,530 average per capita GNP in the United States.[6] The inequality in the worldwide distribution of the gains from economic growth is even more noticeable in a comparison of the richest and the poorest. In 1981 the richest fifth of the world's population had an average per capita GNP of about $10,000, close to 50 times the average for the poorest fifth of the world's people.[7]

Even if per capita growth rates in the developing countries were equal to those in the developed countries, the absolute gap in per capita incomes would continue to grow. However, the average annual rate of growth of GNP in the 73 lowest income countries of the world over more than two decades has been less than that of the 18 richest industrial market economies, thereby widening the gap both relatively and absolutely.[8]

Moreover, distribution of the gains from growth in past years obviously affects the composition of future output from the world's resources as well as the distribution of future gains from growth. Present inequalities of income, by determining the composition of future demand in both domestic and international markets, help determine the share of the world's resources that will be devoted to the production of basic necessities and the share that will be devoted to other goods and services.

Thus, it is not surprising that Catholic social teaching from developing areas of the world, such as that in the Puebla documents, directs ethical criticism to the consumerist mentality that characterizes the societies of the richer nations.[9] It should also be noted, however, that international income inequalities also contribute to differences in public sector expenditures on social goods, such as public health expenditures, which are more than 30 times higher per capita in developed countries than in the developing world.[10]

Ethical evaluation of the economic relationships between the developing and the developed countries of the world is further complicated by the fact that both growth and future distribution are dependent upon distributional preconditions other than past shares in world output and income. I speak of such factors as the initial endowment of economic resources, which includes not only the obvious endowments of wealth, capital and natural resources, but also the size, growth, skills and education of the population. Distributional preconditions also include political conditions, especially those that determine who shall participate in decisions concerning economic allocation and distribution. For many decades the historical distribution of these preconditions supported a doctrine of comparative advantage in international trade that kept the resources of developing countries concentrated on the export of primary products to developed countries.

Finally, the distributional preconditions include cultural factors that influence economic activity. In some Eastern cultures, for example, it is more important to be in harmony with nature than to conquer and dominate nature. For Gandhi this principle also extended to setting limits on the fulfillment of material wants to which the human person should aspire.[11] In Western cultures, on the other hand, the ethical imperative to conquer and dominate nature goes hand in hand with the premise that material wants are unlimited, or at least will always exceed the capacity of existing resources.

Labor and International Markets

Much of the debate about the ethical quality of an international free market economic system overlooks the importance of assumptions about the economic, social and political preconditions that underlie and shape the working of market instruments and mechanisms. Thus, in a simple model of pure and perfect competition a market system left to its own devices tends towards a general equilibrium in which the remuneration of labor, like that of other factors of production, will be determined by the value of its marginal product, that is, the market value of the added output of an additional unit of labor.

If all consumers and suppliers begin with an ethically satisfactory distribution of income, wealth and resources, and if they share the same knowledge about and access to the markets in which they function, and if none of them has sufficient resources, size, political clout or social status to control markets, then an ethically appealing equilibrium can be expected. For example, equal pay for equal effort and skills will prevail at every level of output everywhere in the system. All consumers will pay equal prices and none will pay a price more than the cost of production, including a competitive remuneration for the services of entrepreneurs.

The proper working of the competitive markets will insure that labor is fully employed and that new technology and more efficient forms of production and sale of goods and services will be brought on line as soon as the proceeds can be expected to outweigh the costs. There is a nice ethical dimension to the analysis that increases in productivity and the resulting economic growth will, in the competitive model, accrue either to workers in the form of higher wages or to consumers in the form of lower prices or better products or both. Profits and the return on capital, i.e., interest beyond the minimums necessary to keep entrepreneurs motivated and supply of savings sufficient for equilibrium growth, will be non-existent or at most transitory on the way to an equilibrium in income and growth. All of this is ethically appealing and suggests the way in which economic growth might be equitably transmitted through the international marketplace.

Of course, if, as in the developing world, there is surplus labor, that is, widespread unemployment and underemployment as a precondition, one of the major assumptions of the market model is violated, and the model will not work as predicted. Increases in productivity may raise the average product of labor, but the marginal product of employed labor, which determines wages, will not change. Increased productivity under these labor market conditions may, of course, lead to growth-inducing increases in employment levels, but not to wage increases that are likely to narrow the gap in wage levels between rich nations and poor nations. This is the attraction to international companies of cheap labor in developing countries. However, under conditions of surplus labor prevailing in developing countries, market forces cannot be relied upon to transmit to worker incomes the value added in economic growth from increased productivity or increased demand.

Of course the value added by improvements in productivity may still accrue to consumers in the form of lower prices. But if there is less than perfect competition in the markets for goods and services, that is, if any single firm or small group of firms can control or influence selling prices in some deliberate way, another crucial assumption of the competitive model is violated. This means that there is no reason to expect the gains from increased productivity to be passed along competitively in the form of lower prices to consumers.

Thus, free trade with the developing world makes it possible for the gains from improvements in developing country labor productivity to be retained in the form of profits and returns on capital beyond the necessary minimums, a social windfall for those whose incomes are derived form capital income. If these incomes are spent for the luxury consumer goods that are criticized in Catholic social teaching, there is little opportunity for workers in developing countries to recoup the value added that would have been theirs otherwise, even in a system operating within the assumptions of a well-behaved competitive economic model. This biased market behavior helps to explain ethical criticism in *Laborem Exercens* of the "priority" of capital over labor in contemporary international markets.[12]

Of course some of the non-competitive profits and returns to capital earned in the growth process may be reinvested in further growth-stimulating improvements of productivity. The hope would be that such improvements at least create new jobs, even if wage rates do not participate in the increased productivity. But even this is not assured, since the technology developed for economic growth may well be labor saving to reflect conditions in the labor markets of the most developed areas of the international market system.

However, the realities of international markets complicate the distributional effects of economic activity still further. For example, national barriers to factor mobility, that is, to international immigration, result in further deviations from the norm of equal pay for equal work and skill. A taxi driver in Manhattan earns more than a taxi driver in Bombay, not because he works harder or is more skilled or more efficient in delivering his passengers. He earns more because his opportunity cost is higher, which simply means that he has better alternative employment opportunities than his Indian counterpart. He has better alternatives both because labor is more productive in U.S. markets and because, even in the absence of union or government intervention, U.S. labor is more likely to capture a larger share of productivity improvements in the absence of unemployment and underemployment at rates like those found in India.

Removing barriers to immigration would, of course, tend to equalize wages for comparable work in national markets. Illegal immigration, like that currently found between parts of Latin America and the United States, allows employers in the United States to appropriate at least part of the differential between foreign and domestic wages for comparable work because of the legal inability of immigrants to compete equally in U.S. labor markets.

There is probably no moral or ethical principle that fully justifies, in the abstract, the disparities in incomes for comparable skills and work that currently exist among the nations of the world. However, nothing less than a radical conversion from short-term self-interest to a principle of universal human solidarity would make acceptable the social and political destabilization that a radical reduction in barriers to immigration would create.

International Trade and Equity

The substitutes for immigration in spreading the gains from increases in economic productivity and growth internationally are found principally in international trade of goods and services and international capital movements, such as direct investment and private loans through international capital markets along with various forms of capital transfer from official governmental sources. If workers themselves cannot move freely, the free movement of their products across national boundaries can in principle accomplish some of the same distributional effects. Using the doctrine of comparative advantage, any student of elementary economics should be able to demonstrate how the world's resources will be allocated optimally if countries, rather than trying to be self-sufficient in production, specialize in producing those goods which they produce most efficiently. By exporting such goods in competitive international markets, countries will earn the foreign exchange necessary to import the goods produced most efficiently by other countries.

If the assumptions of the competitive model are realized, this international division of production will utilize the world's resources most efficiently, that is, achieve maximum world output. In addition, free trade should in theory equalize factor payments by bringing about equal pay for equal work across national boundaries. Unfortunately, for ethical evaluation this result holds only under the assumption of full employment in all countries participating in the system.

Moreover, even the theory of free trade is ambiguous about how the gains from specialization will be distributed among the trading partners. Indeed the rigid assumptions of the competitive model do not rule out the possibility that one of the trading countries may capture all the increased income that results from specialization and trade according to the principles of comparative advantage.

The doctrine of comparative advantage was in its infancy a powerful analytic antidote to the inward-looking trade policies of European mercantilist regimes. However, since World War II the less developed countries, especially in Latin America, have complained that the historically determined patterns of international specialization and division of labor are biased against the developing countries in their attempts to increase their share of world trade. Since 1950, for example, the share of the non-oil producing developing countries in the value of total world exports has declined from over 23 percent to just over 11 percent in 1980. On the other hand, the share of the developed countries of the free world in international trade, despite the post-1973 oil shocks, remained about the same.[13] Since 1970 the non-OPEC developing countries have maintained but not substantially increased their export share in the total value of imports by the developed market economies, while the share of their own exports directed to trade with each other has increased by about 50 percent.[14]

It should be noted that the share of total exports of non-OPEC developing countries that goes to the United States, as well as the share of total United States imports that comes from these developing countries, have increased more rapidly than the comparable shares for other developed market economies.[15] Nevertheless, trade with developed economies remains an uphill fight for non oil-producing developing economies, especially as protectionist sentiment grows in the United States just as the developing countries are struggling to increase exports in order to earn the foreign exchange necessary to service the foreign debts that have accumulated so rapidly in the past decade.

In light of the urgency of basic needs for the majority of the populations in developing countries, it is not surprising that ethical criticism is levelled at the composition as well as the excess of exports from developed countries to developing countries. The distribution of domestic income in developing countries, especially those with free market economies, is often as skewed in favor of a rich minority as is the international distribution of income among countries. Hence, consumer imports will tend to reflect the consumption preferences of the rich minority (which often resemble the tastes of their peers in the developed countries), rather than the basic needs of the majority. As a result it can be charged that producers of those goods in the developed countries, including workers, management and stockholders, benefit from the inequalities of distribution in the developing countries. The often criticized consumerism of the developed countries both induces and feeds upon the consumerism of the rich minority in the developing countries.

It is also worth noting that international trade in military armaments during the 1960s and the 1970s increased at a rate only slightly lower than the rate of increase in total world trade.[16] Moreover, virtually all of the arms shipped in world trade come from the developed countries and the great majority of the shipments are to developing countries.[17]

Spokesmen for less developed countries often contend that a major reason for their failure to capture a larger share of world trade lies in the fact that primary products continue to dominate their exports. Despite decades of development and industrialization, the less developed market economies of the world still depended in 1980 on primary products for well over half their exports.[18] It can be argued that the prices of primary products in world markest are too unstable to be a dependable source of income for development. Thus, a price index of over 30 primary products (excluding oil) exported by less developed countries has gone through three cycles with fluctuations averaging 25 to 40 percent each just in the last decade.[19] The international demand for primary products fluctuates during recessions and booms in developed countries, whose business cycles are also tied to one another. On the other hand, supplies of many primary products in world markets are relatively unresponsive in the short run to changes in world demand. The gestation period for coffee and cacao plantings are long, but once mature will be good for a large number of harvests.

In addition it has been argued that the prices of primary product exports of developing countries in world markets, especially of commodities from the tropics where most of the less developed countries are located, tend to deteriorate over time relative to the prices of imports to developing countries from the developed world. The statistical evidence for this long run deterioration in the terms of trade for primary products of developing countries is hard to come by, partly because of the difficulty of separating out the effects both of export diversification and of the cyclical fluctuations in primary product prices mentioned above. Nevertheless, there is evidence that the terms of trade of the non-oil producing developing countries have deteriorated by over 18 percent since 1965.[19] This means roughly that, despite economic growth and diversification of exports from developing countries, a dollar's worth of developing country exports today purchases only about four-fifths as much as it did less than two decades ago.

The long run deterioration in the purchasing power of primary product exports is supported by the argument that over time demand in developed counties for primary products, especially from the tropics, will fail to increase at the same pace as income in developed countries. A doubling of family incomes in the United States, for example, is not likely to produce a doubling of consumption of bananas or pineapples. So too raw materials from the developing countries constitute an ever smaller share of the total value of output in the developed countries as resource allocation in the high income countries shifts to the production of increasingly sophisticated goods. In addition, technological obsolescence has too often erased the market value of major primary product exports, e.g., jute in Bangladesh or nitrates in Chile.

Moreover, the conditions of the markets in which the primary product exports of the developing world are supplied differ from those in which the sophisticated manufactured products of the developed world are traded. This contributes both to short run price instability and to long run deterioration in the terms of trade, that is , the relative prices of exports versus imports, of the developing countries. The prices of primary products in world markets (with the obvious exception of oil) tend to be set competitively outside the control of individual suppliers.

Market conditions governing prices of many of the products that developing countries import from developed countries are, however, quite different. The markets for relatively sophisticated manufactured products are generally dominated by a handful of firms that are sufficiently large relative to market size; thereby they can influence price. IBM surely has more control over the prices of its computers than Juan

Valdes does over the price he receives for his coffee beans. In times of slack demand manufacturers of products with administered prices can respond by holding firm on prices while cutting production where necessary to maximize revenues and/or profits. Juan Valdes has no such choice.

Furthermore, manufacturers with some control over the prices they receive for their products need not pass along the gains from improvements in productivity to the public in the form of lower prices. Instead they can retain those earnings for future investment or distribute the gains to stockholders as dividends or to workers in the form of higher wages, especially in labor markets where unions have adequate bargaining power. Thus, the competitive differences between the export and import markets in which developing countries trade discriminate not only with respect to price but also with respect to potential improvements in workers' incomes. Workers in developed countries have opportunities to share in some of the gains from growth in the developing world in ways that workers in that world do not.

Given these allocative and distributional problems associated with reliance on exports of primary products, it is not surprising that developing countries have sought to adopt alternative trade strategies. International commodity aggreements have been formed among producers of primary products, e.g., coffee, tin and cacao, to give them some control over the prices and quantities of product to be marketed in order to redress some of the short run instabilities and long run imbalances just described.

The success of export cartels, of which OPEC is the most notorious example, depends partly upon the ability of the cartel to keep most of the world's production under its control. However, success depends also upon the willingness of importing nations to respect the cartel and upon the strength of demand for the product in the major importing nations. The United States imports roughly half the coffee produced in the world, so its willingness to live with an international coffee agreement is obviously important for the success of the agreement. Even then, however, the earning potential of the agreement depends upon the responsiveness of consumers to increases in price as well as upon the availability of acceptable substitutes. Even the strength of OPEC has not been immune to these influences.

For all of these reasons it is not surprising that developing countries have sought to diversify their exports in order to capture a larger share of growth in the world economy. They have sought to do so by moving into industrialization and away from specialization in the primary products which have been assumed to constitute most of their comparative advantage in world trade since the days of colonization by the more economically advanced nations. The path to industrialization in the face of a 200 year headstart by the developed world has not been an easy one for the developing nations. The lack of infrastructure, including transportation, communication, power, and research and development capacity, along with the absence of managerial and technical expertise, have created bottlenecks that translate into inefficient, high cost production, not always offset by the low wage costs of a surplus labor economy.

In addition, because the technology of modern production is often determined by the markets of the developed countries that serve the industrial preferences and needs of those countries, modern production processes are not always easily adaptable to the preconditions, social and political as well as economic, that exist in developing countries. Efficient low cost production in a developed country often requires a minimum plant size that is very large relative to resource availability and market potential in the developing country.

The requirements for capital and for management expertise to develop a competitive automobile facility, for example, can easily exceed the resource capacity of a developing country, while the marketing risks faced by a new exporter of autos can far exceed those faced by the dominant firms already in the industry. Moreover, concentration of a disproportionate share of a developing country's limited resources on a single major industry invests that industry with major impact upon employment, wages, political stability and other determinants of growth and the quality of life in the country.

Transnational Industrial Corporations

Consequently, it is not surprising that developing countries have turned to the transnational corporations to plug them into the most lucrative industrial export markets of the world. Between 1960 and 1981 direct investment of United States firms in the industries of developing countries increased by more than 500 percent, from about 11 billion to over 56 billion dollars.[21] According to one estimate, slightly over half the exports of manufactured goods and about one-third of all exports from Latin America to the United States in 1977 originated in subsidiaries of United States companies.[22]

Transnational industrial corporations bring to the developing countries investment capital plus modern technology, management and marketing expertise, direct and indirect employment opportunities, and access to world markets. They bring new products for local markets, on-the-job training and other educational possibilities, as well as demand for the products of local suppliers and new sources of tax revenue for social expenditures.

These can be important features for economic growth and development, but are not easy to appropriate independently in existing international markets. In the absence of other institutional conduits the transnational firms become important transmitters of these elements. Moreover, unlike interest on foreign borrrowing, which must be paid regardless of earnings, repatriation of earnings on direct foreign investments is not an issue until the investments are profitable.

The actual performance of each of these features in the development process of developing countries has, however, provoked serious criticism, including that found in *Laborem Exercens* and other recent social teaching of the Church.[23] Some of the criticism is directed at the cultural impact of the transnationals, especially upon traditional local values through the import of aggressively materialist attitudes and standards and the introduction of consumer products deemed frivolous by local cultural standards as human needs, personal and social. The internationalization of consumption patterns, especially among the affluent minorities of developing countries, contributes to a homogenization of material values that may be destructive to traditional spiritual values and culturally divisive and destabilizing in developing countries.

Much of the criticism is directed, however, at the interactions of the transnational with factor markets, both domestic and international. It is frequently pointed out, for example, that capital movements of transnational companies are not dependable sources of capital for individual developing countries because of the relatively high mobility of capital. The profitability of investments by transnational companies in developing countries is always subject to company re-evaluation against profit opportunities elsewhere in the world, regardless of the long-term implications for development and employment in individual countries. There is little space or incentive in quarterly earnings reports to stockholders for corporate managers to justify non-maximizing behavior on social or ethical grounds.

Barriers to and social costs of free movement are obviously much lower for capital than for labor in international markets. These differences in factor mobility can be added to the distributional biases against incomes of workers in labor markets of developing countries described earlier as evidence for the "priority" accorded to capital over labor in international markets that is criticized in *Laborem Exercens*.

Transnational companies can be expected to seek rates of return in developing countries higher than those in developed countries because of perceived political risks and uncertainties associated with foreign business activity. The desire of foreign firms for political stability also leaves them vulnerable to the accusation of complicity with authoritarian regimes that try to guarantee social peace by violations of human rights in the repression of political dissent, especially among the poor. They may also expect higher operating margins to allow for fast write-offs of capital goods for the same reasons. Obviously, labor market conditions that keep wages low contribute to these objectives and so are a principal attraction for foreign firms.

In addition, foreign firms seek the freedom to repatriate both capital and income (including that portion of value added attributed to rising labor productivity, but not captured in the wage rates of surplus labor economies). They also frequently need the freedom to import necessary inputs not available locally.

These desires and needs obviously require foreign exchange and therefore put pressure on the balance of payments of the host country, which is not necessarily offset by foreign exchange generated by the export sales of the foreign firms. Lacking access to and a complete understanding of the internal accounting procedures of transnational firms, developing countries are understandably critical of the prices they receive for the semifinished products of local subsidiaries that are not sold on the open market, but are shipped to other divisions of the parent transnational for further elaboration. The prices recorded in the developing countries in such cases are obviously administered internally by foreign firms, rather than set competitively in the marketplace.

By operating in markets that are not perfectly competitive in the domestic economies of both the developed and the developing world, transnational business firms thus possess a degree of freedom that makes them international arbiters, not only of the international allocation of resources, but also of the distribution of some portion of the gains from international growth. In the surplus labor markets of developing countries, transnational firms can set wages either to share or to capture the gains from increased labor productivity. In the labor markets of the developed countries they can either pass along in wage negotiations some of the gains captured in the labor markets of developing countries, or they can use the existence of international wage differentials as a bargaining threat in union negotiations.

In product markets they can administer the prices of the output of their foreign subsidiaries as well as the prices of final products in ways that distribute the gains from growth differently among countries and between workers and consumers. The same is true of the distribution of fixed costs, including depreciation schedules. Or they can do some of all the above. Their decisions are, of course, constrained by market expectations, domestically and internationally, as well as by social and political factors, domestically and internationally.

Critical evaluation of the gains from technology transfer by transnationals to developing countries can easily reflect a Catch 22 spirit. The imported technology, for example, may be advanced and sophisticated. In that case it is also likely to be capital intensive, thereby putting pressure on the balance of payments of the host country for repayment of the capital import in scarce foreign exchange without assurance of commensurate benefit to domestic employment or labor incomes.

Or the technology may be relatively labor intensive, as in the transfer by transnational firms of only those parts of the production process that benefit substantially from cheap labor in the host country. Assembly of electronics components manufactured elsewhere, or handwork on textiles are frequently cited examples. In these cases there is in fact little transfer of technology for use by the host country. Even where there is useable technology transfer there are apt to be complaints about the foreign exchange burdens of royalties and license fees.

Transnational Banking

Since the oil crises of the 1970s the importance of direct investment by transnational industrial firms as a source of development capital

has been challenged by petrodollar bank loans. The non-oil developing countries have for a decade been on the receiving end of the recycling of oil producers' windfall earnings by international banks,
especially those headquartered in the United States. By lending to
developing countries some of the huge sums deposited by oil exporters,
the international banks helped to avert a possible international financial crisis occasioned by the sudden transfer of international financial
resources to the oil exporters.

In the process the international banks also recorded paper earnings
that were often more attractive than what was available in the reces-
sionary economies of the developed countries. However, in the same
process the developing countries accumulated debts that were also unprecedented. In the decade between 1973 and 1983 the medium and
long-term international debt of the developing countries increased by
over 500 percent, from 109 to 575 billion dollars.[24] Between 1970 and
1981 the international public debt of 13 major developing countries
increased by a multiple of almost eight, from just over 31 billion to
over 227 billion dollars.[25]

For many of these countries, especially in Latin America, payment
of the debt service in hard-to-find foreign currency has taken precedence
over national development objectives. At the insistence of international
lenders and the International Monetary Fund, countries like Brazil and
Mexico have had to take domestic policy measures to reduce imports
and increase exports in hopes of creating a trade surplus sufficient to
generate the foreign exchange necessary to meet annual debt service
payments.

The policy measures prescribed, including devaluations and contractions of domestic money supplies, have resulted in additonal severe
unemployment beyond that attributable to chronic surplus labor,
reaching over thirty percent of the labor force in some Latin American
countries. Moreover, the resulting improvements in the balance of
payments of the debtor countries have been less than encouraging.
Despite their efforts to increase exports, the debtor nations of Latin
America in 1983 faced interest charges alone on foreign debts that
represented 35 percent of their total export earnings.[26]

In the absence of formal default or moratoria, the balance of the
debt service can be covered in the short run only by additional borrowing. This process of capitalizing interest payment defaults, along
with additional high service charges by the lending banks for the

privilege of "rolling over" the bad debts, creates high—and highly questionable—paper profits on the books of the foreign lending banks, while simply increasing the burden to the borrowers of the unpaid debt.

Additional lending, if it is forthcoming at all from banks in the United States and elsewhere, tends to be for shorter lending periods and at higher and fluctuating rates of interest. Developing countries argue that the desired outcome of their borrowing in the form of competitive exports for world markets requires much more time to generate the necessary conditions for internal development and to remove inflationary internal bottlenecks to economic growth.

Dependency or Interdependence?

Some critics argue that the accumulation of competitive imperfections in international markets for labor, capital, goods and services, along with the behavior of the transnational industrial and financial firms, are cumulatively biased to create a self-reinforcing economic dependency of developing countries on the developed world. It is argued by some that the imperfect international markets for both products and factors of production are interrelated and self-reinforcing in such a way as to prevent the international economy from reducing the growth in economic inequalities between the rich and poor of the world. These arguments go beyond economic analysis of markets to identify social and political relationships that contribute to dependency. Attention is paid, for example, to the natural alliances that form among economic elites in developing and developed countries as well as to the sometimes less than savory links between international business and corrupt, unrepresentative governments in developing countries.

Others retort that the growth of the international economy has resulted in global interdependence. The dependence of the United States and other developed countries on imported oil and the recent relatively rapid growth of United States trade with developing countries, including imports of manufactures, are cited as evidence of interdependence. So too is the stake of many large United States banks in the continued solvency of the major debtor nations of Latin America.

It is also claimed by some that the failure of developing countries to grow more rapidly is due more to failures of domestic organization and commitment than to biases in international markets. They point to the high, relatively non-inflationary growth rates of the Asian NICS (newly industrialized countries), namely, South Korea, Taiwan, Hong Kong and Singapore. These countries have achieved high growth rates largely through success in world markets and with reliance on transnational firms in production, trade and finance. And they have done so with a distribution of income and wealth that is probably less skewed than that of many less internationally involved developing countries.

About all that can be said conclusively in this debate is that the present interaction of domestic development and international markets is not functioning to narrow the development gap for the vast majority of the world's poor. The degree of dependence of any single country, however, is related to a host of cultural, social, political, economic and personal characteristics and relationships, both internal and external, that identify the historical development of that country. This is consistent with the perspective of *Laborem Exercens*, which perhaps more than earlier social encyclicals acknowledges a principle of pluralism of development models within the developing world, involving different mixes of market freedom and deliberate public intervention in the ownership and allocation of resources and in the distribution of income.[27]

Policy Alternatives

The options for international economic policy are as varied as the analyses that support them. As indicated earlier, the international economy has been subject to less international regulation than most domestic economies, capitalist and socialist. Developing countries have responded unilaterally to their disadvantages in international markets with a variety of selective and sometimes conflicting restrictions on trade in goods, services and capital, including tariffs, exchange controls and a plethora of regulations restricting the freedom of foreign investors.

At the same time, there are arguments for even greater liberalization of the international economy. These deal mainly with the removal of protective tariffs and similar obstacles on grounds of efficiency in the allocation of the world's resources. Removal of protective tariffs in the United States on manufactures from developing countries would allow developing countries to earn scarce foreign exchange for development needs and for service on debts to developed countries that cannot be met without inflows of foreign exchange.

Free trade also helps keep prices low for consumers in the United States. However, because surplus labor in developing countries prevents the doctrine of comparative advantage from operating according to the principles of full-employment, competitive market theory trade can also permit developing countries to export some of their unemployment to the United States. This means that tariff removal would have to be accompanied by domestic economic and social policies, such as retraining programs and social subsidies, to preserve equity as far as possible for affected United States workers. Even then it would be impossible to avoid interpersonal comparisons of the benefits to the poor abroad with the disruption of the lives of United States workers. The greater the disruption the greater must be the acceptance of principles of common good and international human solidarity by those who currently benefit from the present system of international allocation and distribution.

Removing protective barriers in the United States and other developed countries, however, is not sufficient to redress the biased allocative and distributional effects of the international market conditions that have been the subject of this paper. I refer especially to the existence in the developing world of surplus labor, imbalances in the mobility of labor, capital and technology, as well as in relationships between markets for commodities and for manufactures, and noncompetitive elements in the economic activities of the transnationals. Consequently, various proposals for deliberate intervention in the international marketplace have emerged in recent decades, and many of them, like commodity agreements, have been the subject of recommendations by six United Nations Conference on Trade and Development (UNCTAD) conferences over the past two decades with a limited positive response by the United States. The most recent UNCTAD conference has proposed a Common Fund to place a floor under commodity prices intended to offset the deterioration in terms of trade of developing countries.

In markets for manufactured goods, developing countries have sought and received to some extent preferential tariffs for their manufactures which compete with those of the developed countries. Such preferences are justified on grounds that costs of production are high until both scale of production and efficiency increase to competitive levels. The burden of such concessions, to the extent that they are effective, falls selectively in developed countries upon competing producers, provoking political resistance or compensatory domestic concessions. Developing countries have also sought contractual agreements to permit additional processing of primary products, especially of minerals, in their countries to capture more of the value added on the way to the final product. Oil refining, copper smelting and instant coffee processing are some obvious examples.

The international economy lacks the tax and transfer mechanisms that are available in the public sectors of domestic economies to redistribute part of the gains from growth in the form of grants, subsidies, educational and social expenditures, etc. To some extent overseas development assistance by developed countries has acted as a substitute. However, as a share of their own incomes, economic aid from the wealthiest developed countries has been far less than domestic social expenditures and income redistribution.

The United States, for example, spent about $600 per capita on public education but only about $25 per capita in 1981 on official development assistance, which was less than the per capita aid expenditures of Canada, Japan and every western European nation except Italy.[28] The share of its gross national product spent by the United States on development assistance declined by about one-third during the 1970s (the development decade!), so that by 1981 only the Soviet Union among the major powers spent a percentage of its gross national product on development assistance less than the two-tenths of one percent spent by the United States.[29] On the other hand, military expenditures per capita in 1980 of $632 in the United States were higher than for any other nation except Israel and four Arab oil nations.[30]

Slightly more than one-quarter of United States economic aid is channelled through multilateral institutions like the World Bank and the International Monetary Fund which attempt to follow consistent, if not universally accepted, lending policies.[31] The remainder, however, is the result of bilateral political agreements and is spent principally on university consulting services and capital goods.

The interrelated character of international markets for labor, capital and final products and their imperfections is not likely to be well served by isolated policy options like bilateral trade and development assistance agreements. Consequently, there have been efforts to introduce more consistently planned and integrated sets of policy options to redress the cumulative biases of international markets against the development of the poorest nations. These approaches to reform emphasize the interdependence of trade, aid and markets for capital and labor within the world economy to achieve growth and distributional equity. Two notable examples of comprehensive schemes for reform of the international economy are the Brandt Commision Reports, *North-South: A Programme for Survival* and *Common Crisis: North-South Cooperation for World Recovery*. These reports have called for an unprecedented level of international economic cooperation, including much greater reliance by individual nations on multilateral institutions for planning and coordination of the international economy. The Brandt Commission reports have received attention in Europe and developing countries, but have been largely ignored in the United States.

All of these policy proposals acknowledge the interrelationships of the international economy and attempt to make those relationships more equitable. All involve redistribution of some kind, whether only redistribution of future gains from growth or more fundamental redistribution of ownership and control of existing resources. In international markets all acknowledge the persistence of self-interest in policy recommendations that seek to reconcile conflicting vested interests. Increasingly the case is made for more global planning in the interest of the long-term peaceful survival of all of humankind.

The challenge of universal equity invariably falls most heavily on the developed countries. Therefore, recommendations for domestic policy in those countries must acknowledge that international responsibility. It is on this point,for example, that the recent pastoral letter of the Canadian bishops, *Ethical Reflections on the Economic Crisis*, is vulnerable. In seeking to find economic alternatives less dependent upon the United States, the Canadian bishops opted for greater self-sufficiency based upon more labor-intensive production for domestic consumption, rather than upon development of high-technology export industries. In this context they recommend more production of textiles for domestic consumption.[32]

Unfortunately, they fail to note the implications of this recommendation. Either wages of Canadian workers will have to fall to keep the prices of Canadian textiles competitive with imports from developing countries, or prices will have to be allowed to rise. If they are allowed to rise, protective tariffs will have to be erected against cheaper imports from the developing countries to keep the Canadians employed. The net result will be higher prices for Canadian consumers and the export of unemployment to textile workers in developing countries. The ethical implications of economic interdependence are not so easily avoided.

The challenge of international equity to domestic policy in developed countries is perhaps nowhere more acute than in the United States which, despite its own increasing dependence on the rest of the world, continues to dominate the world economy. As the recent world-wide recession has again demonstrated, domestic economic policies in the United States reverberate throughout the international economy. We have not yet, however, been able to control our own federal budget, either by generating more tax revenues or by reducing military and other public expenditures.

Borrowing by the government to finance its huge budget deficits drives up interest rates. So too does tight control over the money supply by the Federal Reserve Bank to offset inflationary pressures from the budget deficit. High interest rates in the United States in turn raise the cost to developing countries of their foreign debt service and attract international capital to the United States away from the developing and other developed economies of the world. In 1983, as a result of these forces, Latin American countries became net exporters of capital to the United States and other developed economies in a paradoxical and burdensome reversal of conventional development theory.[33]

Inflation does inhibit growth. And growth in the United States increases domestic demand for exports and makes more palatable redistributive policy measures in behalf of the world's poor. It is not clear, however, that the poor of the Third World are beneficiaries of our decision to accept high interest rates as the price of maintaining non-inflationary high levels of defense spending and other public expenditures.

Moreover, it is unlikely that even enlightened individual self-interest alone will ever achieve the redistribution of income, wealth, control and power that is necessary to narrow significantly the gap between the richest and the poorest of the world. Only a more deeply rooted personal conversion to universal human values of solidarity and a shared common dignity can embrace the scope of cooperative action that is needed for greater equity in international economic life, as Catholic social teaching right up through *Laborem Exercens* continually teaches. For the Christian, that conversion ultimately rests on acceptance of the full implications of the Gospel message of creation and redemption in the love of Jesus Christ.

Notes

1. Cf. Michael Novak, *The Spirit of Democratic Capitalism* (New York: Simon and Schuster, 1982), Ch. IX, pp. 180-181; Michael Novak, "Can a Christian Work for a Corporation," *The Judeo-Christian Vision and the Modern Corporation*, ed. Oliver F. Williams and John W. Houck (Notre Dame, IN: University of Notre Dame Press, 1982), pp. 170-202; and P.T. Bauer, *Reality and Rhetoric: Studies in the Economics of Development* (Cambridge: Harvard University Press, 1984), Ch. 2.

2. John Paul II, *On Human Work: Laborem Exercens* (Washington: United States Catholic Conference, 1981), Ch. 6, pp. 13-15.

3. *Ibid.*, Chs. 4-5, pp. 11-13.

4. *Ibid.*, Ch. 25, pp. 53-56. For an elaboration of this religious view of co-creation see my essay, *"Laborem Exercens:* A Third World Perspective," *Co-Creation and Capitalism: John Paul II's Laborem Exercens*, ed. John W. Houck and Oliver F. Williams (Washington, D.C.: University Press of America, 1983), pp. 174-198.

5. John P. Lewis and Valeriana Kallab, eds., *U.S. Foreign Policy and the Third World: Agenda 1983* (New York: Praeger, 1983), Table C-3, p. 220.

6. *Ibid.*, pp. 219-220.

7. Estimates based on The World Bank, *World Development Report 1983* (New York: Oxford University Press, 1983), Table 1, pp. 148-149.

8. *Ibid.*, pp. 219-220.

9. "Evangelization in Latin America's Present and Future: Final Document of the Third General Conference of the Latin American Episcopate, Puebla de Los Angeles, Mexico," reprinted in John Eagleson and Philip Scharper, eds., *Puebla and Beyond* (Maryknoll: Orbis Books, 1980), Sec. 213, Par. 56, p. 130.

10. Ruth Leger Sivard, *World Military and Social Expenditures 1983* (Washington: World Priorities, 1983), Table III, p. 37.

11. For a commentary see Margaret Chatterjee, *Gandhi's Religious Thought* (Notre Dame: University of Notre Dame Press, 1983), esp. pp. 117-119. See also the theological debate about human creativity and human sin amongst Michael Novak, Stanley Hauerwas and David Hollenbach, S.J., in *Co-Creation and Capitalism*, pp. 13-77.

12. *Laborem Exercens*, Ch. 12, pp. 25-27.

13. Vd. UNCTAD, *1981 Handbook of International Trade and Development Statistics*, p. 25.

14. Lewis, *op. cit.*, Table E-4, p. 246 and Table E-7, p. 250.

15. *Ibid.*, Table E-7, p. 250 and Table E-12, p. 256.

16. *Ibid.*, Table E-1, p. 243 and Sivard, *op. cit.*, Table I, p. 32.

17. Lewis, *op. cit.*, Table F-4, p. 266.

18. *Ibid.*, Table E-2, p. 244.

19. *Ibid.*, Table E-8, p. 251 and Table B-4, p. 196.

20. *Ibid.*, Table B-5, p. 197.

21. *Ibid.*, Table A-9, p. 188.

22. Estimates based on data in ECLA, "Las Relaciones Economicas Externas de America Latina en los Anos Ochenta," p. 39.

23. Cf. *Laborem Exercens*, Ch. 17, p. 39 and Puebla "Final Document," Ch. II, Par. 66, p. 131.

24. The World Bank, *Debt and the Developing World: Current Trends and Prospects* (Washington: The World Bank, 1984), Table 1, p. ix.

25. Lewis, *op. cit.*, Table B-8, p. 200.

26. ECLA, "Preliminary Overview of the Latin American Economy During 1983," Table 15, p. 37.

27. *Laborem Exercens*, Ch. 7, pp. 15-16 and Ch. 14, pp. 30-34.

28. Lewis, *op. cit.*, Table G-4, p. 276 and Sivard, *op. cit.*, Table II, p. 33.

29. Lewis, *op. cit.*, Table G-4, p. 276.

30. Sivard, *op. cit.*, Table III, pp. 36-40.

31. Lewis, *op. cit.*, Table G-8, p. 280.

32. Episcopal Commission for Social Affairs, Canadian Conference of Catholic Bishops, *Ethical Reflections on the Economic Crisis*, section titled, "New Directions."

33. ECLA, "Preliminary Overview . . .", p. 5.

Eleven

Transforming the World Economy: The Crisis of Progress and the Priority of Labor

JOE HOLLAND

ALL THEOLOGY IS ULTIMATELY SOCIAL ETHICS. ALL theology is in its fullness a correlation of two poles—the religious tradition and the social situation. All religious tradition is a reading of the social world, and all theology within the religious tradition is therefore a religious interpretation of the social world.

Further all theology is a strategic act. The theological correlation of the social situation and the heritage of the religious tradition guides the faith community in its worldly journey. How the social context is read, how the tradition is tapped in relation to that context, these are the basic sources for shaping the historical thrust of the religious tradition.

Contempory Catholic social thought refers to this historical consciousness within theology as "reading the signs of the times." It was this biblical phrase which Pope John XXIII used in his letter of convocation for Vatican Council II. The Council itself made the phrase its own, as did Paul VI. And now with Pope John Paul II, the reading has taken greater complexity and depth.

In the Catholic tradition this theological task of historical discernment was canonized by a statement of Pope Paul VI in his 1971 document *Octogesima Adveniens*, referred to in English as "A Call to Action."

It is up to Christian communities to analyze with objectivity the situation which is proper to their own country, to shed on it the light of the Gospel's unalterable words, and to draw principles or reflections, norms of judgement, and directives of action from the social teaching of the Church. (No. 4)

In summary, Paul VI asked faith communities: 1) to analyze their social situation: 2) in the light of the gospels: 3) for purposes of action and reform.

The Cultural Crisis of a Mechanistic Civilization

At its deepest cultural foundation the crisis of the modern world is, I propose, the spiritual exhaustion and social-ecological destruction flowing from absolutizing the mechanistic imagination.

To begin a discussion of trade with culture may seem unnecessarily remote. But what is more powerful in the trading process than the penetration of one culture by another? Trade is not only about economic goods and services; it is also about political structures and power and, above all, about values. We know clearly today that all world cultures are being aggressively reshaped by the commercial expansion of American capitalist culture.

From the long-range perspective this cultural crisis is the culmination of the entire process of Western civilization. But let us leave aside the ancient roots of the modern crisis and look only at its proximate foundation, the modern Enlightenment.

The Enlightenment secularized biblical messianism and linked it to a dramatic expansion of the classical critical spirit. This secularized and critical messianism saw salvation in modern science and made autonomous technology its redemptive act. In sum, the Enlightenment unleashed a Promethean vision of scientific salvation within history.

In no way do I wish to reject all the achievements of modern science and technology. At the heart of its genius, authentic science is a sharing in the religious wonder with which the Creator has endowed humanity. The technological gains which have flowed from this wonder can testify to the marvelous co-creativity in which the Creator has invited us to share.

But creatures can be turned into idols. When science loses its roots in religious wonder, it becomes Promethean scientism — an idol. Similarly, when the roots of technological creativity in the co-creative linkage of humanity and its Creator are forgotten and it poses instead as the act of autonomous redemption, then its energies often shift from creation to destruction.

This, I propose, is what is coming to dominate the main lines of both secularized ideologies in the world economy today. More and more, the consciousness and structures of modernity are collapsing into social, ecological, and spiritual destruction. Of course there are important defenses against this collapse still left in the social fabric, but this I believe is the direction of the main lines of the ideologies themselves. (I prescind here from any creative revision of the main lines of these ideologies.)

But let us turn now to the root source of this idolatrous and destructive energy, the absolutizing of the mechanistic root of modernity. Whereas classical society viewed experience through the lens of an organic (body/soul) root metaphor, modern society came to use the lens of a mechanistic metaphor. All experience — natural, social, psychological, and even sometimes religious — was seen to work like a machine. This perception has been taking deeper and deeper hold in the foundations of Western culture, and extending beyond the West to reshape the globe. It is the underlying vision which came to inform the modern shape of science, be it the physical, biological, psychological, or social science, including economics.

There have been two successive and distinct, though related ideological forms of this mechanistic vision, namely the liberal ideology of industrial capitalism now centered in the American superpower and the Marxian ideology of scientific socialism now centered in the Soviet superpower. There are of course intermediate and revisionist positions between the two, i.e. social democratic, christian democratic, eurocommunist, and various Third World movements, but they do not constitute the political mainstream of the superpower world. Let us speak then of the clearer extremes.

Capitalist Ideology: Priority of the Market

The capitalist or liberal ideology originally saw nature and society as a simple physical machine. It took over the Newtonian-Cartesian scientific model and applied it to politics and economics. The truth was to be found in the parts, not the whole.

Therein is the first difference between the modern liberal mechanistic and the classical organic root metaphors. I can take my lawn mower apart to the last piece, clean it and oil it, and put it back together to run better than before. But if I try to take a living body apart piece by piece, I will kill it. For one the truth is in the parts. For the other it is in the whole.

In the modern capitalist or liberal experience, through the fragmenting differentiation or specialization of liberal science and technology, the sense of the whole has been eroding. One part is isolated from another part, and the two are put into competition. We call this the free market, interest group politics, or the war of ideas. In religious terms, it has brought the separation of faith and life, whose scientific equivalent is the separation of fact and value. Religion is privatized, while the economic structure becomes morally autonomous. This progressive fragmentation of the parts is called liberal freedom.

Of course liberal freedom is a wonderful contribution to human experience. Few of us would want to return to pre-modern authoritarian and theocratic societies. But if liberal freedom becomes the only or final ordering principle of social space, then it proves ultimately destructive. There is no place left for the common good, that is, the vision of the whole.

Polanyi noted this crisis of the capitalist or liberal vision well before it fully matured in our own time.

> . . . the idea of a self-adjusting market implied a stark utopia. Such an institution could not exist for any length of time without annihilating the human and natural substance of society. (*The Great Transformation*, p. 3)

If freedom is the first dogma of capitalist liberalism, the second is progress. The liberal doctrine of progress found a scientific model in Darwinian evolution — the steady but random and ruthless trajectory of the cluster of parts toward higher forms. Capitalist progress is a fragmented and competitive evolutionary arrow, contrasting with the integralist and static cycle of classical society.

But the progressive liberal arrow sets up a dichotomy between past and future. The future was to be built by rejecting the past, in effect separating the two as separate parts. For the Enlightenment, and for the scientistic prejudice generally, the past is the repository of ignorance and superstition to be developed by progress. Not too long ago the Catholic Church was seen by the leading edge of modernity as the most institutionally entrenched vestige of repressive tradition. Sectors of the liberal and socialist intelligentsia still share this anti-Catholic prejudice.

It is this dualistic paradigm of the future against the past and the pluralistic paradigm of the fragmentation of the parts which culturally undergirds the capitalist or liberal development model and gives it legitimation. The center is seen as bringing progress and freedom to the periphery, raising it out of backwardness and un-freedom. The center of industrial capitalism, according to its ideology, would bring social progress to the periphery by freeing up the market, liberalizing the politics, and modernizing the culture. These acts in turn are to unleash the arrow of progress.

Within this capitalist or liberal ideology free trade has been considered the leading agent of development. According to the capitalist theory of comparative advantage, trade promised to magnify productivity. This would in turn break the power of pre-modern authoritarian elites (the landed oligarchy or aristocracy) and free up the ascendant and competitive politics of the modernizing commercial and industrial elites. Finally, free trade would introduce modern education and innovation, shattering the cultural restraints of tradition.

But, I propose, modern freedom and progress pushed to maturity in this way are now producing their dialectical opposite, namely repression and destruction. The arrow of progress turns round like a boomerang into a dagger of death.

In his first encyclical, *Redemptor Hominis*, Pope John Paul II noted this crisis of modern progress. (I have taken the liberty throughout of transforming the pope's sexist language.)

> Humanity today seems ever to be under threat from what it produces . . . it turns against humanity itself, at least in part . . . This seems to make up the main drama of present-day human existence in its broadest and universal dimension. Humanity therefore lives increasingly in fear. (RH, 15)

In the judgement of the Pope what we see being spread across the world, and especially into the "developing countries," is a degrading and regressive progress. It threatens to destroy the earth rapidly through nuclear holocaust or slowly through ecological contamination. In the interim it oppresses human dignity by widening the gap between rich and poor, unleashing a plague of human rights violations and repressing the true freedom of religion. This leads the Pope to the concluding judgement.

> So widespread is the phenomenon that it brings into question the financial, monetary, production, and commercial mechanisms that, resting on various political pressures, support the world economy. These are proving incapable either of remedying the unjust social situations of the past or of dealing with the urgent challenges and ethical demands of the present. (RH, 16)

Later in his extraordinary encyclical *Laborem Exercens*, the Pope points out the fatal flaw in this misguided world economy. The key is that labor has been made subject to capital, forgetting the foundational principle of the "priority of labor." As a result, workers are converted into merchandise, treated as a factor of production, and reduced to pieces of an economic machine. (LE, 58)

This inverts the order of creation and points it toward idolatry and destruction. For this reason, says John Paul II, the church " . . . differs from the program of *capitalism* practiced by liberalism and by the political systems inspired by it." (LE, 14)

Clearly it would seem then that the stress of the capitalist ideology on the principle of free trade, as a morally autonomous principle detached from the social, ecological, and religious values of the human community, cannot be the foundational principle for ordering the world market. For if we allow it to become the primary ordering principle, then we in effect acquiesce in the inversion of capital over labor. Rather, according to Catholic social teaching, labor should determine trade, not trade determine labor.

But if the inverted ideology of capitalism cannot be the guide for the faith community in its worldly journey, what then of the other modern ideology?

Socialist Ideology: Priority of the State

I have come to believe that the ideology of scientific socialism, in spite of the insights it has to offer about equality and the common good, is now strategically bankrupt. For this reason Christians should not accept the ideology of scientific socialism. It also falls into the general crisis of modernity, or the wider crisis of our mechanistic civilization. Thus scientific socialism is not an alternative to the crisis of industrial capitalism, but rather shares in the same wider cultural crisis, with disturbing economic and political consequences.

The modern ideology of scientific socialism, flowing from the foundational work of Karl Marx, attempts to break beyond the mechanistic limits of capitalism and yet in a paradoxical way winds up radicalizing the mechanistic principle. I leave aside here any appraisal of the intention of Marx's original writings or of any attempts to transform socialism, and speak of the contemporary main lines of the ideology, just as I did with capitalism.

The heart of the matter is that while capitalism initially projected a vision of a simple physical machine, scientific socialism, in rebelling against the irrationality of the free market, actually pushed the mechanistic logic deeper to a cybernetic level.

Originally for industrial capitalism the market was free, that is, without overt guidance. Rather the guidance was hidden—the providential invisible hand described by Adam Smith. But for socialism, the guidance became overt. The economy was to be planned. The state, and behind it the intelligentsia, became the scientific mind of the economy.

Thus the socialist ideology anticipated the cybernetic dimension of the modern industrial machine, something the capitalist ideology is only now coming to in its present stage. Through its elitist vanguard (party) and the centralization of all power in the state, the socialist tradition heightened the role of the technocratic or strategic intelligentsia. It was like the modern coupling of the computer to machine. Economics was to be politically guided. Yet the content of economic life followed the same social, ecological, and spiritual erosion as in capitalism, except the erosion was more rationalized.

Scientific socialism still accepted the main lines of capitalist technology—in Marxian terms its means of production. In fact, it has had to feed largely off capitalist technology. Apart from the different initiating factors (the private corporation or the public state) the social and technological absolutizing of material production at the expense of social, ecological, and spiritual communion is similar in the two system.

Both systems, for examples, were committed to Taylorism (time/motion studies), both embraced mass abortion and nuclearism, both have highly militarized systems, both have prioritized urbanization, and both have highly concentrated centers of bureaucratic power (one public, the other private). In essence, both are modern industrial societies. I might add both are increasingly repressing their own workers, though in different ways. In essense both modern ideologies reduce society to a machine of material production, with capital—in public or private form—over labor.

If industrial capitalism began as a practical economic materialism with the economy shaping the politics and culture (the supremacy of the market), scientific socialism shifted the focus to a theoretical political materialism, that is the primacy of politics over economics and culture (the supremacy of the state).

But what of culture? Is it simply the expression of the market or the tool of the state? Or is it not rather the infrastructure within the infrastructure, the deeper foundation of political and economic life? This is the religious vision—humanity with the Creator shaping economic and political life out of the deepest wellsprings of culture. This is the clear position taken by Pope John Paul II in his contemporary cultural deepening of Catholic social teaching.

In terms of the capitalist side of the crisis, the Pope points starkly to the strategic cultural flaw within the new competition growing out of this global stage of industrial capitalism:

> An economy oriented solely to profit would not create a community of persons, nor would it generate a true social culture of responsible participation . . . (Address in Milan, 22 May 1983)

It was the "strategic" error of modern socialism to repeat this error on politcal ground, for if economic competition does not create culture, neither does state power. Only human community creates culture—community with humanity, with nature, and with the Creator. Yet for scientific socialism the class struggle to regain the primacy of labor over capital was waged almost exclusively in political terms as the class struggle between capital and labor over control of the state.

In this struggle, strategy was set by the Left intelligentsia, who theoretically entered into coalition with workers. But the struggle tended to end when the political hegemony of the capitalist class was overcome and the intelligentsia gained control of the state. It was assumed that the state, under the control of the intelligentsia, was the single and only instrument for socialization. The result, however, was not the priority of labor, but a shift from the primacy of private capital to the primacy of public capital—the state over labor.

This shift had both good and bad sides. On the good side, it raised again the principle of the common good, that is a holistic view of society. On the bad side, it mediated the service of the common good only through a centralized state apparatus dominated by the techno-cratic intelligentsia. The common good was perceived exclusively in mechanistic terms of material production, again uprooted from au-thentic social, ecological, and spiritual community. The scientifc socialist state became a modern mechanistic example of the older organic tradition of benevolent despotism with all the risks that en-tails. In theory the primacy of labor is restored, but not in practice. The structure negates it.

Reflecting on this failure of the scientific socialist experience, Pope John Paul II writes:

> For it must be noted that merely taking these means of production (capital) out of the hands of their private owners is not enough to en-sure their satisfactory socialization . . . Thus, merely converting the means of production into State property is by no means equivalent to "socializing" that property. (LE 14)

According to the Pope, the same mechanistic result flows from this alternate model. It " . . . makes the worker feel just like a cog in a huge machine moved from above." (LE 14—language revised)

Even when it is not yet in power, and even when the Left takes soft forms, as in social democracy, the crisis is still present. For despite its powerful and valid critique of industrial capitalism, the Left in-telligentsia normally pursues a path which deepens anti-spiritual secularization, cuts its own members off from their social roots in tradition and community and from their ecological roots in nature, and promotes a libertarian-technocratic culture centered in the in-telligentsia. As a result the mechanistic culture deepens.

Late Modern Ideological Convergence

In sum, both modern ideologies of progress are converting into a common mechanistic crisis. Industrial capitalism began the mechanistic drive though incompletely, for its rationality was hindered by the fragmentation of economic and political functions. Later scientific socialism broke beyond the irrationality of this fragmentation, but only succeeded in deepening the mechanistic logic, bringing the full power of state strategy to the development of the national economic machine. Now industrial capitalism, in its new stage, is converging with scientific socialism as it too creates a strategic state, streamlining and disciplining the national economy for world market competition.

In the First World this appears in soft form with neoconservative governments, as we see in the United States with "Reaganomics" or with future liberal "corporativist" governments. In the Second World we see it also in hard form as in the military repression of the workers movement in Poland.

In both cases, however, the defining imperative becomes national security, which is the collective security of the economic and political machine inverting the cultural principle of the priority of labor. Traditionally under industrial capitalism labor was subject to private forms of capital (via the market) and under scientific socialism to public forms of capital (via the state). In neither case is the priority of labor honored. Now we are beginning to see the convergence of the two forms, that is the *combination of state and markets in a competitive world market system where the national state apparatus provides strategic guidance for the competition.*

We see this ideological convergence of the two forms of denying the priority of labor clearly in the modern ideological cultivation of economic, political, and cultural forms which have amplified technological power beyond any human imagination, yet turned humanity and the earth into mere instruments, sometimes disposable, of secularized rationalization. Still worse, both ideologies aggressively undermine the delicate fabric of human community and solidarity. Above all they directly attack or subtly erode the deepest symbols of the religious Mystery. In scientific socialism religion tends to be politically controlled. In industrial capitalism it tends to be culturally trivialized.

The fruit of this common crisis haunts us daily in the ever proximate act of nuclear war and in the expanding program of mass technological abortion. It haunts us too in the steady erosion of our natural ecological fabric, of the social ecology of family, and of com munal life. Finally it haunts us in the now world-wide attack against authentic labor movements.

We in the capitalist center live intimately with one cultural side of this crisis. We are submerged in the rat race, where time becomes money or power—anything but contemplation and wonder. Culturally we find the consumer society begins to consume our spiritual depth. Human interchange is pressed toward an endless series of "efficient" yet shallow encounters. Most important, the religious Mystery is progressively excluded or still worse manipulated to bless the very path of destruction. Meanwhile we are taught that labor unions are to be despised as corrupt, representing special interests and interfering with economic efficiency.

But above all it is in the Third World that we see the most destructive forms of the crisis. We watch as the gap grows wider between rich and poor, as debt and unemployment mount higher, as the concentration of capital into oligopolistic and conglomerated transnational corporations grows. Our brothers and sisters both in church and labor suffer exile, imprisonment, torture, and death under the national security dictatorships.

Structural Pressures on the Modern State

There are four structural pressures on the modern state coming from the new world market competition and shifting it into the national security mode. These are:

1) *Provide Cheap Labor*: Since every state is moving into competition with every other state, all other things being equal those states which can offer cheaper labor are more attractive to transnational capital. This leads to a world-wide attack on labor movements, directly in the Third World and indirectly in the First World. It also leads to greater pressures to marginalize labor and substitute capital-intensive technology, including robotics.

2) *Reduce Social Spending*: Since the social programs of the social welfare state may be considered part of the social wage, paid for in part by taxation on investments, there is a corresponding pressure against these social programs.

In the Third World, industrialization simply often fails to provide social welfare programs or at best offers state subsidies to basic goods and services like food and transportation. The pressure there is to block social welfare demands on the state and to reduce or even eliminate subsidies aimed at basic needs.

In the First World there are pressures to suspend or at least slow the growth of expansive state social spending. The reason again is to make the political jurisdiction more attractive to transnational capital by being thereby able to offer tax breaks or even direct subsidies to corporations. This negative pressure on the social welfare state occurs at the very time that the production system is marginalizing large pools of labor into structural unemployment and reducing the employed working class to austerity levels. This intensifies the fiscal pressure on the social welfare state precisely when it is already in crisis. Thus the first pressure compounds the second.

3) *Increase Military Spending*: The world market today becomes more polycentric, both because of the recovery of European and Japanese industrial bases after the devastation of World War II and because of the global spread of industrialization through the world factory model of the transnational corporations. As a result the world economy grows more interdependent. At the same time the world polity also grows more volatile, partly because of the weakening of American hegemony, partly because of the global competition itself.

As a result, in the new interdependent and competitive context, states are under pressure—either alone or in coalition—to expand their external military security. They do this to guarantee access to strategic resources, shipping lanes, and foreign markets, and sometimes to protect foreign investments. Of course for many states of the industrial center these functions are not new, but their scale is vastly amplified.

The new Cold War growing up across the East/West axis, and the new militarization of politics on the North/South axis may be seen in part as the fruit of global economic competition over resources and markets by the super-powers and their client states. Also the Soviet bloc is ever more active in the world market system, guiding external economic strategy by capitalist principles.

The expansion of military spending is also fueled by the same technological drive feeding the new stage of capitalism. The very technological gains in transportation and communications, as well as production, through the electronic revolution of miniaturization compels as well the production of ever more sophisticated weaponry.

The arms race has pressed itself to a new stage, further absorbing the limited capital of the society.

The need to streamline social spending is further aggravated by the growing military demands for scarce capital. Thus the third pressure also compounds the second.

4) *Guarantee Political Stability*: When major investors look to a political jurisdiction to make a significant investment, they want to be assured of political stability over five, ten, or perhaps fifteen years, in order to realize the maximum return on investment. In some cases this is already present. But more and more, due to wide ranges of structural unemployment, deepening austerity policies, the growing nuclear and ecological threat, and the general attack on labor movements, there are strong movements of social instability emerging across societies.

Sometimes these movements can be countered in residually democratic nations by "divide and conquer" policies, but increasingly in the Third World at least the solution is found in the turn to dictatorship. Stability is achieved by force, in the name of national security. Thus the new stage of industrial capitalism seems explicitly to be undermining democracy. It has been said that the Alliance for Progress in Latin America, aimed at bringing progress and freedom, began in a context of 17 democracies and 3 dictatorships, only to wind up with 3 democracies and 17 dictatorships.

The expanded role of the military is not the deep cause of this shift. The deep cause is rather in the foundational economic structures of an uprooted and unregulated world market. The controlling elites are no longer landed oligarchs, small entrepreneurs nor the national triumvirate of big business, big labor, and big (social) government, but rather the technocratic state-centered alliance between the new military elites (now part of the strategic intelligentsia) and the elites of transnational capital.

In this state-centered, militaristic, and strategic style of government, we see the cybernetic principle, once limited to scientific socialism, now appropriated within advanced capitalism. Similarly the national security principle, once absolutized only in the communist sphere, now heads toward maximization in the capitalist sphere as well. Indeed this is the source of the negative convergence between advanced industrial capitalism and advanced scientific socialism.

Trade and the New International Division of Labor

This new national security stage of industrial capitalism has led to the maturing of the world market under the global factory model of the transnational corporations and transnational banks. This in turn has led to a new international division of labor, which is the heart of the matter in the present trade debate.

The new international division of labor has been made possible by two related but distinct developments: 1) the technological revolution of transportation and communications; and 2) the steady fragmentation and de-skilling of the production process.

Now, as never before, goods can be moved rapidly and cheaply across the world. In seconds managers can communicate with divisions half-way around the globe. This is the positive side of modern technological development. It is creating, for the first time, the foundations of a world community.

Yet at the same time the industrial labor pool becomes world-wide and ever more subject to capital because of technological de-skilling and fragmentation of production. It is this same de-skilling process which has been turning the worker into a tool (to be bought at the lowest price, and often disposable), simultaneously uprooting the production process from its reproductive communion with society, nature, and the Mystery.

This same instrumentalized labor pool is dramatically expanded because of the capitalization of agriculture, under corporation farming or agribusiness, which displaces large numbers of the peasantry from the land. They then become available for industrial employment precisely because the skilled side of the work process has been removed from ordinary human community. Thus, for example, unskilled Asian peasant young women can be hired to assemble the most sophisticated technological components, but they now play a menial role and are dismissed as soon as they pass out of youth.

The wages of this Third World labor pool are of course quite low. I remember visiting factories in a free trade zone in the Philippines where workers for American corporations were making less than $2.00 U.S. per day. In some of these factories young women were working several days straight, twenty four hours a day with only 30 minutes off for meals. By contrast, when demand slowed, they were simply let go with no unemployment compensation or other social welfare programs.

The factories in this free trade zone were beautifully kept—surrounded by attractive landscaping, air-conditioned inside, but with armed guards and barbed-wire. Outside the gates the workers lived in the most wretched conditions imaginable, often eight young people living in what seemed like a chicken coop, with raw sewage running down the main street. There was no running water in the dwellings, but the Coca-Cola truck came regularly to replenish the canteens.

The thrust of the new international division of labor is to move the more labor intensive industries to the low wage periphery (the Third World) and to keep the capital or information intensive sectors (especially management and finance) in the center (First World). Initially it was industries like textile, garments, and electronics which led the way in the industrial migration. Now it is also heavy industries, like steel, auto, rubber, etc. If robotics deepens, some of these could return, but for the moment the main thrust of the global industrial migration is from North to South.

From a capitalist or liberal perspective it appears that jobs are being brought to the South, while the social dislocations of the North can be handled by re-training and financial compensation. The rich North is seen sacrificing something for the gain of the poor South. But as someone once said, it can also appear that the poor of the North are subsidizing the rich of the South while the poor of the South gain little and the rich of the North continue their power.

Meanwhile, whole communities and industries in the North are devastated by capital flight. Still more workers and communities are threatened that, if they do not make certain wage or tax concessions, they too will be abandoned. Better to take a giant cut in wages than to lose your job. Better to give a big tax subsidy than to lose the industry. Communities and workers are threatened with ecological concessions as well, trading job security for environmental danger. In addition a whole national anti-labor climate arises. The unions, it is said, are keeping America from being competitive. Eliminate the union and then we can really produce.

Meanwhile, Third World governments draw investment precisely by their ruthless social policy. The International Labor Organization, for example, just pointed out a system of Haitian slavery at the foundation of the sugar industry in the Dominican Republic, and that is one of the democratic countries. In other countries, like Guatemala or Chile, strong union leaders are dealt with by murder or torture. The police state promises to keep itself an attractive investment climate.

Yet there is little correlation between the security of the state and the social, ecological, and spiritual well-being of the people. The production surplus is drained off by foreign capital and by the tiny percent of upper income elites who often then invest the money outside their country. Industrialization or de-industrializatin is pursued autonomously, without dealing with the impact on families and the community or the impact on the chain of life across the systems of water, air, and earth or the impact on human dignity and its religious roots. Meanwhile the development model, ordered to external priorities, goes deeper into militarism, inflation, and debt.

Presiding over this new international division of labor are the transnational corporations and the transnational banks. On one hand they are advancing the creative process of human history by networking the entire globe into a single coherent unit. On the other hand, the way this is happening — through an uprooted and unregulated international market where capital and technology have no moral accountability to community — is leading to a downward spiral of social viciousness. This social viciousness is not the fruit of a transnational conspiracy. It is not so much what the corporations do that causes the crisis, but rather what is left out. It is the autonomy of the production process, the fact that development is constructed without explicit rootedness in social, ecological, and spiritual community which is the root cause. It is this which narrows the cultural imagination to mechanistic economics. The result is that capital is inverted over labor.

Because all nations are now in ruthless competition with one another, and because there is no moral control over this structure, the competitive lead belongs to those states which maximize the new technology and best exploit their internal labor pool. But the technological thrust is no longer in service of human community, only of the autonomous imperatives of export-led development. And the exploitation of labor has clearly instrumentalized and victimized that which should be primary in production. As a result all nations are under pressure, to lesser or greater degrees, to begin to match the behavior of the most technologized and the most ruthless competitors. All other values yield before these absolute priorities.

The present debate between free trade and protectionism in this context is a debate over how power will be tilted in this structural context, but not over the context itself. Simply to favor free trade in an uprooted, unregulated, and morally automous global free market is to concede to the downward spiral of social viciousness. Simply to react by protecting one's own industry against world competition could mean threatening the tenuous solidarity which exists among nations today. And both poles of the debate, in the present context, seem to acquiesce in the on-going social, ecological, and spiritual erosion of the mechanistic civilization. Isolated in this sense, the trade debate fails to address the deeper question of the structural context.

Evangelical Response: The Priority of Labor

In this section I will explain briefly one foundational principle and six derivative principles which, I propose, are coming to us from contemporary Catholic social thought with bearing on the social context of the trade debate. This will be followed by some moral conclusions from these principles for the world economy. The primary guiding principle is the now well-known priority of labor from Pope John Paul II's encyclical *Laborem Exercens*. From this foundational principle at least six derivative or supportive principles can be discovered in the Pope's writings. They are:

1. work as creation;
2. creation as building communities;
3. the global solidarity of communities;
4. unions as mediators of community;
5. international institutions as mediators of solidarity;
6. the strategic primacy of culture.

As mentioned earlier, these principles are taken to be contemporary mediations of the healing and transforming presence of the Spirit. They are seen as mediated through the ongoing tradition of Catholic social thought — the church's living memory of the gospel applied to today's world (LE. 3). After reviewing these theoretical principles, we can then turn to the search for practical principles to challenge the mechanistic civilization and to transform the present trade debate.

1. Priority of Labor: the Foundational Principle

For Pope John Paul II, the question of work is key to the whole social question, indeed as he says "the essential key." This is the whole reason for his composing the encyclical *Laborem Exercens.*

> It is in order to highlight — perhaps more than has been done before — the fact that human work is a key, probably the essential key, to the whole social question, if we try to see that question really from the point of view of human good. And if the solution — or rather the gradual solution — of the social question, which keeps coming up and becoming ever more complex, must be sought in the direction of "making life more human," then the key, namely human work, acquires fundamental and decisive importance. (LE, 3-revised)

The problem with work in contemporary society is that since the dawn of the industrial age a dual process has been underway: 1) the discovery and correct affirmation of science and technology as a "basic coefficient of economic progress," and 2) the tendency to reduce the worker to a "slave" of the mechanistic civilization. (LE, 5)

The Pope describes the two sides of this process as the objective and subjective dimensions of work. The objective side is the technological embodiment of the productive achievement. The subjective side is the conscious social relation of the worker to the technology. This distinction is similar to the one made by Karl Marx between the means of production and the relations of production, although in Marxism there is a tendency to reduce the relations of production to the objective dimension as well. Later John Paul speaks of these two dimensions of work as capital (the objective side) and labor (the subjective side).

For John Paul the key to the social question is the fact that modern ideologies have granted capital priority over labor — industrial capitalism through economic forms and scientific socialism through political forms. Both thereby have attempted to exclude the subjective dimension of work, even while heightening the objective dimension. Both thus acquiesce in the modern mechanization of culture.

> However, it is also a fact that in some instances technology can cease to be humanity's ally and become its enemy, as when the mechanization of work "supplants" humanity, taking away all personal satisfaction and the incentive to creativity and responsibility, when it deprives

many workers of their previous employment or when, through exalting the machine, it reduces humanity to the status of its slave. (LE, 5-language revised)

The fundamental question, therefore, to be put to any issue in contemporary economic debate, including the trade debate, is: *"Do the proposed policies protect or restore the priority of labor or not?"* It seems clear from John Paul's wider reflections, and indeed from experience, that the tendency of both modern ideologies is increasingly to invert the priority.

This inversion (capital over labor) is not offset simply by introducing state social welfare reforms into a market economy nor by introducing market reforms into a state economy (welcome as those reforms might be). For, as we have seen, it is not simply the state or the market which is the problem or the solution. A combination of the two, as is now happening in the ideological convergence of the economic strategy of the national security state and the transnational free market, is aggravating the inversion of capital over labor.

The principle of the priority of labor is much deeper. Both the state and the corporation, or the functions of market and planning, are distinct embodiments of capital, of the objective side of the work process. To combine the two is only to combine the public and private faces of capital. Neither one nor the other, nor both together, is a substitute for labor itself.

2. Derivative or Supportive Principles

a. *Work as Creation.* The Christian theological tradition has carried two interpretations of work, one stressing its pain, rooted in sin, and the other stressing its goodness, rooted in creation. John Paul links himself clearly with the good interpretation of work, and sees its sinful side not as integral to the act of work, but rather as the fruit of social sin disfiguring the good creation of work. Sin and pain are not part of work itself, but rather something imposed to disfigure it and impede its creativity.

For John Paul, work is humanity's participation in God's ongoing creation across nature and history. He has embraced modern humanism in this recognition of the creativity of work, but he also transforms it by indispensably linking human creativity to its divine source. Humanity can create through work only because humanity shares in divine creativity.

If work is creation, and if creation is central to humanity's religious dignity, then the phenomenon of unemployment is a great abomination. It is a fundamental denial of the divinely given creativity of human dignity. In such a perspective notions like the leisure society or broad scale permanent unemployment (e.g. so-called structural unemployment), even if reasonably remunerated by a social welfare state, are a denial of the person's God-given call to participate in the social act of creation.

This biblical insight into work as co-creation with the Creator stands in direct contrast to the two modern ideologies. For industrial capitalism, labor tends to be only a factor of production, something to be bought and sold at the lowest price by the private corporation. For scientific socialism, labor tends to be only a class force to be scientifically guided by the strategic intelligentsia. Both thereby secularize and degrade work. One in practice and the other in theory deny its spiritual dignity.

But if work is so endowed with spiritual meaning, what is it that work creates? This brings us then to the second derivative principle.

b. *Creation as Building Community*. This second derivative principle pervades all of the Pope's text and other writings as well. Thus he writes, "For the greater (humanity's) power becomes, the farther (its) . . . community responsibility extends." (LE, 25) The scope of community grows with the power of work.

In another place, speaking of the creative role of unions, he reflects, "It is characteristic of work that it first and foremost unites people. In this consists its social power: the power to build a community." (LE, 20) I believe he means here that community is not simply a good side effect of work, but is rather a constitutive principle. The community is the work, it's deepest product. Work which does not build community is a degradation of work, not faithful to its essence. A parallel in the case of sexuality would be the relation of marriage to prostitution.

Because of this communitarian nature of work, Catholic social teaching has stressed the principle of the common use of goods. Private ownership can never be absolutized as in the liberal sense, nor simply concentrated into giant corporate or state bureaucracies.

Rather the goods of the earth belong to all who labor, and even to those who are denied the right to labor. Thus the Pope writes of this "principle of the common use of goods" as "the first principle of the whole social ethical order." (LE, 19)

One might expand on this principle of work as community-building to suggest that work should not only build up human community, but also ecological and spiritual community. Thus the community which work creates would be at once social (the creative solidarity of labor), ecological (deepening creative cooperation with nature), and spiritual (greater communion with the depth of the Mystery which is the Creator).

The Pope constantly refers to the work community as interacting with nature to creatively reshape it. From the ecological viewpoint perhaps the biblical translation of "dominating" the earth has a harsh ring to it today. A better expression might be entering into creative communion with the earth process.

From the spiritual viewpoint, the social and ecological communion growing out of the work processes becomes, at its deepest foundation, communion with the Creator who is the source of the creativity of nature and history. The Creator, we now realize, continues the process of nature and history precisely in cooperation with the co-creativity of humanity. This is the deepest communion of the experience of work. It is the insight which modern secularism failed to grasp, even while it discovered the enormous scientific powers of the human race.

c. *The Global Solidarity of Communities.* The building of community through work is not a provincial affair. It reaches out to the entire human family. In his speech before the United Nations International Labor Organization (ILO, Geneva, 15 June 1983), the Pope developed this theme of the international solidarity of labor in the global community of work.

He first pointed out how the gross injustices in national context during the early industrial revolution led to "the impetuous emergence of a great burst of solidarity among workers, first and foremost among industrial workers." This was, he says, a "just social reaction" against the "degradation of work" when the "machine was tending to dominate." (ILO, 8)

Today, however, "It is necessary to forge a new solidarity." The Pope calls for a much larger and more powerful solidarity of labor on a global scale. For, he charges, both the old abuses persist and new ones have been created on a wider geographic scale. Now all the great problems of society are "world problems." Therefore there is a need for a world-wide solidarity. (ILO, 8-9)

For this reason, "a new world conscience ought to be formed" where all members of society can consider themselves members of "this great family, the world community." But we should not assume "that people's consciousness of solidarity is sufficiently developed." And so the need to develop a fruitful tension between national consciousness and the new world consciousness. (ILO,9)

The purpose of this world-wide solidarity of communities of work is nothing less than to affirm the priority of labor: "The solution must be found in solidarity with labor, that is, by accepting the principle of the primacy of human work over the means of production." (ILO, 11) But then what are the agents of this solidarity? Of course the Pope praises all the agents—economic enterprises whether public or private, the state, and various social organizations. But he singles out with strategic emphasis two actors—labor unions and international organizations. These are the focus of the next two principles.

d. *Unions as Mediators of Community.* In his speeches across the world, the Pope has given special place to the role of authentic unions. Again he devoted to it his address to the United Nations International Labor Organization. The clearest statement, however, is back in *Laborem Exercens*, where he speaks of unions as "indispensable."

> All these rights, together with the need for the workers themselves to secure them, give rise to yet another right: the right of association, that is to form associations . . . called labor or trade unions. . . . The experience of history teaches that organizations of this type are an indispensable element of social life, especially in modern industrial societies. (LE, 20)

But, the Pope warns, the vision informing the union movement cannot be determined by either of the modern ideologies. His warning, however, is not simply negative, for I believe that he proposes a highly creative vision for a transformed and post-modern world labor movement.

On the one side the Pope warns against the ideology of scientific socialism which reduces the solidarity of labor to the political level of class conflict. The Pope does not mean to deny confrontation in the building of labor solidarity, nor the creative role of politics. Indeed he recognizes confrontation is often present. (LE, 20) But the vision informing the solidarity is deeper than simply a contest over state power culminating only in a centralized state apparatus.

Neither is the aim of the confrontation struggle "for struggle's sake" alone. (LE, 20) Indeed a hyper-masculine military consciousness of struggle can appear sometimes to be the normative pattern of interpretation on the Left. Solidarity is not aimed predominately at eliminating the opponent; otherwise it would only feed off this opposition instead of its own internal life and always need an enemy to function. Rather solidarity must feed predominately off its own positive energy, that is, its own creation of community. (LE, 14)

On the other side, one might add, the union cannot be the narrow bearer of special interests apart from community, as may often be the tendency in the liberal or capitalist tradition. A liberal or capitalist union movement which closed in upon itself, relatively isolated from the wider community, would produce the opposite error from the scientific socialist tendency to reduce community to state-centered politics.

This I believe was sometimes the unfortunate tendency of some elements in the American labor movement during past decades, until a recent policy shift to return to the active building of coalitions with other carriers of community. It paralleled a similar tendency of the Catholic Church, once closely allied with labor and its own working class roots, to grow distant from labor. In essence by growing away from each other, both church and labor lost some of their common roots in the wider creation of community.

The task of the union movement, rooted in the community of work which is the heart of humanity's social experience, cannot be reduced to a special economic interest nor to political struggle, legitimate as they are in their own right. Rather the union becomes a primary bearer of community. It carries the cause of the whole human enterprise, rooted in the divine co-creativity of human labor.

A new form of the labor movement might be described as a communitarian tendency. On one side it would reach back to a rooted community of special craft skills, but with a comprehensive vision bonding all workers and the unemployed in their local community. On the other side it would link the solidarity of its rooted community with networks of other communities of work across the world. Thus both roots in local community and transnational solidarity would be the defining themes of its transformed structures. Such a new vision of the labor movement would offset the uprootedness of modern technology, which has so divorced itself from human community and even turned against it. It would also offset the deepening viciousness of an unregulated world market system which sets workers in competition with each other across the world.

e. *International Institutions as Mediators of Solidarity.* But how is global solidarity, defending the primacy of labor in the creation of human community, to be built up at the global level? It is here that the Pope turns to that theme which has been so important in the whole legacy of modern Catholic social thought and an important antidote to the competitive and chauvinistic nationalism of the modern experience, namely the role of international institutions in creating a world order.

Liberalism or capitalism of course denies the economic need for such institutions, or at best grants them a marginal role in the international free market. But if the primacy and solidarity of labor is to become a global principle, then there must be global institutions to embody this principle. Scientific socialism by contrast has always recognized the need for global solidarity. (We have only to recall the concluding words of *The Communist Manifesto*, "Workers of the world unite! You have nothing to loose but your chains!") But history has shown that this vision, when mediated through a scientific socialist state which eventually achieved the status of super-power, became only a smokescreen for manipulative national interests.

For this reason, international institutions will be truly international only when they both carry a truly international consciousness and have a legitimate structural independence of national centers. The first of such international institutions implicitly recommended by the Pope would be a world labor movement, for such an institutional embodiment would be required for any actual global solidarity of labor. A second international institution would be the United Nations itself, especially its specialized agencies dealing directly with the world of work. Here the Pope stresses the International Labor Organization (ILO), whose conventions have tried to set global standards for the defense of labor. This was the point of his speech at the ILO—to link the church with the "fundamental objectives" of the ILO. (ILO, 1) One might also suggest the eventual regulation of the world market system by the United Nations according to principles of the common good, as for example has been attempted in the United Nations Conferences on Trade and Development (UNCTAD).

f. *The Strategic Primacy of Culture.* This theme of the primacy of culture, I believe, is at the heart of the Pope's whole social and pastoral thrust. For him the achievement of social justice requires nothing less than a fundamental transformation of modern culture and its reductionist ideologies.

It is important to realize how deep is this challenge to transform crisis-ridden modern culture. By focusing on culture the Pope is saying that we cannot try to bring justice into society, into the trade debate, into labor relations, or anywhere else and simply let all else continue as normal. Rather he is saying that the creation of a just order of global solidarity requires the deepest cultural transformation of modern consciousness. One will not be possible without the other. Further the reigning ideologies of industrial capitalism (or liberalism) and scientific socialism (or Marxism) do not in their main lines realize how profound this cultural transformation must be.

Indeed the Pope is talking about constituting a distinct civilization. So deep is the social and spiritual crisis of modern civilization — threatening slow or rapid destruction through ecological contamination or nuclear holocaust, turning against the unborn, the poor, and the elderly, and unleashing waves of human rights violations — that the modern cultural foundations are no longer adequate.

These foundations are no longer adequate precisely because they carry a misconstrued intrepretation of human work. I have already indicated one reason why these foundations lead to the disfiguring of work, namely the mechanistic root metaphor which shapes the whole modern imagination. Thus if the church is to raise profound religious questions about trade, or any modern economic issues affecting the world economy, it would seem indispensable to address the cultural foundations of that economy, that is, the vision and values which guide its behavior. In the American case this means inevitably critiquing the "exhausted" modern ideology of capitalism.

Ethical Norms for the Trade Debate

Before offering any ethical norms, let me repeat my basic frame of reference. The deepest debate is not free trade versus protection, but the structural context within which the question arises. The call of the

Spirit, for the long range, is not to choose one side over another, but to transform the mechanistic civilization out of which the question arises.

Nonetheless, in the short range, we still live in this mechanistic civilization and must work out an interim ethic. It is out of such an interim ethic, hoping in the long run for a deeper transformation, that the following norms are proposed.

Five norms are proposed, one for trade in general, one for the Third World, one for the First World (more narrowly the United States), and two for the overarching world economy. These principles are: 1) *free trade as fair trade;* 2) *human rights and social clauses;* 3) *adjustment assistance and community redevelopment;* 4) *world order and a regulated world market;* and 5) *interdependence and self-reliance.*

I focus on the key question of trade between the United States and the Third World. This means prescinding from the equally problematic trade relations between the United States and other industrial capitalist centers (eg. Japan, with questions of a corporativist economy and an overvalued dollar) and as well between the United States and communist nations (eg. U.S. trade with the U.S.S.R or Poland). Nonetheless these same principles, as in interim ethic, could also be applied to all world trade.

a. *Free Trade as Fair Trade.* In the current trade debate, there is a distinction between the old and new protectionisms. The old protectionism was based on tariffs and obvious export subsidies. The new protectionism is based on a broader range of complex state policies that affect the marketability of products. These latter policies flow especially from a corporativist tendency in advanced industrial capitalism to use the state as the key instrument for rendering the nation competitive. The policies correspond in the widest sense to what is often described as "industrial policy."

In this debate over industrial policy, we see the beginnings of the conflict between the laissez faire and the corporativist strains of capitalist ideology. Initially a restoration of laissez faire, as with neoconservative governments, seemed to offer the most competitive posture for the nation. But it is now becoming clear that the nation needs to undertake more deliberate and positive policies to compete.

In the most obvious sense, the new protectionism includes factors like exchange rates, various state subsidies to investors and producers in certain industries, ecological policies, health and safety policies, consumer policies, military policies, labor policies, even education policies. Tariff barriers may be absent, but the trade may be subsidized in more subtle ways.

I offer no empirical guidance in this matter, but simply wish to point out the wider range of the debate. *If trade is to be free, it seems also that it should be fair*—that is, with state supports relatively balanced on each side. If that is not the case, serious conflicts may ultimately arise, even apart from the old protectionism. The ways nations will compensate for such imbalances may lead to policies which seem further to aggravate the spirit of protectionism, but may in fact be partially justified defenses against more subtle subsidies. But we need much greater sophistication in understanding the wide range of state supports for trade. We also need instruments to weigh them, criteria for evaluation, and institutional forums to arbitrate over them. But this gets us into the fourth norm.

b. *Human Rights and Social Clauses.* We have across the Third World today the subsidizing of competitive exports by the repression and exploitation of labor. Even in our own country we see a strategic attack against labor unions on managerial, legislative, and public opinion fronts. Indeed such an attack is now worldwide. (See for example two reports by the International Metalworkers Federation. TRADE UNIONS UNDER ATTACK, Geneva 1980, and THE STRUGGLE FOR HUMAN AND TRADE UNION RIGHTS, Geneva 1981.) Further, the suppression of the Polish workers organization *Solidarnosc* was in part to retain credit-worthiness with Western banks, and thus preserve a basis for Polish participation in world competition.

Competition in trade, based on the exploitation and repression of labor, I propose, is grossly immoral. It is a direct and obvious denial of the priority of labor. Yet the Third World is filled with repressive governments which crush workers organizations in order to attract foreign investment. In my opinion, it is ethically justified for a nation to penalize trade based on such injustice, no matter what the disadvantage to consumers.

Two tactical policies might be suggested to deal with such situations. On the preventive side, nations could and should write into trade agrements "social clauses" which would protect the rights of labor. If the trading partner grossly violated these rights, as codified in the Conventions of the United Nations International Labor Organization, then the nation would be justified in curtailing or terminating the trading agreement. On the reactive side, it would seem justified to impose a penalty or "justice tariff" based on the degree of exploitation in the offending nation. Thus if the price of competing goods were reduced by x amount of exploitation, a nation might rightfully impose a penalty tariff of x amount. Such cases would have to be adjudicated by some sort of international court so that nations would not make arbitrary decisions. Again the International Labor Organization seems the logical forum.

Such policies, either preventive or reactive, seem unlikely, especially with conservative governments. But I believe, if the world market is not to descend into a downward spiral of social viciousness, they will be indispensable.

This then is the second ethical norm I would propose—*that for free trade to be fair it must include respect for the rights of labor, and that when it does not the injustice may and indeed should be dealt with through social clauses in trade agreements or tariff penalties proportionate to the violation.*

c. *Adjustment Assistance and Redevelopment.* From what I understand in the United States today, most adjustment assistance is an inadequate response, and even that is declining. Even when proposed, it deals with individuals and focuses only on retraining. Might it not be possible, and indeed moraly required, for the state to assist not simply in the retraining of the individuals (in reality often little more than an alternate form of unemployment compensation), but more broadly in the reconstruction or redevelopment of the affected communities? And might not this redevelopment be mediated through, at least in part, workers organizations, since these are the communitarian expression of their voice in work?

It would seem that both these possibilities are moral duties of the state and the corporations involved. Thus the government should not allow a corporation simply to up and leave a community with no responsibility. To do that is to acquiesce in the most autonomous liberal definition of economics. Rather the government should hold the corporation to accountability for a share in community redevelopment. Similarly, the government itself should have some responsibility for this. How the degrees of these responsibilities would be measured, including financial reimbursement, would require further moral and social reflection. But the principle should not be in doubt.

This would mean some form of community compensation paid by a corporation which decides to relocate in order to be more competitive (i.e. capital flight). This compensation should be substantial and proportionate to the damage inflicted on the community by the corporate decision. The compensation, however, would not simply be handed out as welfare payments for unemployment, but would, at least in large part, be redirected to community economic development.

Again, these are not good ideas but moral responsibility. It was the labor of the workers which built up the departing corporation and also which supported the multi-level government. Arbitrary and uprooted decision-making processes cannot be allowed to destroy their community of work. In justice compensation must be made to enable the community of work, perhaps in another form, to continue.

This compensation payment would go to the local community structures, but the wider governmental structures, both state and national, would also have some responsibility to provide financial compensation and supportive services for redevelopment.

Here then emerges an opportunity for tranformative creativity, passing beyond the interim ethic. If the labor unions affected could be brought into play, along with local government and various community organizations, there would be the possibility of creating new economic initiatives organizing capital in cooperative form and probing alternative technologies.

In sum the third ethical norm says that *corporations and governments must contribute to the economic rebuilding of communities injured by departing corporations and foreign competition; and, reaching beyond the interim ethic, that such occasions offer the opportunity for creating, through cooperation with unions, local government, and community organizations new modes of development based on community cooperatives and alternative technology.*

d. World Order and a Regulated World Market. In *Laborem Exercens* we learned from Pope John Paul II that "the first principle of the whole ethical and social order" is "the principle of the common use of goods." The goods of the earth belong to all the human family. For this reason, the world market cannot be left to pure competition. Rather the market needs to be ordered—not eliminated. This is a fundamental and classical principle of Catholic social teaching, namely that markets have social functions and require a social order.

Thus, as the world market matures through the revolution in transportation and communications technology, and through the consequent rise of the transnational enterprise (encompassing both private and public forms), it becomes necessary to regulate and order the world market for the sake of the commonweal of the human family. The precise ordering of this world market is a matter for further social and moral reflection, but again it is the foundational principle that is important here.

Such ordering might include agreements to stabilize commodity trading, global standards for currency exchange, and even orderly marketing agreements. It might also include a future world tax and creation of certain global "commons," as was attempted in the United Nations negotiations over the "law of the seas." Again the criterion for such methods would be the common good of the widest community.

Ordering of the world market becomes possible only with the creation, strengthening, and democratization of international economic institutions. This means first and foremost the United Nations and its councils and agencies which bear on economic questions.

In sum then the fourth ethical norm applied to trade calls for *the democratic ordering of the world market by expanded international institutions according to the principle of the common use of goods, now applied globally.*

e. *Interdependence and Self-Reliance.* The maturing world market is clearly converting all the world into a single economic system. The volume of trade expansion over the past several decades is creating, for the first time in human history, a truly interdependent world. In economic terms, if not yet in conscious political ones, the sovereignty of the nation-state has ended, and with it the modern epoch centered in the rise of autonomous (or "sovereign") nation-states. As Christians we should welcome this, for it reveals the unity of the human family. But if the maturing world market is to be ordered only by the principle of competition, the new consciousness will witness to an unruly and destructive form of the human family. Indeed we are already aware how heightened are military and social tensions in areas of strategic resources like the Middle East and the Caribbean Basin.

Further, the control over the world market is increasingly concentrated in ever larger centers of economic bureaucracies, which we call transnational enterprises and geo-banks. By their investment strategy, these enormous centers of power can shape the rise or fall of whole nations. Does the national principle then completely collapse before the transnational stage, or only emerge in the military competition over strategic resources?

It is here that the Catholic principle of subsidiarity needs to be invoked and applied this time to the economic life of the nation in the maturing world market. While on the one hand the nation is called to ever greater bondedness with the human family, on the other hand it would seem to have a legitimate right and duty to defend its own relative self-reliance in the world system. For if a nation loses all self reliance, it becomes powerless and over-vulnerable before world market forces. It is the same danger faced by intermediate institutions with the totalitarian state, except this time the totality is global.

For this reason, it would seem morally justified for a nation to follow a certain industrial policy which guarantees to some degree a relatively self-reliant industrial base. One frequently hears this argument in regard to military production, but it could also apply to other basic needs like food and energy. Indeed the near total vulnerability in the areas of food and energy of many poor nations constantly lingers under the cloud of catastrophe.

Such self-reliant strategies would only be justified and practical if they were accompanied by other strategies which increased the bonding across the world community and by the mediation of international institutions setting working standards in this area. Otherwise national self-reliance alone could lead to greater international economic tensions, thus shattering the even tenuous international networks.

Thus, the fifth ethical norm, would be that *interdependence and self-reliance should not be antagonistic, but complementary, and mediated by the principle of subsidiarity and by international institutions.*

American Catholicism can mediate these norms to the wider nation by drawing on both its distinct theology of nature and grace, and on the Catholic sense of the world community. These could partially heal the alienated cynicism of the Left and the militaristic nostalgia of the Right. They could help American culture move beyond its often messianic compulsion to be "number one" and to enjoy instead the grace of being a cooperative member of the human family.

Part IV

Cooperation, Priorities and Planning for the U.S. Economy

JOHN W. HOUCK

Two themes were mentioned several times in the discussions — the need for increased participation in economic and political decision-making processes and the need to reduce the "adversarial culture" that exists between workers and managements and between business and government.

> *Our Sunday Visitor*
> December 25, 1983

"It's not our duty to put blame on any one factor or any one group, but to look at labor, management . . . and to challenge them in their decision-making . . . to get a consensus on certain principles."

> *The Toledo Blade*
> December 15, 1983

The odds are that the bishops will not advocate comprehensive central planning. The Church supports "subsidiarity" — the policy of keeping decisions on as local or small a scale as possible, a tenet that militates against broad federal planning.

> *Business Week,*
> December 19, 1983

Inasmuch as the five American bishops are politically left-of-center, it follows that free enterprise is in for a thrashing . . . Thus we can predict with reasonable certainty that their letter will contain the old collectivist gospel.

The Detroit News
December 19, 1983

PART IV, COOPERATION, PRIORITIES AND PLANNING FOR the U.S. Economy, deals with critical issues — the institutional arrangements and processes needed to accomplish the priorities advocated in the first three parts of this volume. But before examining this subject, it will be helpful to summarize what has already been discussed.

I. Work and Employment
   1. The focus is on the centrality of employment as a source of social participation and human dignity as well as income.
   2. Unemployment is currently too high and should not be the trade-off for fighting inflation.
   3. The private sector and government both have substantial roles to play in employment generation and training, but there is disagreement about how much government involvement is helpful.
   4. In our concern about the quantity of work, we should not forget the quality of work life.
II. The Poor and Disadvantaged
   1. The level of poverty in the United States continues to be intolerable.
   2. The poor should not be the scapegoats for campaigns to cut government expenditures.
   3. The need for a safety net is not debatable, but the arguments are over dollar amounts and the effectiveness of delivery systems.
   4. A form of negative income tax is advocated, which will not conflict with the importance of the availability of employment for everybody. The stability of the family must not be eroded by welfare policies.
III. Trade: U.S. and Developing Countries
   1. A major concern must be the ways in which the U.S. economy

and trade patterns impact on developing and very poor countries.

2. For better or worse, we export our culture and values as well as our products.
3. There is a need for some institutional arrangements to protect and develop the poor and disadvantaged nations — similar to what we have internally in the U.S.

There would seem to be strong theological warrants for the emphasis and priority given to the propositions in the above summary. For example, Catholic social teaching argues for the importance of the availability of work for all, as well as an adequate welfare policy providing food, clothing and shelter to those who lack these necessities. Not to so indicate in the contemplated pastoral letter would be a major departure from that tradition.[1] And starting with John XXIII's *Mater et Magistra* (1961), these concerns were extended to the wider world: economic power ought to be an instrument of service and justice not only internally but in any area touched by the U.S. economy.[2]

The Debate About National Planning

But how are we to achieve these priorities in a rational and purposeful manner? Would economic planning contribute significantly? Given the U.S. practice of diffused power and many veto groups, could we expect economic planning to work? Or, would we have beautifully phrased, generalized schemes on paper which are rarely read or implemented. Are we so phobic about even the word "planning" that it would get into the way of consensus-building and cooperation by labor, management and government? There is in the American experience a ready acceptance for "working together" and teamwork, but, it seems, not for planning.[3]

Daniel Rush Finn, both a theologian and an economist, details in his essay several of the pro and con arguments for planning, yet he does not give a resolution of the debate. His prescription:

It is impossible for a conference of bishops to adjudicate the disputes among economists . . . it seems only prudent for non-economists such as the bishops to say that there is not definitive empirical evidence either that all forms of economic planning will reduce the level of economic activity in the nation or that any one form of planning will without doubt increase it.

But if economic planning is rejected as the effective social mechanism, what are the chances of cooperation by labor, management and government? Elmer Johnson suggests that our society is degenerating because of the intensity of the struggle between these three groups. Far too much of our national talent is utilized in the "adversary culture" of litigation and dispute. He advocated some form of "Industrial Cooperation Act," with a commission composed of top representatives from the warring factions:

> Such a commission would be assigned responsibility for identifying the sources of these adversary tensions and proposing new mechanisms of cooperation. Such an act might also establish an ombudsman function for examining long-term problems involving particular government agencies and industries and working out resolutions.

At the symposium his proposal was met with skepticism and even anger from the representatives of organized labor. Robert Harbrant, president of the AFL-CIO's Food and Allied Services Department, attacked as a sin and crime a "$500-million-a year union-busting business" which contends that "unions have no role in American society." Monsignor George G. Higgins, long-time staff member of the U.S. Catholic Conference and observer of the labor-management scene, agreed: "It is utterly fatuous to talk about worker-management consensus without strengthening the right to collective bargaining." Higgins reminded the participants at the symposium that there are few principles in the Catholic social tradition more firmly fixed than the workers' right to organize and to bargain collectively.

In chapter twelve, Gar Alperovitz opens his paper by reviewing some pertinent economic data: a Gross National Product of roughly $3.5 trillion, a per capita income of about $15,000 and an average of $60,000 for a family of four. Even with such astonishing wealth we are told that "we must curtail social programs, that we cannot assist the poor, that we do not have resources enough to assist other nations." Alperovitz rejects such conclusions as "nonsense" and argues rather that we lack two critical elements as a society: first, moral commitment and second, effective, comprehensive national economic planning. Moral commitment will overcome the sham that we are too poor to be either socially just or generous. Planning would be the institutional process essential to overcoming the shortfalls in employment and GNP of the 1970s and 1980s, the crazy quilted pattern of the current planning and marketplace dependence:

> . . . the fundamental point is that the underlying structure of the industry . . . has not been that of the true free market for years. Rather it is an odd, highly integrated system involving government tax programs, expenditure programs, regulations, loans, loan guarantees, etc. — and this strangely planned system not only has not disappeared, but in important respects has grown, even under the Reagan Administration.

Regarding "issues of centralization of power" in industrial planning bodies, Alperovitz argues that the significance of technocratic, elitist control is exaggerated; that the main task is "strategic planning in key areas, not 'total planning.' " He believes that "explicit and democratic" planning will enhance our ability (1) to reach the poor both nationally and worldwide, (2) to achieve full employment and the priority of labor, (3) to facilitate the production of basic necessities at a reasonable price, and (4) to protect resources needed for future generations.

Peter Peterson, the former Secretary of Commerce and persistent critic of the priorities in our economy, does not see any large surplus of wealth available for social justice purposes. Rather, he contends that our economic wealth is being drained away in current consumption by both the wealthy and the middle class, mainly through non-means entitlements like social security, medicine and pension programs. Our society is not saving but consuming. And this pattern will ensure that business competitiveness will decline. Peterson fears that our industrial and human capital will be so weakened that long-term negative consequences are inevitable. He identifies two groups who are hurt by our profligacy: the poor, whose means-test welfare payments have been cut, and future generations, who will be saddled with our current deficits. He argues for a justice which forces stringency and discipline on the politically powerful middle-class and the wealthy.

Two executives of General Motors Corporation — Elmer Johnson, chief cousel and V.P. for Public Affairs, and Marina Whitman, chief economist — explore together whether the market can sustain an ethic. Johnson is less optimistic about market mechanisms — either in an economic or an ethical sense. He argues that we need to temper the "harsh short-term effects of the market system on particular people, industries and regions." Whitman defends markets and economic freedom as essential to progress and the alleviation of poverty:

> . . . it is clear that to try eliminating the disruptive effects of change by erecting barriers to technological advancement and international commerce, to try to "freeze ourselves in time," so to speak, would be to retard rather than to advance the human condition.

Although Johnson rejects "all forms of economic planning that would replace rather than complement the basic functions of the market," Whitman identifies industrial policy with "central planning" and "resource allocation by government," and argues strongly against its adoption.

In the final essay, Daniel Rush Finn proposes a framework of issues within the ongoing debate. In his outline, there are six general arguments against national economic planning: (1) such planning concentrates too much power in the hands of too few people; (2) it may infringe upon the rights of property owners and stockholders; (3) special interest groups tend to dominate planning processes; (4) inevitable bureaucratization would render the processes unworkable; (5) planning breeds inefficiency and would thus produce a lower output and employment level than does the market; and (6) planning subverts consumer sovereignty over the allocation of resources.

These arguments must be weighed against five considerations in favor of national planning: (a) the U.S. government is already responsible for the macroeconomic operation of the economy; (b) foreign governments rely on economic planning to compete against the United States; (c) sheer reliance upon market mechanisms may institutionalize social and racial injustices; (d) the market ignores the social costs imposed upon communities by capital flight; and (e) planning provides for democratic decisions, which are superior to market solutions.

Finally, Finn presents several "background assumptions" concerning economic life and Christianity: the world is a gift, humans are both individual and communals; the problem of sin, and the need for prophetic confrontation about economic matters. He advocates that the bishops strike a prophetic stance by emphasizing "the distributional concerns of Christianity about justice for those whom the market leaves paying the 'necessary' price." He raises the possibility that the trade-off might be harsh: to provide greater security for the poorest twenty percent we might have to sacrifice a higher living standard, and productivity for the rest of us. Neither as a theologian nor economist does he give us much relief from the burden of our religious values.

Values and Issues for Economic Cooperation and Planning

The chairperson and commentator of this panel of essayists was Kirk Hanson, lecturer at Stanford University Graduate School of Business and consultant to several corporations.

I have organized my observations around three categories: priorities, process, and policies. The points of commonality and the points of difference can be summarized under these three topics. What I mean by priorities is the values that an economic system ought to represent and adhere to. By process, I mean the style of planning or political consensus-building by which you achieve those values, and finally the policies that implement and carry them out. I think the process of defining these values is the process of creating the larger moral framework which creates an imperative for change that many have advocated at this symposium.

First, the basic function of the economic system ought to be a concern for the welfare of people and individuals — not just their material welfare, but their freedom, their autonomy, their sense of participation in the society of which they are a part, and a concern more broadly for their psychological, social and spiritual welfare.

Second, a special commitment to provide for the poor and the disadvantaged.

Third, a concern for future generations: Do our present economic priorities and policies address the needs of our children and grandchildren both in terms of human and industrial capital?

Fourth, a special concern for the impact of the U.S. economy, not just on the United States, but on the world, and particularly on the poor and disadvantaged of the third and fourth worlds.

Fifth, a concern for the social and human costs of economic transition — inevitable dislocations which occur as industries decline and new ones are created; and economic shocks—like the energy crisis of the 1970s.

Sixth, a commitment to economic growth and productivity in order to provide an adequate welfare safety net, the material and service needs of our citizens and full employment.

Seventh, a concern for our national and worldwide environment.

Eighth, a recognition that we are essentially addressing concerns in an economy of scarcity, and that the issue is really how we provide for people in an economy that cannot do all things, and that does indeed require trade-offs which ought to be made from some kind of moral base.

I want to point out that not everybody will agree with this list. Certainly Gar Alperovitz would heavily emphasize community integrity and the human cost of plant closings, *or* the value associated with worker participation and control in many "management" decisions, not just as a vehicle toward higher productivity but also as a value in and of itself, *or* that we are an economy of scarcity given in essence a GNP share for a family of four of close to $60,000.

As to process and priorities, I shall be brief. In terms of process, there seems to be a consensus developing that the strength of special interest groups has to be transcended by a sense of the higher common good. Yet there is recognition that special interest groups play an important representational role in an otherwise mass society. As to policies, I would stress the often-forgotten but obvious point: That policies, such things as investments, entitlements or taxes, must logically and realistically follow from the values and priorities we adopt. Too frequently we back off from the necessary but painful policies needed to accomplish our social goals.

Vatican Statements

Leo XIII, *Rerum Novarum*—1891

28. It is a capital evil with respect to the question We are discussing to take for granted that the one class of society is of itself hostile to the other, as if nature had set rich and poor against each other to fight fiercely in implacable war. This is so abhorrent to reason and truth that the exact opposite is true; for just as in the human body

the different members harmonize with one another, whence arises that disposition of parts and proportion in the human figure rightly called symmetry, so likewise nature has commanded in the case of the state that the two classes mentioned should agree harmoniously and should properly form equally balanced counterparts to each other. Each needs the other completely; neither capital can do without labor, nor labor without capital. Concord begets beauty and order in things. Conversely, from perpetual strife there must arise disorder accompanied by bestial cruelty.[4]

Pius XI, *Quadragesimo Anno* — 1931

79. Just as it is gravely wrong to take from individuals what they can accomplish by their own initiative and industry and give it to the community, so also it is an injustice and at the same time a grave evil and disturbance of right order to assign to a greater and higher association what lesser and subordinate organizations can do. For every social activity ought of its very nature to furnish help to the members of the body social, and never destroy and absorb them.

80. The supreme authority of the state ought, therefore, to let subordinate groups handle matters and concerns of lesser importance, which would otherwise dissipate its efforts greatly. Thereby the state will more freely, powerfully, and effectively do all those things that belong to it alone because it alone can do them: directing, watching, urging, restraining, as occasion requires and necessity demands.[5]

John XXIII, *Pacem in Terris* — 1963

53. Individual citizens and intermediate groups are obliged to make their specific contributions to the common welfare. One of the chief consequences of this is that they must bring their own interests into harmony with the needs of the community, and must dispose of their goods and services as civil authorities have prescribed, in accord with the norms of justice, in due process, and within the limits of their competence.[6]

Second Vatican Council, *Gaudium et Spes* — 1965

26. Every day human interdependence grows more tightly drawn and spreads by degrees over the whole world. As a result the common

good, that is, the sum of those conditions of social life which allow social groups and their individual members relatively thorough and ready access to their own fulfillment, today takes on an increasingly universal complexion and consequently involves rights and duties with respect to the whole human race. Every social group must take account of the needs and legitimate aspirations of other groups, and even of the general welfare of the entire human family.

At the same time, however, there is a growing awareness of the exalted dignity proper to the human person, since he stands above all things, and his rights and duties are universal and inviolable. Therefore, there must be made available to all men everything necessary for leading a life truly human, such as food, clothing, and shelter; the right to choose a state of life freely and to found a family, the right to education, to employment, to a good reputation, to respect, to appropriate information, to activity in accord with the upright norm of one's own conscience, to protection of privacy and to rightful freedom in matters religious too.[7]

Paul VI, *Populorum Progressio* — 1967

33. Individual initiative alone and the mere free play of competition could never assure successful development. One must avoid the risk of increasing still more the wealth of the rich and the dominion of the strong, whilst leaving the poor in their misery and adding to the servitude of the oppressed. Hence programmes are necessary in order "to encourage, stimulate, coordinate, supplement and integrate" the activity of individuals and of intermediary bodies. It pertains to the public authorities to choose, even to lay down the objectives to be pursued, the ends to be achieved, and the means for attaining these, and it is for them to stimulate all the forces engaged in this common activity. But let them take care to associate private initiative and intermediary bodies with this work. They will thus avoid the danger of complete collectivisation or of arbitrary planning, which, by denying liberty, would prevent the exercise of the fundamental rights of the human person.[8]

John Paul II, *Laborem Exercens* — 1981

18. In order to meet the danger of unemployment and to insure employment for all, the agents defined here as "indirect employer"

must make provision for overall planning . . . , they must also give attention to organizing that work in a correct and rational way. In the final analysis, this overall concern weighs on the shoulders of the state, but it cannot mean one-sided centralization by the public authorities. Instead, what is in question is a just and rational coordination . . .[9]

American Catholic Bishops' Statements

Pastoral Letter, 1919

In his pronouncements on Labor (*Rerum Novarum*) Pope Leo XIII describes the advantages to be derived by both employer and employee from "associations and organizations which draw the two classes more closely together." Such associations are especially needed at the present time. While the labor union or trade union has been, and still is, necessary in the struggle of the workers for fair wages and fair conditions of employment, we have to recognize that its history, methods, and objects have made it essentially a militant organization. The time seems now to have arrived when it should be, not supplanted, but supplemented by associations or conferences, composed jointly of employers and employees, which will place emphasis upon the common interests rather than the divergent aims of the two parties, upon cooperation rather than conflict. Through such arrangements, all classes would be greatly benefited. The worker would participate in those matters of industrial management which directly concern him and about which he possesses helpful knowledge; he would acquire an increased sense of personal dignity and personal responsibility, take greater interest and pride in his work, and become more efficient and more contented. The employer would have the benefit of willing cooperation from, and harmonious relations with, his employees. The consumer, in common with employer and employee, would share in the advantages of larger and steadier production. In a word, industry would be carried on as a cooperative enterprise for the common good, and not as a contest between two parties for a restricted product.[10]

The Christian in Action, American Hierarchy, 1948

Christian principles should be put into action in economic life. It is not enough to find fault with the way our economic system is working. Positive, constructive thought and action are needed.

The secularist solutions proposed by eighteenth-century individualism or twentieth-century statism issue either in perpetual conflict or deadening repression. Christian social principles, rooted in the moral law, call insistently for cooperation not conflict, for freedom not repression in the development of economic activity. Cooperation must be organized—organized for the common good; freedom must be ordered—ordered for the common good. Today we have labor partly organized, but chiefly for its own interests. We have capital or management organized, possibly on a larger scale, but again chiefly for its own interests. What we urgently need, in the Christian view of social order, is the free organization of capital and labor in permanent agencies of cooperation for the common good. To insure that this organization does not lose sight of the common good, government as the responsible custodian of the public interest should have a part in it. But its part should be to stimulate, to guide, to restrain, not to dominate.[11]

Notes

1. See David Hollenbach, *Claims in Conflict: Retrieving and Renewing the Catholic Human Rights Tradition* (New York: Paulist Press, 1979). See also David Hollenbach's essay, "Modern Catholic Teachings Concerning Justice," in *The Faith That Does Justice*, ed. John C. Haughey (New York: Paulist Press, 1977), pp. 207-231.

2. Dennis P. McCann, "Liberation and the Multinationals," *Theology Today*, Spring, 1984, pp. 52-60; and Donal Dorr, *Option for the Poor: A Hundred Years of Vatican Social Teaching* (Maryknoll, N.Y.: Orbis Books, 1983).

3. George C. Lodge, "Managers and Managed: Problems of Ambivalence," in *Co-Creation and Capitalism: John Paul II's Laborem Exercens*, ed. John W. Houck and Oliver F. Williams (Washington, D.C.: University Press of America, 1983), p. 250.

4. John F. Cronin, *Catholic Social Principles: The Social Teaching of the Catholic Church Applied to American Economic Life* (Milwaukee, Wis.: Bruce Publishing Company, 1950), p. 200.

5. *Ibid.*, p. 212.

6. *The Gospel of Peace and Justice: Catholic Social Teaching Since Pope John*, ed. Joseph Gremillion (Maryknoll, N.Y.: Orbis Books, 1976), p. 213.

7. *Ibid.*, pp. 263-264.

8. *Ibid.*, p. 397.

9. John Paul II, *Laborem Exercens* (On Human Work), *Origins* 11 (Sept. 24, 1981) para. 18.

10. *Catholic Social Principles*, pp. 207-208.

11. *Ibid.*, pp. 205-206.

Twelve

Planning For Sustained Community

GAR ALPEROVITZ

> In order to meet the danger of unemployment and to insure employ-
> ment for all, the agents defined here as "indirect employer" must make
> provision for overall planning . . . they must also give attention to
> organizing that work in a correct and rational way. In the final analysis
> this overall concern weighs on the shoulders of the state, but it cannot
> mean one-sided centralization by the public authorities. Instead, what
> is in question is a just and rational coordination . . .
>
> Pope John Paul II, *Laborem Exercens* (18)

THE UNITED STATES, A NATION OF ROUGHLY 230 MILLION
people, currently enjoys a Gross National Product (GNP) of approximately $3.5 trillion. This breaks down to just about $15,000 per person, or an average of $60,000 for each family of four. Any assessment
of our future must begin with this astounding fact: Self-evidently our
nation can afford an extraordinary life for all its citizens, even with
our massive ongoing wastes of unemployment, inadequate skill training, excessive military spending and industrial inefficiency.

When President Eisenhower held office in 1956, the unemployment
rate was 4.1 percent, currently 8.8 percent of the labor force is unemployed. If we were managing our economy at the Eisenhower level,
the GNP would be roughly $350 billion more than it is now — or $6,000
added to the $60,000 for each family of four — for a total in the range
of $66,000.

We shall return to consider such planning issues as the level of employment which is manageable without inflation and how to increase productivity growth so that output per worker expands. However, in today's political climate even to cite such obvious facts can be startling. The overwhelming perspective of our economic debate is that of necessity and burden: We are told that we must curtail social programs, that we cannot assist the poor, that we do not have resources enough to assist other nations. This is *prima facie* nonsense. Given our extraordinary wealth, the question of what we choose to make of this great nation's economy is not primarily a technical one. *We have what it takes to provide a decent life for all members of our society.*

What is really being said is that we do not *choose* to utilize our great wealth in different ways. At the heart of this choice is not economic inevitability, but a confusion over values and cultural possibilities. I shall argue that in a nation of historically unprecedented wealth the issue of planning — at its core — is an issue of choice, not necessity. And therefore the priority questions of planning are ethical questions.

To the extent that we can clarify our understanding of these issues, we have an opportunity to move forward in our national trajectory and in the expansion of human dignity.

Planning and Freedom: A First Approach

Planning is a confusing subject to the lay person because it means so many things and because it is mystified by ideological posturing. My father, who was an engineer, used to tell of his first university course on mechanical design. He was surprised to find the front of his freshman classroom covered by a photograph of one of those massive, many wheeled locomotives which once dominated transcontinental travel. His professor began the class with the gruff assertion: "Our goal this year will be to redesign this engine." As the young students gasped at the thought, he reassured them: "We shall begin today with . . . one bolt."

The analogy to planning in the vast U.S. economy is by no means exact, but instead of beginning with the largest, most abstract problems, it helps to initiate our discussion by breaking planning down into understandable pieces. We also need to distinguish sharply between *planned government intervention* in the economy (as opposed to the free market) and *coherent planning* as an open, explicit, rational goal-setting process. As we shall see, the former is already the norm in many parts of the economy, and it is to a large extent a growing, not receding phenomenon even under the Reagan Administration. The vital issue is whether the planning we do is made rational, open, explicit and accountable to democratic participation.

A useful point of departure is this question: How have we been faring, relative to our potential, on the course of policies we have been following for the last several decades under both political parties? The answer is poorly by any standard, and extraordinarily poorly by the best standards set by other nations.

Since World War II we have had seven recessions, and our failures have deepened as time moved on: The average unemployment rate for the 1950's was 4.5 percent, for the 1960's 4.8 percent, for the 1970's 6.2 percent, and for the 1980's (so far) just under 9 percent. On its current trend the present recovery may not even top out at the low point of some previous recessions. Even in years of relatively good performance we did badly by important measures: During the sixteen-year period 1959-76 our average unemployment rate was 5.3 percent. Many nations did much better during the same period, as illustrated by the following comparisons:

> France: unemployment 2.5%; inflation 6.2%
> Germany: unemployment 1.2%; inflation 3.6%
> Japan: unemployment 1.4%; inflation 7.6%
> Sweden: unemployment 1.9%; inflation 5.6%

While the massive economic disruptions of the last several years have reduced economic performance everywhere, the pre-1970 period remains a valuable benchmark for both an assessment of the past and of possibilities for the future. Professor Steven Scheffrin has estimated that had the United States matched high levels of employment achieved abroad during the 1959-76 period, we would have enjoyed an additional $3.8 trillion in GNP (and with this an additional $750 billion of federal revenue)! Had we maintained even the 1956 Eisenhower unemployment rate of 4.1 percent we would have enjoyed an additional $2.3 trillion in GNP and roughly $450 billion in additional revenues.[1]

America today remains behind many other nations in the rate of growth of overall productivity, especially of productivity in the crucial manufacturing sector. In fact the rate of growth of U.S. manufacturing productivity in recent years has lagged substantially behind that of every major non-communist industrial nation except Great Britain. In comparison with Japan the gap has been dramatic: From 1970 to 1975 U.S. manufacturing output per worker increased at an annual rate of 3.4 percent while Japan moved ahead at nearly double-time, 6.7 percent. Between 1975 and 1980, as American productivity increased 1.6 percent a year, Japan averaged 7.9 percent, almost 5 times as great an improvement each year. The U.S. rate of growth of real GNP for the decade of the 1980's was a mere 1.75 percent compared with 4.7 percent for Japan. (France averaged 2.3 percent and Germany 2.7 percent.)[2]

Several observations follow from these facts: First, it is a matter of record that other democratic nations have at various times demonstrated the possibility of significantly better economic performance; it is not a matter of conjecture. They have also utilized a variety of more explicit and open planning techniques in achieving their gains. The Japanese, for instance, have maintained their thirty-year sustained record of unemployment in the 2 percent range while drastically restricting imports, providing government assistance to selected industries through a planning agency, allocating credit formally and informally, etc. Moreover, virtually every major industrial country with a higher rate of growth during the 1970's except Japan had a much larger share of government involvement in the economy than the United States — both as a percentage of the GNP and in terms of regulations, loans, loan guarantees, etc. (The percentages were in 1980: Sweden 57.1%, France 45.4%, Germany 42.8%, United Kingdom 40.4%, United States 32.7%, Japan 28.2%.)[3]

It is not my intention to endorse the planning policies of Japan or any other nation at this jucture; but for the moment let us assume (we shall return to the issue) that particular forms of explicit planning can in fact produce a more successful economic record. It is held, however, that the free economy cannot be infringed upon — *else freedom itself will be infringed*. Is this so? If it is, it can be an important, even an overriding objection to further consideration of all forms of planning.

In the first place, such an assertion would mean that the other Western nations in the list with larger government sectors in their economies than the U.S. must all be substantially less "free," a dubious assertion. But let us sharpen the ethical issue: Consider, first, the actual lives of the roughly ten million individuals who today cannot find work and the lives of the members of their families, a group which includes perhaps thirty million people. The actual freedoms of *each* of these individuals when work is not available are dramatically reduced. They may lose their home, their dignity, their health. Those who have jobs (but in a context of mass unemployment *fear* they may lose them) also experience a reduction in freedom: To alter a work pattern, to incur the manager's displeasure, may mean you are moved to the head of the line when the next cutback occurs; it may mean you will lose your job, stop paying the mortgage, put your marriage in jeopardy, destine your children to poverty.

This is not a hypothetical question. The freedoms of the poor *today* are massively curtailed by any standard and have been curtailed for years, day in and day out. If through planning we can significantly increase employment levels and the economic security of only five million (!) of the ten million unemployed, and improve the security of only a fraction of the millions who now work in fear, what is this worth? It is important to consider "sins of omission" in connection with our failure to manage the economy more successfully, especially through an examination, day by day, of the situation of those left out.

"Planning" is too abstract a term. For instance, a good deal of the economic instability in the 1970's which produced our massive unemployment arose because of the disruptive impact of energy problems. If by planning we mean that the absolute freedom of choice, say, of the seven large oil companies which dominate our energy economy is slightly curtailed, what is this worth?

When we talk about planning, we also need to be careful in defining precisely whose freedoms we are talking about. I used the term "the seven large oil companies," but this too is abstract: When we look at freedom of decision-making in such companies, we mean specific men and women, and we mean very small numbers of men and women at the very top who actually make major decisions in the giant corporation. To a much greater extent their subordinates take orders and implement decisions. These institutions are very different from the traditional entrepreneur.

It is useful to select the large oil companies and the energy problem as "one first bolt" in considering general planning because we are extremely vulnerable, again, to a disruption in our overall economy due to inattention to energy planning for the future. The massive price jolts caused by OPEC which destabilized us in the 1970's are likely to do so again in the 1980's. France has just leased to Iraq five Super-Etendard jets which can launch Exocet missiles, and Iran has threatened to close the Persian Gulf in retaliation. Our former Ambassador to Saudi Arabia, James Akins, argues that the chances of a disruption of oil from the Middle East *not* occurring are "about zero" in the coming years. The Lebanon crisis, instability in the smaller Gulf States, terrorism, are all obvious possibilities. The fate of previous bulwarks of stability, from the Shah of Iran to President Sadat of Egypt, is handwriting on the wall. A recent Congressional Research Service study predicts oil prices could shoot to more than $100 a barrel.

In these circumstances sensible planning can be very economical, even if it entails some administrative inefficiency, since reducing instability can save tens of billions of dollars in lost overall economic output.[4] Such planning should include a massive expansion of our strategic petroleum reserve, stepped-up energy conservation programs, a renewable fuels program (including, especially, solar), and standby controls in the event of a disruption. (Note that some of the required policies simultaneously create jobs in insulating houses, building solar collectors, etc.) The current Administration has, however, slowed filling of the strategic petroleum reserve, slashed conservation programs, drastically reduced solar energy programs, and vetoed the stand-by controls which even the Republican Senate thought was minimal protection.

Let us be clear. Planning which helps prevent another massive oil price jolt and destabilization of the economy would definitely limit specific decisions and choices particular individuals in the large oil companies can make. So too might the income of some of the companies and specific individuals be limited. The question is: If such limitations help avoid, or mitigate, the massive economic downswings which follow inflationary price explosions, and if by virtue of such planning the security of several million other individuals is maintained — is it worth the cost? The loss in decision-making flexibility of a few hundred oil executives, I submit, is nothing compared with the loss of dignity, income, family security, meaning and individual integrity of millions of men and women who can be deprived of the means of their daily bread if we avoid prudent planning to reduce disruptions of the economy.

A good case can also be made that individual freedom rests in part upon a healthy sector of individual entrepreneurs in the economy. They provide institutional diversity. They offer vitality, areas for individual initiative, the possibility of "another chance." They maintain opportunities for others who want to be independent of the larger institutions of our society. But this group of people has suffered massively under recent economic policies: Given the recession and depression occasioned by economic programs antagonistic to planning, more entrepreneurs have lost their livelihoods than at any time in our history! If through explicit planning we assure a healthy overall economy the economic freedom of individual entrepreneurs may be increased.

Similarly, in a situation of massive recession and unemployment the economic health of local communities is reduced. Deprived of resources, the school board, the highway maintenance department, the local public health service are all put under severe constraints when the national economy falters. Especially when the local tax base declines and social problems expand, a community experiences a reduction in its capacity to make real choices. Conversely, explicit planning which systematically rationalizes overall national economic management may expand areas for democratic choice and decision-making in local communities.

Preventive Planning

Were I to urge one priority to the Bishops, it would be to help us pierce through the fog which surrounds such fundamental issues associated with planning. The way forward is to demand a specific focus on individuals and communities affected by specific planning decisions, "bolt by bolt." We must ask the questions very concretely to clarify both the economic and ethical content of planning measures, for better or for worse. It is a neccessary subject for technical analysis and a fit subject for religious leaders concerned with the day to day lives of people in their communities.

Let us add more "bolts" on our way to an assessment of "comprehensive and explicit" planning:

There is considerable agreement about the major reasons the economy went into the inflationary spiral in the 1970's and that this turn led to the tough measures which produced severe unemployment.

There are five separate factors which together account for the major impetus for inflation during the decade. If we are willing to adopt appropriate preventive planning policies for the future, at least these sources of difficulty can be reduced.

The first initiator of inflation was the way in which the Vietnam war was financed, when Lyndon Johnson refused to raise taxes to pay for the miltary buildup. Thereafter came the first and second OPEC jolts (followed subsequently by delayed reactions when cattle herds were cut back in response partly to high feed grain prices and partly to high interest rates, leading to subsequent higher meat costs).

Add to this ongoing structural problems in health care and growing housing costs, in part the result initially of speculation in response to general inflation, in part the result of population growth and greater demand (and insufficient supply in specific geographic areas), and in part the result of high monthly financing costs.

Note that each of these factors is quite specific. You can cut the budget all you like and you will not change the fact that the food- and energy-related price jolts arose out of quite concrete problems. The specificity of inflationary problems is also clear in the health care area (which continued to rise in the double digit range even when other parts of the Consumer Price Index fell) and in connection with housing.[5] There is confusion on these issues because the initial jolts (and other sectoral factors) led to subsequent general price pressures, which in turn led to wage demands during the 1970s. Industry-specific problems become generalized throuout the price-wage system of the economy once they are let loose.

Policy-makers in the late 1970's and early 1980's were regularly left *after the fact* with two options: creating a massive recession and/or attacking wage settlements. The Carter Administration turned first to budget cutting (even though it acknowledged this to be more symbolic than real); second, it attacked wages. With the exception of the important symbolic victory in the PATCO strike, the Reagan Administration has relied primarily on recession.

Reaganomics has enjoyed low levels of inflation not only because of the massive recession-depression, but because it has (so far) been extremely lucky in regard to the two jolt-prone sectors and because the effects of the new military buildup have not yet been significantly felt. But this is almost certainly a temporary situation. Preventive planning for the future in each of these areas is absolutely essential.

As I have indicated, over the next period a military blowup in the

Persian Gulf could easily destroy vital oil installations, and an over-throw of the medieval Saudi Government could be disastrous. Even if such events do not occur, a resumption of global economic growth will increase energy demand and could begin to create new cost pressures in the later 1980's.

As to food prices, it appears that we have turned the corner on world food supply and demand in recent years. To the extent that world population and demand grow faster than production, the terms of reference are set for longer term shortages and price increases. At some impossible-to-pinpoint date over the coming decade, poor climatic con-ditions are likely once again to explode price stability into food infla-tion. The "PIK" program has massively reduced grain reserves and the current drought may create a major price jolt as early as next year. So, too, could a resumption of international growth create a price jolt, as rising incomes in the developed nations increase world consumption.

Preventive planning for food price stability, as for oil, requires a particular set of specific measures. Looking ahead to the next few years, it is clear that the United States will ultimately have to join most other advanced industrial nations in its approach to the key grains. The Cana-dians, Australians, and other grain exporters have for some time been unwilling to subject their economies to the full effects of temporary world food shortages. Each, in one way or another, insulates domestic prices from world prices. The measures vary (and can be improved upon); they include a mixture of government reserve, export controls or licensing, and bilateral arrangements to insure protection of cer-tain international consumers (particularly in the Third and Fourth Worlds). There is little doubt that a coherent plan can be put together if there is a will to do so. It is just possible that backing for higher current support levels might be offered in exchange for farmer sup-port to prevent another future inflation jolt.[6]

There is much debate as to how much inflation the military buildup will ultimately generate, once actual contracts for production are turned into bottlenecks in key sectors. Lester Thurow thinks there will be somewhat more; Charles Schultze thinks there will be somewhat less. We are, however, definitely seeing a partial repetition of the Johnson Administration's decision to try to finance a military build-up without a tax rise. Here the first requirement of planning which does not rely on slow growth, recession and unemployment to reduce inflation is a program to trim military expenditures.

The remaining two areas are not so "jolt-prone" (except to the degree that housing costs are indirectly responsive to general inflation and to tight monetary policies, both of which had major recent initiating causes in previous jolts). But here, too, the need for preventive planning is clear.

The fundamental needs in connection with housing are: 1) for an expansion of supply in particular areas and categories of need, 2) for measures to reduce the monthly interest rate component of housing costs at low and middle income levels. On the one hand, a tough-minded assault on overall interest rates is needed: the Federal Reserve Board must be taken on. On the other hand, public housing, subsidy, and other programs which build upon the 1982 Congressional housing proposals are necessary, both to increase production in key areas and to lower monthly costs. (Again note the coincidence between what is requred to deal with inflation and what is required to create jobs.)

In connection with health care, there is a need for strong and comprehensive hospital cost containment measures and for an expansion of consumer-oriented health maintenance organizations (HMO's). Beyond this, if a comprehensive health insurance program is revitalized (as it must be at some point), it will be necessary to strengthen controls, HMOs, and also begin moving down the road towards a salaried public health service, beginning in low income areas.

In closing, I have been struck by this passage from *Gaudium et Spes*:

> Whether individuals, groups, or public authorities make decisions concerning [the] distribution and the planning of the economy, they . . . must realize their serious obligation of seeing to it that provision is made for the necessities of a decent life on the part of individuals and of the whole community.[7]

A sharp focus on preventive planning in connection with the above "big five" inflation problems also helps establish principles which are at least as important and understandable as balancing the budget: the moderation of wasteful and dangerous military excesses and stability in the costs of the necessities of life.

The Free Market Versus Planning?

Let us pause to consider an extraordinary bit of ideological confusion. In each of the five areas we have just reviewed, the fact is that our economy is *already* significantly planned! Moreover, at the same time the Reagan Administration has cut back social programs and approved tax cuts benefitting the wealthy, and despite rhetoric concerning a free market it has either maintained existing planning systems or significantly added to them in many ways. Bearing in mind the distinction between the free market and planned (but not coherent or explicit) government intervention, let us briefly review the facts.

The most systematically planned part of the economy, of course, is the military production sector where virtually everything is dependent upon government directives, contracts, and guidance, and this has been the most rapidly expanding part of the U.S. economy, particularly since the election of 1980. In connection with energy, although there has been decontrol in some areas, the government has expanded direct subsidization and encouragement of the nuclear industry and synthetic fuel industries in recent years. No nuclear reactors would have been built by the free market, for instance, without the Price-Anderson Act which provides public insurance against large-scale risks that "free enterprise" refuses to take. The oil industry also has been significantly planned in important respects since 1922, mainly at the insistence of the big oil companies. In that year laws were passed to use government power to restrict supplies so as to raise prices, and this approach (plus planned tax subsidization) was at the core of policy until OPEC created today's new conditions. During the Eisenhower Administration restrictions (again at the behest of the industry) on the importation of foreign oil were also established to reduce supply and to raise the price.

In connection with agriculture, the Reagan Administration's "PIK" strategy of giving away commodities to reduce production has implemented what is perhaps the largest agricultural planning program in world history—to the tune of $21 billion dollars this year (more than net U.S. farm income!). Despite marginal tinkering it has also maintained the marketing orders which by law force farmers to reduce the production and distribution of dozens of commodities, from milk in the Midwest to fruit and nuts in the West (again to reduce supplies and to raise the prices).

The housing industry as we know it is also literally unthinkable without the massive panoply of tax, loan, loan guarantee, government insurance, credit regulation, and banking regulatory institutions which insure the capital flows to this industry which would not occur if there were a truly free market. (The amount of money which goes into middle class housing through tax provisions also amounts to a plan which indirectly subsidizes this area at costs many times that of programs approved by Congress to aid low income housing directly.) The health industry, through Medicare and Medicaid (and programs which help build hospitals and provide for medical research) is also a significantly planned industry, not a free market. And again the Reagan Administration has only dismantled programs in certain areas, mainly affecting low income people. It has even added to planning by regulations which tightens controls on some medical practices.

This is not to say that specific changes have not occured which have deregulated this or that part of an industry, or that specific measures have been implemented which hurt one or another group. All have occurred. For our purposes, however, the *fundamental* point is that the underlying structure of the industry in each case has not been that of the true free market for years. Rather it is an odd, highly integrated system involving government tax programs, expenditure programs, regulations, loans, loan guarantees, etc. — and this strangely planned system not only has not disappeared, but in important respects has grown even under the Reagan Administration.

A very good test of the reality beneath our confused public dialogue about the free market versus government planning is available. Ask any farmer whether he *really* wants the Government to get out of all agricultural programs; ask a doctor if he really wants to eliminate all government health-related programs; ask a realtor or a banker if he really wants the Government to eliminate all tax, loan, insurance, regulatory, and other programs related to housing; ask an oil industry executive if he really wants the Government to do the same. What you will find is that none of these individuals and groups want to return to the free market. To be sure they want to eliminate government programs and planning which they do not like, but they also, simultaneously, want to expand those government policies, tax programs, etc. which favor their industry. (It is by no means clear, incidentally, that if the free market were achieved it would be more efficient than even the badly managed existing government planning programs. For instance, a totally free market in agriculture would destroy tremendous numbers of farmers in excess production years — farmers we need in normal times; the elimination of all banking insurance programs would mean a return to a pre-Depression situation when banks were unreliable and people rushed to take money out of them in difficult moments; without putting floors under oil production costs, we might eliminate producers whom we need in periods of shortages, etc. The argument that the free market is always more efficient is simply not true in many cases. Whether it is more efficient to plan in ways different from both the free market and existing planning is a matter for concrete investigation case by case.

We shall return to this issue later in connection with other areas of existing and potential future planning. But at this point it is worth reflecting upon the fact that if our odd system of private-public planning is a reality that will not go away even under the Reagan Administration, the real issue is not whether we should plan. We already do. The real issue is how we should plan, for whose benefit, under what circumstances, and by which members of society. It is whether the planning we do shall be made coherent, open, explicit, and publicly accountable. If there can be no return to the nineteenth century of a truly free market, the question of planning as we usually consider it is totally misstated.

High Production Planning

I have begun with the above mundane areas of the economy because I believe they offer much better insight into the general problem of planning than the highly publicized debate over selected aid to such industries as auto and steel (or even some of the "high tech" industries). The average family spends some 60-70 percent of its income on the basic necessities of housing, food, energy and health care. The military budget amounts to roughly 6-7 percent of our GNP. The abstraction, "the economy" is misleading: From the point of view either of society as a whole or the individual family, these five specific areas are by far the most significant part of "the economy." To the extent these areas are planned, "the economy" is significantly planned, for better or worse, in important respects.

Prudent planning to reduce the sources of disruptive inflation in such areas is necessary but not sufficient to achieve stable jobs and overall economic growth. Let us take another step forward.

These days prominent economists on both sides of the political aisle regularly tell the public that we can neither have a robust restimulation of the economy nor a real end to unemployment without rekindling inflation. *If* the recovery continues, many argue that we must make do—*after several years*—with 6 to 7.5 percent unemployment. The consensus position for slow growth is neither pure Reaganomics nor pure Carternomics, but what might well be termed "bipartisan creep-along economics."

The view that a high level of unemployment is necessary, however, is based not on economics alone, but on a *political* judgment about the public's unwillingness to support an aggressive program to target jobs to high unemployment areas, to shape specific job programs for unskilled people, to train them for jobs, to improve productivity, and, in general, to implement coherent planning to offset known potential inflationary problems. In reality it is a political judgment against *planning*, not inflation.

The narrow limits of the current dialogue are illuminated by recalling that only a few years ago even the Carter Administration proposed a $30 billion, two-year net stimulus spending package to put people back to work, at a time when the economy was a trillion dollars smaller than it now is. (In today's larger economy it would take $45 billion to have the same relative impact.) The Carter proposals were put forth, moreover, when only 7.5 percent of the labor force was unemployed.

Nor did serious economists at roughly the same time flinch from discussing a real jobs commitment. As former Congressional Budget Office Director Alice Rivlin put it in 1976: "It does not seem, from an analytical point of view, that there is any magic number below which we cannot push unemployment. It is a question of the will and of choosing the right mix of policies."[8]

Explicit planning for high production must expand the cramped limits of the current debate. First we need to change our definition of success; this requires open goal setting. Unemployment in the 6-7.5 percent range means that Black and other minority unemployment will remain roughly twice that high, and minority youth unemployment will still be at least in the 30 percent range. It also means that the collision course for scarce jobs which is already putting white women (and white teenage kids working part-time) in competition with minorities for lower skill jobs will continue.

While it is true that in recent years more young people and women have entered the labor force (in part because inflation in the 1970s ate into real income), this is no reason to avoid strategies which have as their first premise a job for everyone able to work.[9] The demo-graphics, which are shifting away from hard-to-employ younger workers, will help as we move through the rest of the 1980's. Politics does not dictate creep-along economics. The point of high production planning should be to recast our national dialogue so as to focus on which elements, taken together, are best able to fulfill a commitment to put the economy into high gear and keep it there.

The only way to assure sustained high production is to do it directly. And with business depressed and frightened, with consumers in debt and worried, the only actor capable of leading to full employment is the Federal Government. Since tax cutting is strategically limited, full employment requires a decision that public investment must provide not only counter-cyclical help but also a sustained lift to the economy.

I recently spoke to a group in the Middle West about such matters. A woman in the audience, a retired baker, raised what seemed a simple point: "I remember the Depression," she said. "No one was working. There wasn't any money around. Then, all of a sudden, World War II came and there was plenty of money and plenty of jobs. If we can do that in wartime, why can't we do it in peacetime?"

The question has merit. It is quite clear that we can muster the ability to put people to work in time of war. And when we do so, "there is plenty of money around." Bombs and tanks get built; bombers and rifles come off the assembly line. There is no reason, other than political will—*and the value consensus which either does or does not support an active public role*—that the economy cannot be put into high gear and kept there through a program of insulating homes, educating people, and building roads, mass transit systems, houses, etc. We do not want to have a fully regimented wartime economy, but neither do we need to suffer sustained unemployment in the 8-10 percent range. It is a matter of choice and of measuring the specific benefits (social, economic and moral), of making it happen against the costs of not doing so.

In this regard it is useful to recall that before the massive jolts of the 1970's we did far better than we currently seem to think possible. Between 1960 and 1969 the average unemployment rate was 4.8 percent and the average inflation rate was 2.8 percent. If we adopt measures of preventive planning to obviate difficulties which occurred in the five key areas during the 1970's, there is no reason we cannot minimally return to the trend we were on at that time.

Nor is there any reason we cannot go beyond this conclusion. Those who argue that 6 percent or 7.5 percent unemployment is necessary, I believe, are simply wrong. There is reasonable debate as to whether the "non-accelerating inflation rate of unemployment" (what some economists call the NAIRU) lies somewhere between 5-6 percent.[10] All things else being the same, this is the best rate, it is held, that can be maintained without engendering inflation. Even if one accepts the concept, it is important to recognize that *it assumes no direct anti-inflation planning*. It is, quite simply, what economists think would happen "all things else being the same."

Yet if we so choose, there are many options available which can further decrease inflation, or increase productivity (which permits price reductions because of increased efficiency). Organized labor, for instance, has regularly stressed its understanding that real income depends as much (if not more) on what happens to the non-labor components of sectoral costs as on wage gains: energy costs, land costs, structural waste, interest rate increases, etc. A comprehensive plan should build upon this awareness. It would offer an aggressive attack on the sectoral sources of inflation *in exchange for* labor cooperation in holding wage increases to overall productivity gains. To such a package should be added the tax, social and other programmatic elements of a comprehensive plan as well as the most important ingredient — assurance of an aggressive job programs in the context of a high production plan.

Again, we know that wage pressures are much less in areas where there is substantial unemployment. A coherent plan should also target jobs to communities with slack labor markets. The goal should not be simply national "full employment" (which can mean 2 percent unemployment in Houston averaged with 14 percent unemployment in Detroit). Rather, as the League of Cities has proposed, it should be defined in terms of a minimum level of full employment for each community above a certain size, i.e., "*community* full employment." In this way a social contract should be extended beyond labor and industry to include the communities of the nation. A comprehensive strategy also requires targeting to areas of special need or excess capacity.

This brings us to the productivity question. The only way to raise real income and hold down prices on a sustained basis, obviously, is to maintain a decent rate of growth in overall productivity. In the last several years proposals to raise productivity have been restricted almost exclusively to tax incentives for savings or for investment. But such incentives are wasteful and almost useless in a context of tight money, massive recession, and extraordinary uncertainty about the future. There is little sign, for instance, that the Reagan tax incentives stimulated much investment. Indeed investment went down at the same time tax incentives went up!

The truth is that we have gone about as far as we are going to go on the tax-cutting side in any event. This leaves two tactical options and one strategic one. The first involves reforms in industrial organization (including worker participation and worker ownership) which give people a direct stake in the outcomes of cooperation for higher technology industry. Neither is to be ignored, and I personally favor a forthright expansion of worker participation and worker ownership both on economic and social grounds. But stop-start growth and widespread uncertainly have undermined investment *in general* during the last decade and with capacity utilization at 78.9 percent and unemployment at 8.8 percent, neither approach is likely to do much in the absence of a plan to move the economy into the kind of *sustained* high level operation which engenders ongoing investment in new technologies.

The current "buzz-word" among some Democrats is "industrial policies." These include not only measures to aid high technology industries but also strategies to preserve basic industries. They involve proposals for protectionism and for tax changes to reduce consumption and expand investment. Some discussions encompass more traditional research and development, training, education, and relocation strategies. Such policies are mainly proposed as ways to improve U.S. competitiveness in world trade. For the most part they do not address the jobs or inflation questions directly. (On their own, in fact, some will reduce jobs by introducing labor-saving equipment.)

A program of industrial policies to improve the efficiency of some sectors of the economy can be useful, though it is not without difficulties. But discussing such policies in the abstract avoids the central issue, and overly emphasizing their priority puts the cart before the horse. In the first place, their significance in a giant economy like our own has been greatly exaggerated. More important, industrial policies make sense only in the context of a coherent overall plan: No amount of subsidy can deal with the fact that in a sagging economy both the computer and the steel industries will regularly be in serious trouble. In the zero-sum environment of bipartisan creep-along economics the situation can only worsen, sharpening "either/or" choices. In the context of a strategic plan for high production the overall lift of the economy provides the context for steady and focussed investment in both new technologies and basic industries.

Costs and Benefits

It should be clear that by high production planning we do not mean environmentally destructive planning. Quite the contrary. We need to put people to work insulating our houses and building solar collectors rather than making more large gas-guzzling cars (as we now are). We need to increase economic stability so that local communities are not under pressure to reduce environmental protections out of fear of job losses. We need a particular kind of planning which preserves the resources we need for coming generations, an ecologically sound planning which takes the concept of community seriously and extends it over time, which also includes our children and grandchildren.

Let me also say a word about the Third World at this point. I do not believe that healthy Third World development is possible if the United States economy regularly falters. The single most important element in assisting Third World nations is an American economy which is producing fully, one which imports the goods others produce, one which lowers interest rates and does not strangle world economic growth. We are paving the way for restrictions and totalitarianism when we allow the world economy to collapse. The central requirement of world economic health is high production in the United States. It is also the essential condition of generating enough new domestic resources to help provide development assistance to other nations.

An assessment of the cost and benefits of planning measures requires us to confront additional areas of confusion. If ever there was time, for instance, for serious questioning of the thesis that deficits cause inflation, it is now. The statistical relationship between deficits and inflation has always been virtually nonexistent. But with deficits tripled to the $200 billion range in the last three years and inflation fallen to below 4 percent the simple-minded idea that deficits are the primary source of our problems is increasingly absurd.

Until very recently, in fact, state budget surpluses have more than balanced Federal deficits so that the overall public sector has been in balance. If, as part of a high-production plan, we also clarified those parts of the Federal budget which are not spent on current account and developed the kind of capital budget that every business and many states have, you can even make a case that the Federal current account budget is close to balance now. The lay person understands the difference between what the family spends for food and clothing on current account and the capital investment it makes when it signs a mortgage to buy a house.

Narrowly political attacks on government and government spending have obscured such facts. This is not to say that there are no problems to be dealt with in connection with both short- and long-term fiscal balance. However this question does not involve inflation *per se*, but how to sustain sufficient growth to generate new tax flows, how to reform the tax system so that with decent levels of employment the budget is in reasonable balance in future years, and how to reshape the balance between military and other spending: in short, *how to plan*.

If a preventative inflation plan were to allow us to move more aggressively towards full employment, each additional 1 percent of employment we gain because inflation is *directly* reduced will pay back roughly $25-30 billion in the Federal budget. It will also yield roughly $75-80 billion in GNP. Even now, if we were operating the economy at 5 percent unemployment (to say nothing of the 4 percent mandated by the Humphrey-Hawkins Law recently reaffirmed by such authorities as Otto Eckstein), the Federal deficit would be massively reduced and the overall combined government budget (including states and localities) could be in surplus. If reductions in military spending, major loophole closing, and a bold tax reform package were adopted, there is no reason whatsoever that fiscal problems need block a high production strategy.[11]

In this area the matter of *choice* and values needs especially to be highlighted. We are regularly told that we must cut the budget, cut spending, particularly social spending. The first question is a choice as to which budget needs to be cut, as illustrated by the obvious trade-off between military and social programs. Then there is the question of taxes. I believe taxes need to be raised, but given the loopholes in the present tax system it is self-evident that *if we so choose* we can increase taxes without overly burdening the vast majority of low and middle income groups. The *fundamental* choice, however, is between budget cutting and high production planning which would reduce the need for it.

It is also held that we need greater capital investment in the economy. This is almost certainly true, but the primary source of new capital can only be an expanding economy. As we have seen, if we were at the Eisenhower level of unemployment we would have almost $350 billion more of GNP to draw upon than we now have. Policies which aim to cut spending in the name of saving capital will simultaneously reduce stimulation of the economy and thereby undercut growth, which in turn will undercut the resources needed for both public and private needs. Similarly, increasing taxes (without increasing spending) will also reduce economic activity. Those who urge increased tax programs and budget cuts usually do so in a vacuum. They have not stressed, simultaneously, the need for a coherent production plan to increase the growth of the overall economy.

I wish to underscore that this is not only (or even primarily) an economic choice; it is a political and moral one. We have the where-withal for high production planning, and if we choose such planning we can offset, reduce, and limit the burdens now being urged upon us.

Professor Scheffrin, whose work we cited earlier, made the following estimate in 1976 of the difference between optimal rates of employment and other alternatives for the rest of the century. The waste associated with not achieving high production was calculated in several ways:

—It was roughly $15 trillion ($3.2 trillion in federal tax losses) if the economy grew only at the average rate of growth of the period 1956-76 (yielding an overall average unemployment rate of 9.9 percent) as compared with ongoing Japanese employment levels or 1959-76 European levels;
—$7 trillion on the assumption unemployment averaged 6.5 percent (compared with the same);
—$6 trillion on the assumption unemployment averaged 5.5 percent (compared with the same).

Comparing the losses of what he called a "moderately pessimistic" scenario of 6.5 percent unemployment with a "modestly optimistic" scenario of 5.5 percent unemployment yielded a $1 trillion GNP loss over the period.[12] Such calculations are, of course, only rough estimates. Nonetheless, considering that unemployment has run at a much higher level than what seemed a "moderately pessimistic" projection of 6.5%

when Scheffrin's study was published in 1977, the scandalous order of magnitude of wastes (as compared with the potential of our economy) may well be an underestimate. The waste which might be reduced also gives us a rough sense of the potential gains to offset the inevitable (but much lower order of magnitude) administrative and other inefficiencies of planning.

If a comprehensive plan were put into place which combined tax reform with a commitment to high production (and hence, enough tax flows to eliminate *future* deficits), an answer is also available to fears which have repeatedly unsettled our long-term capital markets. The Federal Reserve Board should be required to accomodate an aggressive expansion in any event, but a major rationale for a tight money policy also disappears in such circumstances. Reducing interest rates is also essential, of course, if we are to bring the dollar back to a more reasonable value against other currencies to restore U.S. competitiveness.

Getting specific about each of the components of an initial planning strategy permits us to contrast some of the additional costs and benefits. For instance, in my judgment, the question of community stability is a central one. Specific planning which helps target tax, loan guarantee, public procurement, and other programs to channel funds to maintain economic stability in specific communities is not without costs. Inefficiencies are likely to appear in bureaucratic management; market inefficiencies will also appear. The costs need to be faced openly.[13]

But that is not the end of the matter. Planning which places a high value on *community* should openly address the costs, their dollar value, and their social value and compare these with the economic and social costs of "throwing away communities" (to use Los Angeles Mayor Thomas Bradley's phrase)—their infrastructure, their housing, their hospitals, and above all their social cohesion. It would include the cost of building new schools, houses, hospitals, sewers and roads in other parts of the country to replace those left behind. It would include the social and efficiency losses to society of the local entrepreneurs who collapse when larger economic forces undermine a local community. It would include the human costs of breaking up families and neighborhoods, an area which even more than others needs to be examined not only by economists but by those, like the Bishops, who have a broader perspective.

Towards Coherent and Democratic Planning

The delineation of major elements of economic management leads to several self-evident questions: Do they add up? How can we best make the pieces fit together? What are the goals we should aim for? Is one mix of policies better than another? Virtually every major American corporation manages its affairs through a process of explicit and open goal setting, the aim of which is coherence and rationality. Only in the economy do we avoid this seemingly obvious management approach, even though, as I have tried to indicate, the real issue is no longer the free market versus planned government intervention.

One reason this avoidance occurs is the vested interests which gain from our present situation. But a final set of concerns about planning reaches to issues of centralization of power. As we have seen, some of these concerns confuse real issues of individual freedom with free market rhetoric. Some ignore the experience of other nations. Some refuse to face the reality of the inextricable relationship between government and the economy in the modern world. Most offer little hope for the future other than a vague and illusory call to return to a 19th century world that no longer exists (if in fact it ever existed in the form described by common generalities). Yet the concerns need to be addressed.

Government as a whole now amounts to roughly one-third of the U.S. economy. Despite repeated criticism of government, the Reagan Administration has not significantly changed its role as a percentage of GNP (though it has obviously changed the priorities involved in that role). The percentage of Federal governement activities in the GNP, in 1979, rose to 22.4 percent in 1980, 22.9 percent in 1981, 24.6 percent in 1982, and is likely to end up slightly higher in 1983.[14] Ronald Reagan also approved the Chrysler bailout (though he did so quietly and with as little public notice as possible). In other industrial areas the Reagan Administration has negotiated an understanding with the Japanese government to reduce the number of autos imported into the United States, again a *de facto* plan quite contrary to the free market. It also has reduced the importation of sugar, steel and motorcycles. As other nations increase the planned assistance they give to key industries in the future, I believe any U.S. administration will be increasingly forced to respond in kind.

The fact that big government is here to stay in the modern world, that there will be no return to the 19th century, does not obviate the issue of centralized power. In fact it defines it more clearly, and fairly cries out for real answers rather than rhetoric.

In the first instance, looked at "bolt by bolt," it is clear that although coherence is critical, we are talking about strategic planning in key areas, *not* "total" planning. There is no need to plan vast sectors of the local, state, and regional economies. Second, I believe a policy which aims to maintain the stability of local communities has an importance far beyond the economic, social, environmental and other considerations so far reviewed. Longer range policy should aim to systematically build up the economic health of local communities *as a political offset to the centralization of power.* To the extent local communities experience stability, more real democratic decision-making can be left to them. In the longer run still, I think the same argument favors substantial regional autonomy in planning in a continental-scale nation like our own.

By reducing instability, as we have seen, planning can also increase the role of the truly free entrepreneurial parts of both the national and local economy. If we are serious about the future, however, we need to look ultimately towards a democratic planning system. This requires going beyond both a preventative anti-inflation plan and a plan for high production to the institutional questions of long-range planning *per se.* Initially it requires a much more effective capacity to assess economic and resource trends and to provide coherent goals, scenarios and options to the goverment and to the citizenry. By making explicit and open what is now implicit and covert, we move both towards greater rationality and greater democracy. Other nations, particularly Japan and Norway, have highly sophisticated planning capacities which at least allow the clear delineation of long-term options. We do not have such a capacity. We need to begin to build one. If planning is not to be technocratic and elite, however, we need to go well beyond foreign methods and simultaneously strengthen the capacity of state and local governments to assess options. And in the Congress we need to have an offsetting capacity to evaluate Executive Branch proposals "checks and balance" style.

Democratic planning ultimately entails the submission to Congress of a coherent economic plan for consideration and ratification. During the mid and late 1970's several planning proposals were introduced in Congress, among them the Humphrey-Javits Bill and the Humphrey-Hawkins Bill (which, after being very substantially watered down, was enacted into law). In Congressional hearings on such legislation, numerous suggestions to increase community and worker participation and to expand democratic processes were offered by business, labor and other supporters of planning. The budget process, though badly damaged by the Reagan Administration, requires Congress to reconcile various specific programs and to pass a comprehensive budget (with its economic implications delineated both by the Administration and the Congress); it too is a precursor to general economic planning.

As we look to the future it is clear that at some point the functions of a new technical planning entity, of the current Council of Economic Advisors, and of the current Bureau of the Budget should be amalgamated within the Executive Branch. Within the Congress a similar bringing together of the power of the Joint Economic Committee and the Budget Committee, along with the support of the Congressional Budget Office, should provide an offsetting capacity. If at the local and state levels we were to develop a capacity to assess the implications of national plans *for states and localities*, we could begin to evolve toward a more decentralized and participatory planning system.

Our national discussion of industrial policies has recently focused on the rather narrow question of whether an independent elite technical agency or a tripartite entity (labor, business and government) should make decisions affecting specific industries. I do not believe the citizens of the United States will allow major decisions to be made about industries which supply the lifeblood of the working family, nor about location decisions which can disrupt entire communities, without participation. Proposals which attempt to "insulate" industrial policy decision-making from the people are likely to be short-circuited.

Moreover, such strategies still leave us mired in isolated "bolt by bolt" problems. Although there have been proposals for a very general coordinating or advisory agency, neither option takes into account the need to carefully integrate plans and decisions affecting specific industries with much larger and much more significant federal program decisions (e.g. tax, spending, regulatory), nor does either attempt to do so in a way which systematically builds democratic processes.

The only answer (difficult as it may be) is to subsume specific industrial policy planning within the larger context of coherent planning and, ultimately, to submit such planning to the overall decision-making processes of publicly accountable elected officials. We need to define clear goals to give guidance to specific industrial policy decisions. As we consider which industries require assistance, we need to know whether we will be building more new houses and mass transit systems or more missiles and nuclear power plants; we need to anticipate bottlenecks and shortage areas; we need to be clear about how much of a steel industry is required for national security and other reasons. We are obviously not yet that far along. But to say as much returns the focus of the planning issue to the value basis of an ongoing consensus.

It is here above all that the role of groups such as the Bishops is crucial: *Unless there is a clear and deeply held ongoing shared value basis for planning goals, it is unlikely that a sustainable consensus for sensible economic decision-making will be achieved.* Without a shared value basis all strategies break down into interest group contention, pork barrel politics, and irrational log rolling. And unless there is agreement on the ends to which economic production is dedicated, the sacrifices and burdens required to achieve high production and high productivity are not likely to be accepted.

When, however, the people are clear about the goals they seek, and have participated in their development, public authorities have solid backing to meet them. *The central issue of explicit and democratic planning is therefore the affirmation of certain key end values as opposed to others.* May I commend to you the following: the priority of human labor and employment, the needs of the poor, access to the basic necessities of life at reasonable prices, the reduction of unnecessary military expenditures, the stewardship of resources needed for the coming generation, the importance of local community, and the greatest possible democratic participation in decision-making.

None of us knows what methods and institutions ultimately will best enable us to plan. Nevertheless, the planning issue, with all its complexities, with its difficult tensions between centralized power, local communities, the market and individuals is before us, both in our own countries, and throughout the world in all the advanced industrial countries. *It will not go away.* As we move through the very brief few years to the new century, we need to create new methods appropriate to our own tradition by trial and error, public discussion and debate, and open dialogue. We need strong policies to sustain essential parts of the national system, but we need policies which, simultaneously, maintain and encourage openness and initiative by individuals, groups and communities. Professor Michael Walzer of Princeton University has offered a useful concept:

> The state must be held tightly to its own limits, drained of whatever superfluous moral content and unnecessary political power it has usurped, reduced so far as possible to a transparent administrative shell (overarching, protective, enabling) within which small groups can grow and prosper. The state is not going to wither away; it must be hollowed out.[15]

Conclusion

Let us stand the planning question on its head: *Not* to plan is absurd on the face of it. In our daily lives, in our families, in our communities, in our corporations, in our local and national institutions it is obvious that we must look to the future and plan ahead. Only in our economy do we say this is a mistake. All the while we quietly continue a trend of planning which is done badly and deceptively in significant part because of our lack of candor. It is time to recognize reality — and common sense. The issue before us is not whether to plan but *how* to plan effectively, by which groups, and toward which goals.

The 1960's and the 1970's are over. So long as the economy malfunctions there will be inadequate resources for all, and the tensions between those who need and those who have will grow. If we allow the decay of our society to continue, who is to say that racial violence will not one day erupt and call forth measures which destroy freedom and democracy? As a former student of foreign policy let me also recall that history teaches that societies under internal tension all too often seek foreign scapegoats as a way to avoid their own problems.

High-production planning offers the only answer for minorities, white- and blue-collar males, and women, who seek real assurances for real jobs. Combined with tax and military reform for future years, it is also the only way to generate the revenue flows needed for a variety of social programs — above all Social Security, an issue which has been relegated to the politics of tax and benefit trimming when its main problems can only be solved by a high-production, tax-producing economy. In the longer term it is the staging ground and learning context for coherent and explicit democratic planning.

People who are not professional economists often avoid economic questions because they are confused, because economists differ in their opinions, because "it is all too complicated." While I understand such concerns, may I suggest that they involve both a form of escapism and of idolatry. Pleading ignorance simply means avoiding the hard work needed to clarify hard issues. And it makes "economics" into an "idol" not to be challenged but in a sense to be worshipped by those with lesser rights or knowledge.

We are not a poor country. Nor are we a rocky island of limited resources like Japan. We are a rich, magnificent continent endowed by the Creator with unbelievable agricultural and mineral resources, protected from invasion by two oceanic moats. Our highly educated and well-trained men and women have demonstrated their willingness and ability to work well and hard. Despite all our problems there is no other nation like us. It simply will not do to say that "economics" *requires* us to do x, y, or z without very careful reflection. No purely technical consideration can be allowed to blur the fundamental fact that the choices this nation makes about its future are its choices alone—for better or for worse.

And they are *our* choices.

Notes

1. *The Cost of Continued Unemployment, Report of the Exploratory Project for Economic Alternatives* by Steven Scheffrin, 1977.

2. *Statistical Abstract* 1981, p. 879; *Handbook of Labor Statistics, Bureau of Labor Statistics,* 1980, p. 467; *Statistical Abstract 1981,* p. 883.

3. *Studies, 1980,* Organization for Economic Cooperation and Development, Paris.

4. See "Social Justice and the New Inflation," Gar Alperovitz, in *New Directions in Economic Justice,* Roger Skurski, editor, (Notre Dame, IN: University of Notre Dame Press, 1983).

5. Despite well known difficulties in the Consumer Price Index (CPI) housing index, any way housing costs are measured they remain a hot spot for future inflation; both because of growing scarcity due to production cutbacks and because of high monthly financing costs.

6. See Barry P. Boswarth and Robert Z. Lawrence, *Commodity Prices and the New Inflation* (Washington, D.C.: Brookings Institution, 1982). See also

various papers by E. Phillip LeVeen available from the Public Interest Economics Center, Washington, D.C.

7. *Gaudium et Spes*, (70).

8. Hearings, Joint Economic Committee, March 18-19, 1976. *Thirtieth Anniversary of the Employment Act of 1946 — A National Conference on Full Employment* (Washington, D.C.: Government Printing Office, 1976), p. 276.

9. For a discussion of the changing definition of appropriate levels of unemployment, see Gar Alperovitz and Jeff Faux, *Introduction*, in the study by Scheffrin previously cited. Also see U.S. Congress, Joint Economic Committee, 92nd Congress, 2nd Session, *Reducing Unemployment to 2%* (Washington, D.C., U.S. Government Printing Office, 1972). The 2 percent goal, incidentally, was affirmed in these hearings by such well-known conservative economists as Herbert Stein and Martin Feldstein.

10. For a useful review see "The Full Employment Unemployment Rate", Isabel V. Sawhill, The Urban Institute, Project Report. Sawhill estimates the unemployment rate consistent with stable inflation at 5-6 percent, and "probably at the lower end of this range." p. 23.

11. See Otto Eckstein, "Disinflation", in *Inflation: Prospects and Remedies*, Center for National Policy, October 1983, p. 22. For a review of "tax expenditures" estimated in 1984 at $388.4 billion, see Appendix C of *Setting National Priorities: The 1984 Budget*, edited by Joseph A. Pechman (Washington, D.C.: Brookings Institution, 1984). For one approach to tax reform see also the essays on tax policy by Harvey Galper in that publication. For a review of corporate tax options see *Inequity and Decline* by Robert S. McIntyre and Dean C. Tipps, Center on Budget and Policy Priorities, 1983.

12. See Scheffrin, *ibid*, pp. xii, xiii.

13. The extent of present market efficiencies and the inefficiencies associated with more direct planning seem to be exaggerated in most discussions. For a review see Barry Bluestone, and Bennett Harrison, *The Deindustrialization of America* (New York: Basic Books, 1982).

14. *The Economic and Budget Outlook, an Update, September 1982*, Congressional Budget Office, p. 35; see also p. 7 of statement of Donald T. Regan before the Joint Economic Committee, July 19, 1983.

15. Michael Walzer, *Radical Principles: Reflections of an Unreconstructed Democrat* (New York: Basic Books, 1980), p. 100.

Thirteen

Justice for the Poor and Between Generations

PETER G. PETERSON

MY THESIS IN THIS PAPER IS RELATIVELY SIMPLE TO STATE and to understand: America's future needs and opportunities are being shortchanged. The Great American Majority—the broad middle class, from faded blue collar to spiffiest white collar—is choosing to consume today and not save for tomorrow. I will argue that this high-consumption, high-debt pattern impacts adversely on both the poor and the young and raises serious questions of justice and equity for us as a society. I will further argue that special interest politics, which has contributed substantially to our present problems, also dooms the chances for successful economic planning in our nation.

Zero Economic Growth by Accident

Ten years ago a favored topic of discussion was zero economic growth; presumably with zero growth came a higher quality of life. The growth skeptic, like British economist E. J. Mishan, would point out that "we might more reasonably be asking if life is becoming more enjoyable or if we are becoming better or more contented people in consequence of economic growth."[1] I was never persuaded that very many people

359

took zero-growth seriously, but it did form a hypothetical context in which we might judge value systems embedded in our economy.

Not long ago I was looking at the economic performance of this country in terms of real income per worker for the last ten to twelve years. I discovered that we have achieved zero growth, however inadvertently and unintentionally. At the same time I was examining the performance of other countries. I looked at Japan, a country that has little land and no resources. During a decade when it imported all of its oil, half of its food and most of its resources, it managed to grow much more, to trade much more and to have earnings growth per worker at much higher levels than the United States.

There are many factors that explain this disparity between the U.S. and Japan, including some structural and some motivational, but there is one factor that I want to emphasize. It seems to me that a decisive difference in comparing the Japanese economy with ours is that while we have been busy mortgaging our future; they have been equally busy investing in theirs. For example, during the Seventies:

—Japan invested nearly three times as much in new corporate plant and equipment (net 9.8 percent of Gross Domestic Product vs. net 3.4 percent in the U.S.)

Japan invested over seven times as much in public "infrastructure" such as roads and waterways (5.0 percent vs. 0.7 percent).

Japan invested 20 percent more in civilian research and development, exclusive of R & D for space and defense (1.9 percent vs. 1.6 percent).[2]

And in all-important human investment, the education of children, 34 percent of their high school graduates have taken Calculus, 30 percent have taken computer related instruction. (Our comparable data would be considerably lower.) Finally the Japanese are now spending about three times as much as we are on the training of children in science education.

Although I am not an economist, I do think there is at least one inexorable law in economics: It is difficult to consume more and save more at the same time. And before we can invest, it is necessary that we save. So when one asks the tough question: "Whose rate of consumption are we willing to cut back temporarily, so that we can invest more?" I am afraid our political system says essentially "not me!"

Our bloated deficits are a prime symptom of our ravenous appetites for publicly subsidized consumption. These deficits on a structural basis now come to 5 or 6 percent of GNP and amount to about $200 billion. These deficits are draining about 50 to 70 percent of an already small savings pool while the Japanese, even in their worst years, have never taken more than about 30 percent of their much larger savings pool for deficits. Despite the cyclical economic rebound this year, the outlook for the budget remains alarming. Even assuming the economy continues to grow rapidly for the next few quarters and then (optimistically) grows steadily at about 3½ percent annually thereafter, annual deficits for 1984 through 1988 are still projected to be in the $200-$250 billion range. These projections require that Congress holds defense budget authority growth to 5 percent in real terms, allows nondefense programs on balance to continue operating at current services levels and does not enact any new tax programs. Right now, the deficit is on a course that appears to be permanently locked in at 5 percent of GNP or more — well above either the postwar average of 0.9 percent or the average of 1.6 percent for the more recent period, 1965-1980.

Table 1

Federal Deficit Projections — Baseline Estimate*
— in Billions of Dollars —

FY1983	FY1984	FY1985	FY1986	FY1987	FY1988
$197.4	$196.2	$199.4	$218.0	$243.0	$244.5

— As a Percentage of GNP —

6.1%	5.6%	5.3%	5.2%	5.3%	5.0%

* Assumes real GNP growth of 5.4%, 3.6%, 3.2%, 3.4%, and 3.4% in fiscal years 1984-1988, no change in tax and nondefense spending policies, and a 5 percent real growth in defense budget authority in each year.

Source: Bipartisan Budget Appeal, Bowling Green Station, Box 9, New York, N.Y. 10004.

Most economists believe a prolonged period of rapid economic growth like that in the period 1962-1966 is highly unlikely, especially

Table 2

Deficits Under Alternative Economic Scenarios

	Baseline Growth Scenario			Record Growth Scenario (1962-1966 Growth)			Slightly Slower Growth Scenario (1976-1980 Growth)		
	Real GNP Growth	Inflation (GNP Deflator)	Deficit	Real GNP Growth	Inflation (GNP Deflator)	Deficit*	Real GNP Growth	Inflation (GNP Deflator)	Deficit*
1984	5.4%	4.2%	$ 196b	6.0%	4.5%	$ 191b	4.5%	4.0%	$ 204b
1985	3.6	4.5	199	6.0	5.2	171	3.4	4.2	209
1986	3.2	5.2	218	5.5	6.1	160	3.4	4.9	229
1987	3.4	5.3	243	5.0	7.2	148	3.4	5.0	257
1988	3.4	5.4	245	4.6	8.3	102	3.4	5.0	264
Cumulative 5 year real growth**	20.5%			24.0%			19.5%		
Average Annual Rate of Growth	3.8%			4.4%			3.6%		

* Deficits were computed by adjusting baseline estimates of revenues for the difference in nominal incomes relative to the baseline scenario and by adjusting outlay estimates for unemployment compensation, food stamps, and other means-tested programs for the difference in the projected unemployment rate relative to the baseline. Finally, estimates for interest on the debt were adjusted, relative to the baseline, to reflect both the effects of higher (or lower) nominal interest rates because of changes in the inflation rate and the effect of changes in the volume of government financing.

** No 5-year period in the 1970s had cumulative real growth as high as 20%.

Source: Bipartisan Budget Appeal.

on top of this year's rebound. For example, the Administration discounted the possibility in its January 1983 budget document. It cited among other things the fact that low capacity utilization at the start of the recovery makes the above average rebound in capital spending, necessary for unusually strong real output growth, an unlikely occurence. It also cited the restrictive effects of high interest rates and the fact that the financial difficulties facing the developing countries will hold down imports from the U.S. and other industrialized nations. More recently, Commerce Department officials have publicly predicted that our trade balance will deteriorate further in 1984. It is hard to envision a sustained period of above average economic growth when our export sector is being decimated. All of this points to rebutting the argument that we can somehow grow ourselves out of this deficit gridlock.

The Long-Term: Bottomless Deficits by the Year 2000 and 2025?

We can see that the grim fiscal outlook is the result of several congruent forces — all converging to push federal spending and deficits to unprecedented levels. Principal among these are: 1) *a rapidly aging society;* 2) *fully indexed and largely unfunded entitlement programs*, in particular health care, going principally to the aged (Joseph Califano, former Secretary of HEW made the following estimates of the percentage of the federal budget going to the elderly: 13 percent in 1960, 25 percent in 1980, a substantial 35 percent in the year 2000, and an unthinkable and unsustainable 65 percent in the year 2025);[3] and 3) *exploding interest costs.*

I will now attempt to indicate what the continued effect of these factors might be in the year 2000 and beyond. Before doing this, it is essential to make the important distinction between a projection and a prediction. Projections are obviously hazardous since many of the variables are hard to assess far into the future. Beyond any errors in estimation, it is especially unwise to equate these projections with predictions. The political system will often change the outcome of the projection. Thus, as seems likely, if the congruence of the three factors mentioned earlier combine to result in taxes, deficits, interest rates, inflation, or unemployment (or all of the above) so high as to be either economically or politically unsustainable, then the projections will not turn out to be good predictions of what in fact happens. At the same time, if such projections, under any reasonable set of long-range assumptions, yield a deficit and spending outcome that is obviously unacceptable, then they fill an important function: They remind us that the longer we wait for structural reform, the worse it gets. There is no way, as we shall see, to avoid the need for reform.

Table 3

Long Range Economic Assumptions Used in
Social Security Trustees' Scenarios* —
IIB ("Intermediate Pessimistic") and III ("Pessimistic")

Year	Real GNP Growth		Inflation Rate		Unemployment Rate	
	IIB	III	IIB	III	IIB	III
1990	3.0%	2.7%	4.0%	5.0%	6.5%	7.4%
1991	3.0	2.6	4.0	5.0	6.2	7.0
1992	3.0	2.5	4.0	5.0	5.8	6.8
1993	2.5	2.3	4.0	5.0	5.7	6.5
1994	2.5	2.0	4.0	5.0	5.6	6.5
1995	2.6	2.1	4.0	5.0	5.5	6.5
2000 & later	2.6	2.1	4.0	5.0	5.5	6.5

* Source: *1983 Annual Report — Federal Old-Age and Survivors Insurance and Disability Insurance Trust Fund*, June 27, 1983.

Because the various social security programs are such dominant factors in these out years and official long-term estimates are required, this is perhaps the best place to start. The most widely used estimates are the Social Security Trustees' Scenario IIB (Intermediate-Pessimistic). I believe their Scenario III (Pessimistic) estimates are the most prudent ones but that will become clearer after looking at the critical variables.

Given the magnitude of the deficits and debt service costs, the assumptions about interest rates are crucial. Here both the long term "intermediate" (nominal interest rates of 6.1 percent, inflation of 4.0 percent, and real interest rates of 2.1 percent) and "pessimistic" cases (nominal interest rates of 6.6 percent, inflation of 5.0 percent, and real interest rates of 1.6 percent) use assumptions that seem to me to be optimistic, especially in light of the large deficits that are projected. Nevertheless, we have used those assumptions.

The resulting budget projections support the case I am making; namely, that even under optimistic sets of economic and demographic assumptions, the spending, tax and deficit levels are simply unacceptable. In spending terms, these projections result in numbers that are 10 to 20 percentage points more of the GNP than record peacetime levels. In tax terms, they would imply tax burdens 50 percent (or more) in excess of record levels, unless interest costs on ever expanding deficits and debt were allowed to explode. Are we seriously suggesting that we are asking our children and grandchildren to accept such destructively high tax levels for programs that *we* put into place? Are we seriously suggesting that future generations or the economy *could* absorb these costs or taxes?

Table 4

Year 2000 Projections of Federal Outlays as a Percent of GNP— Using Social Security IIB and III Scenarios

	IIB			III		
OASDI—Retirement and Disability Part of Social Security	4.3%			4.8%		
HI—Hospital Insurance Part of Social Security	2.0			2.6		
Supplemental Medical Insurance (SMI)	1.0			1.3		
Civil Service/Military Retirement	1.1			1.1		
Other Nonmeans Tested Benefits	0.9			1.0		
Means Tested Benefits	1.9			1.9		
Grants	1.2			1.2		
Other Operations/subsidies Civilian Agency Payroll	1.4			1.4		
Defense*	6.7%	to	9.0%	6.7%	to	9.2%
Interest	3.6	to	4.5	4.3	to	5.4
Total	24.2%	to	27.3%	26.3%	to	29.9%
Deficits as a % of GNP:	4.2%	to	7.3%	6.3%	to	9.9%

* The range gives what happens if (a) defense grows in real terms as fast as GNP after 1988 (low end) and (b) defense grows in real terms by 5 percent each year (upper end). This range for defense expenditures under each scenario causes a range for interest costs.

Source: Bipartisan Budget Appeal.

Projections for the Year 2000

— The *OASDI* and *HI* projections are from the Trustees' report. The SMI projections assume *SMI*, the physician's fees part of Medicare remains equal to about 50 percent of HI. This may be a slight underestimate. SMI has been growing more rapidly than HI, but no projection is available from the trustees on the long-term cost of SMI.

— *Civil Service and Military Retirement* are projected to remain at their 1988 GNP share of 1.1 percent. Federal employment has been flat for over 20 years and is projected to remain so and the real wages of federal workers, on which retirement benefits are based, have not grown. Thus, holding the GNP share constant 1.1 percent is reasonable and may even be a tenth or so too high.

— *Other nonmeans tested benefits* are comprised primarily of unemployment benefits and veterans benefits. The GNP share will probably decline slightly over the 1990s from the 1988 share of 1.2 percent to 0.9 - 1.0 percent, because benefits to World War II veterans will fall.

— Outlay for *means tested benefits, grants to state and local governments* and *other operations-subsidies-civilian agency payments* are simply assumed to retain their 1988 GNP share. This has not been the pattern over the 1980s—as budget restraint has been targeted primarily at these programs. But even if these categories were reduced to *zero*, outlays would still be 20 to 23 percent of GNP under Scenario IIB and 22 to 25 percent under Scenario III.

— *Defense* is a big uncertainty in the projections. For 1988 the defense share of GNP is projected to be 6.7 percent. To retain that share until the end of the century, which is what was assumed for the low end of the range, defense would have to grow in real terms by 2.5 to 3.0 percent annually in the 1990s (IIB) or 2.0 to 2.7 percent (III). The upper end of the range was constructed by assuming defense outlays would continue to grow by 5 percent per year in real terms (as assumed for the late 1980s).

— The interest projection makes use of the assumption that revenues will equal about 20 percent of GNP by Year 2000 together with the projections of spending for other categories. Interest rates that are one percentage point higher than the 6.1 percent and 6.6 percent in scenarios IIB and III would raise the GNP share for interest in 2000 by 0.7 to 0.8 percentage points. Even without this, we can see in Table 4 that interest costs could consume about one out of every six budget dollars in the year 2000.

Table 5

Federal Spending in 2025, As a Share of GNP— Using Social Security IIB and III Scenarios

	IIB			III		
OASDI—Retirement and Disability Part of Social Security	5.6%			6.7%		
HI—Hospital Insurance Part of Social Security	3.2			4.1		
SMI—Supplementary Medical Insurance	1.6			2.1		
Civil Service/Military Retirement	1.1			1.1		
Other Nonmeans Tested Benefits	0.6			0.7		
Means Tested Benefits	1.9			1.9		
Grants	1.2			1.2		
Other Operations/subsidies Civilian Agency Payroll	1.4			1.4		
Defense*	6.7%	to	9.0%	6.7%	to	9.2%
Interest	6.3	to	11.6	11.9	to	18.4
Total	29.7%	to	37.2%	37.8%	to	46.8%
Deficits as a % of GNP:	8.7%	to	16.2%	16.8%	to	25.8%

Source: Bipartisan Budget Appeal.

—The estimates shown for 2025 are more uncertain. The methodology and assumptions used were similar to what was done for the year 2000, with few exceptions. The trustees have published just one projection for HI in 2025—under the IIB Scenario. The Scenario III projection for Hospital Insurance assumes that in 2025 the gap between the estimates of the cost of the HI program under IIB and III (as a percent of taxable payroll) would be the same as in 2005—the last year for which an official projection of HI expenses under Scenario III is available. This is a relatively conservative estimate since it assumes no further deterioration in HI under Scenario III relative to IIB.

—The range for defense makes the assumption that after the year 2000 real defense spending increases will equal real GNP increases—2.6 percent per year under alternative IIB and 2.1 percent annually under Scenario III. This would mean the GNP share for defense in 2025 would equal the share in the year 2000.

—Revenues are projected, under current law, to rise to 21 percent of GNP by 2025. The interest projection uses this estimate as well as the estimate of spending for other categories. Interest rates that are one percentage point higher than the 6.1 to 6.6 percent assumed here would raise the GNP share for interest by 3.4 to 3.9 percentage points of the GNP! Again, even without this, interest costs could consume, depending upon one's assumptions, as much as forty percent of the entire budget.

Again, this is not a prediction, only a projection of what *would* happen *given* an indefinite continuation of current policies. Since it is unlikely that future decades will be entirely devoid of unexcepted and expensive emergencies—one might imagine everything from a natural disaster to a political confrontation abroad—these deficit figures have to be regarded as inherently optimistic. Whereas financing extraordinary expenditures was once the exclusive function of federal deficits, it will in the future be just one more borrowing burden to be added to all the rest. Indeed, so huge are these projected deficits to begin with that it is hard to believe, even without an emergency, that they will actually be allowed to occur. Perhaps the real question then is not *whether* we reform our budget, but *when*: sooner, so that we may plan ahead and enact policy changes in a modest and gradual manner? Or later, after years of economic damage has already been inflicted and we have no choice but to cut spending suddenly, drastically, and painfully?

Given these projected deficits, we are hearing a line of political defense which goes something like this: If you do not face the problem or do not have a solution, why not pretend that there is no problem? Therefore we are increasingly being told that deficits do not matter or that they do not affect interest rates. Space does not allow me to develop my arguments, but I strongly contend that structural and permanent deficits of this magnitude do affect the critical question of investment in our future.[4]

Another view is that we are going to grow our way out of these deficits, but if we look at a scenario of the fastest growth in the history of the U.S., the 1962-66 period (Table 2), we still come up with deficits of over $100 billion. If we examine the international picture, the effects are very serious and they raise some moral questions in my mind. In the first place, one important source of financing these deficits is foreign capital. We are for all practical purposes extracting savings from the rest of the world. I do not understand the moral basis of the richest nation in the world drawing savings from those that are less rich, from savings that would be available to the poor countries of the world. Our overvalued dollar and high interest rates substantially raise the cost of oil (which is dollar denominated) and of debt carrying by these countries. Finally trade protectionism is once again abroad in our land.[5] I trace this to deficits and high interest rates, and it could have a devasting impact on poorer nations attempting to develop if their products and raw materials cannot be sold in this country.

"Bribe the Rich in Order to Help the Poor"

About half of all federal spending consists of benefits to individuals, and typically we think of means tested welfare payments—too often it is believed into the pockets of the unworthy or cheaters—as being the main component of these benefits. But more than two-thirds of this account is made up of non-means test benefits: military and civil service pensions, unemployment compensation, medicare and social security. And if you examine the budget actions of the last few years, you will find the following pattern: The programs that are means tested or based on need, i.e., Medicaid, food stamps, welfare, etc. have been cut three times as much as the programs going to the rest of us. The remaining programs, which by 1985 will be five times as large as the means tested, have barely been touched at all. So while we hear rhetoric about the safety net for the truly needy, I see it as a well padded and protected hammock for the middle and upper income groups. And unless we attack this problem directly by cutting these programs that are growing 15 percent a year compounded, we will never get this fiscal situation under control.[6]

Many of these non-means tested entitlement programs are nothing more than welfare programs in my view, subsidy programs for the middle and upper income groups. In the case of Social Security we have heard euphemisms, such as, "I'm getting back my money," "It is my account," "It is a social insurance program," and so forth. The programs are in fact designed to give everyone, including upper and middle income people, substantially more than they, with their companies' contributions, paid in. We simply cannot afford, in my judgment, subsidies and welfare for the middle and upper income groups.

The argument I sometimes hear is that we cannot cut back on those programs, because if we cut back on programs for the middle and upper income groups, the wealthy will no longer support the programs for the poor. My reply is: "If everyone is going to get on this political wagon, who is going to be left to pull it?" I hope we can get rid of the view in our fiscal and moral calculus that we somehow must bribe the rich to take care of the poor.

These huge entitlement programs raise very serious ethical and moral problems of another kind. It was a German philosopher who once said it is the duty of the old to lie to the young. And Herbert Hoover once remarked, "Blessed are the young for they shall inherit the debt." I remind the reader that we now have something like $7 trillion of unfunded liabilities for the entitlement programs: Social Security, Federal pensions, and military pensions.

These are bills that we are passing on to our children. These entitlement programs (I really do not understand what entitlement means in this context) are now growing at a shocking rate:

Item: Fifty years ago only 4 percent of our population was over the age of 65; today it is 11 percent, and that proportion will double again over the next 50 years. In fact, for the next several decades our elderly population generally, those who receive the benefits, will grow 20 times the rate of our labor force, those who contribute the benefits.

Item: We shall not be able to afford the current entitlements system for the aged. To take the Social Security system as an example, the total payroll — tax today at 13 percent of wages — would have to soar well above 20 percent by the turn of the century and some say as high as 40 percent by the year 2030. If we instead dip into general revenues, the burden would simply switch to the income tax — a burden which would force us to forgo virtually every other important national objective.[11]

I believe we are setting the stage for a very ugly generational conflict because the young will refuse to pay the crushing taxes required to support the aged.

Planning and Regulation

Let me comment on a widely discussed prescription for economic ills: some sort of national economic planning. This proposal implies a set of national premises and logically developed policies proceeding from these premises. Our major assumption, going back to the end of World War II, was that the United States was *the* permanent economic superpower of the globe. We could fund the Marshall Plan and our dollar was as "good as gold." This was a period of enormous optimism:

1. Hunger was going to be eliminated worldwide.
2. Economic growth was guaranteed.
3. We could simultaneously fight a war in Vietnam and against poverty.
4. We could clean up the environment without seriously affecting productivity and industrial investments.

Clearly we believed we could finance every need and say "yes" to every interest group, i.e., aged, white, black, brown, ethnic, male, female, rich, middle class and poor.

In 1971 when I was a cabinet member of the Nixon Administration, Wilbur Mills, then chairman of the powerful House Ways and Means Committee, proposed a twenty per cent increase in Social Security and a one hundred per cent indexing of all entitlement programs. Another example of economic optimism! Neither the President nor the cabinet objected; rather we spent a good part of the time figuring out how the Republican President could get credit for a Democratic Congressional Chairman's proposal: Shouldn't the Amercian flag and the President's signature be on the social security check? I believe this story illustrates what will happen to national economic planning. Even with the best of intentions, partisan political advantage will crowd out economic rationality and concern for the larger common good. Each interest group will mobilize its members to insure that it receives its "fair" share of the economic pie, whether that pie is growing or diminishing.

There is a form of general economic planning that proposes the idea of targeting certain industries to be the growth industries of the future. These designated industries would therefore be heavily subsidized. I have grave doubts whether we have the prescience to predict which industries will be growing ten to fifteen years into the future. Certainly the Japanese record indicates as many incorrect choices as correct ones, and Japan is always cited as the innovator in the area of industrial policy. In addition, I likewise see partisan politics playing the key role in the selection process. One of the most unattractive assignments I was given by Presidential Nixon was to negotiate a textile import quota in 1971 before the 1972 presidential election. In those days the designation was "strategic industries" for national defense, which like "growth industries," obtained special subsidies and protection. Of course the reason textiles were strategic had very little to do with national defense. Election time was approaching; there were two hundred congressional districts in which there were textile mills; the border states (the location of many of these mills) were critical to President Nixon's re-election; the industry had contributed two million dollars to the campaign. Whether it is called "strategic" or "growth," I believe *both* Republican and Democratic Administrations will fall sway to political expediency in their economic planning.

Conclusion

I would like to close by suggesting some basic principles which will serve as a useful guide in thinking about spending, deficits and public policy.[7]

Realism: It is important to realize that the deficits we face are too large. They are not going to disappear even if the economy grows at record rates over the next five years, and they are going to result in substantial and destructive interest rates and, ultimately, inflationary pressures.

Speed: Although realism dictates that the target year for cutting the deficit to 2 percent of GNP should probably be moved back to at least 1986, some action is necessary soon in order to achieve this modified goal. Otherwise, high interest rates and an overvalued dollar will continue to ravage our export industries, and governmental calls on the capital markets will continue to drain off funds badly needed for new investment.

Long-term impact: A multi-year plan, targeting long range goals, is necessary.

Spirit of cooperation and compromise: The uncontrolled and inadvertent growth of so many categories of public spending over the last 15 years is a good reason for us to consider reforms in the way our legislative process appropriates money. At the same time, however, we should not succumb to the cynical view that the only way left to control spending is to hold the entire economy hostage to massive deficits until "the other side" gives way. Without compromise on all sides, and without a civilized determination to resolve our most critical problems, all sides will lose and every one of us will end up poorer and weaker for our efforts.

Focus on investment: The only acceptable policy for the country is to focus on freeing up resources for long-term investment in our future. Reasonable people do not differ on the fact of our extremely meager rate of private savings, the degree to which our tax structure discourages private savings, and the extent to which earnings are in turn consumed by federal borrowing. Here there is no question that the U.S. is way out of line with the other industrial countries. It is one of our most critical economic problems and our success in resolving it will have important long-term consequences for our future living standards.

Fairness and burden-sharing: The lower income groups have so far borne a disproportionate share of budget austerity. It is time for the rest of us to absorb our share. In addition, it is important for us to be fair and honest with our young, most of whom do not realize that they will bear the burden of something like $7 trillion in unfunded liabilities of the social security, Medicare, and federal pension systems. For example, as much as 30 to 40 percent of wages of the year 2025 workers would be required to support the social security system alone. This would be an unsustainable tax, both from an economic and political standpoint.

I can visualize neither a credible nor a fair solution to our fiscal dilemma that does not include a rigorous application, or perhaps I should say *re*application, of the principle of need. For example, of the benefit payments we will have to give up the much cherished notion that we are *all* "entitled" to some benefits and subsidies. The sense of largesse that has flooded our society with red ink is simply incompatible with the Era of Stringency and Scarce Resources which we now confront. Some will argue we will need to go back directly to *means* tested benefits. Others will want to trim off some of the largesse and spending growth going to individuals or businesses that are not in

serious need (through freezes, caps on indexing and benefits, taxation of benefits, etc.). But all of us will have to face the grim reality
of the necessity to distribute economic and political pain. This is
something our political system has demonstrated itself incapable of
doing in recent years. If those choices are not made by us and our
representatives, they will ultimately be made for us by relentless events,
and those who will suffer will be our children—left with a less prosperous America.

Notes

1. E.J. Mishan, "The Wages of Growth," *Daedalus* 102, 4 (Fall
1973), p. 72. This issue of *Daedalus* is a good introduction to policy
debates about a no-growth society.

2. Disparities between American and Japanese investment and productivity are discussed more fully in "The Peterson Prescription," *Harvard Business Review* 62, 3 (May-June) 1984, pp. 66-77.

3. See my article, "No More Free Lunch for the Middle Class," *The
New York Times Magazine*, January 17, 1982.

4. See table and discussion of "Estimated Federal Government
Outlays, Comparison of 1980 and 1985 as Now Projected" in my article "The Coming Crash," *The New York Review of Books*, December
2, 1982.

5. "The Peterson Prescription," *loc. cit.*, p. 77.

6. This argument is developed in my article "The Salvation of Social
Security," *The New York Review of Books*, December 16, 1982.

7. For an overview of these conclusions and some elaboration, see
"Social Security—The Great Debate: Peter G. Peterson Replies to
Critics," *The New York Review of Books*, March 17, 1983.

Fourteen

Industrial Competitiveness, Employment, and the Role of Planning: A Dialogue

ELMER W. JOHNSON
MARINA v. N. WHITMAN

Industrial Policy and Planning

ELMER JOHNSON: LET ME BEGIN BY OFFERING A BRIEF PER-
spective on the issues we are proposing to discuss.

Over the last 20 years or so our society has devoted itself almost
singlemindedly to the protection of various legitimate social interests
that had hitherto been neglected: interests respecting the environment,
safety, pension rights, health care, consumer rights, energy efficiency,
the needs of the poor and so forth. In hindsight it appears this process
ignored the fragility of other very basic social interests—industrial
competitiveness and full employment—and forgot what every good
engineer understands: the unpleasant necessity of trade-offs.

Within the last few years political and business leaders have begun
to focus on the importance of economic goals. Ronald Reagan un-
doubtedly won the last presidential election by doing so. More recently leaders in the Democratic Party have attempted to formulate
and articulate a new "industrial policy," and to this end they have
enlisted the help of Lester Thurow, Robert Reich, Felix Rohatyn,
Irving Shapiro and others.

The Democrats' effort proceeds from the belief that government will have to intervene in the market system to a much greater extent than it has in the past if we are to experience real growth, be globally competitive, and approximate full employment. Douglas Fraser was recently quoted as saying, "Industrial policy is very, very, very important because this goddam free market system doesn't work any longer." (*N.Y. Times Magazine*, 8/28/83, p. 5) Or as Lester Thurow says, "Major investment decisions have become too important to be left to the private market alone, but a way must be found to incorporate private corporate planning into this process in a non-adversary way. Japan, Inc. needs to be met with U.S.A. Inc. . . . The market makes transitions in a painful, clumsy, slow way. . . . " (Ibid., p. 2)

Among the alleged reasons for market failure is that markets have tended to become global, and we are ill equipped to compete effectively with Japan, Inc. That is, in these new circumstances we must be like Japan and have a centralized industrial strategy based on our peculiar strengths and advantages and involving a high degree of cooperation among government, business and labor. The central prescription of industrial policy seems to be some form of government-owned reconstruction finance corporation that will improve upon the market through various mechanisms (loans, guarantees, subsidies, etc.) that would advance the winners at a more rapid rate, while rehabilitating the losers.

So much for the critique offered by the exponents of industrial policy. There is another group, mainly church groups, who focus not so much on our lack of industrial competitiveness but rather on the human tragedy of high unemployment. They begin with the moral point that one's dignity and sense of self-worth are deeply dependent on having meaningful work. Therefore one of the most important goals of economic policy is full employment. And the levels of unemployment that we have experienced in recent years constitute, in their view, an indictment of the market system. Some of them see a new, more pernicious "structural unemployment" referring to the long-term kinds of unemployment caused by new technologies or other developments that require the retraining of workers. These critics admit that they are not technical experts, and they therefore usually do not try to prescribe specific solutions, but most of them tend to prescribe various forms of government intervention.

Well, I have briefly mentioned these two sets of indictments or charges against our market system. I know you too are very concerned over the human tragedy of high unemployment and yet remain an ardent supporter of the free market system. How then do you respond to these charges and assess their diagnoses?

Common Goals and Different Means

MARINA v.N. WHITMAN: The pointed questions you raise have set the stage for our dialogue on industrial policy, the version of national planning that is currently the focus of a warming political debate in this country. After several years of recession, economic stagnation, rising unemployment and growing competitive pressure on many of our major industries, the attention of our political and business leaders alike is focusing increasingly on the need to raise economic growth, expand employment opportunities and enhance international competitiveness. But, within this growing consensus there are, as always, wide differences of opinion on the most effective means of achieving these goals. The novelty of the current political debate on economic issues is that it is concerned not only with questions about the most appropriate mix of overall monetary, tax, spending and regulatory policies, but also about the extent to which government should intervene directly to affect the structure of our economy, that is, the allocation of resources among its various sectors, industries and firms.

Although the nature of current debate suggests a growing recognition that we need to focus our policy discussions on how to make the size of the economic pie grow, and not simply on how we should divide that pie among the many legitimate competing interests that comprise our society, the discussion involves, as you note, differences in priorities as well as in views about the most effective means of achieving both high employment and economic growth. As you have indicated, religious leaders focus primarily on the human aspects of unemployment while business leaders generally express their concerns more in terms of the need for accelerated growth and enhanced competitiveness, a difference in emphasis that is reflected in gradations of rhetoric across the political spectrum.

It may help our discussion if we can establish at the outset a simple common yardstick for assessing the pros and cons of industrial policy in the light of the previously mentioned goals. If the assertion that economic growth and high employment are complementary rather than antithetical seemed self-evident, this effort might appear to be a pointless red herring. But when we focus on the only sustainable source of economic growth—increasing productivity—the link to employment opportunities becomes more complex and even controversial. For there seems to be a growing fear in this country that productivity increases, at least in the form of automation, may reduce rather than increase employment and thus impoverish rather than enrich the human condition. We need to tackle this concern head-on because economic efficiency and growing productivity are important, after all, not as ends in themselves, but rather as a means to increase both human welfare and opportunties in a world of limited resources.

The fact is that real income from work can rise on a sustainable basis only if productivity increases, unless, of course, we are willing to see an increase in the sheer number of hours worked. Output must expand for real incomes to increase and to create new opportunities for an expanding workforce; efforts simply to "spread the work around" do not get very far in enhancing opportunities for meaningful work, as a number of countries are finding to their sorrow.

When we drop back from the aggregate level to look at specific sectors or industries, the link between productivity increases and employment opportunities is most direct and obvious in industries such as pharmaceuticals, communications and synthetic fibers where demand is growing rapidly. In such "growth industries" productivity improvements generally lead to lower prices, a more-than-proportionate increase in demand, and higher employment.

The productivity-employment linkage is harder to trace in slower-growing "mature" industries, where the introduction of labor-saving technology may be essential to sustain output in the face of threatened inroads from imports and from other products competing for the consumer's dollar. In industries such as railroad transportation, steel and petroleum refining where demand may be less responsive to lower prices, productivity increases may go hand in hand with declining employment, although the decline will still be less than if the industry had failed to improve its competitiveness. But even in these cases employment is increased indirectly: As productivity improvements lead to higher real incomes and purchasing power, expenditures are bound to increase somewhere in the economy, creating new employment opportunities in other industries.

American agriculture provides a good illustration of this process. At the turn of the century some thirty million people were engaged in farming in the United States—more than two-fifths of the population at that time. Currently, there are only six million farmers—less than three percent of our population. The transition from the farm to factory was not an easy one, but it illustrates how mechanization created the foundation for economic advancement in this country. If forty percent rather than three percent of our population were required to produce today's agricultural output, income and living standards would be far lower and opportunities for diversity in employment and leisure would be much narrower.

Productivity growth has enabled the average workweek in manufacturing to drop from about sixty hours at the turn of the century to less than forty hours at present, while average weekly wages have increased from less that $10 to over $330. At today's prices the turn-of-the-century weekly manufacturing wage was equivalent to slightly more than $100, or about one-third the current level.

The more we look at the evidence, the clearer it becomes that a dynamic economy creates rather than impedes the expansion of employment opportunities. "Booming" Houston and Dallas actually lose a greater proportion of their existing jobs each year than do "stagnating" New Haven or Buffalo. In the two rapidly growing western cities, however, new employment opportunities more than offset the losses.

The direct linkage between economic growth and job creation is further illustrated by the fact that the countries with the highest rates of productivity advance have also had the lowest unemployment rates. For example, between 1960 and 1981, productivity growth rates in Japan and Germany were among the highest in the industrial world, while their unemployment rates averaged less than two percent. In contrast, in the United Kingdom and the United States, where productivity growth over this same span has been well below average, unemployment rates have been considerably above the average of their major industrialized counterparts. Thus, over the long run the trade-off between increasing productivity and job opportunities is illusory. They are, in fact, complementary.

Where does international competitiveness fit in all of this? Why can't we count on increasing job opportunities for American workers by legislative restrictions on imports, rather than pitting ourselves against Asian workaholics or low-paid workers in the Third World? Tempting as this approach to job preservation may appear to beleaguered firms or industries or communities, when we look at policies from a national, let alone from a global perspective, it becomes clear that an open world trading system gives a powerful boost to the overall economic welfare of both producers and consumers as a whole. International trade and investment expand the range of products available to consumers, hold costs and prices down, and increase global market opportunities for domestic producers.

The competitive challenges created by an open trading system provide us with an effective scorecard for tracking the nation's economic performance — the efficiency with which it uses its resources and the success it is having in raising productivity levels. In addition, policies that focus on encouraging productivity advances and international competitiveness and trade benefit the global as well as the domestic economy. As John F. Kennedy once said, a rising tide lifts all boats. Nationalistic approaches to job preservation, in contrast, deprive workers in other countries of opportunities for economic advancement.

Before I start sounding too much like Dr. Pangloss, let me mention some of the stones in the path. The fact that expanding productivity and trade have triggered rising employment opportunities and living standards in the past offers no certain guarantee that they will do so in the future, that the "electronic revolution" of this century will provide the same stimulus to human economic advancement that other technological advances have in the past. It is always difficult to see precisely where the new jobs created by growth and trade will arise, while the specific individuals, industries and regions suffering job losses as the result of economic change are only too painfully obvious.

There can be no "throwaway people;" we must find ways to reduce the impact of job dislocation on those most directly affected, while recognizing that there can be no progress without disruption and its associated stresses. The question of how best to resolve this painful trade-off is a profoundly important one to which there are no easy or clear-cut answers. But it is clear that to try eliminating the disruptive effects of change by erecting barriers to technological advancement and international commerce, to try to "freeze ourselves in time," so to speak, would be to retard rather than to advance the human condition.

If we can agree that productivity, international competitiveness and economic growth are the basic foundations of job creation, we will have set a common benchmark for assessing a more interventionist approach to our economic problems in the form of "national planning" or "industrial policy." You characterized me, Elmer, as "an ardent supporter of the free market system." That is, on the whole, true, although I firmly believe that the government has a critical role to play in establishing the framework within which that system operates, and also that there are particular (although relatively rare) instances where government intervention is required to make the system work most effectively. My preference for giving market forces relatively broad scope is both philosophical and pragmatic in origin. Philosophically my views on the market system are analogous to those of Winston Churchill on democracy—it is the worst system except for all others. On a pragmatic basis I believe that any set of policies must be judged not by their declared intentions but by their actual, or most probable, effects. It is in that spirit that I will try to analyse the proposals for an industrial policy.

Against this background we might turn to a critical analysis of "industrial policy." In the third and concluding dialogue we might focus on the specific steps that should be taken to better address our unemployment problem in a free market setting.

The Role of Humane Values

ELMER JOHNSON: Before returning to the "industrial policy debate," I want to comment on your response. You point to a widening consensus on specific goals of economic policy: economic growth, expanded employment opportunities and international competitiveness. And your basic argument is that we must pursue all three goals simultaneously because they are complementary to each other. Otherwise none of them will be best approximated or achieved in the long-term. You suggest that even these goals are only intermediate, the ultimate goals of economic policy being to "increase both human welfare and opportunities in a world of limited resources."

You allude to these ultimate goals only briefly, but it is clear from your remarks that you are by no means a free market ideologue. That is, you look on the market system in a pragmatic way as constituting, among other things, the best long-term means of assuring ever-increasing productivity. Productivity, in turn, is the common key to the successful pursuit of your three mutually complementary goals.

The problem then becomes one of tempering the harsh short-term effects of the market system on particular people, industries and regions without undermining the market's fundamental functions of long-term efficiency and dynamism. Accordingly, for example, legislation that seeks to protect our society generally from the rigors of international competition would be the wrong way to proceed. It remains for us to try to figure out the right proposals, whether at the public or private level or at both.

Now that I have summarized your argument I have a few questions. First, I began this dialogue by summarizing some charges against our market system in reference to two goals: international competitiveness and full employment. You have added a third goal that you believe to be essential and to be inextricably linked with the other two: economic growth. And you look kindly on the current widespread agreement that in order to solve the problems of unemployment and declining competitiveness we must focus on ways to make the economic pie grow. I assume, then, that in your judgment constant growth is the most reliable means of meeting the basic needs of the less advantaged members of society, and that you reject quite flatly Thurow's suggestions for changes in distributive patterns (*A Zero Sum Society*). Is that correct?

Second, judging by your strong emphasis on the goal of continual growth, I assume you also dismiss as impractical John Stuart Mill's dream, in his *Principles of Political Economy*, of a stationary state (or as some might describe the ideal today, a stable ecological system) able to produce sufficient goods and services to provide a more-than-adequate standard of living for all. As you will recall, he looked forward to the time when the masses of people could focus more on the higher, non-economic purposes of life. His language is quite forceful:

> I cannot, therefore, regard the stationary state of capital and wealth with the unaffected aversion so generally manifested towards it by political economists of the old school. I am inclined to believe that it would be, on the whole, a very considerable improvement on our present condition. I confess I am not charmed with the ideal of life held

out by those who think that the normal state of human beings is that of struggling to get on; that the trampling, crushing, elbowing, and treading on each other's heels, which form the existing type of social life, are the most desirable lot of human kind, or anything but the disagreeable symptoms of one of the phases of industrial progress.

To bring about his idea the state would have to concentrate not on unceasing growth, but on a "better distribution of property attained, by the joint effect of the prudence and frugality of individuals, and of a system of legislation favouring equality of fortunes, so far as is consistent with the just claim of the individual to the fruits. . . ." (Book Four, Part I)

I recall that John Maynard Keynes also looked forward to the day when

we shall once more value ends above means and prefer the good to the useful. We shall honour those who can teach us how to pluck the hour and the day virtuously and well, the delightful people who are capable of taking direct enjoyment in things, the lilies of the field who toil not, neither do they spin . . . But beware! The time for all this is not yet. For at least another hundred years we must pretend to ourselves and to every one that fair is foul and foul is fair; for foul is useful and fair is not. Avarice and usury and precaution must be our gods for a little longer still. For only they can lead us out of the tunnel of economic necessity into daylight. (*Essays in Persuasion*, p. 372).

Do you economists ever dream dreams like this anymore? If so, was Keynes right that at least another 100 years (from the time he wrote the essay in 1930) would be required before his dream could be realized?

Third, I want to probe a little more deeply into this concept of worker productivity. What are the human values that underlie this concept? After all, the context in which this seminar has been called is that of the Bishops' decision to prepare a pastoral letter that will consist of "a presentation of the Christian principles and vision of the economy and four applications," the first of which is economic planning. The Bishops' Committee asked for the assistance of Notre Dame's Center for Ethics and Religious Values in Business, and the Center has responded by calling this conference. You have argued that increased productivity is the key to job creation and wealth generation. Perhaps that is reason enough to focus on productivity, but your case is even stronger if this focus is also supportive of central human ends. Let me explain.

You and I want to be sure that our economic arrangements serve the more fundamental goal of human welfare, including not merely the "good life" of ever-increasing consumption, but also meaningful work and, I suppose, meaningful leisure. (That word "meaningful" surely saves a lot of time and thought, does it not?) If opportunities for meaningful leisure are to be given any weight in our scheme of values, then it would seem that productivity increases are essential not only to the creation of more wealth but also to the liberation of persons for the pursuit of other, non-economic goals.

The connection between productivity and meaningful work may be more complicated. I have concluded that, generally speaking, a person cannot have a high degree of job satisfaction without also being highly productive at what he or she does. But there are other factors that bear more directly on the quality of one's work life: the challenges presented by technological changes and whether the person has the opportunity and the skills needed to grow and develop in response to such change, the nature of the job itself and whether it fits and stretches the person's particular gifts and capacities, and the spirit of cooperation and goodwill that obtains between him and his fellow workers and between him and his superiors in the hierarchy of management. It is my belief that productivity at its best is largely a by-product of these other factors, and certainly not a substitute for them. At its worst productivity implies an intense, driven, tunnel vision person. We both know people with these qualities who are very efficient in their work but who lead rather tragic lives.

Now, if I am correct in my comments on productivity and meaningful work, and if you are correct (as I am sure you are) in your assertion of the connection between productivity and job creation, then the subject of economic planning or industrial policy cannot be considered wisely except from this perspective of human values and ends. More specifically, the questions we must respond to are these: What role, if any, can be played by economic planning in enhancing the kind of true productivity I have referred to — the kind that thrives in an atmosphere of cooperation and in a context of technological innovation and organizational excellence at the level of the enterprise unit? And what role in this regard must be played by other factors and instrumentalities such as individual leadership, quality of work life, the educational infrastructure, etc.? In other words, what is the proper division of responsibilities in this connection between the public and private spheres?

Finally, since I agree with your emphasis on productivity, and inasmuch as our economic malaise of the last few years has been associated with a serious decline in the rate of productivity gains, it would be helpful to me to hear your explanation of the reason for this decline. It is easier to talk about solutions if we know the nature of the underlying problem.

The Marketplace and Values

MARINA v.N. WHITMAN: Elmer, before returning to the central question of our dialogue—what, if any, role increased economic planning by government should play in achieving the complementary goals of economic growth and high employment?—let me respond briefly to the questions you raised about my underlying assumptions. Yes, I do contend that our most fundamental economic problems are grounded in questions of sufficiency, not simply of equity in distribution. Ignoring the social upheaval that would ensue if our principal prescription for curing our economic maladies was to take from the haves and give to the have-nots, the best that could be accomplished by distributing income evenly would be to reduce the impoverishment of some. The global economy is just not generating sufficient income to provide an adequate standard for all. Remedies that, at best, make the misery of inadequate income more widespread and complicate the task of generating the savings and investment necessary for economic growth are neither socially nor philosophically acceptable. Economic growth is the only means by which we can even hope to satisfy the material wants and needs of humanity.

The dream of satiety may be all very well for John Stuart Mill, reading Latin poetry in his father's study, or John Maynard Keynes, making brilliant stock market choices before breakfast in bed in his London mansion, but it is an elitist vision that has no relationship to the world in which most of humanity lives and works and dreams its dreams. My answer to Keynes is "not yet" and "maybe never" to the notion of combining economic stasis with increasing human welfare.

Regarding your queries related to productivity growth, the economic benefits and increased opportunities associated with higher productivity can be documented. The more human values are difficult to quantify but I think that a convincing case can be made for the view that human development and high productivity are complementary. Better education, for example, is estimated to account for nearly two-fifths of the growth in productivity in the United States. A quality workforce was one of the key factors which permitted war-torn Germany and Japan to rebound so quickly after the Second World War. The point of increasing productivity is, after all, to "work smarter" rather than to "work harder," not to produce the driven automatons you refer to, but to reduce the drudgery associated with work and to make it possible for people to enjoy more leisure without having to give up income in order to get it.

An economic system which focuses on increasing productivity is also more likely to lead to a higher level of self-fulfillment than one that mandates full employment by government decree. A job should provide more than a weekly paycheck. It should give employes a sense that they are making a contribution. This point is illustrated in a recent article on the Russian economy by Leonard Silk. After getting a firsthand look at the indolence, waste and the wretched quality of services in that country, Silk asked rhetorically if the human waste associated with Russia's full employment is worse and more demoralizing than the unemployment in this country.

Turning back to the central question of this dialogue, I think we can agree that higher productivity growth is needed to bring the United States economy out of the malaise of recent years. But how should this be accomplished? Does the fact that the productivity growth rate slipped from 3 percent during the 1950s and 1960s to zero percent over the 1978 to 1982 interval suggest that the government should try to channel funds toward what promises to be the most productive industries? Even if the effort were successful, such a reallocation would be, at best, a partial solution. The fall-off in the productivity growth trends for all the principal industrial nations during the past ten to fifteen years has never been fully explained. It is clear, however, that in the United States a slackening in the rate of growth of investment or perhaps a less-than-optimal allocation of that investment are only two among many factors which contributed to the productivity slowdown. The other principal factors include:

cyclical weakness, a large influx of new and inexperienced workers into the labor force, energy shocks, increased regulatory burdens and a slowing in the growth rate of spending on research and development.

A higher level of investment spending would not be a panacea but it would help. The Bureau of Labor Statistics, for example, estimates that less than one-fourth of the erosion in productivity growth from the 1948-1973 to the 1973-1981 periods was traceable to a decline in the growth of capital spending. The potential benefits of an improved mix of capital spending — a favorite target of industrial policy — are more difficult to document. With the notable exception of the energy sector where price controls on petroleum led to excessive investment in energy-intensive processes, there is no evidence that a misallocation of capital contributed significantly to the productivity slowdown.

Moreover, there are growing signs that U.S. business may not need a government-led industrial policy to raise its commitment to research and development. After remaining essentially flat during the first half of the 1970s, real expenditure on research and development expanded at a 5.3% rate during the second half of the decade. And in 1981 — the most recent year for which international data are available — spending on research and development in the United States was equivalent to 2.4% of GNP, the same as in Japan and only slightly below Germany's 2.7% level.

The underlying assumption of the proponents of industrial policy is that America's "deindustrialization" must be checked. But the assertion that America is "deindustrializing" simply does not stand up to *rigorous* scrutiny. Manufacturing's share of total U.S. output actually increased slightly between 1960 and 1980, rising from 23.5% of gross domestic product to 24.2%. During the 1970s the share of manufacturing declined throughout the industrialized world. But the contractions in Germany, Japan and the United Kingdom exceeded the comparatively small fall-off in the United States.

Nor do the facts support the contention that deep-seated, generalized structural weakness is responsible for our current problems in international trade and unemployment. During the 1970s, for example, U.S. manufacturing exports doubled. This growth was somewhat less than the two and one-half fold increase in Japanese manufacturing exports, but stronger than the performance of such major European countries as West Germany and the United Kingdom. Much of the weakness in U.S. foreign trade during the past few years reflects an overvalued dollar and the deep global recession rather than long-term "structural" factors. The U.S. record in job creation also compares very favorably with that of other industrialized nations. Since 1970 total employment in the United States expanded by more than 25% — more than double the 11% increase in Japan. In most of the major European countries employment either stagnated or actually declined over this same period.

The hard fact remains, of course, that much has gone awry in our national economy in recent years, and much needs to be done to make U.S. business more competitive and to provide meaningful jobs for all who want and are able to work. But I am skeptical that this can be accomplished by policies directed toward assisting or encouraging particular sectors or industries. It does not require complicated analysis to recognize that if the government does begin picking winners by such a process, it is implicitly picking losers as well.

Looking more specifically at the allocation process, Gerard Debreu's recent Nobel award adds further weight to the considerable evidence that societies work better when a large number of economic decisions are made in the market place. The scarce resource of thoughtful political decision-making should be husbanded. Overloading the political process could divert increasing resources to "working the system" rather than to productive output. There is no reason to suppose that the political process would do as well as the marketplace in picking winners and losers.

The postwar performance of the Japanese economy, the model commonly cited by proponents of industrial policy, has been impressive. A high saving rate and large increases in investment have been the major factors in Japan's rapid growth. However, the link between this favorable performance and central planning is ambiguous. The record of the Ministry of Trade and Industry (MITI) in providing administrative guidance to Japan's managers in investment decisions has been spotty. It has had some significant successes, such as the memory chip segment of the semiconductor industry, but it has also had a number of failures. MITI put the Japanese heavily into ship-building, an industry currently operating at 35% of capacity. It discouraged the Japanese auto manufacturers from competing in the export market and Sony from engaging in transistor manufacturing.

Beyond some broad characteristics such as a richly endowed agricultural sector, there are few principles that can identify in advance the specific lines of endeavor in which an economy might successfully specialize. For example, Professor Assar Lindbeck of the University of Stockholm notes that there is no inherent reason why Sweden is a major exporter of ball bearings, safety matches, cream separators and automatic lighthouses. This same point is further illustrated by the observations of Charles Schultze of the Brookings Institute and the Chairman of President Carter's Council of Economic Advisers, who notes that there is no apparent reason why the British excel in chemicals, Japanese in motorcycles and Americans in construction design and management.

The question of whether central planners would be more clairvoyant than individual business planners is in any case merely hypothetical, unless we can be assured that the process would be governed by analytical criteria rather than political expediency. If industrial policies in the United States were to follow the European experience of price supports and non-tariff barriers that subsidize inefficient industries, they would be counterproductive. And, given the fact that our political history and institutions are much more akin to the European model than the Japanese, it seems well-nigh inevitable that our industrial policy would in actuality be controlled more by political jockeying than by a reasoned, analytical decision process. Citing examples from our own experience, Schultze argues that " . . . for every one winner in the race, there are nine losers — you can be sure that the U.S. government's portfolio, twenty years later, would still have all ten."

Moreover, some aspects of industrial policy would "fix what ain't broke." The U.S. venture capital markets for financing new, small, high-tech ventures are the envy of the world. There is a high probability that perverse effects would stem from a politicized credit allocation mechanism. For example, limitations on dividends might reduce the flow of new capital into an industry more than government loans or guarantees would increase it. And such mechanisms are sure to militate against risk-taking and the "right to fail."

The objectives of industrial policy are, of course, indisputable — and no one disputes them. But I doubt that making false choices between "smokestack" and "high tech" industries is the way to increase technical progress. Only if innovation and progress are encouraged and diffused throughout the fabric of our economy will they fulfill their high promise for enhanced competitiveness, increased income and employment, and advances in economic well-being.

Experience suggests that from time to time particular circumstances may produce irresistible pressures for government action to give temporary assistance in some form. But these exceptions should be reserved for extraordinary circumstances; it seems unwise to try to prescribe in advance guidelines or criteria for the conditions under which we could count on such assistance. Rather, government should concentrate on minimizing the likelihood that such situations will arise by its policies shaping the overall economic environment.

In the next stage of our dialogue we might address more specifically what these policies should be, that is, what kind of action government can and should take to improve the economic climate that confronts Americans in their daily lives.

What Can Government Do?

ELMER JOHNSON: I have listened to you carefully and tried to understand (1) your conception of the human goals by which we should orient our thinking about economic planning, and (2) your dismissal of certain kinds of economic planning as being frustrative rather than supportive of these ultimate goals. I would state these ultimate goals of economic policy as being an adequate level of material well-being for all persons and meaningful work for all persons able and willing to work. To approximate these goals you believe we must put almost exclusive emphasis on aggregate growth, with very little emphasis on equity in distribution. My emphasis here would be somewhat different, but let us go on.

You and I are in complete accord in rejecting all forms of economic planning that would replace rather than complement the basic functions of the market, that is, those forms of planning that would command or strongly influence the allocation of capital resources. We both believe that the utilitarian case for the market system is overwhelming if we take seriously these goals of human welfare and full employment.

On the other hand the most ardent free enterprisers, if they are thoughtful, agree that the federal government has an indispensable planning role to play in the realms of responsible fiscal, monetary and tax policy. We would also agree that federal, state and local governments have another set of responsibilities that are not usually thought of as "economic planning;" yet if governments (and our private associations in certain areas) fail to perform these responsibilities well, no form of economic organization will be able to approximate the goals we have been discussing. I am thinking of those broad responsibilities for maintaining the legal, educational, moral and physical infrastructures of our society. This truth is so obvious that it perhaps needs no further discussion, but others have remarked, for example, that our productivity lag as compared to Japan probably has much more to do with Japan's superior primary and educational system than with Japan, Inc., i.e., the so-called partnership between business and government in Japan and its high level of central strategic planning for resource allocation.

I take it for granted that these two areas of government responsibility are not what is in dispute when we talk of economic planning. Accordingly it remains for you and me to discuss whether there are other forms of economic planning that government should be doing and that would complement or reinforce our private market system rather than undermine it. Let me suggest four areas for discussion.

First, many of us have expressed strong concern over the intensity of our adversary culture: management vs. labor, business vs. government, and special interest warfare in general. No other society in history has come close to matching us in this respect. Compared to Japan on a per capita basis, we have twenty times as many lawyers, seven times as many accountants and 20 percent as many engineers. It is difficult for a society to be highly productive when it allocates so many of its best minds to what Arthur Laffer calls the "garbage business." In considering possible solutions to this dilemma, should we be looking at some form of "Industrial Cooperation Act," legislation that would establish a commission composed of top representatives from labor, management and government? Such a commission would be assigned responsibility for identifying the sources of these adversary tensions and proposing new mechanisms of cooperation. Such an act might also establish an ombudsman function for examining long-term problems involving particular government agencies and industries and working out resolutions.

The second area I have in mind is that of intelligence gathering and strategic studies respecting the long-term outlook for key industries and regarding long-term issues as to particular economic functions. Perhaps Brookings and other private think tanks and educational institutions perform these tasks perfectly well without any help from government. Perhaps, also, the large corporations in key industries are better situated than government to bring the best expertise to bear on such matters. Yet the corporation is suspect whenever it purports to speak in the public interest.

Let us take, for example, the question of how our society should be planning over the next thirty years for changes in the way people are transported from place to place. GM currently engages in long-term planning of how cars should be made ten years from now and it has had a major stake in mass transportation studies. But should some government commission be a clearinghouse for assembling private research efforts and proposing long-term solutions that it believes will best serve the public interest?

The third area is one we mentioned earlier. Should federal or state government intervene in order to cushion the effects on human lives of the market's gales of creative destruction? You described the long-term beneficial effects on our society as a whole that derive from technological advance, but you expressed concern over the tragedy of workers who lose their jobs because their skills are rendered obsolete. Can even the largest corporations be expected to shoulder the full burden of retraining such workers and creating or finding new jobs for them? Or are the numbers so great that the only feasible solution lies in a monumental government job retraining agency?

Perhaps there is a middle way. Last summer many corporations were induced by an unusual federal tax credit program to create jobs for unemployed minority teenagers. Should we have a broad system of federal tax credits that induce employers to cooperate with educational and community institutions to motivate, retrain and place workers whose skills have been rendered obsolete? GM director Leon Sullivan is probably more knowledgeable in this area than anyone else I know. He very much favors national planning and a system of national incentives that will bring about a substantial cooperative effort among our corporate, educational and neighborhood institutions. Private industry, he says, just cannot succeed on its own.

Finally, I raise the matter of justice between generations, even remote generations. Technology has given us the power to set in motion chemical processes that can very gradually but steadily degrade and destroy our environment. The real damage may not be felt for three generations. At the same time our knowledge is also advancing, so that we become ever more able to foresee these long-range effects and do something about them, but only if we act on a collective basis. This means national economic planning of some sort, doesn't it? Or do you go along with those economists and others who take a very optimistic view of human resourcefulness and ingenuity, knowing that future generations will somehow devise means out of the mess we leave them?

Pluralism, Accountability and Subsidiarity

MARINA v.N. WHITMAN: We seem to agree, Elmer, on the central issue of this dialogue: that government allocation of resources, whether called industrial policy or by any other name, would not improve on the job done by the market system in achieving the complementary goals of enhanced economic growth and competitiveness, high employment and increased economic welfare. The lessons from European experiences with industrial planning and the gasoline lines, shortages and misallocations of resources that resulted when the United States tried to circumvent the market system in allocating energy supplies — as well as the remarkable advances in energy conservation that appeared promptly once the price mechanism was allowed to operate in that area — all suggest that more interventionist planning would be more likely to inhibit than to stimulate economic growth and employment opportunities.

We both agree as well that the government has an indispensable role to play in fostering these same goals of growth, competitiveness, employment and economic welfare. We agree, too, on many of the kinds of actions that the government ought to emphasize in pursuit of these goals, though we have some areas of disagreement as well. I do think you misunderstand my views about the relative emphasis that should be placed on aggregate growth as opposed to income redistribution. My point was simply that income redistribution without growth cannot possibly resolve the world's economic ills; that whatever degree of redistribution is deemed desirable by society is more likely to be achievable in the context of economic growth than of economic stagnation. Even John Rawls, the philosophical father of the modern redistributionist ethic, agrees that efficiency is a desirable feature of any social system. But distributional issues, important as they are, are a red herring in the context of the question before us. The proponents of industrial policy share with their less interventionist opponents a stated commitment to the importance of economic growth, and the sort of government planning they advocate is focussed on the allocation of resources among industrial sectors; its impact on the distribution of income among individuals would be indirect and, I suspect, quite unpredictable.

As regards the specifics of what government should do to foster a better economic environment, above all, it should pursue macroeconomic—that is, monetary and fiscal—policies that can sustain steady, non-inflationary growth of the aggregate economy. Although the cost in terms of reduced output and employment has been high, monetary restraint and the resulting sharp decline in inflation since 1979 have set the stage for sustainable economic expansion. But a better balance between monetary and fiscal policy is desperately needed in this country. The combination of tight money with unprecedentedly large and persistent deficits in the federal budget have brought about a combination of high real interest rates and an overvalued dollar that is taking a terrible toll on our interest-sensitive capital goods industries and those American producers that face stiff foreign competition both abroad and at home. If this situation persists it could indeed produce "deindustrialization" in the form of a cumulative decline in the competitiveness and prospects of some of our most important traditional industries. Reducing the federal budget deficit would help bring down real interest rates, free more of our limited pool of savings for investment, and alleviate the overvaluation of the dollar, thus stimulating growth and employment and enhancing international competitiveness.

The government's role in a healthy economic environment goes beyond macroeconomic policies, of course. Like most economists I agree with you that there are certain important "goods" (such as clean air and a healthful environment) that must be purchased collectively rather than individually, and which are therefore properly the subject of government regulatory policies. The challenge, of course, is to design such policies so as to maximize their effectiveness and minimize the costs of reaching desired goals, to swim with and take advantage of the currents of market incentives rather than struggle upstream against them, and to minimize the negative impact of such regulations on international competiveness and economic growth.

You are absolutely right, too, about the important role government plays in maintaining the "legal, educational, moral and physical infrastructures of our society." Improved basic education is essential for growth, innovation and international competitiveness, as well as for enhanced self-respect and opportunities for self-fulfillment. Government has a critical role to play in the upgrading of our educational systems, and it is heartening to see the beginnings of renewed national attention to these needs.

Government can also lend effective support to research and development, although the most effective changes in government's role need not necessarily take the form of direct financial support. The adjustment of anti-trust enforcement in this area to the competitive realities of a global marketplace may, for example, be critical in enhancing the R & D capabilities of the private sector. One example of enlightened policy in this regard is the positive attitude taken by the appropriate enforcement agencies toward such projects as the recently formed Microelectronics and Computer Technology Corporation, a joint venture involving twelve leading electronics firms which will spend as much as $100 million per year on research and development.

While encouragement of technological progress is essential, this goal is not best served by the false choices between "smokestack" and "high tech," between old and new industries, between large and small firms that the advocates of industrial policy would have us make. We must remember, after all, that the major customers of the high tech and information-processing industries are other businesses, including prominently the traditional manufacturing sectors. Just as the advances of the industrial revolution were harnessed to improve dramatically the productivity of the traditional agricultural sector, so the fruits of innovation today must be diffused throughout the entire economy if they are to have their maximum impact on productivity, competitiveness and economic welfare.

Government also has a responsibility to help minimize the transitional costs that are the inevitable by-product of economic change and progress. Society cannot take a laissez-faire attitude towards the welfare of workers displaced by technological progress or competitive shifts; there must be a social safety net. But it is essential to balance social needs and a perception of equity with incentives to individuals and communities to make the necessary adjustments.

Greater security of employment has a priority in our catalogue of national goals, but it must be combined with greater flexibility in other aspects of work relationships if it is to be consistent with an enhanced ability to compete. Labor and management must explore together ways of increasing flexibility in work rules and job assignments as well as in total compensation — as, for example, by increasing the role of profit-sharing in the compensation package. Increased opportunities for and acceptance of retraining and relocation can also help minimize the joblessness associated with economic transition and adjustment.

While government can assist retraining and relocation efforts, experience with government-directed retraining programs has been discouraging. Apparently industry is better equipped to define the kinds of training it requires than is the government, and government programs that give incentives to the private sector to create training and entry-level employment opportunities are more likely to be successful. Private industry cannot do the whole job on its own in this area, as GM director Leon Sullivan argued, but neither can government. Effective partnerships are required. Similarly, such public-private cooperation is essential to create a climate conducive to economic rejuvenation in those communities hardest-hit by economic change. New England, for example, has made substantial progress in filling the void left by declining textile employment with growth in "high tech" areas.

Finally, I share your concern, as do many others, with our "adversary culture" and the economic and social costs it entails. Where I part company from the advocates of industrial policy is that I believe the "solutions" they propose would exacerbate rather than alleviate the problem and increase rather than reduce employment in the "garbage business." The inevitable result of a legislatively-established "commission," composed of members representing specific constituencies and appointed by a negotiated political process and operating in the full glare of publicity, would be greater politicization of economic processes and more rather than less adversarial relationships. A government-mandated "Industrial Cooperation Commission" would inevitably give the lie to its name.

What we badly need and what such a mechanism would effectively block is pluralism, multiple approaches, the freedom to try many things, some of which will not work. And this is exactly what is happening now in the private sector. Shocked by economic adversity and intensified global competition, labor and management in one firm after another and one industry after another are seeking to supplement traditional adversarial relationships with new forms of cooperation, such as quality of work-life programs, retraining programs and similar efforts. The process is a difficult and halting one. Ingrained suspicion and mistrust do not disappear overnight, and some backsliding and failures are inevitable, but the commitments are genuine, the efforts widespread, and progress is being made.

Indeed, pluralism, accountability and the availability of alternatives lie at the heart of the issue, it seems to me. Until now I have argued the case for market solutions as against increased government intervention in the allocation process essentially on pragmatic, empirical grounds. But I think more fundamental questions are involved as well, related to maximizing the pluralism and freedom of choice that are the hallmark, not simply of economic efficiency but of a free society.

The notion that market-determined solutions maximize the range of consumer choice, and impose on firms the discipline of accountability to individuals who can "vote" their consumption preferences without at the same time imposing their choices on others is well-known. Less often remarked is the fact that this pluralism, this availability of alternatives, applies equally to people in their roles as workers or producers. These advantages can be fully realized, of course, only in an economy that provides high levels of employment and thus substantial opportunities to earn adequate or better incomes. And government does have the responsibility of devising macroeconomic policies appropriate to achieving this overall framework, as well as to intervene in the allocation of resources in those selected (and relatively rare) cases where it can effectively correct particular market failures. But without freedom for market processes to operate, these advantages cannot be realized at all. The variants of central planning currently being discussed in the United States would not disenfranchise the individual either as producer or as consumer. But they would certainly begin to rig the election process.

In contrast with central planning by government, decentralized market planning diminishes the importance of any single decision.

The fate of an industrial sector is not tied to the blunders of a particular group of planners. Decentralized planning not only offers the individual a variety of alternatives in his role both as worker and as consumer, but it is well suited to the increasing complexity of products and processes. Paraphrasing Friedrich Hayek, even the best and brightest of central planners will be less capable of assimilating the entirety of this growing complexity than legions of decentralized decision makers. A decentralized planning system is, in fact, consistent with the "principle of subsidiarity" set forth by Pope Pius XI in *Quadragesimo Anno* in 1931 and reiterated in many subsequent papal messages:

> It is a fundamental principle of social philosophy, fixed and unchangeable, that one should not withdraw from individuals and commit to the community what they can accomplish by their own enterprise and industry.

Government does indeed have critical roles to play in the effective functioning of the market system. But systematically picking the winners or supporting the losers in the marketplace is not one of them. The goals we seek — growth, employment, competitiveness, economic welfare — cannot be reached via the increased government planning, government subsidies and international trade distortions that currently popular versions of industrial policy would inevitably imply. As Paul Samuelson recently testified before a Congressional committe regarding industrial policy: "It's not good macroeconomics. And I don't think it's defensible social policy." That experienced and thoughtful economists like Schultze and Samuelson, who are acknowledged intellectual leaders within the party that is currently advocating industrial policy, are increasingly making such views known gives reason to hope that the phrase "industrial policy" may soon be relegated to the ranks of oversimplified political buzzwords that have outlived their moment in the sun.

Fifteen

Ethical Dimensions of the Debate on Economic Planning

DANIEL RUSH FINN

AT THE BEGINNING OF HIS RECENT BOOK ENTITLED *THE Ethic of Democratic Capitalism*, Robert Benne reflects perceptively on the frustration felt by careful and responsible people when economic matters are the subject of discussion between ethicists and economists. The mainstream of American economic thought is solidly in favor of the relatively free operation of the market in the economy ("on both economic and ethical grounds", he notes). At the same time most Christian ethicists in the nation are far more critical of the market and far more inclined to restrict the market's functioning by government activity.[1] The problem he alludes to here is not simply one of a difference of opinion between two groups, but more importantly it not infrequently entails a failure to communicate across disciplinary lines and in some cases an inability to do so.

As the discussions among economists and among ethicists of differing perspectives will no doubt illustrate at this symposium, the problem is not simply one caused by talking over the disciplinary fence to others who do not share one's own professional training. It is by no means easy to be clear and careful about the disputes *within* any one arena — to say nothing of the difficulties of spanning two or more of them.

The topic of economic planning is indeed a difficult one to sort out within either economics or ethics. Trying to gain clarity on the ethical dimensions of economic arguments is even more complex. I propose first to present a framework of issues within the ongoing debate on economic planning, employing to a large extent the arguments put forth by economists and practicioners in the field. Following this I will outline briefly what I take to be the heritage of the Christian tradition concerning economic life and will end with a third section treating the ethical issue raised in the debate over economic planning in more detail.

Since the majority opinion in both our history as a nation and, most likely, our current political situation supports the doctrine of a relatively unobstructed market, I will begin with the arguments against and later turn to those in favor of economic planning.

An Outline of the Arguments Against Economic Planning

There is no single argument or even any one set of arguments put forward by opponents of economic planning. This is, of course, not surprising in public discourse, since there is no single perspective or "world view" out of which all citizens operate. Still, it is helpful to distinguish the major objections presented in the public record. What follows is not an exhaustive list, but it covers the principal arguments marshalled in opposition to economic planning. They appear here in order of generality and not of frequency of appearance.

1. Economic planning is but a first step toward totalitarianism.

Many opponents of economic planning view the struggle to contain the influence of government as the primary political problem of the modern world. In quite graphic terms, the Soviet Union stands as the clearest proof of the failure of investing too much power in government. The essence of this failure is not any evil intentions on the part of Soviet planners, but the concentration of power in the hands of a few people who face no counter-balancing power from others. This conviction that power ought to be diffused throughout society has been fundamental to most critiques of economic planning.[2] For some a free market in the economic realm is a necessary (though not a sufficient) condition for political democracy.[3]

The Nobel laureate Freidrich von Hayek warned against the trend toward a greater role for government: "We have progressively abandoned that freedom in economic affairs without which personal and political freedom has never existed in the past."[4] As the title of his book puts it, the move to social and economic planning is "the road to serfdom."

It is worthwhile to note that some of those who object to economic planning attribute its popularity to a theological source. Irving Kristol, for example, argues that millenarianism, what he describes as the religious utopianism of the Judeo-Christian tradition, is the historical attitude behind "the collectivist imperative," the conviction that "Nothing is impossible for a government that *wants* the good of its citizens." The religious impulse to "hasten the end" has in the modern world been joined to science and technology to produce, Kristol argues, more virulent form of this societal disease.[5]

Putting Kristol's words in a more contemporary theological frame, he is warning that the joining of the prophetic with the eschatological creates popular expectations which are infeasible, destabilizing and dangerous. Michael Novak also links to Christianity much of the contemporary interest in a larger role for government in the economy, but where Kristol asserts that even the medieval church had itself to impose "reasonable limitations" on millenial expectations, Novak argues that much of the contemporary interest by Catholic theologians in economic planning (and socialism more generally) springs from an attraction to "authoritarian and unitary systems" of which the medieval feudalism and contemporary socialism are but two historical instances.[6]

Critics of this argument (that planning leads to totalitarianism) object on two counts. The first objection is that the totalitarian regimes to which free market advocates point exist in nations that have never had a democratic tradition, and that things would be quite different if economic planning were undertaken in the United States. (It would probably be much more like the situation in Sweden today.) The second is that many who profess to be horrified by the denial of democratic rights under totalitarian regimes of the left are hypocritical in their denunciations. Many of these same people supported the action of the CIA in overthrowing the democratically elected socialist government in Chile in 1973, opposed efforts to entice or assist the Sandinista government of Nicaragua to hold elections, and have supported numerous non-democratic governments of the right.

The ethical issues implicit in such debates raise some of the most

fundamental questions about human life. Included here are the understanding of the human person (just how individual and how communal?) and of the nature of society as a whole. Also raised here is
the meaning of freedom and its importance in relation to the obligations of citizens. Needless to say, the understanding of government
and its proper function is crucial.

2. Economic Planning is a violation of the right of ownership.

Many who oppose economic planning do so because it represents
an infringement upon the rights held by owners of property, most frequently the stockholders of firms whose activities would be restricted
by such planning. Few who believe in political democracy in the nation would deny that the people, through their elected representatives,
may rightfully limit the rights of property owners (for example, the
invocation of eminent domain in the building of roads and utilities
is widely recognized as legitimate). Still, as all such limitations entail
a trade-off between individuals' rights and the common good, many
Americans believe that the nation has already "gone too far" in curtailing the prerogatives of owners. Usually implicit in this criticism of
economic planning is the presumption that the "rights of property
ownership" apply with equal force to any kind of ownership of property—whether that property be personal effects, a home, or shares in
a firm employing thousands of workers.

Critics of this argument (that planning violates the rights of ownership) respond that the very conception of ownership under our current economic system is inadequate. Economic planning would not,
they argue, violate the rights of owners of factories and other forms
of capital but would rather end the implicit subsidy that firms have
been receiving from society in their ability to impose social costs on
their workers and communities.

The ethical isues raised in this area, then, are the rights of private
ownership and its relation to social justice. Once again, the relation
between individual and community needs serious ethical reflection.

3. Special Interest groups will dominate the planning process.

Even if economic planning could be kept from the road to totalitarianism and even if it did not violate the rights of shareholders, some

oppose it out of the conviction that the process would be subverted from its high ideals by the inevitable effects of special interest groups. Putting it succinctly, any small group with a lot to gain will be more inclined to invest time and money to influence legislators or planners than will a very large group (usually taxpayers and/or consumers) where each person will lose only a small amount. Thus, if ten firms can each gain $1 million if a law is passed, each firm will be willing to send well-heeled lobbyists to Washington to push its cause. Yet if the $10 million cost will be paid by one hundred million taxpayers (at ten cents apiece), it will not be financially worth it to any of the taxpayers even to pay for the cost of a postage stamp to write to a single legislator — and even then the letter would probably have no effect. Even where larger losses are involved, since just *knowing about* the maze of prospective bills is very expensive in both time and money, most taxpayers do not even know when such special interest legislation is being discussed (and they may not even know it after it has been passed!). This is one of the chief reasons why the democratic process does not work as it is "supposed" to.

Skeptics of this charge argue that with or without such planning the nation should engage in democratizing reforms, such as stricter registration and reporting of lobbyists and stronger campaign financing legislation to reduce the influence of special interest money on government. They also characterize as hypocritical those who use the "special interest" argument against economic planning but who also oppose such democratizing reforms.

The ethical issues here are closely related to a prudential judgment concerning the possibilites for authentically democratic and moral decisions in the face of the tendency of special interests to subvert the process. Within questions about the undertaking of democratizing reforms of the political process, "first amendment" rights of freedom must be weighed against the needs of justice which require a reduction in influence of vested economic interests.

4. Bureaucracy in economic planning is an inevitable and fatal flaw.

Even if all of the above problems could be avoided, many feel that the inevitable bureaucratic mechanisms of government would render the process unworkable. For many the planning process in the Soviet Union is but the most obvious example of the inability of any bureaucracy to understand how things actually work at the production site and to anticipate fast-moving changes in the economic realm. If full-fledged economic planning were undertaken in the U.S., the self-serving aversion to risk on the part of civil servants would be certain to leave the nation lagging behind the innovative technologies of the world's industrial leaders. Both the size of the necessary organization as well as the lack of incentives for civil servants to perform in optimal ways stand as hurdles which planning advocates cannot surmount.

In addition, some, such as Hayek, charge that since the planners as a group will have to hold fairly homogeneous views and will need to cajole or coerce agreement from others, "the worst elements of any society" are the ones who are most likely to "rise to the top", since ethically more careful people find such *necessary* tasks offensive.[7]

Critics of these arguments (that bureaucracy is a fatal flaw of planning) generally agree that bureaucracy is indeed a problem that will have to be faced but that planning opponents overstate the problem to see it as reason enough not to undertake economic planning at all. Whatever structures are designed to develop and execute planning will have to be open, accessible and democratically accountable. The problem, however, will not go away and constant vigilance is recommended.

The ethical issues implicit here are again closely related to a prudential judgment about the empirical possibilities for structuring incentives for individuals in the process. There will have to be changes in current structures to weighing job security for civil servants against explicit incentives and oversight to ensure flexibility in changing situations. In addition, there is the issue of developing sufficient consensus within the democratic process to base any economic planning on publicly acceptable goals and procedures.

5. Planning will produce lower GNP and employment than the market will.

The single most frequently heard objection to economic planning is that is will be "inefficient," that is, that is will result in an aggregate level of economic activity which will be lower than would otherwise be the case if planning were not undertaken. Put succinctly, this argument is that because the incentive structure of the market is countermanded in planning, the overall output of goods and services (roughly the gross national product: GNP) will be lower than it could be otherwise. This entails a lower level of aggregate employment in the economy, which in turn means that there are many unemployed people, who must live in poverty because there are not sufficient jobs in the nation.

The key to understanding this criticism of economic planning is the conception of the working of the market which mainstream economists hold and struggle mightily to help others to grasp. By "the market" is meant not the corner grocery but that series of social patterns of interaction between people who have something which others want and those others who are willing to pay in order to get it. The original "owners" (say manufacturers with goods to sell or workers with their labor power) look for the best offer for their product or service, while buyers (say consumers or employers) look for the lowest priced source of what they seek. Competition (with other sellers) keeps owners from charging too much, while competition (with other buyers) keeps each buyer from being able to force sellers to lower their prices unduly. In addition, the hope of profits entices entrepreneurs to research and invest in new products which consumers would like to have or which will help producers make (and then sell) their products more cheaply. Throughout it all consumers are "sovereign" because no producer would make products that consumers will not buy — or at least bankruptcy will keep such an imprudent producer from staying in business for long.

Quite obviously there are two separate assumptions made about all this. The first assumption is that the system does indeed function this way. The second assumption is that it is a *good thing* for our economy to operate in this way. The first assumption is taken by economists to be an empirical question, that is, its accuracy should be able to be tested by observing the actual working of the economy. The second assumption is taken by economists to be a normative question, one where the values of each person are crucial in deciding whether the assumption is the appropriate one. Since proponents of economic planning argue that the first assumption is false and that planning will *improve upon* the performance of the market as measured by GNP, employment or other empirical econmic measures, we will return to this topic in the second section of this paper. The second assumption, a normative one, is deserving of our treatment in greater detail and will be addressed as objection six below.

The argument that economic planning reduces GNP and employment incorporates several assertions about how planning interferes with the interactions of individuals. The market allocates resources to their highest-valued use through the "messages" provided by changing prices. The most dramatic examples of this process are industries which wither away altogether due to major changes in technology. Thus, the way that the buggy industry got the bad news about its imminent demise when the automobile was invented was by means of the fact that people were not longer willing to buy buggies, or more technically, people were no longer willing to pay high enough price for buggies that would cover the cost of producing them. Critics of planning charge that it will lead to the subsidization of obsolescent industries and, in our example, buggies might be produced decades after their usefulness had ceased. As Charles Schultze put it, such planning would require very difficult decisions in favor of some groups and against others, and "these are precisely the sort of decisions that the American political system makes very poorly."[8]

Implicit in this subsidization of "sunset" industries would be a slowing or outright suspension of adjustments (technically termed "mobility") of capital and labor. When consumer choices lead to economic losses for a single firm in an industry, this is a signal that the kinds of capital and labor being used by that firm are, on average, being used more productively by other (more profitable) firms in that industry. When losses appear for a whole industry, this is a signal that the capital and labor used in that industry are, on average, being used more productively in other industries. Thus the contraction or even the death of an industry is not an unqualified failure. Rather it allows those productive resources to move to other industries where they will be even *more* productive. When losses accrue to firms in a particular geographic area such as the "snow belt" due to competition from, let us say, lower-wage non-unionized areas, this is a signal that the higher-cost plants are *less productive* — not in the sense that the workers produce fewer items per hour of work but in the sense that the workers produce fewer items per dollar spent on wages. The hard realities are that consumers, by choosing the least costly of several identical articles, are telling those snow belt workers that they are being paid "too much." By whose measurement of too much and too little? By the only one relevant: consumers' values as made evident in their purchases, a topic to which we will return presently in the next argument against planning. In the meantime, of course, the people involved in the transition are often laid off and usually must get re-training to find another job elsewhere. Ethically sensitive market advocates like Elmer Johnson and Marina Whitman in their essay in this volume, believe that "There can be no 'throw-away people;' we must find ways to reduce the impact of job dislocation on those most directly affected, while recognizing that there can be no progress without disruption and its associated distresses."

Critics of this agrument (that planning will lower GNP and employment) take exactly the opposite view. And since this is one of the central arguments *in favor of* planning in the minds of advocates, this topic will be addressed later in this paper.

6. Economic planning subverts "consumer sovereignty."

In order for anyone to answer the question, "Are the events occuring in our economic system good or bad?" a prior question must be addressed: "*Whose* values are to be used in deciding this and *how* will these values be made evident?" There is a single answer to that prior question which is given by nearly all "advocates of the market" (a shorthand term I will use for those who generally advocate a "free market" solution to economic problems). This single answer is that the values to be used are those of *all* the people in the nation and *the way* these values are made evident is through the explicit choices which the nation's people make when they spend their money to buy goods and services. The process can be seen as analogous to a democratic election where consumers cast votes by their purchases. That is, this position holds that consumer choices are the basis on which to judge whether economic events and the economy as a whole are good or bad. As Marina Whitman put it,

> The notion that market-determined solutions maximize the range of consumer choice, and impose on firms the discipline of accountability to individuals who can "vote" their consumption preferences without at the same time imposing their choices on others is well-known.

Clearly, for anyone who has taken this position, economic planning results in *bad* effects in the economy since political decisions about economic priorities take the place of at least some of the outcomes which the market would otherwise produce based on the choices of individual consumers. Thus Whitman notes that "the variants of central planning currently being discussed in the United States would not disenfranchise the individual as producer or as consumer. But they would certainly begin to rig the election process."

Critics of this argument (that economic planning would thwart the control of consumers over the economy) assert that consumers are anything but sovereign anyway. The possibilities of consumer tastes being shaped by Madison Avenue advertising are well known. In addition, the nation has *always* made decisions about what sectors of the economy should be subsidized (e.g., education and defense) and which should be penalized (taxes on tobacco, prohibition on heroin). The move to democratic economic planning would widen the circle of decisions, but it would not be a novelty to override market outcomes.

The ethical issues involved here include not only *what are* the values which the economy ought to serve, but *who should decide* those values and *how* will their values become effective. Whether democratic political structures or market structures are morally superior (and whether this should be decided based on the qualities of those processes in themselves or based on their consequences) can be decided only by means of moral decision.

An Outline of Arguments in Favor of Economic Planning

As with the arguments against economic planning, there is no single set of arguments employed by all advocates of such planning. Part of this difficulty arises from the fact that there is no single definition of just what economic planning would entail. Such differences account for the fact that the definition of the issue presumed in the Johnson/Whitman paper is roughly that of "an industrial policy," while the definition employed in the Alperovitz paper represents a far more comprehensive understanding of planning which itself finds a simple "industrial policy" inadequate, for quite different reasons, of course. However, we can once again sort out several arguments which define the contours of the case for economic planning in the United States.

1. We *already have* economic planning, so let's do it right.

Nearly every advocate of economic planning asserts that there exists a severe confusion (often termed an "ideological" confusion) in the ongoing debates about planning (See, for example, Gar Alperovitz, this volume). The government is already so thoroughly involved in the operation of the economy that only the ignorant or the dishonest construe the debate to be a conflict between planning and the "free market." Even the most conservative, market-oriented Presidents of the United States over the past twenty years have steadily overseen the inevitable rise in government responsibility for economic life. In addition, the major corporations which dominate the economy do their own quite specific planning and have been quite successful in getting the government to implement policies which correspond to their privately motivated plans for the future.

The cause is not bad political decisions — otherwise people like Ronald Reagan would not have pushed for limitations on free trade in Japanese automobiles or stood for the Chrysler bail-out or for ludicrously low, Congressionally legislated liability limits for nuclear power plants which keep this technology "cheaper" than the *market* would otherwise allow. The cause is, rather, the increasingly socialized technology and economic interdependence which *necessarily* calls forth more collective activity to organize and shape it. As Michael Harrington put it more than a decade ago, we

> . . . need not any longer ask whether the future is going to be collective — if we do not blow ouselves to smithereens, that issue has already been settled by a technology of such complex interdependence that it demands conscious regulation and control. The question is: Will it be a totalitarian, a bureaucratic or a democratic collectivism?[9]

The terminology has shifted a bit, but many who advocate planning are still generally convinced that the options are either a totalitarian, centrally-planned economy (such as the Soviet Union has), or a government-administered, corporately-dominated economy (such as "market advocates" would effect by pretending that the "free market" is operative), or a democratically planned, decentralized economy.

This argument for economic planning asserts that the question is not whether we will plan but rather

> . . . how we should plan, for whose benefit, under what circumstances, and by which members of society. It is whether the planning we do shall be made coherent, open, explicit, and publicly accountable. If there can be no return to the nineteenth century of a truly free market (and the presumption is that there cannot), the question of planning as we usually consider it is totally misstated. (Alperovitz, this volume.)

Critics of this argument for planning respond in one of two ways. The first and most frequent response is that things *may* be too planned already but that is reason enough to *cut back* on government involvement in the economy and not to increase it. The second response, once made by William F. Buckley in a nationally televised debate, is more pessimistic in that it concedes that there is an inevitable trend toward greater planning but finds this insufficient reason to assist the process.

The ethical issues implicit in this debate are one rooted in questions we have already seen arise earlier: the nature of the person, of society, and of government. Also relevant is an interpretation concerning whether "we already have planning now," since the extent of discontinuity and current practice is relevant to any judgment about feasibility and the degree of change required.

2. Our current national economic policy has led us to recessions and high unemployment while our international competitors are already using economic planning to surpass us.

The single most prevalent argument employed in favor of economic planning is the poor performance of the U.S. economy over the last decade or two. The problems in performance come both from the general boom and bust business cycles the economy goes through, as well as from the deterioration of position of the U.S. economy among its international competitors. The extent of the current recovery from our most recent recession is of course unknown, but most economists predict that it will not be as fullblown a recovery as one would ordinarily hope for and expect. Still, the most distressing dimension of the expected recovery for advocates of planning is that it will almost certainly result in a higher rate of unemployment than have previous recoveries. What is more sobering is that this development will be right in line with a clear trend over the post-war era: that the average rate of unemployment after each succeeding recession is higher than it was after the previous one. Economists at times use the technical phrase "full employment unemployment," but we need not deal with the details here. The point is that as the years progress, both the number and the percentage of workers who cannot find jobs in the U.S. economy have been rising.

Looking in more detail at the economy, many advocates of economic planning argue that the nation is going through a process of "deindustrialization," defined as "the widespread, systematic disinvestment in the nation's basic productive capacity."[10] As Barry Bluestone and Bennett Harrison have put it:

> Controversial as it may be, the essential problem with the U.S. economy can be traced to the way capital — in the forms of financial resources and of real plant and equipment — has been diverted from productive investment in our basic national industries into unproductive speculation, mergers and acquisitions, and foreign investment. Left behind are shuttered factories, displaced workers, and a newly emerging group of ghost towns.[11]

In addition, competition from other nations, most particularly Japan and West Germany, has left us importing goods which we formerly produced for ourselves. This means that Asian and European workers are now doing jobs that U.S. workers once held. And these national competitors of ours, particularly the Japanese, engage in considerable government intervention in the economy. Thus it is argued that opponents of economic planning are wrong-headed to assert that less and not more government intervention is the solution to our problems. Among the areas where this is taken to be most important is the decision concerning where to invest — the choice that determines which industries will expand and which will contract. In Lester Thurow's words,

> To compete we need the national equivalent of a corporate investment committee. Major investment decisions have become too important to be left to the private market alone, but a way must be found to incorporate private corporate planning into this process in a non-adversary way. Japan Inc. needs to be met with USA Inc.[12]

While all advocates of economic planning include such public involvement in the investment decisions of the nation, many advocates seek a more coherent policy than "an industrial policy" often entails. As Gar Alperovitz in this volume evaluates such narrower policies:

> In the first place, their significance in a giant economy like our own has been greatly exaggerated. More important, industrial policies make sense only in the context of a coherent overall plan. . . .

Such "high production planning" would target the sectors of housing, food, energy, health care and defense as the foci of attention in the move to raise GNP and lower unemployment and inflation.

Critics of these arguments for economic planning respond in a number of different ways. Most frequently this amounts to a denial of many of the fundamental empirical premises of planning advocates. Many point out that GNP is recovering satisfactorily now and that there has been clear success against inflation, which was, according to the phrase still ringing in our ears, "the nation's number one priority" just a short time ago. They argue that the U.S. economy has been re- markably successful in producing many new jobs; the problem is that we have had a huge increase in the number of people (e.g., working mothers) who are seeking employment. In addition, job training pro- grams would help many of the currently unemployed to retool in order to move into newly expanding industries. Charles Schultze (and others) have argued that "America has not been de-industrializing."[13] And claims about the causes behind Japanese successes are disputed.

The ethical issues involved include the relative importance of overall prosperity for the majority and explicit decisions to improve the lot of the poor and unemployed. Also included is a necessary judgment about the relative moral importance of well-being in the United States and that of other countries competing with the USA. Also necessary is a judgment concerning the moral significance of the alteration of old patterns of human interaction in communities with sunset industries and of the establishment of new communities and social patterns.

3. The unplanned market institutionalizes injustices based on race, gender, ethnicity, and economic status.

One of the central arguments for economic planning is the differen- tial effects among different groups within the nation. Obviously, prob- lems here can endure in spite of aggregate figures about the overall level of economic well-being. Even in the best of economic times it is clear that women and many minority groups *consistently* do less well economically than do white males. The issue is a crucial one but the evidence has been frequently catalogued elsewhere and we need not delve into it here. The argument for planning is that at all times, but especially in the face of high unemployment and a rising proportion of poor in the population, the nation has an obligation to re-structure its economic life to provide greater justice. Opponents of planning who see such differential effects as an unfortunate yet necessary side effects of our highly productive economic system are (for advocates of planning) all too reminiscent of Andrew Carnegie's lament that there do unfortunately exist some necessary costs in economic life which "we" in our society have to pay.

Critics respond in at least two ways. Milton Friedman has argued that where the source of discriminatory treatment is personal prejudice, the undeniable ability of the individual will lead some profit-seeking employer to offer a job simply out of an interest in technical physical productivity in spite of psychological prejudice.[14]

Where the source of differential treatment is the fact that the market rates the contribution of some groups lower than that of others, the nearly universal response of critics of economic planning is that the market system has already provided a tremendous level of economic welfare for these so-called "exploited" groups. The argument is not a new one. As Bernard Mandeville put it in his *Fable of the Bees* nearly three hundred years ago, it is foolish to chastise an economic system which:

> Had carry'd Life's Conveniencies,
> It's real Pleasures, Comforts, Ease,
> To such a Height, the very Poor
> Lived better than the Rich before.[15]

In spite of the fact that the market is taken to be the key to long-term prosperity for the poor, opponents of planning usually recognize some form of short-term relief as necessary. This, and perhaps more, is indicated by the two "ultimate goals of good economic policy" which Elmer Johnson cites:

> . . . an adequate level of material well-being for all persons and mean-
> ingful work for all persons able and willing to work. (Johnson/Whit-
> man, this volume.)

The diversity among market advocates concerning the nature and extent of "the social safety net" (and the size of its interstices) is well known; the Reagan administration clearly feels that in its current condition it is a bit too extensive.

The ethical issues here include some previously cited as well as the nature of justice — in particular the meaning of social justice for public policy. Also important is the moral evaluation of relative poverty and steps such as affirmative action as strategies for redressing injustices short of a more comprehensive economic plan which would include this goal as a constituent dimension.

4. The market inefficiently ignores the social costs imposed upon communities by capital flight.

Of particular concern to advocates of economic planning is the destablizing and destructive effects which not just unemployed people but whole communities experience when factories close or move away. Even mainstream, conservative economists have long recognized that the market operates inefficiently when a private firm's actions entail costs which others (and not the firm) have to bear. Why, it is argued by Gar Alperovitz in his essay, should we allow profit-seeking firms to close a plant in a city in the "snow belt" and move its operations to the sun belt or abroad with no regard for the effects of the move on the schools, hospitals, public services, private service industry, and the social cohesion of the communities they leave behind?

Critics of planning respond that such dislocations (as difficult as they are) are necessary by-products of a valuable process which would be subverted if we tried to freeze ourselves at our current stage of technology—an impossibility in any case since our international competitors would force us to change by their producing products more efficiently through those very same new technologies which we would be striving to forego. Some critics of economic planning would allow for some restrictions or delays imposed upon capital flight by government, but the prevailing attitude of market advocates is well captured by Marina Whitman:

> The imposition of an additional layer of regulatory process creates costs of delay; . . . the natural processes of economic adjustment are lengthened and made more costly and competitiveness is reduced. Second, even where there may be a public interest in maintaining an uneconomic plant or industry, the necessary subsidies are disguised and forced upon individual private sector employers. And third, the efforts of firms to ward off such potenially costly regulations are apt to heighten the sense of alienation between management and public authorities.[16]

The ethical issues implicit here include once again the nature of justice for citizens, the property rights of owners of firms, and the role of government with respect to individual and common goods.

5. Economic outcomes at their broadest level should be in accord with democratic decision.

In one sense this "argument" for economic planning is just a restatement of the basic thesis that economic planning is a good idea. In another sense, however, this is actually an argument separable from that thesis. This is taken as so basic a principle by advocates of economic planning that it is sometimes not explicitly stated or defended in discussion. There are at least two underlying defenses.

The first defense has already been indicated: The conviction that democratic economic planning will lead to more employment and a higher GNP than the market will. The second, however, is that democratic decisions are inherently superior to market solutions because the former are based on the principle that every person counts equally, while the latter allow a wealthy person to have far more influence on the outcome than a poor one. Thus advocates of planning point to a fundamental contradiction between democracy and the unplanned market, and they opt, clearly, for the long-standing principle of the modern era that people have the right to decide the most basic issues of life through the political process.

Critics, as we have already seen, respond to the first defense of this argument by denying that a planned economy will outperform the market. They respond to the second with the arguments we have already seen in the first part of this paper in their concerns about the dangers of special interests, bureaucracy and/or totalitarianism.

The ethical issues here concern the question of which values should be served by the economy—citizens as consumers or as members of the polity. The problem is, of course, complicated by the fact that there are some moral values which must be respected whether consumers *or* voters happen to act on them. The place of democratic choice in the economic realm is at base a moral issue.

Background Assumptions in the Catholic Tradition Concerning Economic Life

Prior to addressing planning or any other economic policy it is helpful to summarize the elements that form the foundation of the ethical tradition concerning economic life within Chrisitianity. They are what might be called six "background assumptions" therein. Some of the background assumptions are not explicitly listed quite this way anywhere in scripture, the early Christian writings or elsewhere. They are part of the unspoken and presumed worldview of the Judeo-Christian tradition. But let us be clear that this does not make them less important; it makes them more important. The captains of two baseball teams may discuss the "ground-rules" at a particular playing field but they both seem to ignore the most basic rules of the game. That the batter is out after three strikes is an unspoken fact. Similarly in describing the stream of thought of a writer or a whole civilization, those insights which pertain to the most basic facts about life sometimes go unstated. But to think clearly on economic matters we must state clearly these very assumptions.

1. The world is a gift and human ownership can never be absolute.

The world—everything that exists—was created by God and God "saw that it was good." This denies any dualism where the material realm would be considered evil and the spiritual realm good. The doctrine of creation left the economic realm—and all others—as arenas where religiously important events occur. In addition, God as creator alone possesses the world and all that is in it as his own (e.g., Deut. 10:14; Ecclesiastes 3:13). We who use or even "possess" material things do so only due to God's gift and only as stewards of what really belongs to him.

As a result, the doctrine of private property throughout the tradition has always allowed only a qualified, not an absolute, ownership. Within Old Testament theology this qualified right of property was, like all else, rooted in the covenant. The many warnings in New Testament and patristic writings against excessive attachment to material things are well known. Parallel with these are instructions concerning the nature of property itself. The *Didache* exhorts the sharing of possessions as a limit on ownership:

> Share your possessions with your brother, and do not claim that anything is your own. If you and he are join participators in things immortal, how much more so in things mortal?[17]

Similarly, Gregory of Nyssa, Ambrose of Milan and most Church Fathers put strong restrictions on ownership based on the creaturely nature of all material things.[18]

In medieval Christianity we find Thomas Aquinas, as a prime example, treating the question of property as intimately related to the doctrine of creation. In Thomas' view, humanity's dominion over material things consists only in the use of them, and even then their use must be for the common good; God alone has complete dominion over their natures.

Whether in the language of Covenant or metaphysics, the tradition has recognized God's creation of the world as circumscribing the rights of ownership. Most modern visions of property rely on the philosophy of John Locke and stress an initial effort of labor as the justification for private possession. This is seen as granting complete control over a thing to the owner of it. The Judeo-Christian tradition *cannot* support such a claim.

2. The human person is both individual and communal.

Crucial to the Old Testament vision of economic life was the fact that Israel was seen as the people of God, a community. Hebraic religion was not primarily a one-to-one relation with God. Rather, God's action created a people of his own, and each Israelite related to the Lord as a member of that people. The argument from New Testament and patristic sources runs parallel. In Thomistic terms, following Aristotle, that very rationality which characterizes the human person renders every human person a social and political being.

As will be made clearer presently, the modern economic conception of the human person tends toward one of a self-defined and complete individual who relates to others to achieve that individual's ends. In contrast, the Christian stresses the community and "the common good" (in addition to the goals of individuals) as robust categories of analysis for an economic ethic.

3. Human life is historical.

The third background assumption refers to the way the Judeo-Christian tradition has looked at the sequence of events from day to day and year to year. Things did not just happen; there was an unfolding of events.

Acording to the Old Testament scholar Gerhard von Rad, this historicizing of experience in ancient Israel began with common celebration by the whole People of Israel of festal events that had been celebrated singly in different places.

> The ideas of history which Israel worked out was constructed exclusively on the basis of a sequence of acts which God laid down for her salvation.[19]

With the later rise of the prophets Israel came to see even *new* events as sharing the same character as the older founding acts of Yahweh in their nation's past.[20] What remained clear throughout was that the everyday life of the believer and the community has a religious significance. Neither the economic realm nor the political nor any other area of human life was an amoral or non-religious affair. This relation of faith and history has led in the modern era to the development of Christian social ethics and the obligation to transform social structures.

4. Sin is a part of human life.

This background assumption is well known to Christians, but its significance for an economic ethic is often overlooked. Good and evil are pivotal categories in economic life. Not every preference of mine is good and just; because I can afford something does not mean it is alright to buy it. Some economic goods are more basic than others. When I obtain a luxury item which I do not need, I use up resources that might have been used to provide the necessities of life to someone else. Relying on "the market" as the sole or even primary economic structure often entails overlooking the power of sin in the world. On the other hand, naive assumptions about ending sinfulness by just simply initiating economic planning or doing away with profit-seeking firms are also discredited.

5. All earthly power is subject to divine authority.

With the development of monotheism in Israel came the conviction that all gods and all earthly rulers were ultimately subject to Yahweh's rule. Not only were the rulers in Israel subject to the Lord but, as the prophets warned, even the Assyrians and Babylonians fulfilled God's will.

In the New Testament Jesus reminds Pilate that he would have no power at all over him were it not given him from above. The very word used in Greek for "power" (*exousia*) denoted a force—whether possessed by Jesus or the anti-Christ—which came ultimately from God. Similarly all earthly power and even what we today would call "social forces" and "social reality" come under the sway of God's domain. Stephen Mott argues that "social reality" is the basic meaning of "cosmos" in the New Testament. "The world" is not primarily a place but rather a system of relationships and values which have come under God's judgment.[21]

A similar theme is found in Thomas Aquinas, where all earthly powers, like everthing else, are to operate in accord with natural law. The religious importance of political and economic life of medieval Christianity cannot be doubted in the face of the detail with which Thomas considers such issues. Of course Thomas—like the scriptural and patristic sources before him—did not appeal to the possibility of democratic social change to improve or abolish evil social structures. The topic will be addressed again later, but it should be noted here that the move to confronting social structures—in addition to moral appeals to those actually in positions of authority—is not really a radical extension. For Thomas and for most of the Catholic tradition, if a situation could be improved by the application of reason, it was a matter for moral virtue.

Most people in the modern world agree, at least in principle, that citizens have the right to shape social institutions by design. The Christian vision of earthly power implies that the shaping of such institutions should occur according to moral standards. While this does not provide any detailed blueprint, it does undercut a number of positions which oppose this effort, such as all libertarian appeals to "freedom of the individual" which are based on the subjectivity and relativity of "personal preferences."

6. The sinfulness, especially that of earthly powers, requires prophetic confrontation and critique.

Because all human effort and all human institutions will be tinged by sin, prophetic confrontation of sin is crucial. The Hebrew prophets condemned the leaders of Israel for deceiving themselves into thinking that they were fulfilling God's law without providing justice to the widow, the orphan, the sojourner and the poor. Christians striving to live out an economic ethic must not only attend their own personal life styles but must also challenge economic structures, confront the powerful and run counter to popular opinion when justice requires it. It is one of the background assumptions of the Judeo-Christian tradition to carefully examine the background assumptions of every era and civilization and to challenge those world views when they form an ideological barrier to full human life.

The Relevance of Moral Tradition to Contemporary Society

Once we come to some determination about the content of the religious tradition concerning economic life, we are still left with the question: What does it mean for us today? This is by no means a simple question, and it is asked by ethicists addressing all areas of moral concern in the modern era.

One of the possible answers given has been that large portions of the tradition *do not* have much to say to us since our situation today is so different from the situation of earlier eras. Michael Novak seems to make this argument when he cautions his readers against too quick an assent to what Church leaders say on economic matters.

> What cannot be assumed in advance is that the writers of ecclesiastical documents have superior knowledge of economics and Christianity and their proper relation. . . . Church leaders are more likely to err in this territory than in most others. The gospel itself provides little guidance, as do theological traditions formed by traditional social orders. So church authorities have only a very weak authority, indeed, for their pronouncements in this area.[22]

Novak indicates elsewhere that he does wish to engage the tradition more thoroughly than this text might indicate, but the sentiments expressed in this passage are shared by a goodly number of people, including many Christians, who do not agree with most of the statements on social and economic life which have been promulgated by many different church bodies. Taken at face value this approach does not brand the tradition as irrelevant, but it leaves its relevance (and its helpfulness) in serious question.

Still, most Christians—including most Christian theologians—who are striving to work out a responsible economic life do turn to the tradition in the midst of an historical situation very different from those situations within which the religious tradition developed originally. The new setting does indeed make a difference in *how* the tradition is relevant. For example, no one is inclined to defend slavery today on the grounds that it was tolerated within Christianity until relatively recently. While there is no simple procedure for making such judgments, ethical reflection needs to integrate the best insights and developments of the modern era with the most fundamental values and principles of the tradition.

A good example of how such "developments" are catalyzed by new insights associated with older approaches is the very existence of bishops' pastorals on economic matters in the first place. More fundamentally, these spring out of what is a new dimension to ethics or moral theology in the modern age: social ethics. There have always been moral standards for social interaction, and there even were moral standards for the operation of what we today would call governments of nations and smaller groups. The scriptures, the Patristic sources, the scholastic and Reformation texts all stand as evidence of this. Still, this was primarily based on moral suasion and paternal admonition. If a king was grossly immoral in his dealings with his people, there was not much that the people could morally do about it. Revolution or assassination was generally considered an unacceptable option. Thomas Aquinas' assessment of tyrannicide was a good example of the way the subject was generally treated.

In the modern world, however, things are quite different. For a number of reasons which we need not delve into here, most modern people understand that the social and governmental structures within which they live are not eternally given or immutable. Forms of government, for example, are seen as ultimately subject to the will of the governed. People have the right—indeed the duty—to shape their government in accord with their best judgment. Sociology, anthropology and the other social sciences have taught us that not only formal, legislated social patterns but informal ones arise out of human interaction and are susceptible to alteration by human initiative. Tyrannicide is still not a preferred form of political change, but today there are many other options for morally appropriate strategies for social and political change.

Some Christians have objected that the tradition does not authorize and will not condone such a "politicization" of the Gospel. After all, it asked, where in the tradition do you find Jesus, the apostles or later church leaders trying to transform secular political structures? The point, however, is that while the development of such social ethical concerns *is* new, it is in accord with the fundamental thrust of the tradition. Prior to the modern era there was indeed a significant moral interest in both political and economic matters; it was just limited to those arenas where Christians had some direct influence. To take just one example, the early Church fathers often addressed matters of economic life style, and many of them like Ambrose of Milan developed social structures *within* the local church for institutionalizing the obligation to help widows, orphans and the poor. How big a leap is it from this to Christian concern in the twentieth century for community organizations and the process and goals of various levels of government?

Not far. Once the realm of freedom was extended to include social structures outside any one community of people, once people recognized that they can reflect on and decide on such structures to a large extent, then the need for clarity concerning the goals for and means of achieving such changes was clearly recognized by thoughtful people. Viewing this development within the Catholic tradition, we must recall Aquinas' principle: "Whatever can be rectified by reason is a matter of moral virtue."[23] Once it became clear in the modern era that social, political and economic structures *could* be "rectified by reason," the extension of Christian ethics into this arena, while a new development, was in continuity with the tradition. While Protestant ethics has not traditionally had the confidence in reason which Catholic moral theology did, a similar development occurred (though more clearly within the Calvinist tradition than in the Lutheran).

Thus, as we consider the moral arguments against economic planning, it is conceptually important to distinguish between those who criticize church leaders on the grounds that there is and should be no connection between Christianity and public economic policy and those whose criticism is based on a judgment that, while there is an important connection, church leaders have it wrong.

Assessing the Moral Issues in the Economic Planning Debate

In coming to a decision on the basic question — whether we should or should not engage in economic planning — an assessment of the moral issues within the debate is a crucial element. It is not, of course, the only crucial element, since as we have seen nearly all participants on both sides of the question make "empirical" assertions which are important to their cases. Thus, both the Johnson/Whitman and the Alperovitz papers assert that their own policy proposals will lead to higher employment and greater GNP. They cannot both be right on this (especially since both papers presume that the difference will be a large one), but their disagreement occurs in spite of their advocating high employment and GNP as values they all hold dear. The assessment of this element in the debate would require a quite different sort of inquiry than the one I have been asked to undertake.

In the previous sections of the paper, particularly those depicting the arguments for and against economic planning, I have attempted to present the relevant arguments for each position in a manner which any advocate of that position would assess as an accurate description. At this point a different procedure is required, and obviously any *answer* to the moral questions raised will presume a particular moral stance. In order to proceed with clarity I will consider several distinguishable but interrelated issues in sequence.

1. The human person and society.

One of the most fundamental issues implicit in the debate over economic planning is the conception of the human person. This presumption is not frequently made explicit within the debate, but as was noted in the earlier sections of the paper, the role of government in society cannot be adequately addressed without some prior understanding of what it means to be a person.

Within the Judeo-Christian tradition the human person has always been seen as both individual and social. Throughout much of the history of Christianity the individuality of the person was underdeveloped. And we saw earlier how a good bit of the resistance to economic planning comes out of the concern that planning advocates, whether consciously or not, are pushing us back in the direction of a lost individuality. That is, this source of resistance to economic planning is based on an historical and ethical judgment that we have not come far enough in supporting and encouraging the individuality of persons and that planning would be a reversion to an unwanted condition of individual dependence on the community.

It is important that Christians, and especially Catholics, recognize the ways that Christian faith has in the past been employed as a means to prevent the development of a healthy individuality. Nonetheless, it is just as important to make a clear judgment against the unhealthy and objectionable forms of individuality which have come into predominance in the modern era.

The very meaning of the phrase, "the person is both individual and communal," includes a notion of a communal self which many (although not all) critics of planning ignore or deny altogether. Included here are those whose political philosophy runs toward libertarianism. Anytime that individual freedom is taken to be the single most important value in society, individuality has been overextended. Milton Friedman promotes this position in the economic and political realm as clearly as anyone when he advocates "freedom as the ultimate goal and the individual as the ultimate reality in the society."[24] Most presuppositions are not made so clear, but need, rather, to be pursued for greater clarity in discussion. For example, within her treatment of economic planning in this volume, Marina Whitman speaks of "maximizing" pluralism and freedom of choice as "the hallmark, not simply of economic efficiency, but of a free society."

Other critics of a greater role for government in the economy argue for an explicitly communal person. As Michael Novak has put it,

> The ideal of the middle-class man or woman is not to be a rugged individual, isolated and alone. To be independent, yes and also self-reliant. Yet also to be an active member of many communities, to be open to appeals from the needy, to be informed about the world at large, and to care about its problems. The middle-class ideal is communitarian. Its manifold activities, charities, and voluntary endeavors can be explained in no other way.[25]

By this account the person is, indeed, communal. Yet this is still not communal enough to be in accord with the Christian vision of the person. All of the communal interactions of this individual appear to be *voluntary*. The person is open, informed and caring about the plight of the less fortunate but there is no clear sense that the person has any responsibilities toward "the needy," much less any obligations of justice to them. Implicit here is a view of the interrelation of persons in society which is somewhat weaker than contemporary sociologists would describe and considerably weaker than Christian faith would require.

It does not seem to me that economic planning is a litmus test capable of separating "true Christians," who are advocates of planning with a proper regard for the commmunal dimension of the person, from others who are critics of planning with an erroneous conception of human life. Still, most arguments against economic planning belie a serious problem in this regard. Some critiques of greater government involvement in the economy, such as that provided by Robert Benne, do incorporate a more robust and a far more arguably Christian understanding of the person.[26] An absolutely minimum ethical requirement is a set of institutionalized social structures which address the economic obligations which persons have toward one another.

2. The ownership of property.

Within the economic realm the understanding of ownership of property is uniquely indicative of underlying moral presumptions about mutual obligations among persons in society. The prevailing ideas about property ownership in the United States are derived from those set forth by John Locke and other seminal thinkers of the early tradition of British liberalism. Most Americans recognize only minimal restrictions on their ownership of goods, and while most would point no further than the laws of the land in defense of this presumption, nearly all actual arguments in favor of this position rely heavily on the liberal tradition. This can be seen in discussions concerning a crucial arena where property rights have not yet been agreed upon: the international seabed. The central defense (other than unconcealed self-interest) for the U.S. rejection of the "law of the seas" treaty was based entirely on the Lockean doctrine of property. As Robert Goldwin put it, "when we say that something (such as the world's oceans) belongs to everyone we really mean it does not belong to anyone." Thus, anyone has the right to mine the ocean floor without regard for the other nations of the world as long as there is no internationally approved treaty covering such mining operations.[27]

Locke, in his *Second Treatise on Government*, begins with the presumption that in their original state all the goods of the earth belonged to everyone as common gifts from God. Since none of these items can be of any sustenance to anyone without their being appropriated by some individual or another, Locke views the labor of each person as creating the rightful claim to whatever that labor appropriates. Thus in a situation where there are no property rights previously established, the fruits of the tree become rightfully mine when my labor picks them from the branches. While it would be irresponsible, Locke argues, for anyone to horde goods and allow them to spoil without their being used, the creation of an unspoilable unit of exchange — money — allows for the justifiable accumulation of wealth without obligation to share it with others.

In more contemporary terms, an extension of this same general understanding leads some today to believe that their right of ownership includes not simply the right to deny a thing to others (and a few even deny a justification for taxation or eminent domain) but to destroy it if they should so wish. While it might be stupid for me to burn down my house or drive my car into the lake, the more individualist conception of property ownership legitimates even this activity, though nowadays anti-pollution laws may impose some limits on this sort of behavior.

As we saw above, a Christian understanding of ownership circumscribes this right far more severely. Recent papal teaching has often used the phrase, "a social mortage," to speak of the obligation inherent in ownership. To the extent that arguments against economic planning rely on a conception of ownership which does not recognize a real and effective obligation of property owners to others, they are morally inadequate. Once again, it is often impossible to tell with precision an author's position on this sort of question in the midst of public debates on economic planning, but resistance to restrictions on capital flight do often seem to grow out of the conviction that the firms involved do *not* owe much to the community when they decide to move elsewhere. Put in economic terms, a more adequate understanding of property ownership would require firms to internalize (i.e., pay for) at least a substantial part of the negative externalities (social costs) which they impose on the surrounding communities by their actions.

3. Justice and the relation between persons in society.

The fact that nearly every advocate of economic planning cites the current situation of the poor and unemployed indicates that judgments about the requirements of justice are integral to debates on planning. Not all forms of economic planning would have to hold distributive justice as a major concern, as the decision rule of the planners *could* be simply to maximize GNP without regard to how different groups are affected. Yet nearly all forms of economic planning currently under discussion in the U.S. include distributional criteria — even if only to soften the blow of capital mobility on the jobs and communities of workers in affected industries.

Justice, in Daniel Maguire's helpful phrase, is "the first assault on egoism."[28] Where selfishness says "To me, my own," justice demands that others be recognized and respected. And why should I respect the other? Why does even the libertarian feel the need to do so? Because the other is also a self, a person like me. From the perspective of anyone of us looking only at our own wanting the respect of the other, this may feel like a desire for "freedom." But from the perspective of anyone of us having an obligation to act in certain ways toward others, it is quite clearly a matter of justice.

The difficulty in discussing justice in many contexts is caused by the popularity of the most widely held fallacy in American life: individualism. It stands as a descriptive fallacy because the whole of modern sociology and social psychology has consistently found that the dependence of the individual on the emergence of the individual from community is undeniable. All this comes as clear counter-evidence to the presumption of British liberalism that the human person is best defined as an individual who owns his or her own person. C. B. Macpherson has termed this phenomenon "possessive individualism," since it is a form of individualism based on the idea that we are most fully human as possessors of our own qualities and capacities, owing nothing (or almost nothing) to society. The outcome, in Macpherson's words, is that

> Society becomes a lot of free equal individuals related to each other as proprietors of their own capacities and of what they have acquired by their exercise. Society consists of relations of exchange between proprietors. Political society becomes a calculated device for the protection of this property and for the maintenance of an orderly relation of exchange.[29]

The effect, then, is that the best government is that which governs least — since government will be no more than one more "market" in which individuals will vie for influence in pursuit of their own ends. Obviously, from the perspective of possessive individualism economic planning is both morally objectionable (as it violates the individual's rights), and is doomed to failure in any case (the inevitability of the special interest effect is obvious once the basic thesis is accepted).

Justice is so crucial an issue here because individualism recognizes only half of what justice actually entails. What it does acknowledge is "individual justice," the standards of justice between individuals who have made explicit agreements (like contracts) or universally accepted implicit agreements (that if I steal from you I must make restitution). What is neglected is "social justice."[30] It deals with the rights and duties involving the character both of persons and of the human community which creates and nourishes the persons who are a part of it. Social justice deals with the relation between individuals and "the common good."

Thus the individualist definition of justice is usually: "To each according to his merits and earned entitlements." But as Maguire has put it, the very basis of this principle for even the individualist requires that a second portion of the definition be added: " . . . and to each according to his need."[31] Why? Since it is the personhood of the other that creates the other's right to "his due" according to merits and earned entitlements, it is only consistent that the personhood of the other also creates the other's right to *whatever* are the basic necessities required for that person to continue to exist with "self-repect and hope."[32]

Thus, even Novak's "communitarian" individual should recognize the rightful entitlement which the poor and unemployed have as a claim upon the rest of us in society. And critics of economic planning must, as a moral minimum, institutionalize the means by which this obligation is fulfilled. Leaving it to "private sector initiatives" is wholly inadequate since this is tantamount to the society's rendering this an optional undertaking. Benne argues that this moral minimum can indeed be accomplished within an unplanned democratic capitalism, relying "as much as possible on the capabilities of the private sector."[33] *His* moral minimum, however, would seem to look like a mild form of planning to some who today oppose a rise in government involvement in the economy.

Whether it is called planning or not, considerably more must be done to reshape the way our society currently distributes income and the prerequisites to earning it. A robust social justice is a moral requirement, and critics of economic planning face a serious problem in structuring this into the economy in ways that respect the working of the market. This problem is not unsolvable due to some *a priori* assumptions. In the midst of an argument opposing planning, for example, Elmer Johnson in this volume has proposed two "ultimate goals" of economic policy: "an adequate level of material well-being for all persons and meaningful work for all persons able and willing to work." If "ultimate" is taken to mean "most basic" (and not "far off and utopian") then critics of planning may be able to provide concrete suggestions for transforming the plight of the thirty six million poor and the ten million unemployed workers in the nation.

4. Sin and the human condition.

It is a fundamental premise of Christian ethics that sin and human limitation appear in all areas of life. In the debate over economic planning Christians on both sides assert that their proposal is more appropriate in light of the reality of sin and the human condition. In *each* case the claim is that to achieve the best possible outcomes under these conditions the economy must be structured so as to be realistic about human possibilities.

Critics of planning argue that planning advocates are "idealistic" and expect as much good to come from the activities of government decision-makers as they see evil coming from the activities of corporate decision-makers. The presumption is that whereas economic planning has high intentions but predictably poor performance, the market is something of the reverse and is the better for it. Adam Smith pointed out that it is not from the goodness of the butcher, the brewer and the baker that we expect our dinner but from their self-interest. The market system may not be the most morally appealing possibility on the face of it, but it takes the power of sin and self-love seriously, allowing for them rather than presuming they will evaporate.

In explicitly theological symbols, Michael Novak argues that

> The point of Incarnation is to respect the world as it is, to acknowledge its limits, to recognize its weaknesses, irrationalities and evil forces, and to disbelieve any promises that the world is now or ever will be transformed into the City of God.[34]

The literal meaning of the passage is one to which even a Christian socialist could assent. Its tone and intended effect, however, seem clearly to entail a dampening of the ethical urge to counteract sinfulness through economic policy.

Proponents of economic planning argue that in allowing and even advocating self-interest on the part of economic actors, the market system allows individuals and large corporations to "compete" on an "equal" footing and that the outcome is no suprise. Communities are torn asunder, millions are unemployed and the wealthy talk about how hard life is during bad economic times. The point to realism is to construct social structures which will channel the self-interest of economic actors to flow in the direction of the general welfare rather than just presuming that the invisible hand will miraculously compress the gravel of self-interest into the cement of the common good.

The Christian understanding of the human condition calls for a hard-headed realism about human possibilites. The more prevalent interpretation of the doctrine of the incarnation leads to an awareness of the high standards which the incarnate Word demands of us all — in both our personal institutional life. Christian belief has always recognized that the person is called to a life of virtue. Yet Christian social ethics recognizes that in the transformation of social patterns that goal is a set of structures within which self-interested activity would be, not the best one could do, but at least above a moral minimum. At the present time self-interest results all too often in morally unacceptable outcomes for society and some fundamental re-structuring is required.

5. Material well-being and its importance relative to social justice.

Market advocates argue that full employment and a robust economy are necessary conditions for ensuring the material well-being of the poor in this country and abroad. They assert also that the capacity of the unplanned market system to produce this level of economic activity is the only hope for doing so, and that economic planning will lower efficiency and slow the technological change which can enlarge the economic pie so that more can go to the poor and unemployed. Yet in the meantime it is acknowledged, many people will have to suffer so that their own long-term prospects and those of others will improve. Since Christians must be commited to improving the lot of the poor, the question arises: how should Christians weigh the prospect of greater material well-being (for the majority at all times and for the poor minority at least haltingly and in the long run) against the possibility of greater justice for the poor?

Supporters of economic planning, of course, argue that it will provide even greater prosperity than the market, but let us for the moment assume that there *would* be a significant loss in efficiency (and thus in the growth in the standard of living) due to planning. Let us ask ourselves a question to assess our convictions about the meaning of Christian values. In comparison to what the unfettered market would otherwise do, how great a drop in the GNP for, say, 1990 should we be willing to concede in order to achieve a significant degree of economic security for the poorest 20 percent in the nation? Should we be willing to agree to no further increases whatsoever in our standard of living as a fair price for greater social justice? Should we accept a 20 percent decline over the next decade?

It is difficult to defend within the Christian tradition any negative answer to these questions. The concern for the poor has been so clear and consistent a theme within the tradition that putting up with a standard of living of two or four or even six decades ago would seem like a price that people should be willing to pay (especially when most of the advances in preventive medicine, in education and the like could be maintained). It seems doubtful that the price would be this high, but the talk of critics of economic planning seem to presume that *any* loss in productivity would be objectionable, especially because the *poor* would suffer directly.[35]

6. The value of democracy and the danger of its subversion.

While democracy has not historically been a major moral concern for the Catholic church, developments in the twentieth century have seen an integration of the traditional concern for the role of reason in moral discourse with the modern perspective of the electorate as the community of responsibility for the political decisions of the nation. The Catholic tradition has most often been preoccupied with determining what the right decisions were rather than who was to make them. Thus along with the development of social ethics came a greater appreciation for political structures which could better ensure good decisions.

The Christian churches have never been inclined to presume that the will of the majority is by definition the morally correct decision. Thus, all the concerns that critics of economic planning advance about the difficulty of the democratic process have an additional weight within Christian ethics. Still, a democratic political system is recognized by Christians in the nation as the best hope for proper public policy.

The system does not work as well as most would like, and both sides of the planning debate are dissatisfied with the way the government in Washington is currently operating. Conservatives have long used this as an argument for reducing the scope of government. Liberals have used it to argue for democratizing reforms. Christian values would seem to require strong support for the latter even on the part of conservatives who prefer the former. The moral right based on "free speech" to influence Congress by spending money would hold far more weight for say, a libertarian than for a Christian. Robert Benne, as *part* of his opposition to a greater role for government in the economy, argues for "limits on campaign contributions and lobbying, disclosure laws, and congressional reforms that diminish the entrenched power of corporate interest."[36]

Just how sanguine Christians should be about the probability of avoiding the subversion of democratic accountability within economic planning is more difficult to assess. Practically speaking, however, there will never appear on a November ballot the opportunity to vote ye or nay on the proposition: "The United States will operate under an economic plan." Rather, in any immediate future the options will include concrete limited proposals—for political reform, for support of worker cooperatives, for broadening the right of workers to organize, for delays and payments required before plants can move from one area to another, and for widening and strengthening the social safety net. These, then, can be assessed individually and the decision to support each step is less cumberson.

The overall principle which Christian ethics requires is that economic life should operate in accord with and service to fundamental human values.

7. The relevance of Christian values to economic life in a secular world.

As we consider the arguments for and against economic planning in the context of a debate *within* the Catholic church (and even perhaps within the conference of bishops), it is important to address the clearly ethical question of the relevance of religous values to economic life in a pluralistic society. The question occurs because not everyone *is* a Christian. The question might even be posed by critics with a mild taunt in their voices: Even if there are such things as discernible and agreed-upon Christian values for economic life, what relevance does religious belief have to public life in a secular society? This question applies to all moral issues within economic life, but it pertains most clearly to the debate about economic planning because the "threat" of one group imposing its own tastes on others is so great there. Since the question can have three distinctly different meanings, I will answer it in three parts.

A. Arguments "from authority" and public discourse.

In its first (and fairly naive) meaning, the question might be re-phrased: "In a secular world what good are arguments and conclusions based on the Scriptures and on theologians who lived in the third century? Are you going to quote the New Testament in front of the city council?" At the core of this first meaning of the question is a confusion between the kind of reasons why any one person or homogeneous group holds a particular conviction and the kind of reasons which "make sense" to a pluralistic community where many different religious or philosophical positions are represented. To understand this confusion we need better to understand "arguments from authority."

When any group with a history has to settle a disagreement or vote on a controversial proposal, the group members on each side of the issue employ as part of their arguments the views of widely-respected leaders of the group in the past and other "authorities" whose wisdom and vision are taken for granted within the group. Thus, for example, where in a Christian group people might quote Jesus or Paul, discussion at a conservative "think-tank" might refer to John Locke or Abraham Lincoln, and in a Marxist gathering one would hear references to Lenin and Marx. Every group—and every individual—recognizes certain "authorities" whose views on particular issues are given more weight than if those same views were held by just an ordinary member of the group. There may, of course, be a disagreement within the group about which side a particular "authority" would really take in a disagreement, but the point here is that every group does appeal to some authorities.

At the same time, however, that a group of individuals comes to a conclusion based on such authorities, it may be necessary to implement that conclusion in a still larger social grouping — as when Christians, Republicans or Marxists try to influence national or even local policy. No matter how important St. Paul, John Locke or Karl Marx were in arriving at those conclusions, it is highly unlikely that anyone will refer to them at a Congressional hearing or a city council meeting. Why? Because in the nation and city they are not universally recognized as "authorities" and the response to quoting them may be: "So what?" This fact of life does not mean that they are unimportant figures, nor does it mean they are wrong. It simply reminds us that in public discourse between individuals or groups which do not share respect for a particular authority, references to that authority will not be at all persuasive.

Recognition of this basic element of social life leads "dovish" Democrats to appeal to Republican president Dwight Eisenhower's warnings about the military-industrial complex and leads Republicans like Ronald Reagan to quote Democratic "authorities" like Franklin D. Roosevelt in presenting arguments on national issues.

We can now see the confusion implicit in the first meaning of the question about the relevance of a Christian economic ethic to a secular society. From the point of view of the Christian it is not only possible but completely reasonable to come to ethical stances employing Christian (as well as "secular") sources even if religious formulations are not later used in discussions in society at large. From the point of view of citizens who are not Christians, since nearly every group or individual in society respects certain "authorities" which are not held in common in society generally, they need feel no surprise — nor threat — when Christians do likewise. The issue at stake ought not to be the difference in the authorities appealed to. We must look elsewhere.

B. The charge of idiosyncratic minority politics.

The second possible meaning of the question of the relevance of a Christian economic ethic to a secular society centers on a different issue. According to this complaint the basic values of this ethic are not widely shared in the United States and the basic insights into how individual and social life works are founded only on religious vision and are not sound descriptions of the human situation which non-believers could agree with. This sort of stance respects the right of Christian stewards to live their lives as they wish but laments the negative effects this minority has when its idiosyncratic convictions are pressed into national or even local politics.

It is a fundamental premise of this paper that the wisdom implicit in the Christian ethic is not the sole possession of a group of eccentric visionaries. In every age proponents of this ethic have been thoroughly immersed in the problems of the "real" world and have proposed solutions which are appropriate to the everyday realities of economic and social life. Look at Amos as he responded to the wealth and hypocrisy of the leaders of his day; look at Ambrose as he brought the acumen of a civil administrator to his new position as bishop; look at Calvin as he set out to restructure the life of the community in so many of its dimensions.

The descriptions of the human person and social life which are implicit in the Christian tradition correspond closely to the knowledge of these phenomena gained by contemporary psychology and sociology. In fact, it is individualism (and in particular the orthodox economic interpretation of human life) which misunderstands many of these realities of life and ignores the scientific insights available on the issues. The individualist description of human life is far too individualistic to be accurate.

When it comes to the basic values in the Christian ethic, these too are neither idiosyncratic nor foreign to American life. The strong sense of the rights of the individual (which requires both respect for individual initiative and support for democratic decision-making in economic life) is widely held. The equally important sense that there must be economic cooperation and communally determined limits to individual assertion is also widely recognized and is apparent in events ranging from cooperative "barn-raisings" on the prairie and American populism to child labor laws and anti-pollution ordinances.

Of course many of us Americans have become quite comfortable with the wealth which our current, highly productive economic system enables us to attain. Thus, it is no surprise that most middle and upper income Americans will resist many changes in our economy which justice requires. This says that there is a lot of work to be done but it does not imply that the Christian economic ethic is un-American or a purely religious utopian dream.

C. Public norms, civil legislation and religious belief.

The third meaning to the inquiry about the relevance of the Christian economic ethic to secular life arises out of a more general question which requires thoughtful response from Christians. The larger query is this: Where should Christians draw the line between those standards for living which should be legislated in societal life (like prohibitions against murder and guarantees of basic standards of justice) and those which individual believers may live out but which should not be made mandatory in society? If economic planning, or economic justice, were simply an embodiment of one particular brand of religious faith, would it be morally appropriate for those believers to push for it against the will of a majority? Against even a minority?

The first thing for us all to recall here is that, historically, there have been a number of different stances taken by Christian communities towards the "secular" world around them.[37] Many early Christian communities and later Christian sects resisted contact and corruption by the non-Christian world around them. For centuries after the Roman emperor Constantine made Christianity the state religion, it was taken for granted as an essential part of society and there was, in a sense, no "secular" society at all. A multitude of Christian standards *were* mandated in civil society at large. There has been no single answer to our question within the Christian tradition and we Christians in our nation in this era will have to develop an answer appropriate to our situation, just as Christians in other times and places have done.

This is no easy task, but it is made a bit less difficult within a pluralistic political democracy like ours by applying two basic "tests" to any proposals for public implementation (such as ours aimed at greater economic justice).

The first test is directed to the tradition: Are the basic values at stake ones which most scholars and thoughtful believers agree have been held fairly consistently in the Christian tradition as standards for responsible communal living (even if they may not always have been implemented as well as they might have been)? The second test is directed to respect for contemporary pluralism: Are the basic values at stake ones which many (even if not all) other thoughtful citizens, operating out of other philosophical or religious positions, also hold as standards for responsible community life, or are those values unique to our own religious convictions?

Clearly, these two "tests" will not solve all problems. There will be debates among Christians as to whether certain values *have* been consistently held. And, of course, not *all* other philosophical and religious positions will agree with us—otherwise there would be no public disagreement! Practically speaking, without fulfilling the first test, only a small portion of Christians and Christian churches will make an effort to implement any proposal. Without passing the second test Christians will not muster the political clout to make a difference. Fundamental respect for the individual (including one's self) implies that each person must act in accord with his or her conscience (even as a "minority of one" on a particular issue). Still, when these two "tests" are fulfilled, there is at least corroboration of one's convictions and an assurance that they are not idiosyncratic within either the Christian or civic communities.

There is an additional meaning of our original question on the relevance of the Christian ethic to economic life which falls under this third section. It represents a significant confusion on the part of many well-meaning Christians who believe that the churches go too far in trying to influence economic structures. It is one of the major charges made by Michael Novak in his book, *The Spirit of Democratic Capitalism*. In Novak's words,

> No intelligent human order . . . can be run according to the counsels of Christianity. . . . To run an economy by the highest Christian principles is certainly to destroy both the economy and the reputation of Christianity.[38]

At the heart of this rebuke is a misunderstanding of the difference between "highest" and "most basic" ethical principles. *No one* is proposing that the highest Christian principles be made mandatory. Selling all you have and giving the money to the poor, giving your tunic also to the thief who would take your cloak, giving up your life for your friends: *These* are the "highest" Christian principles. These are and always have been counsels for individual life but not laws for society.

Rather than these the Christian ethic requires the public implementation of *the most basic* ethical principles which, while they do put limits on the behavior of the wealthy and powerful, guarantee not wealth and power for all people but the basic elements for a life of dignity and hope for even the poorest and least respected members of society. Guarantees of adequate diet at home and due process in the factory and office are crucial. Relief from sexual harassment and racial discrimination are basic rights. Active governmental support of workplace democracy and corporate social responsibility must replace resistance to reform and accomodation to the *status quo*.

It is quite instructive to look to the debate over related economic reforms over the past century. As each and every humanizing reform was proposed, the defenders of a less restricted market claimed that such high-minded, idealistic reform would derail the train of progress and keep it from its ultimate destination of wealth for all people. We now take for granted child labor laws, the forty-hour work week, worker safety ordinances, workman's compensation laws, social security, labor unions and a host of other changes. Yet every one of these was attacked as foolish moralism and was attained only by long and deliberate struggle by low- and middle-income working people. Basic justice has always appeared to the privileged as unrealistic perfectionism. It is not.

Conclusion

Much of the impetus for the current discussion of economic planning in the United States has come from the intensity of the hardships caused by the recent recession and the additional competition to U.S. firms from "more efficient" producers around the world. This international rivalry in particular has led many firms to move their production facilities from one part of the nation to another, or even to another part of the globe. The firms involved feel the pinch of foreign competition and press both labor and government for concessions to lower costs and to increase their competitiveness in the world market. In the face of such competition U.S. workers and their communities are experiencing hard times on most fronts. In accord with the accepted "rules of the game", this hardship is considered by market advocates as an unfortunate side effect of a larger process which has proven itself benign over the long run. From an ethical perspective, however, more is going on here.

It is helpful to make the distinction between decisions to set up "the rules of the game" and decisions made within the game in accord with the accepted rules. Over the past century and a half a long series of economic reforms made by democratic political decisions have had a humanizing effect on economic life under the market system. Few today would return to the world of child labor, the sixty-hour work week and old age without some sort of social security system. The rules of the game for profit-making firms have become stricter. Their options have been limited somewhat, so that their self-interested activity would not have so severe an effect on the less powerful participants in the process.

For a number of historic and technological reasons we are entering an era when the economic productivity of the United States will be continually challenged. It will no longer be as easy for firms to make such concessions to a public morality in this new situation. Giving longer notices before plant closings and paying subsidies to retrain unemployed workers will detract from the firms' profitability and might reduce the nation's economic performance as a whole. Economic planning would constrain the options of these actors even more. The question of planning is whether such constraints are "good" for the nation.

In morality there is an analogy to the economic principle called "Gresham's Law:" the doctrine that "bad money drives out good." In the realm of ethics it is clear that bad morality drives out good. Testimony before Parliament during the last century records the words of well-meaning entrepreneurs who argued that while they wanted to be more kind to their employees, they were being driven out of business by competition from less scrupulous employers (who could offer lower prices to consumers due to the lower costs of an exploited labor force). We are today at the beginning of what appears to be an era where the pressures of competition from "cheap labor" areas of the world (and from Japan and West Germany) are beginning to unravel some of the reforms which allowed the majority some greater security in economic life. This is not to say that government fiat caused the underlying productivity of the economic system, but rather that democratic decisions have humanized what was otherwise a brutal process.

Within the rules of the market economy (and for that matter any other as well) economic actors are given the right to seek their own self-interest. When, however, the rules of the game are themselves the subject of debate, self-interest is not by any means an adequate rationale. Market advocates too often speak as if we are justified in overlooking this moral fact when discussing how governments and individuals should act in light of the new economic situation. It is certain that nearly no one would propose re-establishing the patterns of child labor that were prevalent during parts of the nineteenth century in England — but it is undeniable that children from families in poverty may be an economically attractive source of unskilled labor. The point is that market advocates — and *especially* market advocates — should be strongly supportive of restrictions on such unfettered "freedoms" of profit-making firms. The reason is that they hope to leave an arena wherein the firm's self-interested pursuit of efficiency will be morally acceptable. This can only be possible when morally objectionable behavior is explicitly forbidden. Unfortunately, the public appearance and legislative effect of all too many firms is one of continual resistance to making the rules of the game stricter. This, of course, is not literally true of all firms, but the difference between legitimate self-interest within the game and the need for a broader vision in setting the rules of the game appears to be lost in many contexts.

It is impossible for a conference of bishops to adjudicate the disputes among economists concerning the effect of planning or not planning. Equally articulate, intelligent and well-trained economists are in dispute on the issue. A majority vote of the American Economics Association would almost certainly oppose planning, but it would probably also oppose "supply-side" economics. While as an economist I have an opinion on the debates within the discipline, it seems only prudent for non-economists such as the bishops to say that there is not definitive empirical evidence either that all forms of economic planning will reduce the level of economic activity in the nation or that any one form of planning will without doubt increase it.

Where, then, are we left? Most definitely with the distributional concerns of Christianity about justice for those whom the market leaves paying the "necessary" price. Democratic economic planning to provide greater security to the poorest twenty percent in the society would be crucial — even if this lowered productivity and the standard of living. In addition, greater encouragement to workers to organize (even within church-run schools and hospitals) is needed. Beyond this, the recent ethical tradition calls for a widening of democratization of both the political and economic realms. Thus explicit policies to support such activities as worker-owned cooperatives and increased worker participation in management would be important. It is a very Lockean conception of property ownership that defines the owners of the buildings and machines as the only rightful overseers of a social organization where many thousands spend a third of each working day. West German and other European legislation on "co-determination" is a model from which much can be learned.

On the whole, then, the Christian ethic finds acceptable neither doctrinaire advocacy of the market nor dogmatic allegiance to government of societal life. Yet as John Paul II has forcefully reminded us, the focal point of a suitable economic ethic takes "the priority of labor" over the inanimate elements in the production process. The exact meaning of this for our economy cannot be told with precision from some pre-existing blueprint. Yet the directions in which it leads us are clear.

Notes

1. Robert Benne, *The Ethic of Democratic Capitalism: A Moral Reassessment* (Philadelphia: Fortress Press, 1981), p.4.

2. See, for example, Robert Nozick's *Anarchy, State and Utopia* (New York: Basic Books, 1974). For an integration of this view with a theological defense of the market, see Michael Novak, *The Spirit of Democratic Capitalism* (New York: American Enterprise Institute/Simon and Schuster, 1982), where Novak argues that three distinct systems — the economic, the political and the moral-cultural — must co-exist without anyone taking precedence (see especially, chap IX). See also his essay "Can a Christian Work for A Corporation?" in *The Judeo-Christian Vision and the Modern Corporation*, ed. Oliver F. Williams and John W. Houck (Notre Dame, IN.: University of Notre Dame Press, 1982).

3. See Milton Friedman, *Capitalism and Freedom* (Chicago: University of Chicago Press, 1962), esp. chap 1, "The Relation Between Economic Freedom and Political Freedom."

4. Freidrich A. Hayek, *The Road to Serfdom* (Chicago: University of Chicago Press, 1944), p. 13.

5. Irving Kristol, "Utopianism, Ancient and Modern," in *Two Cheers for Capitalism* (New York: Basic Books, 1978), p. 149-53.

6. Novak, *Spirit*, pp. 285.

7. Hayek, *The Road to Serfdom*, pp. 138-140.

8. Charles Schultze, "Industrial Policy: A Dissent," *The Brookings Review*, Fall 1983, pp. 9-10.

9. Michael Harrington, *Socialism* (New York: Bantam Books, 1970), pp. 2-3.

10. Barry Bluestone and Bennett Harrison, *The Deindustrialization of America: Plant Closings, Community Abandonment and the Dismantling of Basic Industry* (New York: Basic Books, 1982), p.6.

11. *Ibid.*

12. Lester C. Thurow, *The Zero Sum Society* (New York: Basic Books, 1980), pp. 191-92.

13. Schultze, "Industrial Policy," p. 4.

14. Friedman, *Capitalism*, chap. 7, "Capitalism and Discrimination."

15. Bernard Mandeville, "The Grumbling Hive: or, Knaves Turn'd Honest," in *The Fable of the Bees*, (London: Penguin), p. 69.

16. Marina v.N. Whitman, "American and European Perspectives on Unemployment: Cyclical and Structural Aspects," Seventh Annual Marion O'Kellie McKay Lecture, University of Pittsburgh, April 28, 1983.

17. *Didache* 1.4.8: *Early Christian Writings*, quoted in Willian Walsh, S.J. and John P. Langan, S.J., "Patristic Social Consciousness—The Church and the Poor," in John C. Haughey, *The Faith That Does Justice* (New York: Paulist Press, 1977).

18. Cf. Gregory of Nyssa, *Love of the Poor* and Ambrose, *On the Duties of the Clergy*.

19. Gerhard von Rad, *The Message of the Prophets* (New York: Harper and Row, 1962), p. 83.

20. *Ibid.*, p. 89.

21. Stephen Charles Mott, "Biblical Faith and the Reality of Social Evil," *Christian Scholar's Review*, vol. 9, #3, 1980.

22. Michael Novak, *Toward a Theology of the Corporation* (Washington, D.C.: The American Enterprise Institute, 1981), p. 6.

23. Thomas Aquinas, *Summa Theologica*, I-II, q.84, a.1.

24. Friedman, *Capitalism*, p. 9.

25. Novak, *Spirit*, p. 155.

26. Benne, *Ethic*, see chap. 3 ("Love and Human Moral Striving") and chap. 9 ("The Challenges of Justice").

27. Robert A. Goldwin, "Locke and the Law of the Sea," *Commentary*, June 1981, p. 47.

28. Daniel C. Maguire, *A New American Justice* (New York: Doubleday, 1980).

29. C.B. Macpherson, *The Political Theory of Possessive Individualism* (Oxford: Oxford University Press, 1972), p. 3.

30. Maguire, it should be noted, distinguishes social justice from distributive justice, both of which I am subsuming here under the notion of social justice.

31. Maguire, *Justice*, p. 60. The reader should note that Maguire makes apologies for the sexist language in the traditional (and succinct) formulation of justice.

32. *Ibid.*

33. Benne, *Ethic*, p. 233.

34. Novak, *Spirit*, p. 341.

35. Objections from critics of economic planning that redistribution is impracticable since it couldn't be done on a world scale would seem to beg a crucial question. It would seem that anyone who is concerned about the productivity of the United States in competition with the other nations of the world might not mind if redistribution began only within the USA (see the essay by Johnson/Whitman, this volume).

36. Benne, *Ethic*, 216-17.

37. For a thorough investigation of relation the of Christianity and the secular world, there is H. Richard Niebuhr's famous *Christ and Culture* (New York: Harper, 1961). See also Part One, "The Theology of Co-Creation" in *Co-Creation and Capitalism: John Paul II's Laborem Exercens*, ed. John W. Houck and Oliver F. Williams (Washington, D.C.: University Press of America, 1983).

38. Novak, *Spirit*, p. 352.

Contributors

GAR ALPEROVITZ is Co-Director of the National Center for Economic Alternatives in Washington, D.C. He also serves as the Senior Economic Advisor to the National Economic Recovery Project, and has previously been a Legislative Director in the U.S. Congress and a Special Assistant in the Department of State. A Marshall Scholar, Dr. Alperovitz has testified before numerous Congressional Committees and has lectured at Cambridge, Harvard, Notre Dame, and the Brookings Institution. He received his Ph.D. in political economy from the University of Cambridge and has authored several books and many articles. Dr. Alperovitz has recently published *Rebuilding America* with his Co-Director, Geoffrey Faux.

ERNEST BARTELL, C.S.C. is Executive Director of the Helen Kellogg Institute for International Studies of the University of Notre Dame. He also serves as Overseas Mission Coordinator for the Priests of the Holy Cross, Indiana Province (C.S.C.). He has been the Director for the Fund for the Improvement of Post Secondary Education of the U.S. Department of Health, Education, and Welfare, and president of Stonehill College. Father Bartell earned a Ph.D. in economics from Princeton University. His published works include *Economic Problems of Nonpublic Schools, Metropolitan II: An Econometric Study of Potential and Realized Demand for Higher Education in the Boston Metropolitan Area*, and *Costs and Benefits of Catholic Elementary and Secondary Schools*.

445

C. FRED BERGSTEN is Director of the Institute for International Economics. He has served as Assistant Secretary of the Treasury for International Affairs, Under Secretary for Monetary Affairs, and Assistant for International Economic Affairs to Dr. Henry Kissinger on the Senior Staff of the National Security Council. Dr. Bergsten has been a senior fellow at the Brookings Institution, Carnegie Endowment for International Peace, and Council on Foreign Relations. He received his Ph.D. degree from the Fletcher School of Law and Diplomacy, Tufts University. Dr. Bergsten has published many articles and books, including *American Multinationals and American Interests* and *Toward a New World Trade Policy.*

DANIEL RUSH FINN is the Chairperson of the Department of Economics and a member of the Department of Theology, St. John's University, Minnesota. He is a member of several professional societies, and currently serves as the Chairperson and Convenor of the Subgroup on Economic Justice of the Religious Social Ethics Working Group for the American Academy of Religion. Dr. Finn received his Ph.D. in social ethics and an M.A. in Economics from the University of Chicago. He has addressed the Institute on Pastoral Ministry of the Archdiocese of St. Paul, the Minnesota Catholic Conference, and the Association for Social Economics. He has published *Empowering the Christian Economic Ethic.*

JOE HOLLAND is an associate of the Center of Concern in Washington, D.C. He is a founding member of the Religion and Labor Conference, serves with the National Catholic Conference on Interracial Justice, the Catholic Theological Society of America, and others. Mr. Holland is completing work on his Ph.D. in social ethics at the University of Chicago. He has published numerous pamphlets, articles, and reviews, and his books include *The American Journey* and *Social Analysis: Linking Faith and Justice.*

DAVID HOLLENBACH, S.J. is Associate Professor of Theological Ethics at Weston School of Theology in Cambridge, Massachusetts. He earned his Ph.D. at the Yale University Divinity School. Father Hollenbach is the author of *Claims in Conflict: Retrieving and Renewing the Catholic Human Rights Tradition.* He served as a consultant for the Bishops' Committee drafting the pastoral letter on *Catholic Social Teaching and the U.S. Economy*.

JOHN W. HOUCK is Professor of Management and Co-Director of the Center for Ethics and Religirious Values in Business at the University of Notre Dame. He was a Luce Foundation Lecturer on "Religion and the Social Crisis" at Wake Forest University. He has lectured and conducted workshops on the role of religious and humane values in business at several universities and management groups. A former Ford and Danforth Fellow, Dr. Houck earned his J.D. degree at Notre Dame, an MBA from the University of North Carolina at Chapel Hill, and a master of laws from Harvard. In addition to articles and reviews, he has published *Academic Freedom and the Catholic University*, *Outdoor Advertising: History and Regulation*, *A Matter of Dignity: Inquiries into the Humanization of Work*, and with Oliver F. Williams, C.S.C., *Full Value: Cases in Christian Business Ethics*, *The Judeo-Christian Vision and the Modern Corporation*, and *Co-Creation and Capitalism: Pope John Paul II's Laborem Exercens*.

ELMER W. JOHNSON is Vice President and Group Executive in charge of the Public Affairs Staffs Group for General Motors. He continues as a limited partner of the Kirkland and Ellis law firm in Chicago. He has served as a lecturer at the University of Chicago Law School, where he received his law degree, and has more recently lectured at colleges and universities on various ethical aspects of the economic order. Mr. Johnson has been a consultant to major multinational corporations in regard to their codes of conduct. He has served on the boards of the Chicago Lyric Opera and Children's Memorial Hospital, and is currently a trustee of the University of Chicago. He is co-author of *Can the Market Sustain an Ethic?*

F. RAY MARSHALL is the Bernard Rapoport Centennial Professor of Economics and Public Affairs at the University of Texas at Austin. He is the President of the National Policy Exchange, and serves on the Steering Committee of the Economic Policy Council of the United Nations Association, the Citizens' Commission on Civil Rights, and many other organizations. Dr. Marshall was Secretary of Labor with the Carter administration. He earned his Ph.D. at the University of California at Berkeley and holds several honorary degrees. Dr. Marshall has published many articles, monographs, and books, including *Labor Economics*, *Labor Markets*, *An Economic Strategy for the 1980's* and the forthcoming *Lagging Productivity Growth in the United States: Lessons from Abroad*, co-authored with Diane Werneke and Arvil V. Adams.

DENNIS P. McCANN is a member of the Department of Religious Studies at DePaul University in Chicago. He received his ST.L. degree from the Gregorian University in Rome and his Ph.D. from the University of Chicago Divinity School. Dr. McCann has published *Christian Realism and Liberation Theology* and has recently completed *The New Messiah? A Future for Practical Theology* with Dr. Charles Strain.

MICHAEL NOVAK is resident scholar at the American Enterprise Institute, Washington, D.C. He has received degrees form Stonehill College, the Gregorian, and Harvard University. He has been an advisor in national political campaigns, and was chief of the United States Delegation to the Human Rights Commission in Geneva. Among his books are: *A Theology for Radical Politics: Ascent of the Mountain, Flight of the Dove*; *Belief and Unbelief*; *The Experience of Nothingness*; *The Rise of the Unmeltable Ethnics*; *The Guns of Lattimer*; and *The Spirit of Democratic Capitalism*.

GRACIELA OLIVAREZ is the former director of the U.S. Community Services Administration. She has served as a senior consultant to the United Way of America, director of the University of New Mexico Institute for Social Research and Development, director of planning for the state of Arizona, and director of the Arizona State Equal Opportunity Office. Her life-long concerns include the problems of poverty, juvenile delinquency and minority education. Dr. Olivarez is a graduate of the University of Notre Dame Law School.

RUDY OSWALD is the Director of the AFL-CIO's Department of Economic Research. Mr. Oswald received his B.A. from Holy

Cross College, his M.S. from the University of Wisconsin, and his Ph.D. from Georgetown University. He attended the University of Munich as a Fulbright Scholar. He is a member of the Advisory Committee on Trade Negotiations and the Services Policy Advisory Committee to the U.S. Special Trade Representative; and a member of the Labor Research Advisory Council to the Bureau of Labor Statistics of the U.S. Department of Labor.

PETER G. PETERSON is a member of the investment firm of Peterson, Jacobs & Company and former Chairman of the Board of Directors, Lehman Brothers Kuhn Leob. He is a director of several corporations. He has served as the Assistant to the President for International Economic Affairs, U.S. Chairman of the National Commission on Productivity, Secretary of Commerce, and Ambassador and Personal Representative of President Nixon. Mr. Peterson received his MBA from the University of Chicago. He has published *Marketing: Readings in Market Organization and Price Policies.*

JOSEPH A. PICHLER is president of Dillon Companies, a division of the Kroger grocery retail chain. He is the former Dean of the College of Business Administration, University of Kansas. He serves as a member of the National Board of Consultants for the National Endowment for the Humanities. Dr. Pichler received his Ph.D. from the University of Chicago and his undergraduate degree from the College of Business Administration, University of Notre Dame. He has published numerous articles, and co-authored *Inequality: The Poor and the Rich in America* and co-edited *Ethics, Free Enterprise, and Public Policy.*

MARINA von NEUMANN WHITMAN is Vice President and Chief Economist at General Motors. She is a member of the board of directors of Manufacturer's Hanover Trust Co. and of the Procter and Gamble Co., and is a trustee at Princeton University. She has served in the past as both a senior staff economist and a member of the Council of Economic Advisors and as a member of the National Price Commission. Dr. Whitman has also been associated with the Council on Foreign Relations, the Group of Thirty, and the Trilateral Commission. She received her Ph.D. in economics from Columbia University. Dr. Whitman has published numerous articles and books, including most recently *Reflections of Interdependence: Issues for Economic Theory* and *International Trade and Investment: Two Perspectives.*

OLIVER F. WILLIAMS, C.S.C. is Co-director of the Center for Ethics and Religious Values in Business and on the faculty of the Department of Management at the University of Notre Dame where he teaches and researches in the field of business, society, and ethics. He holds a Ph.D. in theology from Vanderbilt University and has had the experience of a research year at the Graduate School of Business Administration of Stanford University. He is co-author of *Full Value: Cases in Christian Business Ethics* and co-editor of *The Judeo-Christian Vision and the Modern Corporation* and *Co-Creation and Capitalism: John Paul II's Laborem Exercens.* Father Williams has published articles in numerous journals including *Theology Today*, *California Management Review*, *Harvard Business Review*, and *Business Horizons.*

Index